Histories on Screen

BLOOMSBURY RESEARCH SKILLS FOR HISTORY

A series of detailed research skills guides for advanced undergraduates, postgraduates and researchers in the field of history.

Published:

Using Non-Textual Sources, Catherine Armstrong (2015)

Forthcoming:

Elite Oral History, Michael Kandiah (2018)
Primary Sources in British Archives, Simon Trafford (2018)

Histories on Screen

The Past and Present in Anglo-American Cinema and Television

EDITED BY
SAM EDWARDS, MICHAEL DOLSKI AND FAYE SAYER

Bloomsbury Academic
An imprint of Bloomsbury Publishing Plc

B L O O M S B U R Y
LONDON · OXFORD · NEW YORK · NEW DELHI · SYDNEY

Bloomsbury Academic

An imprint of Bloomsbury Publishing Plc

50 Bedford Square	1385 Broadway
London	New York
WC1B 3DP	NY 10018
UK	USA

www.bloomsbury.com

BLOOMSBURY and the Diana logo are trademarks of Bloomsbury Publishing Plc

First published 2018

British Library Cataloguing-in-Publication Data
A catalogue record for this book is available from the British Library.

ISBN:	HB:	978-1-4742-1704-0
	PB:	978-1-4742-1703-3
	ePDF:	978-1-4742-1705-7
	eBook:	978-1-4742-1706-4

Library of Congress Cataloging-in-Publication Data
Names: Dolski, Michael, 1978- editor. | Edwards, Sam, 1981- editor. | Sayer, Faye, editor.
Title: Histories on screen : the past and present in Anglo-American cinema and television / edited by Michael Dolski, Sam Edwards and Faye Sayer.
Description: New York : Bloomsbury Academic, 2018. | Series: Bloomsbury research skills for history ; 3
Identifiers: LCCN 2017021638| ISBN 9781474217040 (hardback) | ISBN 9781474217033 (pb) | ISBN 9781474217057 (ePDF) | ISBN 9781474217064 (ebook)
Subjects: LCSH: History in motion pictures. | History on televison. | Motion pictures–United States. | Motion pictures–Great Britain. | Television–United States. | Television–Great Britain. | BISAC: HISTORY / General. | HISTORY / Europe / Great Britain. | HISTORY / United States / General.
Classification: LCC PN1995.2 H575 2017 | DDC 791.43/658–dc23 LC record available at https://lccn.loc.gov/2017021638

Series: Bloomsbury Research Skills for History

Cover design by Steve Stacey

Typeset by Fakenham Prepress Solutions, Fakenham, Norfolk NR21 8NN
Printed and bound in Great Britain

To find out more about our authors and books visit www.bloomsbury.com. Here you will find extracts, author interviews, details of forthcoming events and the option to sign up for our newsletters.

CONTENTS

FIGURES

CONTRIBUTORS

Nicola Bishop is Senior Lecturer in English with Film and Television at Manchester Metropolitan University and a Senior Fellow of the Higher Education Academy. Her PhD was in English and history and her research to date has focused on the representation of lower-middle-class clerks in middlebrow works by authors including Arnold Bennett, Victor Canning and H. G. Wells. She has published on ramble/rural fiction of the early twentieth century, the works of Agatha Christie and literary representations of the office, and is currently writing a monograph on representations of the lower middle class in literature, on television and in film.

Michael R. Dolski earned a PhD in history from Temple University in 2012. Along with Sam Edwards and John Buckley, Dolski co-edited *D-Day in History and Memory: The Normandy Landings in International Remembrance and Commemoration*, which explored international commemoration of the D-Day battles. He wrote *D-Day Remembered*, a book that analysed American remembrance of that invasion and its impact on US politics and society. Over the past five years, Dolski has researched, written about and presented on the Korean War. He drew upon moving imagery sources in all of these research endeavours. Dolski works as a US government historian involved in accounting for unresolved casualties from previous military conflicts. He resides in Alexandria, Virginia.

Sam Edwards is Senior Lecturer in American History at Manchester Metropolitan University and was previously Fulbright Distinguished Scholar at the University of Pittsburgh. His research explores popular culture representations of conflict (specifically in film, television and literature), commemoration and memory, and the cultural history of conflict. He is a contributor to a new volume examining constructions of militarism on American television (Froula and Takacs, eds, *American Militarism on the Small Screen*), and he is author of *Allies in Memory: World War II and the Politics of Transatlantic Commemoration* and co-editor of *D-Day in History and Memory: The Normandy Landings in International Remembrance and Commemoration*. His current research project explores the place and purpose of counter-factual narratives of the Second World War in Anglo-American popular culture. Sam is a Fellow of the Royal Historical Society and a Senior Fellow of the Higher Education Academy.

Tilman Frasch is Reader in Asian History at Manchester Metropolitan University. He studied South Asian history, European history and Indian languages at Heidelberg University, from which he received a doctorate with a thesis on the city and state of Pagan (Myanmar) in 1995. His research areas include South and Southeast Asian history (with a focus on the history of Myanmar), epigraphy, Buddhist studies, urban history and history of technology. Among his recent publications are 'Tracks in the City: Electricity and Mobility in Singapore and Rangoon, c.1900–1930s' (*Modern Asian Studies*, 2012), 'Buddhist Councils in a Time of Transition: Globalism, Modernity and the Preservation of Textual Traditions' (London Routledge, 2014) and 'The Coming of Cacao and Chocolate to Ceylon' (2014).

Nicholas Gebhardt is Professor of Jazz and Popular Music Studies at Birmingham City University. His work focuses on jazz and popular music in American culture and his publications include *Going for Jazz: Musical Practices and American Ideology*, the edited collection (University of Chicago Press, 2001), *The Cultural Politics of Jazz Collectives* (New York: Routledge, 2015) and *Vaudeville Melodies: Popular Musicians and Mass Entertainment in American Culture, 1870–1929* (University of Chicago Press, 2017). He is the co-editor of the Routledge book series *Transnational Studies in Jazz* and *The Routledge Companion to Jazz Studies*.

Michael Goodrum is Senior Lecturer in Modern History at Canterbury Christ Church University. His research interests include representations of heroism, gender and national identity in American history. He is the author of *Superheroes and American Self Image* and co-editor of *Firefly Revisited* (London: Rowman and Littlefield, 2015), and his articles have appeared in the journals *Social History*, *Literature Compass* and *Studies in Comics*, as well as in a number of edited collections. He is currently in the process of co-editing another volume, on representations of gender in superhero narratives, and articles on a range of topics in American and Anglo-American history.

Sarah Ilott is Senior Research Lecturer in English Studies at Teesside University, where she specializes in postcolonial literature. Her first monograph – *New Postcolonial British Genres: Shifting the Boundaries* – analysed four new genres of literature and film that have evolved to accommodate and negotiate the changing face of postcolonial Britain since 1990: British Muslim Bildungsromane, gothic tales of postcolonial England, the subcultural urban novel, and multicultural British comedy. Developing on research begun in the final chapter of her monograph, she is now researching the way that discourses of British multiculturalism are reflected and refracted in screen comedy (cinematic and televisual) since the 1970s. Her wider research interests include the work of British novelist Helen Oyeyemi, the politics of representation, particularly in relation to minority religious and ethnic identities, and genre fiction and film. Her work on gothic literature, Subcontinental literature and cinematic comedy has been published in the *Journal of Commonwealth Literature*, the *Journal of Postcolonial Writing* and *Postcolonial Text* respectively.

Marcus Morris is Lecturer in Modern European History at Manchester Metropolitan University, where he teaches a range of courses that focus on the social and cultural history of Britain and Europe in the twentieth century. He places particular importance on film as a learning tool in these courses. His research – which has featured in *Cultural and Social History* and *Historical Research* – focuses on the labour and socialist movements in Britain and Europe in the late nineteenth and early twentieth centuries. He has published on the social, cultural and political histories of these movements, including the centrality of class to their activities and their problematic relationship with national identity. He is currently working on the labour movement and internationalism, and has a number of publications forthcoming on their response to the First World War. He is also working on the legacy of Thomas Paine's ideas in Britain and is co-editor of the forthcoming *The Legacy of Thomas Paine in the Transatlantic World*, to be published by Taylor and Francis.

Corinna Peniston-Bird is Senior Lecturer in Cultural History in the Department of History at Lancaster University with a particular interest in research and teaching with a wide variety of primary source materials. Since 1998, her research and teaching has centred on gender dynamics in Britain in the Second World War, with an emphasis on the relationship between memories and cultural representations. Previous publications include 'Of Hockey Sticks and Sten Guns: British Auxiliaries and their Weapons in the Second World War' (*Women's History Magazine*, 2014), '"All in it Together and Backs to the Wall": Relating Patriotism and the People's War in the 21st Century' (*Oral History*, 2012), with Penny Summerfield, *Contesting Home Defence: Men, Women and the Home Guard in the Second World War* (Manchester University Press, 2007), as well as one co-edited special issue with Wendy Ugolini, 'Silenced Mourning' (*Journal of War and Culture Studies*, 2014).

Lydia Plath is Senior Teaching Fellow and Director of Student Experience in the History Department at the University of Warwick, where she teaches courses on US race relations and racial violence. She is the co-editor with Sergio Lussana of *Black and White Masculinity in the American South, 1800–2000* (Cambridge Scholars Press, 2009). The chapter in this volume is part of a wider project on the ways in which American slavery has been represented in American film and television in the twentieth and twenty-first centuries.

Faye Sayer is Senior Lecturer in Public History and Community Archaeology at Manchester Metropolitan University, where she teaches undergraduate and graduate units in historic environment studies, public history and community archaeology. She has worked as a Finds Liaison Officer in commercial archaeology and has directed numerous community archaeology and heritage projects nationally and internationally, including in the US and Australia. Her experience in the field also led her to become a Time Team Archaeologist for five years until her appointment at MMU. Her doctoral research focused on the effects of community archaeology and she is currently undertaking research into the wider impact and value of public heritage programmes. Recent publications include *Public History: A Practical Guide* (Bloomsbury Academic, 2015); 'Can Digging Make You Happy? Archaeological Excavations, Happiness and Heritage' (2015) and 'Politics and the Development of Community Archaeology in the UK' (*The Historic Environment*, 2014).

Jonathan Spangler is Senior Lecturer in Early Modern European History at Manchester Metropolitan University, and Fellow of the Royal Historical Society and of the Higher Education Academy. He did his first degree at William & Mary in Virginia, then worked for several years in Washington, DC and New York City developing museum and corporate exhibitions, before completing a DPhil at Oxford University in 2003. His doctoral research focused on the foreign princes in seventeenth-century France, notably the Lorraine-Guise, about whom he has published articles, a monograph (*The Society of Princes* (Farnham: Ashgate, 2009)) and a co-edited volume (*Aspiration, Representation and Memory* (Farnham: Ashgate, 2015)). Recent work has focused on spreading this study more widely, exploring the role of aristocratic 'trans-regionalism' in border regions between France, Germany and the Low Countries. Current book projects include a study of the high nobility of Lorraine under its last independent dukes (1660–1737) and a comparative study of the role of 'Monsieur' – the younger brother of the king – in the French monarchy. He is a committee member of the Society for Court Studies and co-editor of its journal, *The Court Historian*.

Amy Walling is a postgraduate researcher, having recently completed a MA in public history and heritage at Manchester Metropolitan University. Her research focuses on museum studies; the use, communication and display of heritage and history in modern society; and community heritage. She has worked on numerous public archaeology and history projects, including HLF-funded community archaeology projects such as 'Bones Without Barriers' and 'Headlands to Headspace'.

ACKNOWLEDGEMENTS

This book began with a collection of what in time became connected conversations; with colleagues, with students, with friends, with like-minded people encountered at various conferences over the last few years. These conversations were about film – its worth, value and *use* in historical teaching and research. And in time, as a result of these conversations, the idea for this book was born: a book which would seek to draw upon some of the methods of the dedicated film historian while also exploring how such methods might be incorporated into the activities of those outside the confines of the sub-discipline. In short, the idea was for a book about the use of film *in* history, broadly conceived. Our first debt of thanks, therefore, goes to all those who have contributed to the genesis of the idea, especially students and staff at Manchester Metropolitan University, where two of the editors (and several of the contributors) are privileged to work.

Our second debt of thanks must go to Rhodri Mogford, our commissioning editor at Bloomsbury. Rhodri not only prompted us to pin down the concept for the book; he also commissioned it. Most importantly, he supported it throughout, with all the patience and understanding that this demanded. Thanks should also go to his assistant at Bloomsbury, Emma Goode, for similarly being helpful and understanding throughout.

Finally, we must thank the many contributors to this project for their time, their input and their expertise. Particular thanks must also go to Amy Walling, a postgraduate researcher at Manchester Metropolitan University, who worked with supreme dedication and diligence to turn fourteen chapters written by eleven contributors into a cohesive and coherent whole. Without her, the patience of Rhodri and Emma might well have been put even further to the test.

Sam Edwards, Michael R. Dolski and Faye Sayer
April 2016

Introduction

Sam Edwards and Amy Walling

Film history has come a long way since the pioneering work of those such as Robert Rosenstone, Jeffrey Richards and Michael Paris in the 1980s and 1990s.[1] Having first emerged from among and within social history in the 1960s, the sub-discipline was powerfully affected by the 'cultural turn' at the end of the twentieth century (which saw historians address anew the place and power in society of 'culture', broadly conceived). The result was the consolidation of a certain approach to interrogating film, and a certain research method: the 'new film history'. Central to this approach is the idea that the conventional methods of the historian – archival research, wide reading in the secondary literature, comparison with other primary source material – remain pertinent to the historical analysis of film. Today, this method is best exemplified by the work of those such as James Chapman, Thomas Doherty, Mark Glancey and Mark Connelly.[2] Aside from the scholarship of these figures, the 'New Film History' is also well served and well explained by several engaging introductory texts and guides.[3] In comparison, the historical scholarship connected to television is rather less well developed. Histories of television have often been histories of television *networks*, or of specific programmes, or of the political function of television during certain historical moments (for instance, the Cold War). Nonetheless, some recent scholarship in television history has sought to bring together key ideas and methods, while others have exemplified the critical analysis of the 'small screen'. Take, for example, the work of Gary Edgerton, Peter Rollins, Mia Treacey, Anna Froula, Stacey Takacs, Ann Gray and Erin Bell.[4]

This volume owes much to the scholars noted above, their ideas, insights and methods. But it also sets itself a slightly different task. This is not a history *of* film and television, nor does it purport to outline an agenda for the engaged examination of the film industry, cinema production process, or of the technologies of sound and image. Aimed at the undergraduate teacher and student, and with contributions from experts in military history, imperial and postcolonial history, social history, cultural history, literary history, gender history, public history, popular history, music history, and of course film history, this volume seeks to provide an accessible and engaging introduction to the use of film and television in the classroom, and in undergraduate research projects. In Part One, the volume begins with three chapters outlining some of the key issues connected to the historical study of film.

In Chapter 1, Michael Dolski, drawing upon the general approach developed by the 'New Film History', works through the ways in which the moving image might be interrogated as a 'primary source' – an audio-visual text shaped by the context and chronology within which it was produced. In Chapter 2, Faye Sayer, a public historian very familiar with television production processes, takes up the discussion and outlines the ways in which film and television offer publicly consumable historical narratives. Put differently, Sayer demonstrates that when understood on their own terms, film and television can be readily assessed as 'secondary sources'; retrospective narratives of the past which invoke, use and assimilate various other sorts of 'source material' in an effort to communicate a very particular concept of 'accuracy' and 'authenticity'. In the last of the 'introductory' chapters (Chapter 3), Sam Edwards unpacks and explains an alternative way to approach the moving image: as a memory 'resource'; that is, as a popular culture artefact which increasingly carries the burden – at least in North America and Europe – of constructing and communicating collective memory. Edwards identifies and explains the origins of the idea of 'collective memory' before highlighting some of the questions, challenges and benefits of incorporating film and television into histories of memory.

Part Two contains various 'case study' chapters, organized according to focus and approach. Here, the emphasis is on showing and interrogating the theories and ideas introduced in the introductory chapters via eleven case studies. The subjects, topics and cultures covered by these case studies are by no means exhaustive, and there are many issues which thus remain unaddressed. But the Anglo-American and Anglophone focus of the case studies does help ensure clarity, consistency and connection. As will become apparent, several of the chapters are – deliberately – in dialogue with each other (with topics such as nationalism and identity frequently revisited), and indeed several continue and develop lines of enquiry initiated in their counterparts.

Thus, Chapter 4, authored by Marcus Morris, explores the extent to which film might be analysed as a means to work through some of the often tricky and complex issues connected to the historical, social and economic category of 'class'. By surveying a variety of different cinematic products, from the early twentieth century through to the dawn of the new millennium, Morris shows how British discussions of class have been mediated through film, and how such films thus reveal a profound change in British social history – from a relatively 'homogenous' national community (albeit stratified by class) to a contemporary multicultural society strained by the rise of the regions. In Chapter 5, Corinna Peniston-Bird develops some of these ideas further, but with a twist: here the focus is not on the way in which film has mediated British conceptions of class, but how they have provided a 'model' for another fundamental category of analysis: gender. By close analysis of various Second World War era films Peniston-Bird shows that such productions offer a 'rich source material for the study of gender and war'. Chapters 6 and 7 then turn attention to the ways in which films broach, question and mediate another powerful structure of the modern era: race. Via a close reading of the early twenty-first-century box office hit *Bend It Like Beckham* (2002), Sarah Ilott explores what a film can reveal about contemporary constructions – and discussions – of identity, gender and multiculturalism in Blair's Britain. In Chapter 7, meanwhile, Lydia Plath, adopting an alternative approach in order to explore a very similar issue, offers a broad yet detailed historical survey of the ways in which African-American slavery has been depicted in popular cinema. In doing so, Plath is able to show the ways in which the portrayal of slavery was inextricably connected not just to contemporary racial stereotypes, but also to contemporary race relations. As such, the vocal protests raised within the African-American community in response to some of the films discussed (such as D. W. Griffiths' *Birth of a Nation* [1915]) were as much about the present as they were about the past.

The next section moves from examinations of the moving image as contemporary document, text or political 'mediator' to discussions of what Treacey has referred to as 'screen history'.[5] Here, the focus is on the ways in which film and television construct their own historical narratives in ways peculiar to the power and potential of the medium. To this end, this section highlights the history-making potential of four popular genres: documentary, the historical epic, the musical, and the war film. In Chapter 8, Tilman Frasch provides an engaging study of the role played by Pathé newsreels in the first half of the twentieth century in the celebration and popularization of imperial imagery and ideals. Frasch argues that such sources have been under-used and under-exploited in the historiography of empire, and that they offer an important resource through which to test (and challenge) the long-established Porter/Mackenzie debate.

In Chapter 9, Jonathan Spangler turns our attention to a popular film and television genre: the 'epic', which in recent years has often been drawn to the glamour and glitz of the early modern age. Through detailed knowledge of the period Spangler is able to identify the extent to which such epics, albeit made for money and entertainment, are nonetheless able to provide valuable insights into certain aspects of the famously 'foreign' past, for instance the 'interiority' of the Tudor mind. Chapter 10, meanwhile, offers a thoughtful and thought-provoking examination of the relationship between the Hollywood musical and (American) historical consciousness. Through close examination of script, screenplay and context, Nicholas Gebhardt is able to tease out the ideas of past and present explored by Dorothy as she skips down the yellow brick road. And in Chapter 11, Michael R. Dolski offers a thorough and comprehensive assessment of the potential of war films and television shows (focused on D-Day) to be used in the classroom (and in research) as historical narratives which shed light on important aspects of D-Day historiography.

The final section of the book further develops some of the ideas raised by Sayer and Edwards in Part One. In Chapter 12, Michael Goodrum undertakes a provocative – and persuasive – reading of the Sam Rami *Spider-Man* films produced in and around 9/11. Through close and careful analysis, Goodrum draws attention to the politics of the superhero in American culture, and he charts the ways in which an altered contemporary context demanded a reappraisal – and a reconstruction – of the superhero's power and place in that culture. In Chapter 13, Sam Edwards shifts the discussion from the role played by the 'screen' in the construction of identity to the construction of memory. By focusing on a historical event oft depicted on British television – the First World War – Edwards demonstrates that televisual representations do not constitute 'myths' imposed on the 'truth' (as some critics have contended). Rather, First World War-focused television productions are better understood as 'sights of memory' that mediate contemporary, and ever-changing, perceptions of the past. Significantly, Edwards also argues that although such 'mediated memory' has lost the 'site-specificity' of earlier eras, in an intriguing turn some recent television productions have nonetheless offered a revealing critical commentary on the very politics of memory. Finally, in Chapter 14 Nicola Bishop explores the ways in which television history has become central to modern historical consciousness, and identifies and outlines a 'typology' of history-focused programming. Picking up on some of the ideas raised by Sayer in Chapter 2, Bishop concludes that the question of whether or not TV history can be 'good' has less to do with the medium and far more to do with the method. The challenge, in short, is for the discipline to embrace the history-telling potential of modern mass media.

This volume explores and explains key theoretical ideas, and it demonstrates how such ideas can be used and applied by historians, teachers, students or simply interested individuals. It aims to show that an examination of moving images is useful not only to explore already established connections, such as the inter-relationship between wartime propaganda and films, but that they can also be employed to investigate a wide variety of topics and time periods.

Notes

1   See, for example, R. A. Rosenstone, *History on Film, Film on History*, 2nd edn (New York: Pearson, 2012); R. A. Rosenstone, *Visions of the Past: The Challenge of Film to Our Idea of History* (Cambridge: Harvard University Press, 1995); J. Richards and A. Aldgate, *Best of British: Cinema and Society from 1930 to the Present* (London: I.B. Tauris, 2002); J. Richards, *Films and British National Identity From Dickens to Dad's Army* (Manchester:

Manchester University Press, 1997); M. Paris, *From the Wright Brothers to Top Gun* (Manchester: Manchester University Press, 1995); M. Paris (ed.), *The First World War and Popular Cinema* (Edinburgh: Edinburgh University Press, 1999).

2   See J. Chapman, *The British at War: Cinema, State and Propaganda, 1939–1945* (London: I.B. Taurus, 2000b); T. Doherty, *Projections of War: Hollywood, American Culture, and World War II*, rev. edn (New York: Columbia University Press, 1999); M. Glancy, *When Hollywood Loved Britain: The Hollywood 'British' Film, 1939–45* (Manchester: Manchester University Press, 2013); M. Connelly, *We Can Take It! Britain and the Memory of the Second World War* (London: Routledge, 2004).

3   See, for example, J. Chapman, M. Glancy and S. Harper (eds), *The New Film History: Sources, Methods, Approaches* (New York: Palgrave Macmillan, 2007); J. Chapman, *Film and History* (London: Routledge, 2007); M. Hughes-Warrington, *History Goes to the Movies: Studying History on Film* (London: Routledge, 2006).

4   G. R. Edgerton and P. C. Rollins (eds), *Television Histories: Shaping Collective Memory in the Media Age* (Lexington: University Press of Kentucky, 2001); M. Treacey, *Reframing the Past: History, Film and Television* (London: Routledge, 2016); A. Froula and S. Takacs, *American Militarism on the Small Screen* (London: Routledge, 2016); A. Gray and E. Bell, *History on Television* (London: Routledge, 2013).

5   M. Treacey, *Reframing the Past: History, Film and Television*. London: Routledge, 2016.

PART ONE

Thinking about film and television

CHAPTER ONE

The moving image as primary source: Author, text and context

Michael R. Dolski

Film can be history too

As an eager and impressionable undergraduate student, I once had the opportunity to enrol in a popular course on the Second World War. The professor, a respected military historian, approached instruction in a variety of engaging ways. Ever the showman, he would come to class in period garb, display paraphernalia collected over a lifetime of study, and draw students in through the use of film in the classroom. Glancing around the overfilled large lecture hall in the first week of class, I was shocked to see some of the undergraduate elite, that is in American universities – the student-athletes of a prominent football university – settling in for a taxing exploration of one of the most complex events of recent history. In retrospect, my surprise was mere naiveté; the Second World War is such a popular staple in American culture that over-enrolled university courses are standard. Still, there was something more going on here, as the professor had gained a reputation around campus for making history come alive. Rather quickly, I developed an appreciation for one key ingredient to the success of his warlock's brew of approachable, engaging, yet critical undergraduate instruction: film.

I have to acknowledge that it was more the ways in which these films became part of the overall educational process that stood out at the time and since. The professor used these sources to elucidate certain topics in ways that I simply had not been exposed to prior to this experience. For instance, while a secondary student, my history teacher turned to Ken Burns' wonderful, though still somewhat problematic, *The Civil War* (1990). We sat for weeks on end and watched without discussion, interaction, or anything beyond jotting down a few notes that likely missed the intricacies of content and presentation. Jump ahead a few years, and the aforementioned university professor used film in such a different way that it was hard to grasp at first. The films were launching pads for us to explore various topics. Invariably, discussions of content would be interrupted by some pedantic debate concerning uniforms or availability of some minor piece of equipment (these were war films, after all). Yet the professor would bring us back to topic by challenging all to think deeper, to ponder what the film showed us about a place and time that yielded such a production. Films were often employed in juxtaposition with one other, like the American-made *Wake Island* (1942) versus the Polish-generated *Kanal* (1957). In one, a small band of jaunty heroes fought to the bitter end, but displayed the prowess of a society capable of inflicting major damage on opponents even when caught unawares. In the other, a forlorn group of individuals attempted to deal with horrifying events over which they seem to have no power, with all dying, going insane, or committing suicide by film's end. Even more telling, all the losses in the latter film had absolutely no discernible impact in the grand scheme of things. The discussion moved beyond just considering the events portrayed on screen. We had to delve into what the moving image provided us to better understand what happened but also how depictions of those events shaped our conceptions of the past and present.

The class was a wonderful success. I learned a great deal about the Second World War and embarked upon a journey that took me through graduate school to become a professional military historian. My academic training often exposed me to dirge-like lamentations about the adverse influence of moving images on critical public engagement with history. The almost perfunctory rejection of moving images as educational sources proved inclusive, taking to task Hollywood blockbusters, documentary productions, or decontextualized film stock created at the time of the event conveyed. Despite such vocal reservations, the professoriate by and large in my experience has employed film regularly in the classroom. At times, it is brought out merely to discuss the flaws in a given piece. More commonly, however, it seems that film's place in the classroom is something more – a supplement to promote a deeper understanding of the past, an aid for students to help visualize the strange pastness of things described in text or by mouth.

The intent of this volume is to help undergraduate instructors and students by exploring constructive and meaningful uses of moving images for history education. One popular teaching guide enjoined instructors to encourage 'students in a life-long learning process' by developing 'interest in further learning and provid[ing] a base of concepts and skills that will facilitate further learning and thinking'.[1] Incorporating film analysis into classroom instruction, in a critical and rigorous manner, is one way to engage lifelong educational endeavour. It may help draw in students to the subject matter (moving images can be rather engaging after all) as well as the process of thinking critically about history.[2] The introductory chapters cover several different aspects of this process. In this initial chapter, we will examine the use of moving images as primary sources. We will consider the nature of moving images as sources and then evaluate some of the stumbling blocks encountered when drawing on this source base. The chapter will conclude with an acknowledgement of some of the most compelling benefits gained through rigorous use of these sources.

Moving images as sources

Since the late 1980s, a small but growing band of interested persons has worked to connect critical historical scholarship with examinations of moving image material.[3] Literary and film theory both provide deep readings of film sources, and we would be wise to acknowledge such contributions.[4] Historical inquiry, however, can and should lead the interested to ask other questions of this subject matter. In addition to exploring the nuances of underlying meaning or the structural techniques of expression, the historian must also ponder what the moving image source tells us about the past depicted as well as the moment of genesis for the image. Although the list of titles attending to film and history has expanded recently, there are a variety of approaches displayed among these works. Authors tend to pursue one of several courses that I have roughly separated into the following categories:

1   a discussion of a particular source's contents and then a consideration of its adherence to established historical records, or what usually leads to *history **versus** the moving image*;[5]

2   treatment of the processes for recording images over time, or a *history of the moving image*;[6]

3   an eclectic mélange of productions that *en toto* purports to provide a glimpse into the social or cultural underpinnings of a time and place, or *history **through** moving images*.[7]

This categorization does not imply overly rigid boundaries, as one work or author may cross liminal zones. The intent in describing existing scholarship in such terms is to highlight the predilection to follow specific questions and answers when engaging with moving images as sources.

It is best to acknowledge the benefits of pursuing *all* courses in an integrated approach to historical education. We are compelled to treat the moving image as another source available for the pursuit of historical understanding. Rigorous employment of such a source base must include an assessment of its overall accuracy, examination of its manner of creation, and exploration of ways in which it reveals facets of society. This blended analytical framework will push us beyond simplistic usage of film in the classroom. That means eschewing the tendency to either create a quick history versus film comparison of moving image to some ostensibly more credible source, or a just as limiting exposure to moving images without critical engagement of them as a source. In the former case, one rejects the validity of such sources, usually without fully addressing their power. In the latter, one overly empowers such sources, usually without completely investigating their value and limits.

Discussion too often falls to extremes. Some scholars and educators purport that there is no merit in using films to promote understanding of the past. Alternatively, following the arguments of those such as film historian Robert Rosenstone, the argument advances that moving images are just as credible (or even more credible) as any other source.[8] The moving image simply is another vehicle for constructing the past in this postmodernist view, which tends to neglect any coherent review of the ways in which the portrayal emerged in the first place or the potential ramifications of that production process. Moving images are indeed a type of source worthy for exploring the past. That being said, these sources must be treated to some standard of critical evaluation, just as any other potential source material. Historian Jay Winter sensibly cautioned that '[f]ilm is never the same as text, and the ways in which cinema presents past events are never direct or unmediated'.[9]

This chapter will explore the use of moving images as primary sources. As an example, one could bring to the classroom portions of the block-buster 1998 film, *Saving Private Ryan*. If the object is to present some of the battle sequences as a means to educate on the nature of combat in the Second World War, this film is used as a secondary source – something created after the events portrayed. The same film could be used to discuss the conceptualization of warfare by American society in the late twentieth century; the film now becomes a primary source – something created at or nearly at the time of the events concerned by a participant or observer of those events. Moving image primary sources can include a wide range of material, from imagery captured as events unfolded before the camera (think of the famous Zapruder film of John F. Kennedy's assassination), through documentary films (such as Ken Burn's *The Civil War*, mentioned above), to popular entertainment and money-making ventures like, once again, *Saving Private Ryan*. The variance emerges with the questions posed to these sources.

With that distinction in mind, as one primer on historical study and education sensibly remonstrated, 'Neither written nor nonwritten primary sources can be taken at face value'.[10] One must look beyond the surface depiction of the past offered by any source matter; viewers must ask questions of the 'author', the source's place in the historiography of the events concerned, the cultural context of the time, the production process, and the ancillary features of presentation that affect viewers' perceptions.

The power of moving images to shape our understandings of the past perforce demands rigorous engagement with this material. As one sharp analyst of history through film argued, 'history films, even when we know they are fanciful or ideological renditions of history, have an effect on the way we see the past'.[11]

Incorporating film content into history education requires advanced preparation and a degree of flexibility. The best approach is to manage expectations from the outset, to understand what moving image sources can and cannot provide for historical understanding. One must preface exposure to such source material in an educational setting with some precursory consideration of content and generation of questions that should be asked and answered through viewing the material. Do not treat a moving image in a learning environment as mere filler – there must be some sort of preparation to extract maximum benefit. One must assess the objective sought from engaging with a source and then select suitable material by recognizing inherent differences in content as well as type (segment or whole source; film, television, or something else; etc.). The remainder of this chapter will discuss common challenges encountered when using these sources to educate about the past, and provide recommendations to confront such challenges. The desire is to establish a framework for the focused case studies that will follow the introductory chapters.

'Author'

The most common fault of film analyses (literary and film theory as well as historical critique) is the assumption that there is a single author of these products. The extreme point of this approach is evident with auteur theory, wherein the analyst hones in on the individualizing impact on film production of a given director. It seems there is an attempt to treat films too much as written sources that have one or a small handful of creators responsible for the end product. As with other sources, say a political speech, one could assess the knowledge, experience, biases and motivations of a sole/small group of creators (speechwriter or film director) in order to analyse critically the material. The downfall to this approach is that film productions are rarely the result of a lone individual's input and overarching vision.

The complex and collaborative nature of film production often demands the efforts of many participants, all of which can shape the final product. In the relatively infrequent occasions of moving images created by a lone agent at the time of the event displayed, this matter is of somewhat lesser importance. The astute investigator should still ponder questions of editorial influence, ways in which distribution may have altered content, and so on. Even here one must ask the standard questions of any creator of primary material, such as their access to pertinent information, their biases and their motivation in creating and releasing this content. These questions become increasingly difficult to answer with authority as an accretion of author-like personalities play a role in a given product.

The one figure often singled out for attention when analysing film content is the director. Directorial influence is certainly of paramount concern when evaluating a film as a primary source and a director's declared objective must be taken into account. Oliver Stone's intent to challenge power hierarchies and representations of truth through his conspiracy theory laden analysis of the Kennedy assassination in *JFK* (1991) could be used to ponder post-Watergate/Vietnam unease with political authority.[12] Steven Spielberg proclaimed a desire to honour his (Jewish) mother with the 1993 film, *Schindler's List*, which *inter alia* depicted the suffering of Jewish people in the face of almost unspeakable evil.[13] That objective and the way it transferred to celluloid offers something for students eager to explore representations of the Holocaust in American culture.[14] One must probe deeper than declared intentions to assess the full range of directorial motivation and capability to speak with authority about the events concerned. Most film analyses start and stop with the director, which is an acknowledgement of the profound influence this role plays in shaping moving images. Yet subjecting this role alone to such a review leads to an incomplete analysis of any source.

Aside from directors, the role of producers or other executive figures (for television, documentary and major theatrical releases) must be considered. Executive personalities play a major role in selecting content or approving/ disapproving interpretation of content in major news media programmes. This hidden input potentially shapes public perceptions of contemporary events. Hollywood executives often shape films by rebranding them to fit a target audience, such as with the 1956 film *D-Day, the Sixth of June*, which originally did not have 'D-Day' in the title.[15] Executive decisions also play a major post-filming influence, as evident with Sam Fuller's masterpiece, *The Big Red One*. Fuller shot over 4.5 hours of film, but officials at Lorimar Pictures cut the production to 2 hours for the theatrical release.[16] Such decisions heavily influenced this production, which merits full evaluation.[17]

As one of the primary conduits of information to viewers, the influence of actors and/or narrators also deserves consideration when evaluating moving images as sources. Consider the manner in which actor George C. Scott lent his own interpretation of the subject to the silver screen when filming the 1970 movie, *Patton*. The end result was a bombastic, larger-than-life character, which was the intention of the movie's makers, but also one that went well beyond the original desire due to Scott's personal take on the man.[18] If one were to bring *Patton* to the classroom in order to discuss American ambivalence about warfare in the 1970s, then a full appreciation for the iterative and multi-sourced development of the character is a requirement. Actors breathe life into the characters they portray, just as narrators do with the written text they read aloud.

The scriptwriter is also often just as important an author to film as any director or producer. Whether the script takes form as intertitle frames in the pre-sound era, narrative content for a documentary, or the dialogue (and blocking and setting) for created scenes, these authors are of monumental importance when evaluating a moving image. Often this function is performed by individuals that bring their own views, experiences and intentions to any collaborative venture. One such example, in two different productions, is Paddy Chayefsky, an erudite member of the Hollywood screenwriting community, and also a Second World War veteran.[19] Chayefsky played a major role in developing the script for one of the last theatrically released documentaries, *The True Glory* (1945), helping set the grim tone of this work.[20] His influence extended even further, as evidenced by the irreverent and caustic denial of military glory presented in *The Americanization of Emily* (1964). Chayefsky's authorial presence, as a scriptwriter for each project, heavily structured both of these films.

A full consideration of the author(s) for any moving image is the *sine qua non* for any source assessment. The collaborative nature of film production obviously makes this a far more difficult process than that for a single-authored document. Yet, as with textual sources, eschewing the requirement to evaluate authors risks incorporating flawed material into the educational process, passes over key learning opportunities, or simply abdicates education in preference of entertainment. By setting the scene with 'author' related information, one can help develop techniques for critical evaluation of source material as well as expand knowledge bases by accessing visual depictions of subject-specific content. In the end, one should review and discuss the authors' access to information, their background experiences, their motivation in creating the image, what pushed them to distribute the document, and ways in which their biases (either stated or unstated) potentially shaped the final product.

Genre (and historiography)

The following chapter will deal with historiography and film more directly, which is fitting an exploration of moving images as secondary sources. For the moment, we must address the relationships among moving image sources, or the ways in which a larger body of work influences individual components. When discussing film or television, the proper term for this concept may be genre. As we ponder moving images for historical thinking, the concepts of genre and historiography function in similar ways. Historiography connotes the history of the history, or the conversations that historians have about the past. These discussions ultimately influence individual historical works by setting the research questions and shaping the manner in which answers are derived.[21] Genre conventions set boundaries of discussion and presentation while also informing productions by the nature of (filmic) conversations that predate a given piece. Considered in that light, genre does function in a historiographic capacity when incorporating film works for historical analyses.[22] Film productions do not appear from thin air without background input; genre suggests the collective knitting together of pieces in conversation or relationship with one another. As film historian Janine Basinger describes it, 'Each is a part of a larger, remembered whole'.[23] Another analyst of historical film employed Baktin's concept of 'genre memory' to describe the effect of 'shaping the way the past is reenacted, illustrating the way genre forms recall past usages while making their resources available for the present'.[24]

Genre acts to establish expectations for filmmakers and audiences alike. To assess a single production without investigating such influences on the process of production risks missing major determining factors.[25] For instance, an American-made war film set in and produced during the past few decades may function well as an example of contemporary approaches to warfare as well as cultural representations of such matters (consider the 2001 film, *Black Hawk Down*). However, any consideration of content and presentation in such a film must also pay heed to the evolution of the combat film genre. This progression established conventions that heavily influenced any individual contribution to the discussion. *Black Hawk Down*, although set in Somalia during a 1993 military clash between UN (primarily US) military forces and locals, is plainly influenced by standards of Second World War combat films. While focusing on a small squad of people drawn from across America, the story follows somewhat reluctant citizen-warriors that presume to do good through the use of military force, encounter extreme adversity, overcome it through collaboration (and self-sacrifice) and validate America's world mission of preserving order and decency.[26] Admittedly, these are just some readings possible for the film. Nevertheless, such conventions emerged over time and become almost required features for any new offering.[27] These sources are in conversation with their forebears, even if only implicitly, and that conversation will influence the production and reception of any individual work.

Readers may interject that genre really applies only to major entertainment fare. Such an argument may have merit, to a degree. The underlying point, however, is to ponder ways in which a larger body of moving images relate to one another, how these relationships set conventions, and ask what effect those conventions have on individual pieces.[28] Cast in that light, 'historiography' of moving images applies to all such potential sources.

For instance, the 1973 British documentary on the Second World War, *The World at War*, set new conventions for the medium by focusing on ordinary people presented through interviews and oral testimony, mixed with stock footage and voiceover narration. Many subsequent documentaries borrowed this presentation style, which shows the impact of conventions and the constructed nature of even documentary sources (see Chapter 14 for more discussion of this).[29] Documentaries generated after the early 1990s have exhibited what is now often called the 'Ken Burns effect'. Burns made popular a type of documentary film production that included incorporation of still pictures in dramatic fashion (zooming in, panning to affect motion), high-quality music and voice narration, and even on-screen scholarly discussion.[30] The approach was sentimentalizing, yet proved salable and major documentary productions since have tended to follow suit.[31]

One should examine the use of oral history in these productions just as with moving image sources in general, such as news broadcasts. Uncritical incorporation of witness observation should elicit concern.[32] As with all persons, witness or participant tales should be assessed for bias and accuracy; these people may have stated or unstated motivations that influence what they recount. *How* a production employs such testimony is also a point of consideration when evaluating it as a potential source.

Thinking historiographically will push students of history to consider the ways in which a body of work – through overall argument/approach, through establishment of boundaries/norms – influences the depiction of events in any moving image source. With moving image sources in particular, one must also consider ways in which transmission affect the messages conveyed. Grouping similar shows together for a television broadcast or a film review may influence the perception and reception of content contained in any single piece. A relational analysis will help situate a given source within a larger context of other, similar works while also probing the ways that dissemination (by linking to other sources or editing content) shapes understanding.[33]

Context

Moving beyond an assessment of evolutionary argument will further strengthen (and likely complexify) any overall evaluation. Cultural-historical context should factor into an evaluation of any moving image source. The lack of real objectivity or fundamental truthness of facts means that source material must be rigorously questioned in order to uncover the full range of bias in input and presentation.[34] One must move from a consideration of the relationship between separate works, to an assessment of how works relate to one another *over time*, with the understanding that shifts in the cultural environment will also affect these sources.

This line of inquiry is one of the more challenging facets to explore with due rigour, but is also one of the most promising veins to mine. Through this level of analytical endeavour one can demonstrate how societies express themselves (in this case via moving imagery) while at the same time assisting with the development of critical analytical skills for those exposed to the material. One scholar posited: 'Even visual language systems (photography, cinema and television) operate by connecting images with culturally conditioned concepts and not by automatically reflecting the immanent meaning of things.'[35] Visual sources only reveal their meaning through a process of interaction between viewer and source; this engagement is profoundly influenced by cultural factors. As historian Gordon Wood explained, 'Intellectual activity in a culture is not a one-way flow between the great minds and passive recipients; it is a discourse, a complex market-place-like conglomeration of intellectual exchanges involving many participants all trying to manipulate the ideas available to them'.[36] That wide-ranging interaction constitutes the contextual environment of the past.

Cultural context plays a tremendously significant role in film production and consumption. At times, that relationship between context and content is straightforward, while at other times the viewer must expend more intellectual energy identifying those connections. Common approaches include broad historical reading in the time of source production and viewing, investigation into the intentions and actions of the 'authors' noted above, and research into the reactions of viewers (critics, popular press, interest groups). Approached in this comprehensive manner, a student of history will be able to assess the (at times unbidden) influences on the creation of a moving image and evaluate its impact on audiences. Only discussing the content of a moving image source misses the point that some of these images prove far more powerful or widely encountered than others.

Film historian Robert Burgoyne explored the social imperative to depict, work through and reinterpret the tragic events of the 11 September 2001 terrorist attacks in the United States via two Hollywood films: *United 93* (2006) and *World Trade Center* (2006). In both, he found 'a narrative arc that emphasizes human agency and collective heroic action in the face of overwhelming catastrophe'.[37] The desire to find power, to celebrate individual ordinary citizens turned heroes, to show a light at the end of a dark tunnel in these two works reveals, as Burgoyne argues, something about American society in that period (for an alternative examination of post-9/11 film culture, see Chapter 12).

Another example of context is available with a consideration of major war films made after the Vietnam War. In a time of increasing cynicism in America, with domestic and international acts of violence abounding, war films took a darker turn to reflect this cultural atmosphere. With something far from victory obtained in Southeast Asia, American war films began to exude a rejection of authority and prior visions of military glory, as evidenced in Vietnam-related works *The Deer Hunter* (1978) and *Apocalypse Now* (1979), as well as Second World War title *The Big Red One* (1980).[38]

Context is not everything. Contingency and idiosyncratic approaches project onto moving image sources. The point is to help explore some of the major lines of inquiry open to all interested in using moving image sources for historical understanding. To remove an object from its historical context risks eroding the multitudinous (and sometimes rather subtle) ways that time/place factors shape those that produce – and those that consume – such material.

Production factors

Intentions are only part of the story, and one must also consider limitations or restrictions that affect the generation of moving images; a director or scriptwriter may wish to depict a certain event, but due to technological limitations or budgetary factors feel incapable of delivering the desired result. For this reason the 'history of moving images' line of analysis proves most requisite. Thinking in terms of historical evolution will lead the interested viewer to consider means of film making as well as constraints on content, expression and dissemination. These factors definitely influence the final product and must be evaluated when conducting a source analysis.

Drawing on the work of film and history scholars, one can easily find a treatment of technological and public policy factors relating to the production of moving images.[39] The technological capabilities of film recording devices, which earlier were bulky and largely immobile and thus led to more static scene settings, must be considered. As camera and lighting technology advanced, more innovative and mobile production opportunities materialized, shaping major commercial entertainment as well as amateur activities. To demonstrate the latter, consider the absence of personal recording devices in the early twentieth century, the smattering of cameras first without and then with sound recording capabilities available in mid-century, and then the explosion of visual/audio recording devices available for personal use by the end of the century (first as standalone products, now incorporated into multi-functional handheld devices). Recording is just one side of the story; means of accessing these sources have changed radically, from mediated settings such as nickelodeons then theaters, to home viewing with increasing personalized control (think of the VCR and then DVR shifts),[40] and now highly individualized access possibilities with Internet and satellite technology.[41] Technological innovation that afforded the expansion of opportunities to capture aspects of life should be considered. One should also ponder how representative moving image stock is of whatever it is purportedly displaying.

Viewers must treat moving images as any other source and evaluate them by considering the author's access to knowledge, the ability to convey that knowledge (in this sense technological issues are a concern) and intentions behind distributing the knowledge. For commercial ventures, the means devoted to the task of producing films have radically changed over the past century. Understanding this evolution will help students of history better evaluate and more rigorously employ moving images as sources for their understandings of the past. For example, the ability of motion picture production companies to recreate scenes of major warfare has shifted from something more evocative to a far more graphically explicit presentation; partly a reflection of social mores (thus the continuing importance of cultural context), partly due to changing possibilities with production factors – budgets, filming capabilities and post-filming additions such as Computer Generated Imagery (CGI). There is an evolving relationship between the means to display something and the desire to do so.

Censorship is one intervening factor in the relationship between production and consumption of moving images. Major commercial film ventures in the United States, for instance, experienced a high degree of self-regulated censorship that dictated the bounds of acceptability from the 1930s to the mid-1960s.[42] Censors focused their attention primarily on sexual innuendo or social subversion, but also established finite limits on bloodshed permissible for war films. Assessment of a moving image source as a potential reflection of contemporary culture must also factor in the influence of censorship, an example of cultural input. Using war films once more, production companies often do not have access to many of the major material requirements to set scenes, such as military vehicles, and traditionally have depended upon government assistance or access. This can lead to overt censorship, as expertly covered by film historian Lawrence Suid.[43] For documentary productions or imagery created at the time of the event, censorship is still a significant factor.[44] Documentaries are subject to regulation and production organizations have to face concern over distribution, which may be hindered if flouting social or cultural mores. War-related documentary films, particularly those created during the conflict, will tend to follow demarcated boundaries of content and expression.[45] The viewer must interrogate the source to uncover all of the – at times stated, at other times unstated – agendas in operation.

Evoking the past

There remains one final area of concern for the use of moving image sources to advance understanding of the past. The above categories have suggested the need for a critical evaluation of moving images as sources, just as one would expect with any source material – only refined to reflect the realities of this particular medium. For this final consideration a more nebulous concept is required. Viewers must learn how to conduct deep readings of this source material. This thought relates to the notion of historiophoty advanced by Hayden White wherein viewers must assess the full range of visual and (when applicable) audio effects that feature in a moving image (for further discussion of this, see Chapter 14).[46] Or, as Rosenstone sensibly cautioned, 'To change the medium of history from the page to the screen, to add images, sound, colour, movement, and drama, is to alter the way we read, see, perceive, and think about the past'.[47]

Beyond assessing the main characters or the primary action in centre focus, viewers must consider the overall admixture of sensory stimuli that combine to create the particular presentation of the past. Rosenstone warned to avoid assuming 'that the audience only learns from the central story and the fate of individual characters', and instead to remember that these sources offer 'an experience, the presentation of a world whose moments, characters and images – particularly if they are strong – are capable of staying with the viewer long after the specific plots and resolutions have disappeared'.[48] The camera demands many elements for a convincing display of the past and seldom do filmmakers (professional Hollywood to amateur videographers) leave things to happenstance. With recreated scenes, 'actors assume the roles of historical characters and provide them with gestures, movements, and voice sounds that create meaning', which may have no evidentiary foundation.[49] To set a scene, requires artistic licence in the presentation of the myriad material effects and idiosyncratic mannerisms that the camera demands and audiences expect; 'Language is a very important sign system used by television, but words are not the only symbolic signs that television [or other moving image sources] uses'.[50]

The ambience presented in a moving image helps convey messages and will influence the reception and reaction of viewers. Consider the frequent use of rain to evoke a feeling of sadness in film productions, or the instantly recognizable 'Imperial March' that accompanies the on-screen presence of key villainous characters in the *Star Wars* series. Weather effects, music, lighting, action or stillness, colour versus black-and-white, cluttered or relatively empty frames, and countless other choices influence our perception of content in moving images. Seemingly ancillary features can heavily shape the presentation of a depicted event. Content editing capabilities further add to the arsenal of tools available to creators of this source material. The purposeful employment of such techniques and/or features in any assessment of a moving image source must be considered. As White admonished, 'Modern historians ought to be aware that the analysis of visual images requires a manner of "reading" quite different from that developed for the study of written documents'.[51] A full 'reading' of moving images necessarily includes consideration of all these elements.

Seeing the past: Payoff

After gauging the litany of analytical challenges moving image sources offer, one may be dissuaded from relying upon them in any exploration of the past. That would be folly, as these sources present many robust possibilities for the conscientious researcher. As Rosenstone argued, 'Film has given us tools to see reality in a new way – including the realities of a past which has long since vanished from our sight'.[52] The most significant payoff offered by this source base is the ability to visualize the material in ways that textual or audio renderings simply cannot emulate. Students are more likely to connect with and 'feel' the past they study once able to visualize the events, the people, the settings under consideration.

With great potential comes great responsibility. Moving image sources present many possible uses for an individual to explore the past. Yet there are dangers only outlined above. Some major problems with these sources reside in the ability to simplify, distort, fabricate, or unduly arrogate authority (by imprinting on audiences). As one historian indicated, critics of moving image sources argue that this source base can be 'a useful vehicle for arousing interest or sensitizing viewers to a problem, but [it is] a poor mechanism for presenting detailed, balanced, and comprehensive coverage of a subject'.[53] As he continued, however, 'Films use different techniques to explain the past, but the truths conveyed in images are not necessarily in conflict with the truths conveyed in words'.[54] The dangers of simplification or distortion can be mitigated with proper care. Students of the past must prepare for the successful analysis of any moving image source. Through a consideration of issues broached above, a rigorous analytical approach will permit viewers to achieve that *critical* assessment of a moving image source that is requisite for its use in any educational endeavour.

There is no magic formula that lends itself to easy, straightforward, yet suitably rigorous analysis of any source, let alone a moving image. Preparatory work is required for the selection of suitable material and then critical engagement with that material. Background research, reading and consideration will help establish expectations and inform questions to ask of the material. Familiarity with the content and context of creation will enable viewers to grapple with the potentials and pitfalls that arise with any source. A holistic approach to moving image analysis will strengthen the process of thinking-viewing-incorporating this information. The three approaches delineated above should be combined to consider the accuracy of content, the technical and informational capabilities of the image's creators, and the cultural input that shaped the final product and its reception.

An additional complicating factor is that many of the moving images available for use as a historical source were not created to preserve the past; the makers had entertainment or profit-seeking motives in mind. Television audiences are fickle and have a wealth of content to choose from, while major filmmakers have come to rely on certain stock approaches that prove reliably popular and financially lucrative.[55] Popular preference engenders repetition, with multiple airings of films and television programmes or repeated access of Internet content.[56] That factor alone could prompt an investigation into reasons why certain sources are more popular than others. Reception and audience understanding were only lightly touched upon in this chapter. A cautious student of the past will admit that even the most rigorous analysis of a given source does not provide the researcher with the full range of interpretations other viewers derived from their encounter with the material.[57]

These reservations and aspirations apply to all popular moving image sources like major commercial films, news media, stock television fare, or the ever-expanding variety of content available on the Internet. The vast majority of these sources arose as a path to profit for some interested party. The expectation for self-censorship (to boost audience acceptance) or shading or distortion of the past should lead all students to be cautious when relying on these sources. That caution should not lead to paralysis or deny outright the due consideration of potentially beneficial material. Although, as one critic castigated, television is middle-class 'conformist, sells things, and has hidden authors', he still acknowledged that it has the power to bind us together in a global community.[58]

In closing, there are two principal ways that moving images can serve as primary source material for historical education. The first is as a filmic record of the people and places of the past or events as they unfold. The second is as a cultural lens through which one can view contemporary society at the time and place of creation. One can also glean something about the society that views these images, that uses them to access the past. As historian Jerome de Groot suggested, 'How a society consumes its history is crucial to the understanding of contemporary popular culture, the issues at stake in representation itself, and the various means of self- or social construction available'.[59] These sources are just as versatile, just as robust, and just as potentially misleading as any other material available to the interested student of the past. As another historian argued, 'As a stimulus for thought and feeling, as a visual text addressing broad problems, as a foray into historiography, or as a sensitive reconstruction of times, places, people and events, films can promote new ideas'.[60] With proper accord, due caution and rigorous inquiry, they can provide useful answers to a host of profound questions. The real trick is in determining which are worth asking in the first place.

Robert Rosenstone once seemed like a solitary figure championing the cause of moving image material as worthy of serious historical inquiry. Now, moving images often provide input into history as understood by the student, teacher, scholar and public at large. Despite the work of the previous decades, much scholarly work remains to be done in the effort to promote critical inquiry of the past with the use of moving images as a serious, widely accepted source base. 'Almost a century after the birth of the motion picture,' as Rosenstone himself once lamented, 'film presents historians with a challenge still unseized, a challenge to begin to think of how to use the medium to its full capability for carrying information, juxtaposing images and words, providing startling and contrastive mixtures of sight and sound, and (perhaps) creating analytic structures that include visual elements.'[61] This volume serves in the quest of extending Rosenstone's call for serious treatment of moving image sources, with critical rigour. The chapters that follow each provide a more focused study to assist in this overarching goal, putting into practice, in various ways, the ideas and methods discussed above.[62]

Notes

1   W. J. McKeachie, *McKeachie's Teaching Tips: Strategies, Research, and Theory for College and University Teachers*, 11th edn (New York: Houghton Mifflin Company, 2002), 11.

2   P. B. Weinstein, 'Movies as the Gateway to History: The History and Film Project', *The History Teacher* 35 (2001): 27–48.

3   Rosenstone issued an early call to arms in, 'History in Images/History in Words: Reflections on the Possibility of Really Putting History onto Film', *The American Historical Review* 93 (1988): 1173–85.

4   A sound starting point for any individual interested in unpackaging the underlying meaning and structure of sources, including written as well as visual, is found with the work of Jacques Derrida. Derrida's sometimes dense philosophizing was monumentally important for launching deconstruction (peeling away content to find deeper meaning), particularly in the United States. A solid baseline assessment of his work is found in S. Glendinning, *Derrida: A Very Short Introduction* (New York: Oxford University Press, 2011). Regarding introductions to the other theoretical approaches mentioned, see J. Culler, *Literary Theory: A Very Short Introduction*, 2nd edn (New York: Oxford University Press, 2011); P. Barry, *Beginning Theory: An Introduction to Literary and Cultural Theory*, 3rd edn (Manchester: Manchester University Press, 2009); R. Stam, *Film Theory: An Introduction* (Malden, MA: Wiley-Blackwell, 2000); L. Braudy, *Film Theory and Criticism: Introductory Readings*, 6th edn (New York: Oxford University Press, 2004).

5   A prime example of this approach is offered by S. Ambrose, '*The Longest Day* (US, 1962): "Blockbuster" History', in *World War II, Film, and History*, ed. J. Whiteclay Chambers II and D. Culbert (New York: Oxford University Press, 1996), 97–106.

6   See, for instance, L. Suid, *Guts & Glory: The Making of the American Military Image in Film*, rev. edn (Lexington: University Press of Kentucky, 2002).

7　R. Sklar, *Movie-Made America: A Cultural History of American Movies*, rev. and updated (New York: Vintage, 1994).

8　The clearest example of this argument appears in R. A. Rosenstone, *History on Film, Film on History*, 2nd edn (New York: Pearson, 2012).

9　J. Winter, 'Film and the Matrix of Memory', *The American Historical Review* 106 (2001): 863.

10　J. R. Benjamin, *A Student's Guide to History*, 10th edn (New York: Bedford/ St. Martin's, 2007), 105.

11　Rosenstone, *History on Film*, 5.

12　R. Burgoyne, *The Hollywood Historical Film* (Malden, MA: Blackwell, 2008), 125–46.

13　'Steven Spielberg', *Inside the Actors Studio*, dir. J. Wurtz, Bravo Channel, 1999, VHS, accessed at the UCLA Film and Television Archive, Los Angeles, California.

14　For more on the subject of the Holocaust in American culture, see H. Flanzbaum (ed.), *The Americanization of the Holocaust* (Baltimore: Johns Hopkins University Press, 1999); or P. Novick, *The Holocaust in American Life* (New York: Houghton Mifflin, 1999).

15　Letter, Charles Brackett to Robert J. Wright, 6 March 1957, Folder Charles Brackett papers 1.f-[21] D-DAY, THE SIXTH OF JUNE – correspondence, Charles Brackett papers, Special Collections, Margaret Herrick Library, The Academy of Motion Picture Arts and Sciences, Beverly Hills, California. Hereafter referred to as MHL.

16　R. Schickel, 'Belated Victory: *The Big Red One*', *Time*, 21 July 1980, Folder The Big Red One Lorimar/United Artists 1980 Warner Bros. 2005 Also Known As: THE BIG RED ONE: THE RECONSTRUCTION (REVIEWS & MAGAZINE ARTICLES), Core Collections, MHL.

17　*The Big Red One*, as many of the films mentioned in this chapter, could serve in either capacity as a primary or a secondary source. In the former, it could help portray post-Vietnam understandings of war in American popular culture. In the latter, it would stand along any other secondary source analysis of combat and daily life of American soldiers during the Second World War.

18　Suid, *Guts & Glory*, 273–7.

19　S. Considine, *Mad as Hell: The Life and Work of Paddy Chayefsky* (New York: Random House, 1994), 17–23.

20　M. Paris, 'Reconstructing D-Day: 6 June 1944 and British Documentary Films', in *The Normandy Campaign 1944: Sixty Years On*, ed. J. Buckley (New York: Routledge, 2006), 207–9.

21　The historiography of film has been a topic of scholarly attention for some time. For an earlier example of this work, see C. F. Altman, 'Towards a Historiography of American Film', *Cinema Journal* 16 (Spring 1977): 1–25.

22　In fact, as Rosenstone argued, 'What we too easily ignore ... is the extent to which written history, and especially narrative history, is also shaped by conventions of genre and language'. See his article, 'History in Images', 1180.

23   J. Basinger, *The World War II Combat Film: Anatomy of a Genre*, updated filmography by J. Arnold (New York: Columbia University Press, 1986; Middletown, CT: Wesleyan University Press, 2003), 1.

24   Burgoyne, *The Hollywood Historical Film*, 14.

25   J. Feuer, 'Genre Study and Television', in *Channels of Discourse: Television and Contemporary Criticism*, ed. R. C. Allen (Chapel Hill, NC: University of North Carolina Press, 1987), 113–33.

26   T. Doherty, 'The New War Movies as Moral Rearmament: *Black Hawk Down* and *We Were Soldiers*', in *The War Film*, ed. R. Eberwein (New Brunswick, NJ: Rutgers University Press, 2005), 214–22; J. Mathews, 'Maneuvering in the Theaters of War: Tales of 2 Battles Pushed Ahead', 8 November 2001, *Daily News (New York)*, LexisNexus Academic (accessed 8 April 2010).

27   Basinger, *The World War II Combat Film*, explores the evolution of the American combat film genre.

28   R. C. Allen, 'Introduction: Talking about Television', in *Channels of Discourse* (Chapel Hill: The University of North Carolina Press, 1987), 3.

29   J. de Groot, *Consuming History: Historians and Heritage in Contemporary Popular Culture* (New York: Routledge, 2009), 149–54. On *The World at War*, cf. T. Downing, 'History on Television: The Making of *Cold War*, 1998', in *The Historical Film: History and Memory in Media*, ed. M. Landy (New Brunswick, NJ: Rutgers University Press, 2001), 294–96.

30   S. Rosenheim, 'Interrotroning History: Errol Morris and the Documentary of the Future', in *The Historical Film: History and Memory in Media*, ed. M. Landy (New Brunswick, NJ: Rutgers University Press, 2001), 316–17.

31   Burns was building upon the work of predecessors and any full evaluation of documentary films as primary sources should trace these interconnections. R. Kennedy, 'The Still-Life Mentor to a Filmmaking Generation', *New York Times*, 19 October 2006. Available online: http://www.nytimes.com/2006/10/19/arts/design/19lieb.html?_r=0 (accessed 23 December 2014).

32   Downing, 'History on Television', 295.

33   S. R. Kozloff, 'Narrative Theory and Television', in *Channels of Discourse*, ed. R. C. Allen (Chapel Hill: The University of North Carolina Press, 1987), 45. For a telling critique of uncritical employment of Internet-provided and heavily edited film clips to 'learn about' warfare, see D. Finkel, *Thank You for Your Service* (New York: Farrar, Straus and Giroux, 2013), 227.

34   P. Novick, *That Noble Dream: The 'Objectivity Question' and the American Historical Profession* (New York: Cambridge University Press, 1988).

35   Allen, 'Introduction', *Channels of Discourse*, 12.

36   G. S. Wood, *The Purpose of the Past: Reflections on the Uses of History* (New York: Penguin, 2008), 20.

37   Burgoyne, *The Hollywood Historical Film*, 148–68 (quote on 149).

38 Suid, *Guts & Glory*, 295–423; W. Hagen, '*Apocalypse Now* (1979): Joseph Conrad and the Television War', in *Hollywood as Historian: American Film in a Cultural Context,* ed. P. C. Rollins (Lexington: University Press of Kentucky, 1983), 230–45; P. C. Rollins and J. E. O'Connor (eds), *Why We Fought: America's Wars in Film and History* (Lexington: University Press of Kentucky, 2008), Chs 17–19; and M. Anderegg (ed.), *Inventing Vietnam: The War in Film and Television* (Philadelphia: Temple University Press, 1991).

39 Suid, *Guts & Glory*, is the best example of relevance. Cf., Burgoyne, *The Hollywood Historical Film.*

40 For a consideration of public engagement with the past through home viewing due to VCR capabilities, see R. A. Beaumont, 'Images of War: Films as Documentary History', *Military Affairs* 35 (1971): 5–7.

41 De Groot, *Consuming History*, 3–9.

42 L. J. Leff, 'A Test of American Film Censorship: *Who's Afraid of Virginia Woolf?* (1966)', in *Hollywood as Historian,* ed. P. C. Rollins (Lexington: University Press of Kentucky, 1983), 211–29; S. Prince, 'A Brief History of Film Violence', in *Violence in Film and Television,* ed. J. D. Torr (San Diego, CA: Greenhaven Press, Inc., 2002), 21–8.

43 Suid, *Guts & Glory*. For a recent example, see N. Wapshott, 'Hollywood Moguls Enlisted to Bolster War Effort', *The Times,* 10 November 2001.

44 On a related point about wartime censorship in general concerning the Second World War, see T. Doherty, *Projections of War: Hollywood, American Culture, and World War II,* rev. and updated (New York: Columbia University Press, 1999), 133, 233.

45 As an example, consider F. Capra's *Why We Fight* series (1942–4) that presented the Second World War as a world-saving contest between fascism and democracy. For more on wartime censorship and Second World War moving images, see G. H. Roeder, Jr., *The Censored War: American Visual Experience During World War Two* (New Haven, CT: Yale University Press, 1993), 43–66.

46 H. White, 'Historiography and Historiophoty', *The American Historical Review* 93 (1988): 1193.

47 Rosenstone, *History on Film*, 186.

48 Ibid., 169.

49 Rosenstone, 'History in Images', 1181.

50 E. Seiter, 'Semiotics and Television', in *Channels of Discourse: Television and Contemporary Criticism*, ed. R. C. Allen (Chapel Hill, NC: University of North Carolina Press, 1987), 20. Seiter also cautions that '[i]t is important to remember that TV is a sign system, and, therefore, can be used to lie' (23). For more this analytical approach, see D. Chandler, *Semiotics: The Basics,* 2nd edn (New York: Routledge, 2007).

51 White, 'Historiography and Historiophoty', 1193.

52 Rosenstone, *History on Film,* 179.

53 R. B. Toplin, 'The Filmmaker as Historian', *The American Historical Review* 93 (1988): 1215. He also warned, 'The public does not expect an

introduction to historians' debates when watching a film about the past',
but 'by their presentation of evidence and attempts to draw conclusions' the
films are taking sides (1218).

54   Ibid., 1226.

55   See de Groot, *Consuming History*, 153; R. B. Toplin, 'Hollywood's D-Day
from the Perspective of the 1960s and 1990s: *The Longest Day* and *Saving
Private Ryan*', in *Why We Fought: America's Wars in Film and History*, ed.
P. Rollins and J. E. O'Connor (Lexington: University Press of Kentucky) 313;
and Feuer, 'Genre Study', 119.

56   For instance, consider the multiple airings of *The World at War*, described
in Downing, 'History on Television', 295. In addition, repeated theatrical
re-releases and television airings of *The Longest Day* (1962) display its
popularity while also suggesting questions about why audiences flocked
to this source just as much as what it is they derived from viewing it. See,
M. R. Dolski, '"To Set Free a Suffering Humanity": D-Day in American
Remembrance' (Ph.D. diss., Temple University, 2012), 147–53.

57   Allen provided a few thoughts regarding audience reception in his chapter
'Reader-Oriented Criticism and Television', in *Channels of Discourse*,
(Chapel Hill: The University of North Carolina Press, 1987), 74–112.

58   B. Cummings, *War and Television* (New York: Verso: 1992), 22–33. Cf.,
Allen, 'Reader-Oriented Criticism', 108. More damning assessments abound,
though, as evidenced by M. A. Doane's rebuke of television's destructive
impact on popular understandings of history. As she wrote, 'Television, too,
has been conceptualized as the annihilation of memory, and consequently
of history, in its continual stress upon the "newness" of its own discourse'.
See Doane, 'Information, Crisis, Catastrophe', in *The Historical Film:
History and Memory in Media*, ed. M. Landy (New Brunswick, NJ: Rutgers
University Press), 274.

59   De Groot, *Consuming History*, 2.

60   Toplin, 'The Filmmaker as Historian', 1226.

61   Rosenstone, 'History in Images', 1184.

62   Most of the examples in this chapter referred to American war films, which
is an indication of my areas of interest and expertise. Nevertheless, the
questions posed and the caveats provided will apply across the board to
moving images of all types intended for many purposes.

CHAPTER TWO

The moving image as a secondary source: Truth, authenticity and narrative

Faye Sayer

Overlooking 'popular history'

The history presented in moving images has often been overlooked, under-valued and disregarded by many historians; considered nothing more than populist entertainment. For some, film and television misuses and misin-terprets 'History' for commercial gain, with scant regard for historical accuracy.[1] Students might even be instructed that this sort of 'history' is not a valid historical source and should not be used for research purposes. This chapter will not debate the validity and potential of the moving image as a primary source, as discussed in Chapter 1.[2] Rather, this chapter will show the value of the moving image as a secondary source of historical information, supporting the critical deconstruction and interpretation of the complex narratives within moving images as a form of history. It will explore the moving image as a current narrative for alternative historical perspectives, which understand the interweaving interpretations of the past, and which acknowledge history's contextuality. As such, this chapter seeks to explore the positive and negative implications of using films and television as secondary evidence for historical research; considering criti-cally whether moving images can ever be regarded as 'good history'.

Historical stories are frequently communicated via television and film as a form of entertainment, acting as secondary sources of historical information, for both the public and historians. These moving images can provide broad public and academic access to primary source material. The dynamic and interweaving historical narratives presented within moving images provide, and document, diverse visual and audio interpretations of history. As such, these mediums of historical communication can transcend beyond normative, often singular, linear academic narratives.

The 'history' portrayed in films and television often represents multiple perspectives that reflect the diverse human experiences of the past. Using these mediums as secondary sources can illustrate the overarching complexities of historical interpretation. For example, they can demonstrate the impact of drawing from incomplete evidence and of portraying the past through a medium often used for fictional narratives. Concerns regarding the accuracy of sourcing are confounded by the lack of 'scholarly apparatus' contained within moving images; i.e. footnotes, citations and referencing. The analysis of moving images as a historical source requires the historian to effectively 'reverse engineer' both its production by filmmakers and consumption by the audience. A keen analysis must also consider the social and political frameworks in which these moving images are produced. Yet it is not only a critical analysis of the historical framework at the basis of the creation of moving images that is important; this *must* be supplemented by an analysis of the techniques of cinematography, camera work and music, factors that influence meaning.[3]

This chapter, and several of the subsequent ones (particularly Chapters 7, 9, 10, 11 and 14), seek to explore the historical use and validity of 'moving images', specifically film and television, as secondary sources for interpreting and accessing the past. This critical exploration of moving images seeks to encourage, and in many senses enable, the reader to deconstruct films and television as a historical secondary source. By deconstructing the production and consumption of this historical medium, this chapter aims to inspire the reader to discuss and debate issues relating to historical truth, authenticity and narrative construction. This chapter will also examine how films and television programmes can, when used cautiously and through the critical lens of a historian, provide a mechanism to understand diverse and often untold historical narratives.

Secondary sources

The moving image as a secondary source (a source that has been produced to record a historical event, time period, or person after that event, time period or person has occurred) is still often undervalued and viewed with disdain by some in the historical establishment.[4] Some historians have been distrustful about the use of materials such as films and television programmes as secondary documentary sources, and as such have not included them in their historical research.[5] This distrust potentially stems from an inherent conservatism that thwarts some elements of the profession: a lingering conservatism in both research approaches and in source hierarchy. The reticence of some historians to utilize moving images as source material could also be a result of time limitations in researching and analysing already extensive written materials.[6] The resistance of some historians to utilize moving images as a secondary source could also be related to a lack of appropriate analytical skills and confidence to tackle this still developing area of research.[7] These skills include developing structuralist based models for analysis that enable historians to critically deconstruct the various components which produce the final moving image as a document. Deconstruction requires historians to consider not only the date of production and authorship of the source, its points of view and narrative, but also visual, linguistic and stylistic content and elements.[8] This requires historians, as with any historical source, to consider moving images through various critical lenses. These lenses include reliability, credibility, truth, objectivity and authenticity. This chapter will focus on deconstructing the authenticity, truth and narrative of these sources. This method of deconstruction enables historians to decode the iconic and logistic visual messages contained within moving images and to understand the value of moving images as useful secondary sources.[9]

Authenticity

Authenticity, for many historians, has become synonymous with concepts of 'truth', 'fact' and 'evidence'. The authenticity of historical evidence, of secondary sources, is judged on their perceived historical reliability, objectivity and truthfulness; critically, on the 'proven' factual accuracy of the source.[10] This is an accuracy that can be verified by primary source evidence, such as first-hand accounts and official documentation from the time. In assessing the authenticity of moving images as secondary sources, historians often make judgements based on a personal assessment of whether the moving image provides an accurate portrayal of the period, event or person it aims to represent. This analysis is based on a comparison between visual and audio elements presented on screen with that which is regarded as historical or even archaeological fact, such as first-hand 'primary source' written documentation. Resultantly, the analysis of authenticity frequently relates to the nature of evidence, to what historians perceive as trusted, reliable and credible sources. Research into a secondary source's authenticity thus relies heavily on the influence of 'trusted' and 'authentic' primary historical source material used when creating this secondary source. Conversely, first-hand accounts, such as oral testimonies, are frequently regarded by historians as subjective and problematic; their integration within moving images seen to jeopardize the authenticity of these secondary sources.[11]

When film history first began to develop in the 1970s and 1980s, some historians branded moving images as inauthentic, fictional historical re-creations.[12] Despite the significant work done over the last three decades, this critique of films and television as a historical source still lingers in some quarters. In part, this is based on the conventional historical method, which relies upon a variety of both primary and secondary historical evidence; for example, oral history testimonies, personal biographies, official records and scholarly articles. These primary and secondary historical documents are frequently used alongside contemporary fictional visual and narrative elements. But these fictional elements reflect modern conventions and on-screen characters have to be 'created' to appeal to the modern consumer. It is these fictional traits that enable the viewer to form emotive and cultural connections with moving images. As such, many historians questioned the authenticity of historical media, criticising it for simplifying, sensational- izing, romanticizing and 'disneyfying' history.[13] These critiques were often grounded in criticisms of the commercialization of the past, with the media industry accused of 'using' history for purely for entertainment purposes, to generate revenue through viewing figures rather than providing the public with an authentic, educational and worthwhile portrayal of the past.[14]

This judgement of the authenticity of moving images as secondary sources is in direct juxtaposition to authenticity as viewed by the public. The public often base judgements of authenticity on cultural and popular stereotypes and national myths.[15] To the public viewer, authenticity is based on an alternate set of criteria to that of historians, with emotivism, nostalgia, accessibility and personal connectivity being central. As a result, moving images portrayed on the 'big screen' are often regarded as providing a more publicly accessible and authentic representation of the past.[16]

The idea that films and television dramas not solely based on traditional 'factual' 'documentary evidence' fail to offer an authentic representation or even re-creation of the past still persists in some quarters.[17] Yet in the last few decades, historical films and television programmes have nonetheless begun to challenge such traditional views of authenticity. The production of history by the film and television industries has directly confronted academic beliefs regarding the values of more diverse historical sources to interpretation and research, and as such has brought into question the hierarchical nature of conventional historical research. For example, films such as *Schindler's List* (1993) have challenged ideas that moving images are inauthentic historical secondary sources. This film attempts to create an authentic treatment of the Holocaust, using historical facts and first- hand accounts.[18] As Chapter 14 explores, through working with historians in their development, writing and production, documentaries, previously judged as unworthy source material, have begun to be merited for their ability to amalgamate large quantities of primary and secondary history material and as such provide a tool for education, for instance *The Great War* (BBC 1964) and *The World at War* (Thames Television 1973).[19]

For many historians, and indeed members of the public, different types of media history are believed to have different levels of authenticity. For example, historical television documentaries such as Lucy Worsely's *The Age of Regency* (BBC 2011) and Simon Schama's *A History of Britain* (BBC 2000–2) are often regarded as more authentic, truthful and accurate portrayals of history than dramas and films (see also Chapter 14).[20] Television documentaries are often assumed – by both the professionals and the public – to provide unbiased scholarly representations of the past, perhaps due to the fact the presenters of these programmes are professional historians.[21] They are praised for their ability to present multiple forms of evidence and interpretations accurately.[22] Furthermore, many television documentaries – though not all, as Chapter 14 discusses – do not employ the use of visual techniques such as re-enactment and reconstruction to recreate the past; such techniques are often associated with entertainment rather than education, and as a result are critiqued by professionals for perpetrating inaccurate portrayals of the past.[23] Yet, nonetheless, documentaries do simplify history. They are often based on one historian's viewpoint, 'the presenter', on the study of one person, event or time period, and resultantly they often do not present multiple or complex interpretations of history. The history presented in this format can serve to fulfil the political, social and economic agendas of the historian 'presenter'; to provide wider impact for their research, to market and publicize their work and to develop their own career.

Conversely, popular cinematic historical films, for example *Kingdom of Heaven* (2005), or television dramatizations of history, such as the BBC's *The Last Kingdom* (BBC 2015), are regarded by some historians as inauthentic, untruthful and inaccurate representations of history.[24] These films and television dramas, despite working within a backdrop of historical narrative, are in reality based on minimal and sometimes inaccurate historical and archaeological research; they lack factual evidence.[25] The recent plethora of biographical films, such as *The Iron Lady* (2012) and *Lincoln* (2013), illustrate how authenticity is also based on the subject, i.e. the particular historical figure.

As Chapter 9 discusses, historians often assess the authenticity of films and television programmes based on a series of visual cues and their appropriateness to the period. This includes: personal adornments, for example costume design, hair styles, jewellery; set design, such as locational and architectural elements recreated or used in filming; linguistic traits, for example the language and terminology used. These details are compared with historical and archaeological knowledge, for example written documents, illustrations, paintings and artefacts that can be linked to the period being portrayed. If the style of dress is not in keeping with the time period then the programme or film could be regarded as an inaccurate representation of the past.

As illustrated by BBC1's *The Last Kingdom*, authenticity is not merely about visual or aesthetic accuracy; rather authenticity is also about personal experiences and connections, which the consumer uses to construct nostalgic links to the past.[26] As such, the definition of authenticity is dynamic and changeable; like the past, it is not frozen or monolithic.[27] Authenticity is contextually constructed; it is based on the cultural experiences and perspectives of the viewer. To be regarded as authentic by the public often requires historical media to draw on popular historical narratives and stereotypes. Authenticity also requires the programme or film to enable the public to interact with the sensory visual and audio material presented, to generate new human experience.[28]

The inaccuracy of a secondary source is perhaps harder to identify than that of a primary source. For example, for a director and producer of a historically based film, the historical representation is authentic to their wishes. As a secondary source regarded within its newly created temporal and social context, media history is a reflection of modern history, of interpretative changes based on context. As such, history as portrayed on television and in films serves to represent cultural trends, dominant political paradigms and social changes of a period and place; and in some cases of a specific person, producer, director and writer. As a result, the moving image becomes an accurate representation of history in its current context.

Truth

Truth is associated with fact. The belief that something is true relates to a certainty in the evidence being accurate. Subsequently, if a historian believes that a secondary source, such as a moving image, is truthful, they are suggesting that the source has accuracy in its interpretation and presentation of the past. Consequently, documentaries that are based on presenting 'historical' factual evidence, such as *The Great War* (BBC 1964), are often deemed 'truthful' (see also Chapters 13 and 14), as opposed to films or television dramatizations such as *Deadwood* (HBO 2006), which could be considered fictional modern mythologies and popular recreations of historical ideas.[29]

Producers and directors of historical films and television series rarely claim to want to reconstruct or recreate historical truth, despite the search for truth being the dominant ideology in the discipline of history. Perhaps this is because this popular media seeks to move away from 'traditional' scholarship and resonate with a wider audience in which truth is not the dominant ideology; rather escapism, connectivity and entertainment are.[30] Popular media can seek to explore untold truths. The interplay between truth and fiction enables new narratives to be heard, narratives that represent the history of not only the elite and heroes but of those forgotten or underrepresented in primary sources, for example minority groups and slaves.[31] For instance, *12 Years a Slave* (2013) explores an autobiographical story of the history of slavery in Southern America before the Civil War and displays the impacts of slavery on African-Americans and their treatment by their owners from an angle unrecorded in the historical annals, stories that were unwritten, unheard and deliberately subdued (see Chapter 7). On the other hand, *Band of Brothers* (HBO 2001) uses interviews with survivors, personal journals and letters to tell the story of the soldiers of the US Army 506th Regiment of the 101st Airborne Division, rather than the formal records and official documents from commanders and leaders (see Chapter 11).

Truth is a concept of functionalism, yet visual media in its current form was created in a postmodernist framework of multiple interweaving stories of the past, based on both tangible and intangible evidence, on interpretations of fact and the addition of fictional elements to create a story. For historians examining media as a historical secondary source, it is essential to move on from the idea of 'truth' supported by primary normative 'tangible' evidence. This requires a movement away from the modernist, rationalist, absolutist framework of historical analysis, from belief in absolute 'evidential' proof, to a postmodernist framework of the social construction of knowledge; of the contextualist, relativist idea of truth as essentially being non-existent.[32] As Nietzsche suggests, 'there are no facts, only interpretations'.[33] Examination and analysis of media as a historical secondary source or primary source is based in relativism, in understanding that this is a social construct representing a contextual viewpoint.[34] Perhaps historical television programmes and films should not be regarded as either truthful or untruthful, rather they should be seen to represent the grey area in-between the two; the unproved and un-testimonied history. They therefore serve as a critical construct of the point in time at which the media was created.[35]

History as historical media is influenced by external factors and personal biases of the producer, which affects their interpretation of the past. This considers the wider public involvement in the creation and production of history, which is part of understanding history's creation. For example, it has been suggested that films are also art; therefore filmmakers are less motivated by facts while historians are often driven by the need to find them. It is this lack of dialect between the two arenas that thwarts our understanding of this type of source.[36]

This new approach requires historians to consider not only how and why history was created in this form, but the broader influences on history, including national and international political, social and culture frameworks in which moving images exist and are created. This moves away from acceptance of historical media based on representing absolute truth to an analysis of accurate, authentic representations. Furthermore, studies such as the Present the Past Project (US) and The Past Project (AUS) suggest that the public do not trust historical films and television as much books and museums, even though films and television are the dominant form of historical knowledge interface for the public.[37] This is a salient point for historians; perhaps historians should be less concerned with truth when examining this popular historical medium and focus on how this medium provides a unique cultural representation of history and the complex myriad of interwoven historical stories that television and films can present.

Narrative

Creating historical narratives in moving images requires a system of enquiry and interpretation that work within the media industry's conventions.[38] In order for history to be accessible and have a coherent message, the creation of history in moving images requires multi-faceted, complex and contradictory narratives to be interweaved and presented in a linear and uncluttered form.[39] The complex narratives of history are simplified to enable a singular story to be presented within a limited timeframe. These mediums present historical stories that remove historical contradictions.

The creation of moving images moves beyond constructing the beginning and end of a story to investigate the middle ground, the humanistic drivers for events and periods.[40] In order to create characters, filmmakers need to understand the motivations for their actions rather than merely the action and its consequences.[41] The result is a complex socio-cultural construct of history that is combined with imagination and storytelling.[42] The difference from this and other narrative discourses is the types of evidence used. Empirical historians rely on written primary sources and other verifiable material evidence; filmmakers create a story through a montage of the past. This combines oral history, generational stories, memories and photographs with empirical historical facts to create a more artistic history. These constructs require imagination, flexibility and empathy.

The central plot of moving images is based on historical events, people or periods, yet this history is edited, the less interesting parts removed if perceived not to add to the overarching narrative.[43] In its place narrative content is added that builds relationships between characters, and critically, relationships between the public, 'the viewer', and these characters and actions in history. This enables connections to be formed and emotions to be expressed. In this sense media history is rewritten, reconceptualized history, which is often imagined, sometimes misconceived and frequently recreated.

Historical narratives on-screen are created through the use of various visual, stylistic and linguistic elements. Visual elements include costumes, lighting, screen design, locations, facial expressions, body language, static imagery and camera movements; while audio elements include scripted conversations and dialogues, background noise and sound clips. For each element a choice has been made by the writer, director, producer, actor and film crew; this directly relates to the pre-existing overarching narrative framework, they are visual narrative codes that seek to convey and impose emotions on the viewer. These choice elements and the narrative codes imbedded within them are not accidental; rather these elements are integral to the narrative. Historians should consider moving images as narratives, to be 'read'. As with any form of material cultural record from the past, the treatment of moving images requires critical deconstruction in order to piece together the life biography of this postmodern construct of the past. By exploring the narrative of the moving image within the context of its life history, history can be analysed and utilized by historians; as a source that provides a visual metaphor of popular cultural memory of history and a medium to communicate messages and interwoven themes within the complex and multi-faceted historical primary sources.[44] The analysis of moving images should seek to explore the motivation behind its creation, construction and production and finally its public consumption; this can only be achieved through the systematic deconstruction of its complex narrative strands.[45]

In the majority of instances, historical media does not aim to perform as a history lesson for the general public. Neither is it supposed to act as a research article seeking to provide a historical synopsis of an idea for professional consumption.[46] The historical narratives presented within moving images are, as previously discussed in Chapter 1, important primary sources that are equally valuable as secondary source material.[47]

Moving images can act as a cultural commentator and provide historians with unique insight into popular culture and public values attached to history.[48] It is a way to uncover recent pasts and past representations (as discussed in depth in Chapter 3). Moving images should be treated like an artefact with a complex biography.[49] Yet, in order to access this contextual information historians are required to draw on their skills as detectives, to understand complexities of interpretation and to engage in critical analysis as they would when evaluating traditional textual resources.[50]

All historical narratives, whether an academic book or television programme, represent the point of creation and reflect the creator's ideology.[51] Yet, media history is fundamentally different from normal academic prose in its creation, communication format and perception. Historical narratives presented in moving images are often accused of being inauthentic, of lacking truth and falsifying history; as Downing suggested media history is 'certainly not real history'.[52] Yet what is real and truthful about media history, as with all histories, is that they are stories, created in the present, from multiple interweaving strands of information. This is never complete, rather it is a hybrid between fact and fiction; the difficulty is finding a balance between the two.[53]

The concept that moving images are narratives which sacrifice accuracy over entertainment in part originates from the 'anti heritage movement', which might be perceived as the 'anti popular narrative movement'.[54]

Proponents of this movement suggest that 'heritage', often perceived as 'popular history', such as television and films, dilutes historical authenticity and exposes history to external non-professional biases, which can result in historical manipulation.[55] Academia's fear of the unknown world of media and of losing control over history impacts on this perception. This is a result of a lack of understanding by many historians of the production and creation of moving images, and as such their potential as a medium of communication and as a historical source, a situation which has arisen due to a lack of communication and collaboration of film and television industry professionals with historians and vice versa.[56] However, in recent years the media industry has begun to collaborate with historians to alter this inauspicious relationship. Collaboration has helped to bridge the narrative gap between the two professions and as such alter and realign the historical narratives presented in moving images. This has resulted in programmes that have both popular appeal and entertainment value, but also in some cases, moving images that have become regarded as valid and accurate secondary sources of historical information and as reliable educational resources.[57] This new rapport has increased the historical validity of the moving image and its value as a secondary source to both the professionals and the public, particularly in relation to historical documentaries.

Similarly to historical textbooks, the lines between human interpretive fiction and historical 'fact' are often blurred, as are the lines between artistic representation and historical scholarship.[58] Analysis of the media narrative requires an engagement in a new kind of historical discourse, one based upon deconstructing and decoding the interwoven tangible and intangible stories that are regarded as 'evidence'. This requires the 'reader' of moving images to look not only for what is missing and inaccurate, but also for what is present, subconsciously hidden and accurate.

The Last Kingdom

The recent television dramatization *The Last Kingdom* (BBC1 2015) of Bernard Cornwall's fictional novel series *The Saxon Stories* (2004–) saw the re-creation of the Viking invasion of Saxon England in the ninth century. This sought to tell the historical story of the Viking and Saxon relationship, specifically focusing on Wessex's defence against the Viking invasion. This narrative is delivered by a central character 'Uhtred', a son of a Saxon noble man captured by the Vikings and reared as a 'Dane'. The popular television series provides an illustrative example of the value of historical media as a secondary source. It highlights issues relating to authenticity, truth and narrative and resultantly the complexities of using moving images as a historical source.

The programme was commissioned by the BBC, a publicly funded television channel, and was first aired in America. The first episode portrays the Vikings' arrival in England, specifically focusing on the history recorded in the Anglo-Saxon Chronicle, the invasion of Northumbria. It presents the viewer with violent scenes of Vikings raping, killing and pillaging Saxon settlements. These actions are based on some primary historical documentation, which includes the Vikings' first noted arrival in Northumbria and the killing and pillaging at places such as Lindisfarne: 'in the same year on 8 January the raiding of heathen men miserably devastated God's church in Lindisfarne island by looting and slaughter',[59] and the settling in winter camps: 'Here the army took winter-quarters at Turc's island'.[60] It is worth noting primary sources from this period are limited to those recorded and provided by Christians, often monks. When this is combined with archaeological evidence, few sites (with the exception of Ridgeway Hill[61]) suggest aggression and violence.[62] Rather they indicate evidence of integration, such as the winter camp at Torksey, Lincolnshire (UK) or the Norse burial site at Cumwhitton, Cumbria (UK).[63]

This historical television production portrays the Vikings' violent 'pagan' aggression against the peaceful 'Christian' Anglo-Saxons. This imagery draws on the current popular stereotypes of 'Viking' invaders, stereotypes that are taught at school and presented in other popular media including the recent The Vikings (HBO 2014) and Horrible Histories Vicious Vikings (1994) by Terry Derry.[64] As such, this narrative represents current sociopolitical trends, enabling the viewer to form connections between past and present events. This includes nationalistic fear of mass immigration on 'English' culture, of attempting to understand alternative religious faiths beyond Christianity and of recent threats from the 'terror' of foreign groups such as Islamic State of Iraq and the Levant (ISIL). In doing this, The Last Kingdom has similarities with crusader films, such as the Kingdom of Heaven, in its treatment of the exotic, unknown and different, but also in its idealist undertones of acceptance and understanding from the central protagonist 'Uhtred' of both the Christian 'Saxons' and Pagan 'Vikings'.[65] Principally this programme seeks to utilize historical sources and historical narratives to entertain the viewer. This is popular television; it seeks to be entertaining to the public, while appealing to popular myths and nationalist cultural stereotypes. As suggested by Smith, this historical recreation serves to appeal to modern viewers' tastes and cultural beliefs.[66]

Deconstructing this moving image through a structuralist framework provides further evidence of the accuracy of this historical recreation and the validity of this moving image as a secondary source. For example, visually The Last Kingdom utilizes lighting to create darkness around the Vikings, and light and space around the Saxons, suggesting potentially evil foreboding Vikings and culturally developed Saxons. Locationally, the sites chosen such as Winchester are historically and archaeologically associated and evidenced Saxon places. Stylistically, the costume design appears moderately factually accurate, but has been adapted to fit modern fashions.[67] For example, the Saxon broaches worn by the men are historically accurate, as archaeological excavations of similar period sites indicate, yet stylistic trends such as the shields date a couple of centuries later.

These stylistic, locational and visual aspects of the source are unlikely to be aspects of historical accuracy or inaccuracy of which the public are aware. The popularity, high viewing figures of over 2.5 million, and positive broadsheet reviews, such as Runcie's in the *Daily Telegraph*, suggest that for the public this historical narrative is authentic and accurate enough.[68] Yet within this are vignettes of truth (as conventionally understood); the Vikings did undertake raids, they did have winter camps, there is a use of accurate names based on historical literature.

Conclusion

At the beginning of this chapter ideas regarding film and television being 'good history' were discussed; the idea that good history on television provides an accurate narrative based on primary evidence that recounts an unbiased and factually truthful version of history. The mechanisms for analysing history presented in moving images should not be limited to evaluating the accuracy of visual elements, but to assessing if the version of history portrayed can help understand the construction of history in the present. Determining what is 'good history' in moving images is far more complex, it requires techniques of deconstruction that often go beyond the normative historical skills, including understanding the underlying motivations of the producer and of the consumer, alongside deconstructing 'factual' elements from which the moving image has developed.

The 'true' aim of many historical films and television shows is to produce an academically credible account of the past that balances entertainment and education in equal measure, and which appeals to its audience; in this respect, television is not for academics. For the professionals this historical media is produced to appeal to, and be consumed by, the masses, those without the depth of knowledge, critical understanding and perhaps scepticism and cynicism for sources integral to the discipline of history. But historically focused audio-visual media should not simply be judged on ideas of 'truth' and 'accuracy' as defined in academia; rather they should be judged on their ability to capture the interest and the imagination of the public in the historical discipline, to provide them with a platform for further study.

Moving images which use history as a backdrop employ complex narrative codes that have the potential to provide a resource for historians. These films and television programmes have the potential to provide valuable secondary sources of historical information that can have an impact on current historical research, not only in terms of knowledge but also in relation to practice.

In recent years especially, popular historical media have impacted on the public; on their knowledge of historical events, people and times, and on the values they attach to the past. Perhaps most critically for the discipline, the history as produced and consumed in moving images has impacted on the practice of history, on the perceived value of different forms of historical evidence, on the nature and hierarchy of sources, and on its mediums of presentation. The moving image has a wider impact on historical knowledge creation and re-creation, and as a result it is vital that historians develop and deploy the skills and methods needed to deconstruct and critically analyse this secondary source as history, rather than regard it as just popular fiction.

Notes

1   P. Smith, 'Introduction', in *The Historian and Film,* ed. P. Smith. (Cambridge: Cambridge University Press, 1976).

2   See M. Dolski, Ch. 1 this volume.

3   M. Ferro, 'Does a Filmic Writing of History Exist?' *Film and History: An Interdisciplinary Journal of Film and Television* 17 (4) (1987): 81–9.

4   Smith, *The Historian.*

5   Ibid., 5.

6   Ibid.

7   Ibid.; M. Ferro, 'The Fiction Film and Historical Analysis', in *The Historian and Film,* ed. P. Smith (Cambridge: Cambridge University Press, 1976), 80–94.

8   W. Hughes, 'The Evaluation of Film as Evidence', in *The Historian and Film,* ed. P. Smith (Cambridge: Cambridge University Press, 1976), 49.

9   Ferro, 'Does a Filmic Writing of History Exist', 81.

10   F. Sayer, *Public History: A Practical Guide* (London: Bloomsbury Academic, 2015).

11   L. Jordanova, *History in Practice* (London: Bloomsbury Academic, 2010), 92; Sayer, *Public History.*

12   Hughes, 'The Evaluation of Film', 64, 66.

13   N. Ascherson, 'Why "Heritage" is Right-Wing', *Observer,* 8 November 1987.

14   C. Holtorf, *Archaeology is a Brand! The Meaning of Archaeology in Contemporary Popular Culture* (Oxford: Archaeopress, 2006).

15   Smith, *The Historian*; Ferro, 'Does a Filmic Writing of History Exist'.

16   Sayer, *Public History.*

17   Hughes, 'The Evaluation of Film'; Smith, *The Historian.*

18   C. Classen and W. Kansteiner, 'Truth and Authenticity in Contemporary

Historical Culture: An Introduction to Historical Representation and Historical Truth' *History and Theory* 47 (2) (2009): 3.

19 J. Isaacs, 'Television History', *History Today* 58 (9) (2008): 17.

20 J. Richards, 'Signposts: History Films', *History Today* 61 (10) (2011).

21 De Groot, *Consuming History,* 147.

22 Ibid.

23 N. Ascherson, 'Why "Heritage" is Right-Wing', *Observer*, 8 November 1987.

24 T. Downing, 'Bringing in the Past to the Small Screen', in *History and the Media*, ed. D. Cannadine (New York: Palgrave MacMillian, 2004), 12; T. Hunt, 'How Does Television Enhance History?' in *History and the Media*, ed. D. Cannadine (New York: Palgrave MacMillian, 2004), 88–102.

25 N. Ascherson, 'Why "Heritage" is Right-Wing', *Observer*, 8 November 1987; R. Samuel *Theatres of Memory: Past and Present in Contemporary Culture* (London: Verso, 2012).

26 N. Graburn, 'A Quest for Identity', *Museum International* 50 (3) (1998): 13–18

27 W. Morris, 'At Henry Parkes Motel', *Cultural Studies* 2 (1998): 11.

28 Ibid.

29 R. Rosenstone, *Visions of the Past: The Challenge of Film to Our Idea of History* (Cambridge: Harvard University Press, 1995).

30 C. Holtorf, *Archaeology is a Brand!*

31 R. Rosenstone, *History on Film, Film on History* (New York: Pearson, 2012), 6.

32 S. Blackburn, *Truth: A Guide for the Perplexed* (London: Penguin Books, 2006).

33 F. Nietzsche, *The Will to Power*, ed. W. Kaufmann (London: Weidenfeld and Nicolson, 1967).

34 Ibid.

35 Rosenstone, *History on Film*, 140.

36 J. Barrett, *Shooting the Civil War: Cinema, History and American National Identity National Television and Civil War* (New York: I.B. Tauris, 2009), 3.

37 J. Warren-Findley, 'History in New Worlds: Surveys and Results in the United States and Australia', *American Studies International* XLII (2/3) (2004).

38 Sayer, *Public History*.

39 Isaacs, 'Television History'; Richards, 'Signposts: History Films'.

40 S. Crofts, 'Not a Window on the Past: How Films and Television Construct History', *Film and History: An Interdisciplinary Journal of Film and Television* 17 (4) (1987): 90–5.

41 Crofts, 'Not a Window on the Past'.

42 Sayer, *Public History*.

43 Barrett, *Shooting the Civil War*, 5; Crofts, 'Not a Window on the Past', 93.

44   A. Dawson, *Historical Insights: Focus on History: Hollywood For Historians* (Coventry: History at the Higher Education Academy, 2009).

45   Rosenstone, *History on Film*.

46   Barrett, *Shooting the Civil War*, 3; M. Hughes-Warrington, *History Goes to the Movies: Studying History on Film* (London: Routledge, 2006).

47   See M. Dolski, Ch. 1 this volume.

48   Rosenstone, *History on Film*.

49   J. O'Connor, 'Special Report. The Moving-Image Media in the History Classroom', *Film and History: An Interdisciplinary Journal of Film and Television* 16 (3) (1986): 49–54.

50   J. Tusa, 'A Deep and Continuing Use of History', in *History and the Media*, ed. D. Cannadine (New York: Palgrave MacMillian, 2004), 123–40.

51   D. Lowenthal, *The Heritage Crusade and the Spoils of History* (Cambridge: Cambridge University Press, 1989).

52   Downing, *Bringing in the Past to the Small Screen*.

53   Ibid.

54   N. Ascherson, 'Why "Heritage" is Right-Wing', *Observer*, 8 November 1987; Samuel, *Theatres of Memory*.

55   Samuel, *Theatres of Memory*; Sayer, *Public History*, 62.

56   Isaacs, 'Television History'.

57   Ibid.

58   Rosenstone, *History on Film*, 27.

59   Anglo Saxon Chronicle: Peterborough Manuscript, AD 793.

60   Anglo Saxon Chronicle: Peterborough Manuscript, AD 872.

61   The excavations as Ridgeway Hill, Weymouth, revealed the mass grave containing fifty decapitated skeletons, predominantly male from Norse regions. Skeletons revealed defensive wounds relating to battle.

62   L. Loe, A. Boyle, H. Webb and D. Score, *'Given to the Ground': A Viking Massive Grave on Ridgeway Hill, Weymouth* (Dorset: Dorset National History and Archaeology Society, 2014).

63   J. Richards, and D. Hadley, 'Viking Torksey: Inside the Great Army's Winter Camp', *Current Archaeology* (2013); C. Paterson, A. Parsons, R. Newman, N. Johnson and C. Howard Davis, *Shadows in the Sand: Excavation of a Viking-age Cemetery at Cumwhitton, Cumbria* (Lancaster: Oxford Archaeology North, 2014).

64   Sayer, *Public History*.

65   Richards, 'Signposts: History Films'.

66   Smith, *The Historian*.

67   Hughes, 'The evaluation of film'.

68   C. Runcie, 'The Last Kingdom, BBC Two, Review: "The thinking person's Game of Thrones"', *Daily Telegraph,* 23 October 2015. Available online: http://www.barb.co.uk/whats-new/weekly-top-30? (accessed 15 February 2016).

CHAPTER THREE

The moving image as memory: Past and present on screen

Sam Edwards

So far, the introductory chapters to this book have examined how the moving image can be interrogated as a 'primary source' (a visual/audio-visual text which offers a record of a specific time and place) and as a 'secondary source' (a visual/audio-visual narrative interpretation of the past). This chapter develops these ideas further by connecting these two approaches to the historical analysis of film in order to outline and explore a 'third way': moving image as 'memory'. To do so, this chapter first discusses the idea of 'collective memory', which originated in the early twentieth century, before then shifting to discuss more recent thinking, thinking which has drawn particular attention to the growing importance of film and television in producing and popularizing understandings of the past. In this sense, and as Chapter 2 also discusses, while the moving image is indeed often used in order to communicate *History*, recent decades have also seen it purposefully deployed as a vehicle – or 'vector' – of commemoration.[1] As such, some films and television programmes – especially those connected to the great events of history – can be viewed as 'sights' of memory; audio-visual *memorials* designed to communicate a particular image and idea of the past. As this chapter explains, such commemorative activities make perfect sense: the moving image, the modern idea of 'memory', and the very technology of cinema are all early twentieth-century contemporaries. Seen in this light, audio-visual 'sights of memory' have much in common with their more traditional counterparts – memorials and monuments – and can certainly be analysed as such. But, at the same time, they are also suggestive of an important shift in the form and function of 'memory', a shift which demarcates twentieth- and twenty-first-century 'memory' from that of previous eras.

On collective memory: Origins and beginnings

The origins of the idea of 'collective memory' can be traced to the early twentieth century, and to the work of the French scholar, Maurice Halbwachs, a pupil of the eminent sociologist Emile Durkheim.[2] Like his mentor, Halbwachs was drawn to explore the ways in which human societies worked, and he was particularly intrigued (again like Durkheim) by the rites and rituals through which certain social groups constructed and celebrated their collective identity. Durkheim, like many other late-nineteenth-century sociologists and anthropologists operating in the great age of Empire, found the ritual dynamics of supposedly 'primitive' peoples especially fascinating, and this became the subject of an exhaustive tome: *The Elementary Forms of the Religious Life* (1912).[3] For Halbwachs, who lived and worked in urban France, the rituals, symbols and structures of 'civilized' European societies were equally revealing. After all, Halbwachs bore witness to an era of great change in these societies: new industrial processes fundamentally altered the rhythms of life, economies and populations expanded, cities were built, empires were conquered and new nations (Germany; Italy) created. It was amid these profound shifts and changes – and, partly in response – that a new 'religion' was cultivated in the industrialized West: the religion of the nation state. As Hobsbawn, Ranger and Anderson have all famously suggested, nationalism itself developed into a form of civic religion during these years: 'national' traditions were 'invented', monuments to national heroes were dedicated and national identities were 'imagined'.[4] For Ernst Renan (another French scholar of whose work Halbwachs was familiar) such activities produced a new architecture of 'myth' – a landscape of memory filled with sites at which citizens were invited to remember *their* past.[5]

Halbwachs went beyond identifying that a monument to a historical hero might be used as a shrine to the nation; he was moved to interrogate exactly how such sites 'functioned' in order to explore the ways in which the past featured in the present; how it was 'recalled' and remembered. The results of his thinking were profound, and continue to shape contemporary understandings of memory. The crux of the matter concerned his assertion that remembering was *always* social, and thus memory was *always* a product, a construction, of a group. For Halbwachs, 'remembering' was a learned social skill demanding specific 'tools', and it was the product of an act of communication which could only take place in a group. To 'remember' was to communicate, and the result of such an activity was, by definition, 'collective'. Halbwachs believed that such acts of collective remembering might take different forms, and might involve different collectives defined in different ways (class, race, gender, nationality, age, status, belief etc.). Regardless of such variety, he asserted that the key consistency concerned the social dynamic which shaped the act of remembering, with the result being 'collective memory'. This idea represented a significant intervention in contemporary thinking: the other key scholar then interrogating the workings of human memory was Sigmund Freud, a psychologist who was, understandably, drawn to a rather more individualized view on how people remember (the ideas of Freud and Halbwachs were in nearly every respect, polar opposites).[6]

When compared to the currency of Freud's work, the contemporary response to Halbwachs, idea was much less than it deserved or demanded. Moreover, with a bitter irony, Halbwachs would be killed by the evil excesses of twentieth-century nationalism: he was murdered by the Nazis in a concentration camp for the crime of being a socialist, and a scholar. Thus, it was not until the *late* twentieth century – the second great age of 'memory' – that Halbwachs, work began to receive the attention of another generation of scholars similarly witness to a contemporary obsession with the past. If Halbwachs lived and worked during the great age of nationalism, which culminated in the carnage – and commemoration – of the Great War, then by the 1980s citizens of the post-industrial and post-national world were again preoccupied with questions of memory and identity. In Central and Eastern Europe, old identities and memories – of the Soviets, of Stalin – were dismantled and replaced (literally in some cases: among the first acts of the new 'free' governments of the post-Soviet age was the destruction and removal of unwanted monuments of the former regime). In the West, with the Cold War won, the victor powers embarked upon an 'orgy' of commemoration, celebrating themselves by remembering the past.[7] With the old 'pole stars' of nationalism and socialism seemingly now gone, many pluralistic and multicultural Western societies also became consumed by a new wave of identity politics as those previously overlooked, ignored or even disenfranchised asserted themselves in the present by invoking and inventing a past.[8] In France, birthplace of both memory and modernity, regional identities were discovered and celebrated;[9] in Britain, a newly resurgent Scottish nationalism drew media attention, and in the United States, museums and memorials to the dispossessed and defeated – for instance, Native Americans – were built and dedicated with federal approval. Little wonder, given all this activity, that many scholars in Europe and North America were increasingly drawn to the study of commemoration, and especially to the ideas of Halbwachs (and indeed of Freud). Little wonder too that many of these scholars used Halbwachs' thinking in order to offer new critical interpretations of a wave of activity with which Halbwachs had been very familiar: the memorialization of war.

Boom and bust? Collective memory critiqued

The 1980s and 1990s saw the publication of several landmark texts exploring and interrogating twentieth-century war memory. Perhaps foremost among this scholarship was the work of those such as Jay Winter, Daniel Sherman, James Young, Marita Sturken and Sarah Farmer, all of whom examined the ways in which dedicated commemorative objects and structures functioned as what Winter termed 'sites of memory': locations at which social collectives formed, gathered, grieved and *remembered*.[10] This work would inspire and produce a veritable 'memory boom', with even Winter noting – with concern – that 'memory' had become the historical signature of the age, and that some scholarship increasingly lacked both terminological precision and conceptual rigour.[11] If some of the leading practitioners were worried, then elsewhere the criticisms were even more strident. In 1992, two scholars – Noa Gedi and Yigal Elam – passionately argued that existing theories of the ways in which social groups make sense of their past, theories which include the well-established idea of 'myth', made a new term – collective memory – unnecessary.[12] To be sure, 'myth', as term and theory, offers much of interest to the historian, and little wonder then that many have, and still do, use this term when examining the purpose and form of rites and rituals, or when interrogating certain historical assumptions and misconceptions.[13] Moreover, according to Gedi and Elam, the concept of myth helps to preserve the 'conscious-subconscious dichotomy', that is, 'it separates the sphere that is dominated by factors "beyond our control" (psychological or mental fixations, inherited notions, traditional or conventional stereotypes) from the one that is susceptible to new ideas and therefore constitutes the playground of the great drama of change. And change is after all, history's main concern.'[14] Using the term myth thus ensures that the historian concentrates on that which is appropriately their field of enquiry: the social, the world beyond the mind, rather than carelessly blundering into that of which we have no knowledge – the subconscious, the psychological.

A second key criticism proceeded from a very similar line of thought. Simply put, several of the most robust attacks on the idea of collective memory contended that its use by historians was inappropriate because 'memory' is always and only something 'personal' and 'individual', thus its application to the social realm is misplaced. Consider, once more, the words of Gedi and Elam:

> It must be quite clear that any definition of 'memory' would revolve around the ability to retrieve some impression of some past experience or some past event that has had some impact on our minds. In any event memory is a personal human faculty that is related to actual personal experience.[15]

Wulf Kansteiner, likewise identifying this problem, suggested that 'many inquiries into collective memories commit a tempting yet potentially grave methodological error: they perceive and conceptualize collective memory exclusively in terms of the psychological and emotional dynamics of individual remembering'.[16] Some of the most important work in the field of memory studies has certainly taken this approach, at least on a superficial level. Henri Rousso's landmark and much-cited text *The Vichy Syndrome*, even employs a psychological term in the very title.[17] Marita Sturken's excellent discussion of the politics of remembering in contemporary America, a politics to be witnessed, among other places, at the Vietnam veterans' memorial, similarly makes use of psychological terminology, this time drawn from Freud's work on screen memories and repression.[18] For Kansteiner, the problem is that on the scale of the collective, these terms, and the assumptions they carry with them, can be misleading. Another theorist of collective memory has also suggested that when discussing 'social forgetting', that is, the ways in which groups cast aside aspects of their past, 'we are best advised to keep psychological or psychoanalytical categories at bay and to focus, rather, on the social, political, and cultural factors at work'.[19]

Such criticisms – which persist in some quarters today – demand careful consideration. Let us deal, first, with the idea that collective memory is a theoretically redundant concept. In this view, collective memory represents an unnecessary intrusion into an area of study already well provided with appropriate terms and theories, among which is the idea of myth, use of which ensures that historians remain focused on the social rather than the individual, a distinction which the term memory, says this criticism, confuses. This is a pertinent point, but from another perspective we might suggest that rather than being a weakness, the blurring of the distinctions between the social and individual which accompanies use of the term memory is among its must useful attributes. Employing the concept of collective memory – rather than myth – invites us to ponder the interactions between the social, cultural, political, and the personal, individual, psychological.

Such interactions are not just receiving the attention of historians (and sociologists); considerable recent research in psychology is likewise concerned with reconsidering these problematic boundaries. Building on the pioneering work of F. C. Bartlett – who was among the first to argue that memories are not 'stored' unaltered in the brain, but are 're-excited' in the process of recall and that this process is controlled by the attitudes and 'schemata' of the present – contemporary psychologists have likewise sought to displace the prominent position previously given to theories of memory 'imprinting'.[20] These researchers contend that rather than remembering being the retrieval of a 'trace' 'imprinted' at the instant of an event, it is better understood as a present-orientated act of *construction*.[21] Thus, memory is not only a *personal* human faculty, but a human activity framed by a social dynamic. The concerns of the present, concerns which are psychological, political, social and cultural, provide not only the impetus to 'remember', but also, in Bartlett's terms, the 'schemata' by which memories are organized. Current thinking suggests that schemata are externally acquired supra-individual mechanisms used in order to process and understand various types of information.[22] The schemata used to organize, or construct, memories of the past are socially acquired rather than originating somewhere in the cognitive networks of our minds. This idea of memory 'construction' can also be found in the research of numerous other psychologists. Worthy of mention here are those theories that argue we should conceive of memory in terms of a 'network of nodes with associative connections';[23] in this view, memories are constituted by a mass of cognitive pathways made up of partial traces which are interlinked and interconnected. When we remember, therefore, we attempt to activate a particular cognitive pathway. However, such pathways are not clearly marked roads but, rather, mingled connections of traces any number of which may come to bear on the memory we eventually construct. 'Recall', therefore, 'amounts not to retrieval but to reconstruction'.[24] Indeed, one reason why we recall so little from our early childhood is that we simply do not know 'how' to remember. In layman's terms, this refers to the fact that constructing a memory is very much like telling a story, but it is not until later childhood that we finally develop the narrative skills, or sense of emplotment, necessary to undertake this work of *construction*. As such, we can confidently conclude that memory is most certainly not *only* personal or individual in content and form. As one psychologist has succinctly written:

> We recreate or reconstruct our experiences rather than retrieve copies of them. Sometimes in the process of reconstructing we add feelings, beliefs, or even knowledge we obtained after the experience. In other words, we bias our memories of the past by attributing to them emotions or knowledge we acquired after the event.[25]

Making and mediating memory: Remembering and representing the past with the moving image

Note the various terms frequently employed above: schemata; narrative; image; impression; representation; discourse; construction; production. All are certainly apt when used to explore the place and purpose of certain physical 'sites of memory'. Memorials are, after all, visible structures which offer a representation of the past and which encode the political discourse

– that is, the 'language' – of a particular group at a particular moment in time. As Daniel Sherman explained, when outlining the focus of his prize winning history of the construction of memory in post-1918 France:

> Just as individual memories constitute a fund of images and impressions – sensory as well as conceptual, auditory and tactile as well as visual – through which we seek out and recast our pasts, the discourses of collective memory and the practices of commemoration represent a society's past to itself.[26]

If such ideas and terminology dovetail nicely with traditional sites of memory, then they are even more fitting when employed to understand the role played by the *moving image* in shaping popular understandings of the past. This connection makes perfect sense: if Maurice Halbwachs lived and worked during the great age of Victorian and Edwardian memorial building, a fact which surely influenced his theory of collective memory, he also witnessed the birth of cinema and the emergence of the 'Dream Palace'. Yet despite these chronological and conceptual connections, the role of film and television in the construction of collective memory has nonetheless been subject to considerable critique. Central to many of these critiques has been the argument that the very nature of audio-visual material actively mitigates against the process of remembering. In fact, more than one scholar has contended that film and television are the cornerstones of a postmodern culture of amnesia; an age not of memory, but of *forgetting*.[27] As Mary Anne Doane has argued, television delivers the 'annihilation of memory, and consequently of history' due to its 'continual stress upon the 'nowness' of its own discourse'.[28] In this view, *History* and *Memory* are understood to be oppositional representations of the past: the former is considered, evidenced, solid, authentic and 'true'; the latter is fluid, fickle and forgetful.

This view of the relationship between film, television, popular culture, history and memory was in many respects characteristic of the 1980s and 1990s. This was the age in which academic history felt the full force of the postmodern assault; the age of Hayden White's pointed critiques of the 'truth' claims of story-telling historians;[29] the age in which the challenging scholarship of Foucault,[30] Derrida and Barthes[31] was assimilated into academic discourse; and the age – especially in the United States – of a presidential administration (Reagan's) which continuously displayed an easy disregard for the 'facts' of history.[32] The response in some quarters was defensive. Reeling from the attack, some historians endeavoured to mark out their territory anew in an effort to defend the integrity of their discipline. The practice of history was revisited, refined and restated, and the line between 'History' and 'Memory' demarcated.[33] Moreover, the idea that these two representations of the past were distinct reached right back to Halbwachs himself, and was reaffirmed by some of the most notable scholars of the late twentieth century. Henri Rousso argued that history and memory existed in tension, while Pierre Nora contended that 'History' was in fact engaged in an assault on memory.[34] In time, however, more nuanced understandings have emerged, and the most recent scholarship recognizes that the boundaries between 'History' and 'Memory' are at best 'entangled'. As Emily Rosenberg has written, 'Memory and history are blurred forms of representation whose structure and politics need to be analysed not as oppositional but as interactive forms'.[35] Similarly, Jay Winter once more:

> History and Memory overlap, infuse each other, and create vigorous and occasionally fruitful incompatibilities ... In virtually all acts of remembrance, history and memory are braided together in the public domain, jointly informing our shifting and contested understandings of the past.[36]

Hardly surprising, given such 'infusing' and entangling, that historical scholarship on collective memory is now laced with explicit – and occasionally implicit – references to the ways in which our ideas of the past often take the form of *images*. Take Marita Sturken's *Screen Memories*; or Iwona Irwin-Zarecka's *Frames of Remembrance*; or Winter's own connections between Great War French remembrance and French cinema.[37]

But the crucial intervention which drew together, assessed and articulated these connections was provided by Andrew Hoskins. Writing in 2001, Hoskins identified the emergence of what he termed 'new memory': a presentatist and postmodern mediation of the past dominated by the moving image, and by new electronic technologies of communication and dissemination. Hoskins countered the established critique of television – that it was present obsessed and produced only forgetfulness – and instead argued that in a mediated age, television had become 'the very "stuff" from which new memory was forged'.[38] Indeed, rather than cultivating a culture of amnesia, Hoskins contended that 'new memory, in some ways, is the satiation of memory'.[39] Similarly, film scholar Amy Holdsworth has persuasively argued that 'in the British televisual landscape at least, memory and nostalgia lie at the very heart'.[40] Movies, media, modernity and memory: all 'invented' at the turn of the twentieth century; all bound together, inseparable bedfellows. In short, film and television have powerfully affected not only our perception of the present, but also our historical consciousness (see Chapters 9, 10, 13 and 14) and thus our 'sense' of the past. Below, I work through some of the ways to interrogate the role of the moving image in order to unpick the construction of collective memory.

Film and television as constructions of collective memory in the twentieth century

As Chapter 1 identifies, and as Chapter 2 develops, film and television are invaluable sources for the historian of the twentieth and twenty-first centuries; the camera 'captures' and such moving imagery can be interrogated in ways not entirely unfamiliar to the historian. But such source material can also be analysed in a subtlety different way. Visual and audiovisual material does not just offer a depiction of 'what happened'; it can also offer a record of what people *think* happened, of how they made sense of a certain issue, event, person or moment. Here, the connection between film and twentieth-century conflict, especially the Second World War, is particularly revealing.

By the start of the Second World War, the movie industry was fully established and powerfully influential in the popular culture of all present and future belligerents. In the United States, the 1930s had witnessed the Golden Age of Hollywood, a laissez-faire era in which a handful of studios dominated the film production process, controlled the activities of the major stars, and offered powerful visions of the American past and present. In Germany, in contrast, a technically sophisticated and innovative cinema was co-opted by a regime obsessed with performance politics and intent on controlling popular perceptions of the world, and of the future. Between these two poles of private enterprise and state authority was the British film industry, partly independent, partly subject to control and censorship. Regardless of the specific dynamics between state and industry, all belligerents made skilful and sustained use of film. The age of Total War demanded the enlistment of all the state's resources; the film industry was no exception. In America, after initial reluctance on the part of the major studios to intervene in contemporary politics,[41] Hollywood mobilized on behalf of the national war effort. Notable directors – John Ford, Frank Capra, William Wyler – enlisted and famous stars – Jimmy Stewart, Clark Gable – volunteered. In Britain, a dedicated Army Film Unit was created, and influential film records of major campaigns created (*Desert Victory*, 1943). In Nazi Germany, the motion picture became a means to document and diffuse the great conquests of the *Wehrmacht*.[42] In short, film and event, moment and motion picture, were entangled *in the instant*. Hardly surprising, therefore, that film would become central to popular perceptions of the conflict while it happened (see Chapters 5 and 11). Hardly surprising, too, that film would also become central to collective memory of the conflict in later decades. The war was mediated as it unfolded; and it has been memorialized via the very same technology (and sometimes even by the same people).

Mark Connelly's work on British collective memory of the conflict is particularly useful in this regard. Through a detailed and exhaustive survey of popular culture, especially of film and television, Connelly traces the construction and communication of recurring images of Britain's war.[43] For Connelly, such a survey reveals the 'sheer homogeneity of its popular culture artefacts', and so confirms that in Britain a 'collective national memory' of the Second World War does exist.[44] Similar work abounds elsewhere. Take Geoff Eley's work on film, the war and British collective memory; John Bodnar's examination of the role played by film in American constructions of the Second World War past; or Merecedes Camino Maroto's identification of the dynamic relationship between film, memory and the Spanish Civil War.[45]

As these scholars (and others) have demonstrated, the close connections between the film industry *and* the state – produced and consolidated by the 'total' wars of the twentieth century – ensured that film played an unusually powerful role in shaping understanding of conflict *as it happened*, and would similarly play an unusually powerful role in the subsequent construction of collective memory. By tracing the nature of the stories told, their plots and politics, historians of memory have attempted to chart how popular perceptions of certain historical events – especially war – have been constructed and reconstructed through the mechanisms of mass media. But this is not to say that this dynamic *only* applies to the Second World War and film; the overall concept and method might be applied elsewhere.

Mediating memories: Analysing the moving image

As we know, collective memory is a construction, the product of social agency. In Irwin-Zarecka's words: 'A collective memory – as a set of ideas, images, feelings about the past – is best located not in the minds of individuals, but in the resources they share.'[46] 'Memorials' therefore, are an example of a specific type of 'resource' shared by the members of a particular group, and which offer a record of what Halbwachs would understand as that group's collective memory. Historically focused films and television productions can similarly be understood as a collectively produced 'resource' offering an audio-visual representation of the past. That said, it is important to be careful with such ideas: films do not 'determine' what people think about the past; they do not 'define' all that a person might think or feel as they watch; they do not offer a concrete and irrefutable statement encompassing *all* views and thoughts on a subject. Rather, collectively produced resources such as a film offer a means through which to 'establish the likely range of meanings' associated with a certain historical event or episode.[47] But what specific issues should the historian address in order to uncover this 'range of meanings'? Here, some of the ideas already broached in Chapters 1 and 2 – albeit with a slight twist – remain important. Crucially, all are familiar within the well-established methodology of the historian.

Authorship and reception

As Chapter 1 explains, and as Chapter 2 affirms, it is now generally accepted that no film has a single 'auteur'. Certain important figures might exercise greater or lesser influence (the director, the producer, a headline star) and some individuals have exercised a powerful controlling role (the likes of John Ford, Alfred Hitchcock, Darryl Zanuck and Steven Spielberg come to mind). Nonetheless, the production of a film is a complex and collaborative endeavour subject to multiple and occasionally competing interests and inputs. The first task for the historian interested in examining the role played by film in the construction of collective memory is to identify and disentangle those involved in its production. The essential ideas used to make sense of a more traditional memorial (such as a monument) hold true: when people combine to commemorate, they argue, dispute, disagree and, eventually (if the 'resource' is to be realized) compromise agree. The seeming unity and clarity of the film (if it's any good) – like the solidity of a stone monument – denies this fluidity, and denies the politics of the production. The first task, then, is to rediscover this politics. Who was involved? What did they set out to achieve? In what ways does the film in question express the attitudes and assumptions of the collective who drove its production?

If identifying the 'author(s)' of a film or television production is problematic; identifying the audience, and their response, is even more so. Tracing *reception* to a film remains a persistent challenge: viewing is certainly not the same as accepting. For the historian of memory interested in using films this is an especially important issue. Failure to engage with the issue of reception risks producing an overly 'reductive' reading. As Jay Winter has commented in a critique of the use of film in studies of memory:

> One of the unfortunate features of the memory boom is the tendency of commentators to term any and every narrative of the past events a constituent of national memory or collective memory understood as the shared property of the citizenry of a state. Nowhere is this more evident than in the case of film. Time and again the claim is made that the way cinema presents the past somehow passes in an unmediated manner into something termed memory.[48]

Winter's critique demands that when we explore the role played by film and television in the construction of collective memory we give due attention – as Halbwachs would similarly have demanded – to the precise *collective* involved. A sensible approach is to carefully identify exactly who was involved in the production, and to whom it was directed. In conventional studies of collective memory, which have often been 'site-specific', it is reasonably straightforward to both see and demarcate these lines; they are physical sites around which visible collectives gather for the deliberate purpose of remembering together. The fact that films (and television) are a form of mass communication problematizes this, and makes it far harder (if not impossible) to identify a specific 'receptive' group bounded in time and space. But this problem also offers potential. For while Winter's reluctance to accept films as suggestive of an abstraction like 'national' memory demands conceptual rigour, we might respond that the very 'abstract' nature of national memory (and national identity) in actual fact means that film – mass produced and mass consumed – becomes a uniquely useful resource. As Benedict Anderson has famously argued, national identity is in essence an imaginative construction, for no national community (unless it's very, very, small) can ever combine and connect in space (see also Chapters 4 and 13).[49] Instead, therefore, the construction of national identity is dependent on the production of connections in time. The past – history – is a tool to be used in order to make an abstraction feel 'real': we bind ourselves as Britons, or Americans, or whatever, by investing in the notion of a collective past. For Victorians, this would result in the elite sponsored construction of monuments to carefully selected historical heroes. Today, the construction of national identity is pluralistic and achieved through many means, but central are surely the media of mass communication, which due to their very nature have peculiar access to nearly everyone.

While the relationship between film, television and national memory and identity demands careful assessment, these audio-visual forms are among the key mechanisms of communication through which Anderson's theory is surely realized. Film and TV are just the sort of memory 'resource' through which members of a twenty-first-century national community can witness their essential sameness visually expressed. That said, to access responses to these resources demands care and patience: audience figures; ratings; box office returns; reports and reviews in the popular press are all useful sources through which to explore responses to particular films and television productions (and to chart and check their popularity). An additional technique, used by Connelly, is to trace the various contacts and connections between audio-visual productions in order to identify recurring themes, images and impressions. Here, the principle idea is that the frequency with which something *recurs* through time is suggestive of its prevalence, power and perhaps its acceptance (although note the caveats).

Narrative and characterization

Narrative is central to the telling of a story *and* to the recounting of a memory. As noted above, in many respects the construction of a memory *is* the construction of a story. In this sense, analysing film as a memory 'resource' is in some respects more straightforward than analysing a more traditional monument. In the latter, the 'story' might demand unpicking inscriptions and 'reading' the design, where as in a film, the story is foregrounded. The skill is to identify the *way* in which the story is told. Who has (or where is) the narrative centre? What drives the plot? What is included and what is ignored? What is assumed and what is revealed? To take a revealing example: *Tora, Tora, Tora* (1970) and *Pearl Harbor* (2001) are both 'about' the Japanese attack on Hawaii on 7 December 1941. Both are suggestive of American perceptions of the attack, and the event at the centre of each is obviously consistent. But the specifics of the *story* told differs significantly. *Tora, Tora Tora* complicated established American understandings of the attack by including – in a clear suggestion of the changed cultural landscape, post-Vietnam – the view and motives of the 'enemy'. *Pearl Harbor* assimilates aspects of this approach, while also romanticizing the narrative and offering – like *Saving Private Ryan* (1998) – an emotional 'Good War' era homage to the 'Greatest Generation'. Similarly, the characterization of each film is notably distinct. *Tora, Tora, Tora*, like many of the Second World War focused 'epics' produced by Hollywood in this era (e.g. *The Longest Day* [1962], *A Bridge Too Far* [1977]), is especially interested in high politics and military strategy. *Pearl Harbor*, in contrast, is drawn to the 'ordinary' heroes who loved and lost. Same event; different perspective; different narrative; different characters. At this point, we should also acknowledge an important distinction between assessing film as a work of memory and interrogating it as a – secondary – source of history. In the latter, and as Chapter 2 explained, issues of 'authenticity' and 'accuracy' are frequently at the fore (even if, as was argued, the criticisms which duly follow are often misplaced). But when examining a cultural artefact – like a film – as a memory 'resource' differences with conventional historical 'truth' actually become key points of interest. Put differently, the actual or perceived *wrongness* of a historical film becomes among its most important, interesting and revealing qualities for such 'inaccuracies' tell us much about contemporary attitudes and assumptions.

Context and chronology

As noted above, the differences between films based upon the same event can be readily explained by engaging with the most fundamental aspect of the historian's method: the role of context and chronology. No expression of human creativity can escape *time*. Place and moment *always* shape the production of any cultural artefact, and a film is no different. That is not to say that films are a mere 'reflection' of the society in which they are made, nor can they be 'reduced' to their context. Such a concept was popular in the 1970s, but film historians have since comprehensively challenged this simplistic reading, drawing attention to the fact that the use of 'mirror' metaphors deprives films of their 'active' role in society; films become passive recipients of some idea or way of thinking. Current research privileges the idea that films 'mediate' social and historical reality. As film historian James Chapman explains, thinking in these terms 'allows for a more dynamic relationship between films and the social processes that produce them'.[50] For the student of memory, this is a particularly useful approach. While the 'reflectionist' school of film history once attempted to recover from film a certain 'view' of society (and hence found use in the 'mirror' metaphor), the historian of memory is already primed to accept the complex and contested nature of collective memory, and can readily accept the idea that a film *mediates* such complexities. As we know, *mediation* is central to the very construction of collective memory.

Acknowledging the idea that films 'mediate' social, cultural and political concerns also returns the historian to familiar methodological territory. As Chapter 1 explains, to understand the issues being 'mediated' demands contextualizing the source; this is at the heart of the historical discipline. Interrogating filmic or televisual mediations of history demands tracing the various links and connections between the moment and the 'memorial': what cultural conventions does the film expose and exploit? It is useful to think in terms of *encoding* operations: how does the film 'encode' – *write in* – certain ideas, values or assumptions? What underlying political attitudes are mediated? Is the 'politics' of the production apparent in the specific vocabulary of the script, or in the framing of the narrative? Or both? This latter issue again returns us to some of the important connections between film and memory. As we know, collective memory is a present-orientated work of construction, and filmic and televisual representations of the past clearly betray this fact. The importance of offering a contemporary audience an experience that makes sense, which they can understand, and which appeals, ensures that films *must* deliver stories of the past from the perspective of the present. Failure to do this will surely lead to box office problems or poor reviews. Thus, film and television clearly expose to study an integral feature of the construction of memory – the shaping role played by the present.

Conclusion: Film, TV, memory and mediation

The past decade has seen the historical discipline enthusiastically engage with the potential of visual and audio-visual material. This is fitting. The early twentieth century was profoundly shaped by the development and popularization of the 'moving image'; the post-1945 period was similarly reconfigured by the commercialization of television; and the early twenty-first century has been comprehensively remade by new technologies of online mediation, technologies which have firmly established the moving image as the prime means through which many people learn about – and 'capture' – their world. No historical account of the twentieth century (and after) can be complete without acknowledging the central role played by moving images in helping (and hindering) individuals and communities to make sense of their moment.

This realization has had important implications for all historians, but especially for those working in a similar area of contemporary academic growth: memory studies. Since at least the 1980s, this area of research has attempted to recover less the historical 'reality' of the past, than historically specific *perceptions* of the past-present connection. Understandably, early work was drawn to the ways in which previous cultures and societies have expressed their commemorative visions on landscape, in the form of memorials and monuments. But more recently, historians of memory have interrogated the dominant form of mass communication – and mass commemoration – of the modern and postmodern age: the moving image, especially film and television. Such interest is profoundly logical; the moving image and the very concept of 'collective memory' are historical contemporaries. As David Williams has suggested (see Chapter 13), the birth of cinema and all that this bequeathed (in terms of technology) should be rightly understood as calling forth a new, distinct, 'age' of memory.[51] Modern 'memory' therefore *is* filmic and televisual; we remember and reflect not just via the moving image, but also through it. In this sense, and as Andrew Hoskins, Amy Holdsworth and Steve Anderson have all identified, our very cognitive processes have been reshaped by the technologies of mediation to which we have been exposed.[52] As such, the moving image is not merely a 'vector' of memory; in so many respects, it *is* memory, and the cinema, television set and online database are the over-flowing memory resources of our supposedly 'amnesiac' culture. Interrogated carefully and critically, their 'contents' has much to tell us about our world, our present, and our ever-changing understandings of the past.

Notes

1   See N. Wood, *Vectors of Memory: Legacies of Trauma in Postwar Europe* (Oxford: Berg, 1999).

2   M. Halbwachs, *On Collective Memory* (London: University of Chicago Press, 1992). Translated and with an introduction by L. A. Coser.

3   E. Durkheim, *The Elementary Forms of the Religious Life* (Oxford: Oxford University Press, 2001 [1912]).

4   See E. Hobsbawm and T. Ranger (eds), *The Invention of Tradition* (Cambridge: Cambridge University Press, 1983); B. Anderson, *Imagined Communities: Reflections on the Origin and Spread of Nationalism* (London: Verso, 2002).

5   Ernst Renan, 'What is a Nation?', 11 March 1882. Available online: http://
    ucparis.fr/files/9313/6549/9943/What_is_a_Nation.pdf (accessed 30 April
    2016).

6   See P. Hutton, 'Sigmund Freud and Maurice Halbwachs: The Problem of
    Method in Historical Psychology', *The History Teacher* 27 (2) (1994): 145–58.

7   G. Eley, 'Finding the People's War: Film, British Collective Memory, and
    World War II', American Historical Review, 106 (2001), 818–838.

8   J. Winter, *Remembering War: The Great War between Memory and History
    in the Twentieth Century* (London: Yale University Press, 2006), 34.

9   See P. Nora, 'General Introduction: Between Memory and History', in
    Realms of Memory: Rethinking the French Past, Volume I, ed. P. Nora and
    L. Kritzman (New York: Columbia University Press, 1996).

10 See J. Winter, *Sites of Memory, Sites of Mourning: The Great War in
    European Cultural History* (Cambridge: Cambridge University Press, 1995);
    M. Sturken, *Tangled Memories: The Vietnam War, The AIDS Epidemic, and
    the Politics of Remembering* (London: University of California Press, 1997);
    J. Young (ed.), *The Art of Memory: Holocaust Memorials in History* (New
    York: Prestel, 1994); D. Sherman, *The Construction of Memory in Interwar
    France* (London: University of Chicago Press, 1999); S. Farmer, *Martyred
    Village: Commemorating the 1944 Massacre at Oradour-sur-Glane* (London:
    University of California Press, 1999).

11 See Winter, *Remembering War*, 51.

12 N. Gedi and Y. Elam, 'Collective Memory – What is it?', *History and
    Memory* 8 (1) (1996): esp. 30–5, 43.

13 See, for instance, the work examining the 'myth' of the blitz: A. Calder, *The
    Myth of the Blitz* (London: Pimlico, 1992); C. Ponting, *1940: Myth and
    Reality* (Chicago: Ivan R. Dee, 1993); M. Smith, *Britain and 1940: History,
    Myth and Popular Memory* (London: Routledge, 2000).

14 Gedi and Elam, 'Collective Memory – What is it?', 32.

15 Ibid., 43.

16 W. Kansteiner, 'Finding Meaning in Memory: A Methodological Critique of
    Collective Memory Studies', *History and Theory* 4 (2) (2002): 185. See also
    A. Confino, 'Collective Memory and Cultural History: Problems of Method',
    American Historical Review 102 (5) (1997): 1386–403.

17 H. Rousso, *The Vichy Syndrome: History and Memory in France since
    1944*, trans. A. Goldhammer (Cambridge: Harvard University Press, 1996).
    But we should note that Rousso explains in his introduction that he uses
    psychological terminology only as a metaphor, 11.

18 Sturken, *Tangled Memories*, esp. 3–9.

19 I. Irwin-Zarecka, *Frames of Remembrance: The Dynamics of Collective
    Memory* (New Brunswick: Transaction Publishers, 1994), 116.

20 Perhaps the most famous example of the idea that memories, particularly of
    traumatic or emotionally intense events, are 'printed' is the so-called 'Now
    Print!' thesis offered by Brown and Kulick in their discussion of 'Flashbulb
    memories'. For a discussion, and critique of this idea, see U. Neisser,

'Snapshots or Benchmarks', in *Memory Observed: Remembering in Natural Contexts,* ed. U. Neisser (San Francisco: W. H. Freeman and Company, 1982), 43–9.

21   See, for example, U. Neisser and L. K. Libby, 'Remembering Life Experiences', in *The Oxford Handbook of Memory,* ed. E. Tulving (Oxford: Oxford University Press, 2000), 315–32.

22   P. Di Maggio, 'Culture and Cognition', *Annual Review of Sociology* 23 (1997): 266.

23   J. McClelland, 'Connectionist Models of Memory', *Oxford Handbook of Memory*, ed. E. Tulving and F. I. M. Craik (New York: Oxford University Press, 2000), 583.

24   Ibid.

25   D. Schacter quoted in Winter, *Remembering War,* 4.

26   Sherman, *The Construction of Memory in Interwar France,* 2.

27   See, for instance, A. Huyssen, *Present Pasts: Urban Palimpsests and the Politics of Memory* (Stanford, CA: Stanford University Press, 2003); A. Huyssen, *Twilight Memories: Marking Time in a Culture of Amnesia* (London: Routledge, 1995).

28   M.A. Doane, 'Information, Crisis, Catastrophe', in *Logics of Television,* ed. P. Mellencamp (Bloomington: Indiana University Press, 1990), 226–7.

29   See H. White, *Metahistory: The Historical Imagination in Nineteenth Century Europe* (Baltimore: Johns Hopkins University Press, 1975); H. White, 'Historiography and Historiophoty', *The American Historical Review* 93 (5) (December 1988): 1193–9.

30   See, for instance, M. Foucault, 'Film and Popular Memory', *Edinburgh Magazine* 2 (1977).

31   See especially R. Barthes, *Mythologies* (London: Grant and Cutler, 1994). Originally published in 1957, but not published in English until 1972.

32   See H. Johnson, *Sleepwalking Through History: America in the Reagan Years* (New York: Anchor Books, 1992); see also W. H. McNeil, 'Mythistory, or Truth, Myth and History and Historians', *American Historical Review* 91 (1) (1986): 1–10.

33   See, for instance, R. Evans, *In Defence of History* (London: Pimlico, 1997).

34   See, for example, Rousso, *The Vichy Syndrome,* 3–4. Rousso essentially understands Memory and History to be oppositional, with the former being the subject matter of the latter. However, he later qualifies this distinction by suggesting that historians are always situated *within* collective memory and are themselves thus a 'vector' of memory. For a rather nostalgic critical lament of the historian's role in the destruction of memory see P. Nora, 'General Introduction: Between Memory and History', in *Realms of Memory: Rethinking the French Past*, Vol. 1, ed. P. Nora and L. Krtizman (New York: Columbia University Press, 1996), 1–20.

35   E. Rosenberg, *A Date Which Will Live: Pearl Harbor in American Memory* (London: Duke University Press, 2003), 5–7.

36   Winter, *Remembering War*, 5–6.

37   Sturken, *Tangled Memories*; Irwin-Zarecka, *Frames of Remembrance*;
     Winter, *Sites of Memory*, esp. 133–43.

38   A. Hoskins, 'New Memory: Mediating History', *Historical Journal of Film,
     Radio and Television* 21 (4) (2001): 342.

39   Ibid., 344.

40   A. Holdsworth, '"Television Resurrections": Television and Memory',
     Cinema Journal 47 (3) (2008): 142.

41   See B. Urwand, *The Collaboration: Hollywood's Pact with Hitler* (London:
     The Belknap Press of Harvard University Press, 2013).

42   For details of the wartime film industries in the United States, Britain and
     German, see: T. P. Doherty, *Projections of War: Hollywood, American
     Culture and World War II* (New York: Columbia University Press,
     1999); C. R. Koppes, *Hollywood Goes to War: How Politics, Profits and
     Propaganda Shaped World War II Movies* (London: I.B. Tauris, 1988);
     M. Harris, *Five Came Back: A Story of Hollywood and the Second World
     War* (London: Canongate, 2015); A. Aldgate and J. Richards, *Britain Can
     Take It: the British Cinema in the Second World War* (Edinburgh: Edinburgh
     University Press, 1994); J. Chapman, *The British at War: Cinema, State and
     Propaganda, 1939–1945* (London: I.B. Tauris, 2000); D. Welch, *Propaganda
     and the German Cinema, 1933–1945* (London: I.B. Tauris, 2001).

43   M. Connelly, *We Can Take It! Britain and the Memory of the Second World
     War* (London: Routledge, 2004).

44   Connelly, *We Can Take It!*, 3.

45   G. Eley, 'Finding the People's War: Film, British Collective Memory, and
     World War II', *American Historical Review* 106 (3) (2001): 818–38;
     J. Bodnar, '*Saving Private Ryan* and Postwar Memory in America', *American
     Historical Review* 106 (3) (2001): 805–17; Rousso, *The Vichy Syndrome*;
     M. C. Maroto, *Film, Memory and the Legacy of the Spanish Civil War*
     (London: Palgrave Macmillan, 2011).

46   Irwin-Zarecka, *Frames of Remembrance*, 4.

47   Ibid.

48   Winter, *Remembering War*, 183.

49   Anderson, *Imagined Communities*.

50   J. Chapman, *Film and History* (London: Routledge, 2007), 93.

51   D. Williams, *Media, Memory and the First World War* (Montreal: McGill
     University Press, 2009), esp. 7–14.

52   See Hoskins, 'New Memory: Mediating History'; Holdsworth, '"Television
     Resurrections": Television and Memory'; S. Anderson, 'History TV and
     Popular Memory' in *Television Histories: Shaping Collective Memory in the
     Media Age*, ed. G. R. Edgerton and P. C. Rollins (Lexington: University of
     Kentucky Press, 2001), 19–36; M. Landy, *The Historical Film: History and
     Memory in Media* (London: Athlone Press, 2001).

PART TWO

Using film and television: Case studies

CHAPTER FOUR

'The way we are': Class and Britishness on film

Marcus Morris

It is somewhat of a cliché to talk of Britain as being a nation obsessed with class; a generation of politicians, such as John Major and Tony Blair, have told us that we now live in a classless Britain. It is perhaps more pertinent now to say we are a nation obsessed with just what it is to be British and whether we have a shared national identity, especially when that same generation of politicians often seem focused on identifying supposedly 'British' values in order to ensure that they can buttress and sustain them in an unstable age of political devolution and Brexit. However, it would be more accurate to say that we are a nation obsessed with both. Britain is a nation still divided by class and it remains a primary identifier for many people, while there seems to be ever-more debate on how we should identify ourselves as British. It is no surprise, then, that British filmmakers have frequently focused on exploring the conjoined issues of class and national identity (as the Danny Boyle-directed Opening Ceremony of the London Olympics so powerfully revealed). Thus, films are an excellent device for illustrating and interrogating how these divided identities have been constructed, contested and communicated during the twentieth century (and beyond).

These identities have not just been central to how we view ourselves as Britons, but also to historians (and those of many other disciplines) who have used them as categories of enquiry when looking at the nation's past and present. Class, for a generation of historians, was the single most important form of social categorization and formed the basis of those historians' understanding of social, economic and political change. This emphasis has now been questioned, but it remains an important, if highly debated, focus.[1] National identity as a focus for academic study is a later development, and first emerged in the 1970s and 1980s just as conventional conceptions of the nation state became subject to the changes wrought by new political and economic supra-national forces and institutions (e.g. the European Union and so-called economic 'globalization'). Nevertheless, the idea of national identity is equally contested, with little agreement as to how British national identity was formed, when it was formed, what it is today and whether the collective identity that is Britishness still has a place in modern Britain.[2] These are some of the most difficult categories for historical inquiry and are thus discussed in a complex and ever-changing literature. It is a debate often conducted in the abstract, confused by obscure terminology and discipline-specific theory; a debate where ideology, political persuasion and the contemporary context massively impact the conclusions that are reached. Film, as a mediating form of mass communication, is a great way to explore these complex interactions between class, national identity and culture.

Film gives context to that discussion; it helps illustrate the debates and divides that permeate the literature, adding clarity. Moreover, film provides perspective on these identities beyond just those of academics and other social commentators. As a collaborative cultural production (see Chapters 1 and 2), films expose more or less the views of directors, screenwriters, actors, critics and, of course, audiences, among others. Looking at films over an extended period of time thus shows the evolution of those views, demonstrating the changing nature of class and national identity in Britain. This chapter will look at what British film (and it will be primarily 'British' films that are focused on, in the sense of being British funded, produced and directed) can add to our understanding of these identities as categories of enquiry. Such identities are the focus for many British films and are often – and perhaps uniquely – bound together in the same films in the British context. By examining selected films produced from the 1940s through to the turn of the twenty-first century, the chapter will also illustrate the evolution that has taken place in British society with relation to these identities, with British films moving from a mediation of homogeneity and unity in British society to a mediation of heterogeneity and disunity.

The most complex of categories

Jerry White has noted that 'we all know class and classes exist, but it and they elude both scientific definition and enumeration. Whatever conceptual pigeonholes we painstakingly build, the infinite variety of human experience spills messily over the crosswalls'.[3] Class is one of the most contested of social categories and has been understood in a number of often contradictory ways.[4] It can be difficult to determine the class identity of any individual or group; difficulty arises from the challenges in defining class. Should class be defined by economics, by social and cultural criteria, by individuals' mind-set, by their moral values, by their accent or education, or by a combination of all of these? There is no definitive answer and class therefore has multiple meanings, while it remains subjective and fluid, as it is, in many ways, an artificial construct. There is a difficulty in determining collective class identities and in deciding the nature of the class structure and class divisions in society. This is perhaps all the more difficult in a nation obsessed with class. Traditionally, Britain has been divided into three classes, with each class sharing a supposed collective identity: working, middle and upper. This is a structure many still talk of today, but clearly it has never been so simple. Do these classes really have the required coherence and homogeneity? Are class characteristics and class boundaries really so clear cut? Are identities shared or individual? Is the British population truly class-conscious in the way suggested?

The social structure of modern Britain is both more elaborate and more integrated than our traditional way of looking at society allows. As Arthur Marwick noted, 'classes evolve and assume their particular shape in response to long-term historical processes, structure, cultural and political', while 'class influences historical developments and in turn is affected by those developments'.[5] Nevertheless, Britons have invariably made sense of the world around them, which was not only or always the British Isles, through class structures and rhetoric. The class groupings we may subscribe to may be constructed or imagined, but that does not make them any less 'real'. When considering the uniqueness of Britain's obsession with class, the sociologist Stein Ringen wrote that 'what is peculiar to Britain ... is not the reality of the class system and its continuing existence, but class psychology: the preoccupation with class, the belief in class, and the symbols of class in manners, dress and language'.[6]

Film can help us answer, or at least provide examples for, a number of these questions and issues. Film is a historical product that both shapes and reflects the world around it; in this sense, film *mediates* the social and historical realities in which it is produced. Of course, like any historical source, it tells a selective story about its subject and one that is carefully (and often purposefully) constructed. However, class, as we have seen, is about constructing boundaries and British films often focus on establishing, emphasizing and reinforcing just such boundaries. Even with definitional difficulties, it is indisputable that class permeates British films. Indeed, films help overcome those difficulties of terminology. This is because in film, as Philip Gillett has noted, 'the cues are visual and aural – and almost entirely qualitative'.[7] To the traditional signifiers of class, film can add the visual minutiae of social stratification that makes those signifiers all the more meaningful. In short, if class is a 'construction', then film – as itself a media of creative production – is a key location through which to witness the constructive act at work. As with any source, though, we must still ask certain questions of films: who is leading the construction? Whose class assumptions are we watching on screen? Is the audience aware of those assumptions? What are the responses of the audience?

British films have undoubtedly tried to embrace all classes, but this has not made cinema attendance a classless leisure activity. As Robert James found in his study of early cinema, 'what films cinema-goers went to see, and where they went to see them, was determined by, and also helped to determine, their social and cultural identity'.[8] Moreover, there was often a social distinction between audiences (primarily working-class) and filmmakers (primarily middle-class), which means we must be careful to not read against the grain and impose our interpretations on contemporary audiences. Nevertheless, films tell us much about inter-class differences, as well as intra-class differences, and the class structures that allow for these. In this sense, they help further untangle the problems of categorization. Some films, especially those of an earlier period, focus on little more than crass class stereotypes. The positive reception of those stereotypes, however, can tell us a great deal about class structure and the acceptance of that structure. Yet, as society developed, so did representations of class and particular class groupings especially and this is why it is such a useful tool for historians.

Debates on class may have been prominent for longer, but equally contentious is the issue of national identity. Ever since Ernest Renan asked 'what is a nation' in 1882, there has been much disagreement on defining the nation and on how national identities are formed (see also Chapter 3). Traditional definitions tended to focus on criteria such as language, religion, borders, territories and race. However, these categories have become increasingly problematic over the course of the last century. Borders and territories have changed, multiple languages are spoken in the same country, the racial makeup of nations has altered and many religions coexist with state secularism. The question of identity is further complicated by the reality that we take on multiple identities, with national identity sitting alongside a myriad of others. Linda Colley has thus suggested that 'identities are not like hats. Human beings can and do put on several at a time.'[9] Where agreement has been reached, is that these identities are not stable and are constantly constructed and reconstructed. Perhaps the most influential take on this is Benedict Anderson's *Imagined Communities*, where he describes the nation as an 'imagined community' (see also Chapters 12 and 13). As it is impossible for everyone in a nation to know everyone else, all forms of relation (such as a shared national identity) larger than those involving face-to-face contact are imagined and invented. They may share recognition of certain values and characteristics as being distinctive to them, but this is primarily a media construction.

Historians (and those from other disciplines) now seek to understand the making and unmaking of national identity and the changes and continuities that have affected that process. In the British context this study has been heightened by a sense of crisis, developed since the 1970s, over what it is to be British. Academic interest has been accompanied by a more populist interest, with newspaper and magazine articles, documentaries, debates and politicians all tackling this issue. This has been further sharpened by

Britain's relationship with Europe and America (especially complicated in the wake of Brexit), the troubles in Northern Ireland, the growing nationalist movements in Wales and Scotland and the associated independence referendum, criticism of traditional institutions, changing moral values and the discord and divide sowed by the Thatcher years.[10] In such a context, many focus on a so-called decline of British national identity; Richard Weight, for example, writes about the end of Britishness, while Robert Colls suggests that though there may be a British state, there is now no such thing as a collective British identity.[11] Others, however, take a less definite view about such a decline. Paul Ward, in particular, has argued that people have been actively engaged in the construction of British national identity and that it is a flexible identity, which has made Britishness a resilient force.

Film has become central to the construction and reconstruction of British national identity, while also playing an important role in providing representations of what it means to be British. Indeed, film is one of the key cultural forms that creates the imagined community of Britain (see also Chapter 12). In this sense, Andrew Higson has noted how,

> individual films will often serve to represent the nation to itself. Inserted into the general framework of the cinematic experience, such films construct imaginary bonds which work to hold the peoples of a nation together as a community by dramatizing their current fears, anxieties, conceits, pleasures, and aspirations.[12]

Films thus build on and naturalize existing identities and representations, while also producing new identities and representations of the nation. They play a crucial role in defining and disseminating national identity, values and character. Of course, they will not disseminate only one national identity and the variety of British identities presented is illustrative too. British national cinema thus mediates historically specific understandings of the nation, but we have to question whose nation and which nation and understand the context in which cinema is operating.[13] This chapter will demonstrate how filmmakers have engaged with ideas of national identity in the ever-changing context of modern Britain and amid the ever-growing number of identities that the average Briton assumes and expresses.

From unity to divide: Forming a consensus in war

In 1927 the British government passed the Cinematograph Films Act, forcing British cinemas to show a quota of British films, in order to stimulate the nation's declining film industry in the face of American dominance. The government had clearly recognized the importance of film to Britain and her internal and external identities; a committee formed to investigate the effects of the Act concluded that film 'is undoubtedly a most important factor in the education of all classes of the community, in the spread of national culture and in presenting national ideas and customs to the world'.[14] The Act was largely unsuccessful in its aims, but indicated that the political elite had woken up to the power of film in establishing and expressing national identity, demonstrating a particular identity to the world, inculcating certain values and expectations, and potentially as a means of social control. It is no coincidence then that in the early years of mass cinema going and filmmaking in Britain, standard representations of class, the social structure and British identity tended to be produced.

British films of the 1920s and especially the 1930s followed an important pattern. These films focused on images of homogeneity: an established and accepted class structure; a nation happy with its lot; shared cultural values and norms between and across classes; and a clear vision of what it was to be British that was to be cherished. In providing such imagery and promoting such an interpretation there was one clear purpose: to maintain the status quo. In some ways this was an image of consensus, but a consensus of being happy with your position. Attempts at class description were often little more than crass stereotype and films were often infused with condescension and even contempt towards the working classes. Few films would attempt to challenge these ideas. *Love on the Dole* (1941) was among the first to contest these somewhat lazy portrayals of working-class struggles. The film was directed by John Baxter and was based upon a 1933 novel by author Walter Greenwood (who also authored the film's screenplay). Through the changing fortunes of the Hardcastle family (featuring Deborah Kerr as 'Sally' and Clifford Evans as 'Larry'), the film questions the acceptance by the working class of the 'system' and examines feelings of entrapment, first by their work and then by their unemployment. In essence, it is a social analysis of a different Britain, alienated by struggle and by intra-class and generational differences. An interesting counterpoint to *Love on the Dole* can be found in *Brief Encounter* (1945), which focused on similar issues but this time within the middle classes. Directed by David Lean at the very end of the Second World War, the film is now somewhat of a national icon, but when first released many questioned its ability to speak for them, their class and their understanding of British national identity. Nonetheless, it has been called the 'definitive document of middle-class repression', a comment on a particular kind of Britishness, a particular moment in Britain's history and the feelings of a particular class at that moment.[15] With both, though, there remains a certain resignation to the status quo and an acceptance that existing class structures and expectations will not change.

These challenges to this contemporary consensus on class and identity are suggestive of the time in which they were produced, but, significantly, they were not indicative of most films from this period and certainly not those produced during the Second World War. Indeed, rather than encouraging 'questions', the war accentuated the further projection of consensus, and stimulated robust depictions of what it was to be British. Of course, historians of the period have vehemently questioned this consensus and the associated idea of the 'people's war'.[16] Moreover, for many, the reality in terms of experience was surely quite different, and far more complex. As the post-war eviction from office of Prime Minister Winston Churchill so publicly revealed, Britain was in many respects still a deeply divided nation, with class at the heart of that divide. However, film historians such as Mark Connelly and James Chapman have persuasively shown that there was a consensus between the government and many filmmakers to produce propaganda pieces that would reinforce messages of unity and a national community. Most films produced during the war stressed a nation pulling together in the face of an evil enemy, stoicism, individual sacrifice and a willingness to prioritize national need over personal gain. In appealing to national collectivism, such films were reliant on familiar national images, stereotypical visions of society and generalized portrayals of national characteristics.[17]

Many films produced during the war made these appeals (see also Chapter 5). Some are forgotten, some received critical acclaim and some are regularly the focus of historical analysis. However, all are useful in terms of what they show about contemporary constructions of class and national identity. A number of films, such as Noel Coward and David Lean's *In Which We Serve* (1942) and the Graham Greene inspired *Went the Day Well* (1942), attempted to reinforce and normalize the social differences, where communities worked together through an understanding and acceptance of their respective positions within the context of nation, region, gender and class. Here, in short, were clear efforts to emphasize consensus. A greater number of films, though, were more concerned with minimizing class differences more generally and suggesting that all the classes were in this together and were making equal sacrifices. Frank Launder's *Millions Like Us* (1943), for example, was set in an aeroplane factory and centred on the interaction between female workers from different classes, whose boss (Charlie) insisted that there was no time for class distinctions, especially when upper class Jennifer felt the work beneath her. The characters are normal and recognizable, something emphasized by the title. Elsewhere, a more common theme among wartime films was to portray images that were identifiably British, emphasize supposedly British characteristics and promote a cohesive national identity. Indeed, on occasion, even Hollywood engaged in this project: William Wyler's *Mrs Miniver* (1941) is a painstaking effort to celebrate heroic British stoicism and national unity in the face of German attack.

The aim of many of these films was to present an image of Britain that was worth fighting for and highlight how being one community or family would be vital to victory. For instance, *Went the Day Well* saw the war as an attack on traditional English values, when German troops in disguise attack a quiet, rural and symbolic English village. The villagers fight back, though, demonstrating the determination and heroism of the British people and illustrating what is being fought for. A similar vision of England can be seen in Michael Powell and Emeric Pressburger's *A Canterbury Tale* (1944), a rather enigmatic and unusual film, in which the war is only a backdrop and the setting is the beautiful Kent countryside. The film celebrates an English identity that is distinctively moral, spiritual and free, as opposed to the tyranny of fascism. *This Happy Breed* (1944), meanwhile, yet another David Lean contribution, celebrated the perceived central characteristics of Britishness: stoicism, humour and resilience. These were to be defended at any cost, as emphasized by one of the grittier films of the war, Humphrey Jennings's *Fires Were Started* (1943). In emphasizing the heroism and determination of the British people who tackled the fires of the Blitz, this film also highlighted the need for sacrifice, with the death of one of the main characters (see also Chapter 5). However, these films also suggested that these sacrifices would lead to a new future, and potentially to new ideas of Britishness, where traditional social hierarchies and attitudes might be challenged.

From unity to divide: Challenging the consensus amid post-war upheaval

Films historians have tended to agree that the social cohesion and unified national community presented in wartime was gradually challenged over the next half-century or so. As the post-war world emerged, it did so in a way that questioned the images and identities constructed in wartime propaganda. As a result, some filmmakers, especially in the 1950s, were wary of such changes and harked back to a pre-war world, pre-war ideas and traditional social hierarchies and expectations. As such, the late 1940s and 1950s have been seen as the climax of middle-class British cinema, which was nostalgic, unadventurous and stressed stability. The best example of this is probably the Ealing comedies, such as *Passport to Pimlico* (1949), *The Titfield Thunderbolt* (1953) and *The Ladykillers* (1955), which stood for continuity and decency, while celebrating community, consensus and supposedly British eccentricity. A number of backward-looking war films were also produced, which rejected some of the key ideas of wartime films. Films such as *The Cruel Sea* (1953), *The Colditz Story* (1954) and *The Dam Busters* (1955) focused on the exploits of individuals, invariably middle-class men, and celebrated them as national heroes, eschewing notions of 'people's war' collectivism. However, British society was changing, especially towards the end of the 1950s, and this meant changing representations of class and Britishness in film, with the most important examples seen in the films of the British 'new wave'.

The 'new wave' consisted of a small body of highly influential films, which have inspired contemporary critics and many historians alike, films that reflected a cultural revolution born out of a rapidly changing context.[18] Britain was recovering from war and entering a period of affluence, full employment and materialism, especially for the working classes. It also saw the death of empire, the emergence a distinctive youth culture and the revival of an intellectual left. The old class structures, identities, values and certainties were increasingly questioned, mocked and rejected. The 'new wave' films played on those feelings by focusing on the lives and aspirations of the young and working class in a fresh, unpatronizing and rounded way. The narratives often centred on characters who desired to be free from restraint and respectability, and who were individualistic, prioritizing personal interests over the greater general good. In doing so, they were clearly challenging notions of class consensus, collective class experience and a shared Britishness. Such 'new wave' films shared common visual and thematic characteristics that reflected their rejection of the status quo: 'black-and-white photography, melancholy jazz scores, northern locations (Blackpool, Salford, Bolton, Bradford, Wakefield, Morecambe, Manchester), and recurrent images of steam trains, cobbled back streets, gasometers and railway viaducts in a gritty landscape.'[19] This was all in stark contrast to wartime propaganda films and the nostalgia of the 1950s, which was central to their appeal.

The 'new wave' can be criticized as an idealist construction of working-class lives and locations from middle-class auteurs, which say little about the reality of those lives and thus are an outsider's view. Nevertheless, even if they are a middle-class perspective, they still represent the changing perspectives in society and how film can illustrate those. The first film of the 'new wave' was Jack Clayton's *Room at the Top* (1959). Based upon John Braine's 1957 novel of the same name, the film sought to expose the fallacy that Britain was a classless society and show how new tensions were developing around class identities. It illustrated the reality that a working-class boy with the desire to succeed and better his position could only do so by sacrificing his self-respect, personality and happiness, even in this new world of affluence. The working-class lead character, Joe, finds himself fighting against a patronizing upper class, a middle class anxious to maintain their position and the status quo and sections of the working class that were conservative and conformist, who press him not to rise above his station. Sexual desire and relations, a key feature of many of the 'new wave' films, further complicate this opposition.

Many critics and historians regard Karel Reisz's *Saturday Night and Sunday Morning* (1960) as the standout film of the 'new wave'. It focuses on Arthur, a young machinist in a Nottingham factory with money in his pockets, who is determined not to lead the same life of domestic drudgery and sterility that those around him do. The film depicts a previously unknown working-class world in a frank manner, pulling few punches about the realities of such lives, but creating a working-class (anti) hero to challenge the middle-class ones that had gone before. In the end, Arthur comes to the realization that he is essentially powerless and settles for such a life. However, the film illustrates the questioning of traditional class expectations and identities, with Arthur defining himself through consumption rather than occupation. He is also seeking an escape from the class expectations that most succumb to, including his own parents. The regional setting is important too; it challenges the notion of a single Britishness and a national community, introducing the idea of there being more than one Britain.

These themes were echoed in a number of films that were part of the same 'new wave' challenge. *A Taste of Honey* (1962), directed by Tony Richardson, is a moving and stylistic film essentially about outsiders and how those characters respond to being outside of 'respectable' society. The main character is a Mancunian teen (Jo), pregnant by a black sailor, who we see attempting to deal with an uncertain future. She is helped by a gay couple, who further distance her from the world of respectability. Elsewhere, John Schlesinger's *Billy Liar* (1963) is a 'new-wave' comedy, which focuses on a young man (Billy) looking for an escape from his dull provincial life. He dreams of a fantasy life, but like many in the audience is unable to escape the humdrum of the ordinary. But the bleakest and perhaps most powerful film of the period is surely Lindsay Anderson's *This Sporting Life* (1963), which tells the story of Frank Machin, a tough Wakefield miner, who becomes a rugby league star. The choice of sport is important: rugby league was seen (and still is to some extent) as a northern, working-class sport with limited national appeal. The narrative is one of

FIGURE 4.1 Saturday Night and Sunday Morning *(1960)*

the impossibility of happiness, the inability of people to communicate and class. It tells a complex class tale, though, with class frustration, confusion and manipulation all shown. And like many of the films mentioned above, at its heart is an attempt to probe the inner motivations of working-class characters in a thoughtful manner. Above all, it is this that demonstrates changing attitudes to class in Britain.

This Sporting Life was a commercial failure and saw the end of this brief 'new wave' in British cinema, but their impact and legacy would nonetheless last much longer. In fact, other films towards the end of the 1960s would focus on similar issues. The most influential and iconic of these was *Kes* (1969), which still meets with critical acclaim today. This was an emotional and amusing story of a young Barnsley boy's (Billy) respect and love for the kestrel he trains (Kes), which inspires a renewed interest in life. Directed by one of the most politically engaged and provocative of post-war British directors, Ken Loach, the film offers a critique of the education system and the way in which it stifled the talent of many working-class children, guiding them down the well-trodden path of previous generations in terms of occupation and aspiration. As such, it provides a critical commentary on the status quo, and on a social system which still sustains traditional hierarchies. Collectively, these films can be seen to explore a tension in contemporary British society, a tension between change and continuity, the new and the old. This was an era in which social change and growing affluence (at least in some quarters) produced challenges to traditional social boundaries, but at the same time there is an understanding that the established hierarchies of power and privilege have not changed. Meanwhile, the very regional focus of these films implicitly questions the idea of a national community, but they do not then provide any answers as to what this means for British national identity.

From unity to divide: Depicting a divided Britain in the age of Thatcher

The election of Margaret Thatcher in 1979, the policies she introduced and the anger she caused provided the next great challenge to British social structure and Britishness. Many British films from the 1980s to the present day depict a divided Britain and one where the question of identity has become even more complex. Thatcher's stated aim was to transform society, where individualism (and the private) would be privileged over collectivism (and the public), and where a deserving, productive population would prosper over an undeserving, unproductive population, with the population divided into wealth creators or wealth consumers. In doing so, as David Monaghan has noted, 'she inevitably lent a new sense of urgency and even crisis to perennial debates about national identity, class relationships, and the economic order'.[20] Some filmmakers chose to focus on the 'beneficiaries' of Thatcherism, the upwardly mobile working class and the expanding middle classes. However, the majority of British films explored the growing social division and the effects on the working class, seeing them as victims of harsh economic conditions, unemployment and the further erosion of traditional class identities. In particular, many films illustrated the specific effects on men of the shift to a post-industrial economy, a shift which in some regions would have profound consequences for long-established employment practices and gendered constructions of identity.

The director Alan Clarke, for instance, examined and critiqued contemporary divisions in society in a number of films, many of which were controversial and celebrated in equal measure. *Made in Britain* (1983) and *The Firm* (1989) directly attacked the Thatcherite greed-is-good mentality that seemed to define the decade, criticising the desire for individualism at the expense of collectivism and giving a voice to the marginalized, forgotten and unpleasant characters in British society. Elsewhere, *Rita, Sue and Bob Too* (1986), ostensibly a comedy about a married man's illicit affair with two teenage babysitters, examines racism, domestic violence and the growing gap between the home-owning beneficiaries of Thatcher's transformation and those left in Britain's sink estates, stuck in a cycle of poverty. The film identifies the decline of traditional working-class values and way of life with the collapse of traditional heavy industries primarily in the North of England (the film is set in Bradford) and the associated unemployment, rather than affluence or the erosion of class distinctions. Similar themes can be seen in *Letter to Brezhnev* (1985), which, though not directed by Clarke, is set against a backdrop of a 1980s Liverpool blighted by unemployment, poverty and decline. It shows characters, especially the central character Elaine, seeking an escape from this world, but also the constraints that mean many will never be able to aspire to anything other than these lives.

The production of films that address the erosion of traditional class identities did not cease with the end of Thatcher's government and were a central theme in a number of popular films of the 1990s and 2000s. Indeed, the working class has continued to be the focus for filmmakers commenting on the social divisions in society today. Commercially, an upper-class comedy like *Four Weddings and a Funeral* (1994) may have been more successful, but is limited on what it tells us about class in Britain (or, rather, it offers a vision of 'Englishness' more geared towards American consumption). In contrast are those films that continue to examine the ways in which working-class identities (and to a lesser extent, middle-class identities) are constructed, challenged and contested in contemporary society. *Brassed Off* (1996), *The Full Monty* (1997), *Dockers* (1999) and *Billy Elliot* (2000) are all important examples. In such films, working-class identity is explored as fractured, split and complicated by various inter- and intra-class factors: alliances between workers and owners in *Brassed Off*;

FIGURE 4.2 Rita, Sue and Bob Too *(1986)*

changing economic relations between men and women in *The Full Monty*; opposition between fathers and sons in *Dockers*; and those willing to cross the picket line and those not in *Billy Elliot*. Their styles differ significantly, though comedy has a place in all, but they are centred on interrogating the same issues and ideas.

Moreover, *Brassed Off* and *The Full Monty* both share a nostalgic sentimentality for what working-class life once was, and both contemplate the ways in which old communities and identities are disintegrating; a point of criticism for some commentators. Nevertheless, along with the others, these films ponder the toll exerted on particular communities by 1980s era economic policies and deindustrialization. *Billy Elliot*, for example, even takes this further by suggesting the essential futility of working-class struggle. These films recognize the challenge to working-class traditions, and masculinities in particular. In this, they share a link to the recent wave of football hooliganism films, such as *Football Factory* (2004) and *Green Street* (2005), both of which illustrate the fears of working-class men emasculated in contemporary British society by societal feminization and masculine domestication, the shift to a service economy and the shift away from the man as producer.[21] Many of these films are thus consciously aiming to reinstate the importance of class politics and traditional class identities. Interestingly, though, they once again tend to do this in a regional setting, which highlights a further challenge to these identities: the evolving idea of what it is to be British.

Since the 1990s Britain has looked increasingly different, politically at least, with devolution and the creation of parliaments and assemblies, for Northern Ireland, Scotland and Wales. It could have looked permanently different if independence campaigners had won the 2014 Scottish independence referendum, and to some extent will after the recent Brexit vote which has demonstrated stark division within the country. These shifts have added to the complexity of contemporary Britishness, a fact acknowledged by several recent films. For instance, in some films images of British national identity are often now centred on ideas of heterogeneity and transnationality, while some also project national and regional identities that challenge the traditional notions of all-encompassing Britishness. Two of the best, if controversial, examples of this are *Trainspotting* (1995) and *Human Traffic* (1999). They suggest an end to homogeneity in British national cinema, indeed an end to the very idea of a national British cinema, with the projection of multiple and unstable (national) identities. Both films reject traditional notions of Britishness, as well as Scottishness and Welshness, and the images that had been traditionally used to represent them. They respectively question the relationship of Edinburgh and Scotland and Cardiff and Wales to the rest of Britain. That they both do this through the highly emotive issues of drug use enhances the challenge to the normal cultural signifiers. Along with other Scottish, Welsh and Northern Irish films, they are part of a cultural decolonization, reimagining both the constituent parts of the United Kingdom and the very idea of Britain itself.[22] They are not alone in this, for there has been one further challenge to the idea of Britishness.

For many one of the greatest challenges to Britishness and the idea of a homogeneous identity had been immigration and the associated multiculturalism of Britain. The emergence of films from the 1980s onwards that focused on these different communities have questioned the idea of a national community and a national cinema that can reflect a nation as diverse as modern Britain. Moreover, they suggest that rather than thinking in national terms we should think in transnational terms or focus on the local and regional through specific communities. Many of these films have chosen to focus on the British Asian community in a regional setting (such as West Yorkshire, Greater Manchester and the West Midlands) as one with multiple identities. Films like *My Beautiful Laundrette* (1985), *Bhaji on the Beach* (1993), *Brothers in Trouble* (1995), *My Son the Fanatic* (1997), *East is East* (1999) and *Bend It Like Beckham* (2002) have at their centre narratives of contested identities (see also Chapter 6). They display the complexities of the main characters' allegiances and relationships, with generational, gender, ethnic difficulties all impacting on a conflicted sense of cultural belonging. These films demonstrate that for many people in modern Britain, Britishness is not simply or easily defined and there is certainly no longer a consensual vision – mediated in cinema – of British national identity.

Understanding the way we are

It is clear that modern Britain seems at odds with itself: we are a nation as socially divided as ever before, while resurgent regionalism, the movement to devolution (and possibly independence) and the vote to leave the European Union has made us question more than any time in recent memory what it is to be British. Yet, class and national identity are still identities through which many Britons define themselves. Much of the academic literature on such issues, though, just adds to the complexity of already complicated issues. It is here where film can be particularly useful. Films tell us much about inter-class differences, as well as intra-class differences, and the class structures that allow for these, while also providing visual clues to the nation's under-standing of class at a particular moment. Indeed, films are central to the very construction and reconstruction of British national identity; they mediate the very ideas through which Britons – and others – make sense of themselves. As this chapter has suggested, therefore, by looking at specific films over an extended period, we can see how constructions of Britishness, and of class, have changed through time in response to evolving political, cultural and economic conditions. Such a survey suggests that Britain – especially after 1945 – has shifted from a homogenous and unified nation with an estab-lished social hierarchy and accepted national identity to a heterogeneous and divided nation, with a confused class system and a complicated national identity. Of course, the process was not quite as simple as this, but film does at least provide suggestive routes into the maze of changing identity constructions, affirming the extent to which Britain has long been, and still remains, a nation obsessed with what we are and what we are not.

Notes

1   A good overview of these developments can be found in J. Thompson, 'After the Fall: Class and Political Language in Britain 1780–1900', *Historical Research* 39 (1996): 785–806; K. Navickas, 'What Happened to Class? New Histories of Labour and Collective Action in Britain', *Social History* 36 (2011): 192–204.

2   For an overview of these debates see P. Ward, *Britishness since 1870* (London: Routledge, 2004).

3   J. White, *The Worst Street in North London: Campbell Bank, Islington Between the Wars* (London: Routledge and Kegan Paul, 1986), 27–8.

4   For an overview of these in the British context see: J. Benson, *The Working Class in Britain 1850–1939* (London: I.B. Tauris, 2003); D. Cannadine, *Class in Britain* (London: Penguin, 2000).

5   A. Marwick, *Class: Image and Reality*, 2nd edn (Basingstoke: Macmillan, 1990), 373.

6   Quoted in Cannadine, *Class*, ix.

7   P. Gillett, *The British Working Class in Postwar Film* (Manchester: Manchester University Press, 2003), 15–16.

8   R. James, 'Popular Film-going in Britain in the Early 1930s', *Journal of Contemporary History* 46 (2) (2011): 272.

9   L. Colley, *Britons: Forging the Nation 1707–1837* (London: Vintage, 1996), 6.

10   For a fuller discussion of this see Ward, *Britishness*; J. Richards, *Films and British National Identity: From Dickens to Dad's Army* (Manchester: Manchester University Press, 1997).

11   R. Weight, *Patriots: National Identity in Britain 1940–2000* (Basingstoke: Macmillan, 2002); R. Colls, *Identity of England* (Oxford: Oxford University Press, 2002).

12   A. Higson, *Waving the Flag: Constructing a National Cinema in Britain* (Oxford: Clarendon Press, 1995), 7.

13   For an overview of the literature on British national cinema see S. Street, *British National Cinema*, 2nd edn (London: Routledge, 2008).

14   Quoted in J. Richards and A. Aldgate, *Best of British: Cinema and Society from 1930 to the Present* (London: I.B. Tauris, 2002), 1.

15   M. Williams, 'Brief Encounter', in *Fifty Key British Films*, ed. S. Barrow and J. White (London: Routledge, 2008), 56.

16   See A. Calder, *The Myth of the Blitz* (London: Pimlico, 1992) and C. Ponting, *1940: Myth and Reality* (Chicago: Ivan R. Dee, 1993).

17   See M. Connelly, *We Can Take It!: Britain and the Memory of the Second World War* (London: Routledge, 2004); and J. Chapman, *The British Can Take it: Cinema, State and Propaganda* (London: I.B. Tauris, 2000a).

18   See J. Hill, *Sex, Class and Realism: British Cinema 1956–1963* (London: BFI, 1986).

19   Richards, *Films*, 149.

20   D. Monaghan, 'Margaret Thatcher, Alan Bleasdale, and the Struggle for Working-Class Identity', *Journal of Popular Film and Television* 29 (1) (2001): 2.

21   See N. Rehling, '"It's About Belonging": Masculinity, Collectivity, and Community in British Hooligan in Films', *Journal of Popular Film and Television* 39 (4) (2011): 162–73.

22   For a further discussion of this see M. McLoone, 'Internal Decolonisation? British Cinema in the Celtic Fringe', in *The British Cinema Book*, 2nd edn ed. R. Murphy (London: BFI, 2001), 184–90; J. Hallam, 'Film, Class and National Identity: Re-imagining Communities in the Age of Devolution', in *Past and Present*, ed. J. Ashby and A. Higson (London: Routledge, 2000), 261–73.

CHAPTER FIVE

Were fires started? Exploring gender in British cinema of the Second World War

Corinna M. Peniston-Bird

In British cinema of the Second World War, the impact of the exigencies of war on existing constructions of gender were explored on screen for a mass audience.[1] Film was one among many visual representations of gender in the public domain in the war, co-existing with photography, fine and popular art, propaganda posters and cartoons. Sometimes the focus on the wartime challenges to traditional roles was overt, for example, in the three feature films on women in employment, *The Gentle Sex* (1943) on the ATS, *Millions Like Us* (1943) on munition workers, and *The Lamp Still Burns* (1943) on nursing.[2] However there are many more examples where masculinities and/or femininities were the unwitting testimony of the film, not its overt subject matter (e.g. *Cottage to Let* [1941]; *Went the Day Well* [1942]; *Fires were Started* [1943]). All representations were of particular significance in a period in which lived gender identities and public expectations were in flux. As Halloran argues, such representations 'provide models for identification, confer status on people and behaviour, spell out norms, define new situations, provide stereotypes, set frameworks of anticipation and indicate levels of acceptability, tolerance and approval'.[3] We cannot generalize how individuals reacted to these models, although there have been interesting attempts to explore audience responses.[4] However, we can explore the filmic representations of gender identities and their possible implications for recasting, resilience and resistance.

The following chapter discusses feature films set in the contemporary world of Britain at war rather than on the popular historical melodramas of the time: the former permit the assumption that audiences were supposed to recognize the reality of the world the men and women inhabited, the roles they undertook and the manner in which they related to each other.

Their possible function to provide potential role models is more evident than in the playfully escapist fare, alluring though its fantasies might have been.[5] Ministry of Information (MoI) shorts are also not under discussion, because their relationship to the reality depicted and their construction of the intended audience differ from that of feature films.[6] Policy towards feature films in the war changed over time, from an emphasis on fantasy to one on contemporary issues and everyday life featuring everyday people.[7] What was presented to the British public was shaped by the approach taken to gender by the MoI, the British Board of Film Classification, the Films Division and the ideas committee, but filmmakers had some latitude too. This chapter explores the product more than policy or the industry, however, because that reflects the likely point of first contact, then and now. As will be argued, representations of both genders were marked by unresolved tensions, albeit of different natures. They suggested the limits of the imaginable.

Gender, film and the discipline of history

While film studies has multiple methodologies to offer students of film, from film aesthetics to auteur theory, the issue for the historian is how to approach film from a disciplinary perspective, while acknowledging the specific character of the genre.[8] 'New Film History' has sought to bring these elements together.[9] This approach is marked, according to its practitioners, by the central importance it accords to primary sources, both filmic and non-filmic, and its attention to films as cultural artefacts. Some elements are familiar to historians, who are versed in the methodologies demanded by primary sources: the significance of authorship; of date, context of and purpose behind production; detailed analysis of content; intended audience and reception. There are therefore aspects of researching film with which historians are clearly comfortable, and their attention to the dimension of time means they have much to offer: as Murphy argues, 'Films need a context, whether as the work of a particular director, the product of a studio or ... as part of a cycle of films emerging from a particular society over a particular period'.[10] The narrative and script can also be readily reproduced and analysed in prose. Such emphases may not do the genre full justice, however, if they fail to engage with the nature of film as moving pictures of shadow and light, viewpoint and scale.[11] As Annette Kuhn argues, 'the starting point for the student of film always has to be *within the frame*, focusing on that which falls within and beyond the boundaries of the screen and on the distinctive experience of film and its relationship to reality'.[12]

The gender historian has of course a further particular focus, and there have been some excellent explorations of the implications of films from the

Second World War period, drawn upon below.[13] As this research suggests, the conventional historical methodology underlying source analysis can be readily complemented by additional questions to stimulate the exploration of the representation of gender identities within film. These encompass issues specific to individual films such as the arc of the narrative; the visual and aural dimensions of the film; and the relationship created between film and audience; but also broader issues encompassing the seven years the British were at war, such as film genres, repeating types and recurring themes, all addressed through the lens of gender.

Plot, characterization and dialogue

Historians' research questions can be nuanced to engage with gender in film. In terms of the plot, what roles are taken by men and by women? What function does each character serve? Whether in lead or supporting roles, how does their presence advance the narrative? For example, in *A Canterbury Tale* (1944) and *Millions Like Us* women are central to the narrative, in the former through the individual character of the Land Girl Alison Smith (Sheila Sim), in the latter through a collective of six (and more). In *Ships with Wings* (1941), however, the two female characters Celia Wetherby (Jane Baxter) and Kay Gordon (Ann Todd) largely serve to reveal the personalities of the men and underline the reckless virility of Lt Dick Stacey (John Clements).[14] How is gender inflected by class, age, marital status, regional and national identities, the latter a frequent emphasis for gender historians? For example, in the war we find the first films set in working-class environments which do not merely resort to the stock comedy characters of music hall, but permit their inhabitants to be more three-dimensional: contrast, for example, *Old Bill and Son* (1941) (Old Bill himself is based on the cartoon character of the First World War created by Bruce Bairnsfather) with the later *Millions Like Us* or *Waterloo Road* (1945). Nonetheless, with Sue Aspinall, we can still question the extent to which we are being introduced to a working-class point of view and the qualifications of those describing the working-class milieu: 'the unfamiliarity of middle-class writers, directors, producers and actors with working-class life militated against any radical change in the images they produced.'[15]

How and when do men and women speak, to whom and of what? The modern paucity of the roles granted to women on celluloid has been highlighted by the Bechdel test, in which viewers are invited to ask three cumulative questions of a film: does it feature more than one female protagonist; do they have a conversation; do they have a conversation pertaining to anything but men? [16] Variants have been added, such as whether the protagonist is even named, and the character development

of strong female characters across the story line.[17] With the exception of
films on the Armed Forces, the majority of films discussed permit their
female characters names and some agency; even the melodrama *Love
Story* (1944) which concentrates on the rivalry between two women, Lissa
Campbell (Margaret Lockwood) and Judy (Patricia Roc), for the love
of Kit Firth (Stewart Granger) allows them both professional identities
and skill (Campbell as a pianist; Judy as a stage director).[18] The subject
matter of conversations between men, and between members of the
opposite sex, are of course equally rich subjects of investigation for the
gender historian. Both *Waterloo Road* and *Millions Like Us* (1943), for
example, offer insight into the characters of the main protagonists and the
conduct of contemporary romantic relations through the halting dialogue
between the lead couples. In their first conversation alone, Celia Crowson
(Patricia Roc), who has recently taken up work in a factory, and Fred
Blake (Gordon Jackson), a young Scottish Flight Sergeant, reveal their
well-matched inexperience and shyness. Celia nearly scares off Fred with
her attempt to appear more experienced and sophisticated than she is and
has to backtrack into self-contradiction. Fred Blake offers a representation
of military masculinity which allows for youth and innocence. He is hardly
the dashing Royal Air Force (RAF) Lothario of popular imagination, and
stands in marked contrast to the multiple representations of confident
male promiscuity in uniform as depicted, for example, in both *Ships with
Wings* (of the Fleet Air Arm) and *We Dive at Dawn* (1943) (of Royal Navy
submariners).[19]

In *Waterloo Road* the freshly married couple seek and give reassurance
in the following charming gauche interchange. It is part of a flashback to
their wedding day which reassures the audience of Tilly's (Joy Shelton)
sincere love for Jim (John Mills) and provides an insight into her yearning
for a home and children that helps to explain their subsequent marital
problems. They are seated side by side in a railway carriage: throughout
this dialogue we see the two characters in medium close-up.

> Tilly What are you thinking Jim?
>   (*She looks into his eyes; he looks away at a shoe in his hand, clearly
>   prevaricating.*)
> Jim (*Focusing on shoe in an over-concentrated and therefore
>   unconvincing fashion.*)
>   Er, I don't know. I was just, just wondering, what are we going to
>   do with this?
> Tilly I suppose we could leave it under the seat.
>   (*She is prepared to take him quite seriously, glancing between the
>   shoe and his face.*)
> Jim (*Avoiding her gaze.*)
>   Yes, I suppose we could.
> Tilly What were you wondering Jim?

(*She smiles a soppy smile into the mid-distance; he glances between her and the shoe.*)

Jim Whether you feel the same as I feel.
(*She looks at him.*)
When I look at you, I mean.
(*He focuses on shoe.*)

Tilly (*Looking him in the eye, hopefully.*)
How do you feel?
(*He returns her gaze, which increases the comedic impact of his response.*)

Jim My stomach sort of turns over.

Tilly (*Slightly taken back.*)
Oh. Does it?

Jim Yes.
(*Looking at her.*)
(*She smiles.*)

Tilly It's the same with me too.

The endearing humour of the scene is entirely dependent on the interplay of the lines with the making and breaking of eye contact.

Both *Waterloo Road* and *Millions Like Us* depict the first conversations of working-class newlyweds as awkward, shy and affectionate: in contrast, the scene in which the factory foreman Charlie Forbes (Eric Portman) refuses to propose to the upper-middle-class Jennifer Knowles

FIGURE 5.1 *Tilly and Jim converse in the train,* Waterloo Road *(1945)*

(Anne Crawford) shows the two of them as articulate and self-reflexive. Gill Plain (who offers an exemplary analysis of John Mills in film) analyses the relationship between dialogue, class and gender in *Waterloo Road*, describing Jim as the 'archetypal, inarticulate working-class male, the man of few words who gets the job done ... the virtuous working classes are silent. Those who talk too much have ideas above their station, as is demonstrated by Ted Purvis'.[20] Such analysis suggests the potential value of deconstructing the different dimensions to gender representation in film drawing on filmic and historic methodologies for reading sources.

In and out of the frame

The issue of spatial location is significant in gender theory and beauti-fully exemplified in film. Where are characters shown both in terms of environment and frame; and how do they inhabit and move through space? Take, for example, the gendered qualities of the ideology of separate spheres, of the construction of the male-dominated public and the female-dominated private domains, mapped in wartime on to the Battle Front and the Home Front.[21] To return to *Waterloo Road*, taking a wider perspective of domestic and exterior shots in the film as a whole, Tilly is clearly trapped in her domestic environment, shared with the in-laws and a lodger, and by her sullen inability to articulate her unhappiness except in anger. She blossoms as she traverses the streets of London in Ted's company, eating in a crowded pub, dancing in a glamorous club: and yet we are to believe that her claustrophobia would be resolved by a home and family of her own.

Windows and doors often suggest the liminal space where the outside and the domestic worlds meet. Men and women are frequently depicted divided by them, as in the First World War poster 'Women of Britain say "Go!"' and in film never more strikingly than in *The Gentle Sex*.[22] Mrs Sheridan (Mary Jerrold) is a veteran of the WAACs in the First World War. She had met her husband while she was driving ambulances on the Western Front, but he died of his injuries in 1930, leaving her to raise their son alone. Like his father, David Sheridan (John Justin) is a pilot. In one scene, we see him bid farewell to his mother. In a striking piece of staging, he does so through an open window: he stands in the front garden, a road behind him; she sits on her sofa in her living room. The house between them underlines how they are separated by his wartime role, but also positions her – elderly, vulnerable, widowed – firmly within the home. He inhabits the outside world, the village and church for whose values he fights in the background, his head silhouetted by the sky which will determine his fate; his feet, presumably, in a flower bed.

A further dimension of the visual concerns the physicality of the actors chosen and the manner in which they are shot to represent their gender identities. Sue Harper offers an analysis in her discussion of the wartime Wicked Lady roles, whom she describes as a small but intense and innovatory group of women drawn from a variety of class backgrounds who wanted to lead their own lives:

> They are the only group to experience the pleasures of consummation outside the law. Most of Margaret Lockwood's wartime roles, Patricia Roc's character in *Love Story*, Jean Kent's and Anne Crawford's roles – all these represented women who were physically confident, with fast, balanced movement and a poised, symmetrical carriage. Their gaze pattern is firm and still, and is often focused on the middle distance rather than on their male partners.[23]

In the Second World War, women had to negotiate a rhetoric of antithesis which focused on their physical presentation: they had to avoid dowdiness to maintain morale, both their own and that of men; but not appear as glamorous as to invite questioning of their morals.[24] As Antonia Lant observes, outside of melodrama, the sexualized woman can only appear in minor characters: Dot (Jean Gillie) in *The Gentle Sex* or Phyllis (Joy Shelton) in *Millions Like Us*; and although the latter is not deterred from nor punished for her overtly flirtatious behaviour, it is her 'ordinary' sister who finds love and marriage (and widowhood).[25] Underplayed femininity, however, could also be read to suggest the acquisition of more masculine traits. Elizabeth de Cacqueray notes the female leads in *A Canterbury Tale* and *Went the Day Well* are not presented as particularly pretty, but 'ordinary everyday women' – and speculates whether this perhaps serves to distance them from their sexual attributions and play down their femininity, which 'qualifies them better for an approach to the symbolic and the wielding of power'.[26]

Rich analysis can also follow from comparisons of filmic representations of the same actor's physical attributes across his or her oeuvre. It is telling, for example, to contrast the representation of Stewart Granger's physicality in *Waterloo Road* with, say, his swash-buckling Nino in *Madonna of the Seven Moons* (1945) or *Love Story*, in which Granger plays Kit Firth – engineer, damaged pilot and romantic hero. In the latter, Granger's athleticism is emphasized in scenes which show him climbing and diving off the Cornish cliffs and rowing about bare-chested. Emphasis on his vitality reinforces the tragedy of his pending loss of sight, caused by an explosion while on active service in the RAF. When Hilary Clarke (Rosamund John) spurns Laurence Rains (Stewart Granger) in *The Lamp Still Burns*, her choice of duty over romance is all the more striking, not only because of her loathing of the petty regulations of the hospital, but given that Rains is played by Granger. In contrast, in *Waterloo Road*, Granger's athleticism and broad-shouldered physique is rendered part of the chancer Ted Purvis's untrustworthiness and vanity, as exemplified by his love of his own reflection. This is underpinned by his flashy suit and dandy bow-tie, and is juxtaposed with the lithe, functional, uniform-clad body of John Mills as the cuckolded soldier, Jim Coulter. (John Mills had himself foreshadowed the depiction of Purvis as the young Bill Busby in *Old Bill and Son* when we first meet him as a sponging drifter unable to hold down a job, clad in a loud stripy suit, dark shirt and white tie. He is redeemed by rejoining the Army and finding a worthy purpose in life.) Tilly thaws under Purvis's attentions and his linguistic skills in playing to her thwarted dreams, but when he does succeed in kissing her, the mildly inebriated Tilly cannot stop laughing and excuses herself, 'I can't help it, you look so funny!' Although the viewer can empathize with unhappy Tilly's vulnerability to Purvis's wiles, his depiction ensures his physical appeal is as tarnished as he is, a message reinforced by his ultimate defeat in the climactic fist-fight between the rivals and the revelation that he has the medical condition he faked to avoid conscription: it is no coincidence this is an affliction of the heart.

Guiding audience responses

How are audiences invited to respond to the individuals shown on screen? Viewers first meet Ted Purvis as he avoids his tax responsibilities, he then speaks openly of his female conquests (a woman who comments on Tilly playing hard-to-get is rewarded with a comment along the lines of 'makes a nice change' and a dismissive smack on the posterior) and later his distraught heart-felt plea for a settled domestic life is followed with a wink and a thumbs up to a passing acquaintance who has asked how things are going. Not a single character has anything positive to say about him. Andrew Spicer argues that 'Audiences clearly took great pleasure in the ways in which Rogues, drawn from all strata of society, dodged responsibility' but this is more apparent in comic films, such as *Let George Do It* (1940): Ted Purvis is punished for his betrayal of community values at the end of the film by suffering a heart condition that will mean he has to give up all that is dear to him (including womanizing and alcohol) if he is to survive.[27]

An important but elusive dimension of the audience response is cumulative, created by the sum total of characters adopted by certain actors. Even where audience members cannot immediately place where they have seen an actor before, the latter's previous roles leave a legacy of instinctive trust or distrust, sympathy or antagonism. Effective filmmakers can draw upon this when casting to take short cuts with characterization or to play with it: most effectively, for example, in *A Cottage to Let* when an audience predisposed to venerate a pilot and familiar with Mill's work to date were doubly astounded to discover that it is Flight Lieutenant Perry, played by John Mills, who proves to be the dastardly traitor. Audiences of the twenty-first century are more likely to have seen an actor's repertoire in a random order through repeats on television. They may therefore be more familiar with the variety (or not) of roles undertaken by actors across the entirety of their careers: Eric Portman, for example, played both heroes and villains convincingly in a screen career which spanned three decades, as did Alistair Sim.

Exploring wider themes: Tensions within and between the genders

It is well established in the secondary literature that the exigencies of war presented a profound challenge to conventional constructions of gender roles and identities. Nonetheless, the characteristics of military masculinity were not so much a departure from as an amplification of hegemonic masculinity, particularly given the contemporary emphasis on what Sonya Rose has termed 'temperate masculinity' which incorporated civilian values and distanced British militarism from that of the German enemy.[28] Jeffrey Richards has explored the emphasis on the 'common man' so fundamental to the waging of the People's War, and Andrew Spicer also details how the war mobilized a specific form of cinematic hero characterized by his 'unexceptional ordinariness'.[29] He was permitted individuality, but not individualism – like Flight Officer Peter Penrose (John Mills) who is the prosaic, indistinctive and modest lower-middle-class hero of *The Way to the Stars* (1945).[30] Just as the nation was personified by groups incorporating English men, Scots or Welshmen, the 'common man' could also be a composite character co-created by the collective identity of a diverse band of men brought together by war service, so that 'the characters make sense across the spectrum of the group as a whole and not when isolated and taken in opposition to each other'.[31]

Service in the military still constituted a new role for most British men, however, and multiple films showed the journey from civvies to uniform, amateur to professional, from self-interest to group cohesion, personal development to the better for finding a worthwhile purpose (as noted above, for example, in the context of the young Bill Busby in *Old Bill and Son*). According to Geraghty, forces films suggested that the greatest threat to masculinity was whether courage would hold; the solution lay in membership of the group, which meant that the individual did not require exceptional bravery.[32] The obvious example of this is the young stoker (Richard Attenborough) in *In Which We Serve* (1942): when he deserts his post, his Captain (Noel Coward) blames not him but the collective for having failed him. Such films addressed the theme of courage and fear by offering role models, the possibility of redemption, and the collective as the solution, not only to fear but also to efficiency. As Gerachty points out, the group also provided a source of emotional support to its members, an observation true of both genders. For women this is exemplified through the inevitable bereavements in both *Millions Like Us* and *The Gentle Sex*. The collective as solace is underlined in the former by mass singalongs as the panacea to loss as in the closing frames Celia joins Gwen in song, her friends framing her. Ironically, 'Waiting at the Church' is first heard in the film at Celia's wedding, when Gwen sings the punchline to Fred: 'My wife ... won't let me'.[33]

The responsibilities of wartime roles and the priority that should be accorded them were also underlined through representations of relationships between the sexes. *Waterloo Road* is exceptional in permitting Jim to act in dereliction of his duties in order to save his relationship: more commonly, however, men were expected to leave their loved ones and concentrate on their duties. This is powerfully represented in *The Bells Go Down* (1943) when Bob (Philip Friend) does not leave his post to check on his pregnant wife, prioritizing quenching a fire over maintaining the home he has prepared for the baby. Women, in contrast, were to wait in trepidation, preferably use the time wisely (even old Bill's wife Maggie [Mary Clare], who has spoken passionately against the cost of war for women, becomes a drill sergeant), and to live under the shadow of an uncertain future fulfilling their obligations as wives, (elided with) mothers. Although the challenges of maintaining domestic relationships are addressed, as Gledhill and Swanson observe, men must choose war, women babies. Rather than attracting detailed exploration, women's new experiences and working lives largely served as the background to their involvements with the opposite sex. Gledhill and Swanson conclude that

> Despite the centrality of women's desires to these narratives, and the potential for women spectators to retrieve enjoyment from them, they need to show women as better off within the home because of their new freedoms. Their desires can be fulfilled only when they are directed inwards in the confirmation of family unity and continuity through motherhood.[34]

The importance of these gendered choices of war and procreation co-existing was a recurring theme, as exemplified by Iris Winterton (Renée Asherson) who argues the case with feeling to Penrose (Mills) in *The Way to the Stars*, a date that suggests attention was turning to the reconstruction of the post-war world. The only film to allow its female protagonist to choose the male priority of duty over romance is *The Lamp Still Burns* in which the heroine Hilary Clarke (Rosamund John) is a trainee nurse. Tilly's work in *Waterloo Road* is clearly drudgery, no female's job appearing as appealing or fulfilling in that film. Yet the resolution for both Tilly and the post-war nation is motherhood and domesticity, and although the film has argued throughout that is her natural domain, even there Dr Montgomery (Alistair

Sim) is more expert, as he chides her at the close of the film for wishing to cuddle her crying son, for fear of creating another Hitler. Harper offers a damning indictment:

> The actresses' function was to remind audiences, on behalf of the government, of the supposed advantages accruing to patriarchal structures and the ills likely to befall those who challenged them. What should be stressed is how much is missing from the ratified women in MoI films. They do not laugh; they do not move with any sensual grace; they do not enjoy their own bodies or anyone else's. They are respectable, and never reckless in love. Half of their identity has been sliced away, in the interests of the state. [35]

Films set in the contemporary world could not ignore the consequences of the new demands made of women, exemplified by the introduction of the conscription of unmarried women between the ages of twenty and thirty in the National Service Act (No. 2) of December 1941. These women were deemed mobile, that is, they could be required to leave the home, whereas mothers of children under fourteen were deemed immobile. Filmic representations of mobile women share certain characteristics with the depictions of conscripted males: the emphasis on disparate characters finding succour in a collective that could accommodate class and individual traits and personal antagonisms, for example. It is worth noting that the gendered collectives seldom meet in communal cooperation: the intersection is primarily individual and/or romantic. As Penny Summerfield convincingly argues, wartime policies, particularly regarding mobile and immobile women, suggested that, unlike men, women could not be removed from the home and it still remain a home.[36] This is substantiated by the representation of Celia's father and widower Jim Crowson (Moore Marriott) in *Millions Like Us*, who begins the film attempting to rule the roost over his daughters and daughter-in-law. The women leave the home to serve the war effort in the variety of ways open to them (in civilian occupations and the auxiliary forces); he accepts their departure as his patriotic duty and remains at home. It ceases to be a welcoming one: despite being widowered when his children were teenagers, Jim cannot meet the challenge of heating the home, coping with the housework or cooking for himself. He returns to his chaotic home one evening with fish and chips, but loses his supper to the cat as he attempts to dry with the table cloth the dirty plate he retrieved from a perilous stack in the sink.[37] Paul Elliot argues that

> The old, the weak and the wicked were beyond the bounds of the hegemonic mode and therefore provided alternative expressions of masculinity both for those who were fighting and (perhaps more importantly) for those on the Home Front.[38]

However, although we have seen this to be true of Ted Purvis, characters like Jim Crowson may be included for comic effect, but they are not always so far beyond 'the bounds of the hegemonic mode' as exemplified by Jim's under-stated service in the Home Guard, a 'front-line duty' after Dunkirk, as Jim remarks. Although cartoonists played with the possibility of role reversal – men taking over the home while women were out at work – *Millions Like Us* held this position open for women on their return.[39]

In the representation of women, the greatest tension represented in film is thus the reconciliation of the implications of the new roles for women (outside the home, with greater opportunities for freedom) with symbolic and traditional constructions of subservient femininity (keeping the home fires burning). If films were to encourage women in their new roles, the latter had to be presented at least on one level as positive, valuable, valued; if old values were to be defended, women had to be kept firmly in their places. The result was, as Gledhill and Swanson observed, 'a struggle between two contradictory pressures'.[40] The satisfaction women derive from their jobs is often ambiguous: seldom so for men. 'Half-Pint' (Betty Miller, played by Joan Greenwood) in *The Gentle Sex* is at first frustrated at the gulf between her hopes and her experience:

Betty (*Sobbing*)
    I want to go home ... I can't scrub floors, clean my own shoes and peel potatoes, I've never done things like that before.
Anne (Joyce Howard)
    Neither have I, dear, but we'll be going in together.
Betty But I so wanted to do something exciting, physical. I wanted to get away on my own and be tough and independent.

Luckily Betty learns to find satisfaction in polishing her shoes, and does end up serving with a 3.7-inch anti-aircraft gun battery. Meanwhile, although Anne is destined to lose her fiancé, her future is predicted by Erna Debruski (Lilli Palmer) to nonetheless involve marriage within five years, then lots of children: 'And you're not going to be very interested in the outside world.' Anne denies the latter, but, as Sue Aspinall argues, 'the resolution of narratives often performs the task of restoring the status quo and reintegrating women into the patriarchal order. However sensitively emotional conflicts are described, if they are always resolved in favour of their existing order of things that order begins to seem immutable.'[41]

Elizabeth de Cacqueray explored the evolution of power relations between men and women in film, to determine whether women lost or gained power, or indeed remained stationary in the war. Her analysis focuses on the uses of space, the distribution of power between men and women as represented in language and speech acts, and the role of women in progressing the narratives. She concludes: 'Traditional stereotypes are significantly modified but although women as represented appear to gain access to increased powers, supreme power seems to remain a masculine prerogative.'[42] This conclusion offers filmic evidence of the double helix theory of gender relations in war. Margaret and Patrice Higonnet introduced the iconic metaphor of the double helix to explain why despite the potential, neither World War led to significant change in the distance between sexes, in male dominance and female subservience:

> The female strand on the helix is opposed to the male strand, and position on the female strand is subordinate to position on the male strand. The image of the double helix allows us to see that, although the roles of men and women vary greatly from culture to culture, their relationship is in some sense constant.[43]

This theory finds substantiation in the conclusions of Gledhill and Swanson, who find that in wartime film it is men who regulate ideas, narrative and action, whereas women are the focus of regulation and, once they adopt their 'proper' role, support for the men.[44]

It is easy to identify in film the strategies of containment that would limit the potential for change, such as the rhetoric of transience encapsulated by 'for the duration'. The alternative possibilities of reading transience, however, should not be overlooked. At the climax of *Love Story*, for example, the two lovers conclude that however unlikely their future happiness is (given that he is a pilot, and she has been given but few months to live), they must live for the moment:

> **Kit** Happiness such as we can have is worth grasping. Even if it is only for a day, an hour. If you can stand on the highest peak for one moment, you have what most people strive in vain for all their lives … We're all living dangerously. There isn't any certainty anymore. There's just today, and the hope of tomorrow. Oh, darling, please, let's take all the happiness we can, while we can. Don't be afraid.

Joan Simpson (Barbara Waring) in *The Gentle Sex* is advised by a Staff Sergeant whom she consults about her ambitions to take it 'as it comes, day by day'. More usually, however, women were to take responsibility for the future while men fought for the present. Women's ultimate commitment to home and family, even if temporarily suspended, meant that femininity in and out of uniform was not in conflict.[45] This was not the case, however, for wartime masculinities.

Although one would not know this from wartime films, the largest gendered collective of the war effort was the civilian male: when the Armed Forces were at their peak of 4,653,000 in 1945, over twice that number – 10,133,000 men – remained on the Home Front, and not all were too old, too young or too infirm to serve.[46] The significance of their civilian roles to the war effort had been established in the *Schedule of*

Reserved Occupations which listed the occupations (and ages) which exempted men from conscription.[47] These men are largely invisible: in most of the films mentioned thus far, the age of the civilian men depicted usually precluded any question that the more appropriate place for them would be the Forces, however much they may hanker to be part of this war: Old Bill (Morland Graham) in *Old Bill and Son*, a veteran of the First World War, finds a way back in, spurred on in part by his son's uniformed service and even more so by his informally adopted daughter's. Individuals with unique skills of value to the war effort could be heralded in film, such as R. J. Mitchell (Leslie Howard) in *The First of The Few* (1942) or the scientific boffins of *Cottage to Let* although Alan Trently (Michael Wilding) is clearly better suited for work that requires genius not physical co-ordination. A positive representation of the male civilian collective can be found in *The Lion has Wings* (1939) which includes a long segment on the contribution of industry to provide aircraft and weapons. However, although we see a range of working men in passing, young and old, including some impressive physical specimens, the camera is more likely to focus on the machinery churning out quantity and quality munitions, and the men are clearly subservient in the wartime hierarchy peaked by the RAF in this period of battle for dominance of the skies. Also, much of this footage clearly predates the war: later visual representations confirm that the environment did not remain single-sex.[48] This too threatened the masculinity of men on the Home Front and may explain why we do not see both sexes serving side by side as a collective, even if films like *Millions Like Us* allow brief glimpses of men and women sharing the work place (three men share the on-site air raid shelter with the more numerous women).

We have already noted the negative construction of Ted Purvis's parasitic roles on the Home Front running a gambling establishment and hairdressers. It is really only Sam (Mervyn Johns) in *The Bells Go Down* who grants any complexity to the common criminal, but Sam is also serving in the Auxiliary Fire Service, a uniformed service of such proximity to the war effort that the representation of its members (here, and in *Fires were Started*) can readily be paralleled with narratives set in the Armed Forces.[49] The young man in civvies was more challenging to represent, as we see in the representation of the wartime bureaucrat.[50] In *Love Story*, for example, two civilian men are pitched against each other in one brief scene: the older, no-nonsense Yorkshireman Tom Tanner (Tom Walls), in Cornwall to investigate mines in the area, and a young man 'from the Ministry' (uncredited). The precise Ministry is not disclosed, but the implication is that it makes no difference:

Mr Tanner Now listen me lad, you can't put that over on me ...
    I've had them all try, prospector with salted goldmines, company
    promotors who wanted to do me out of brass I'd earned.

Young man from the Ministry But Mr Tanner, as a representative of the Ministry I must insist. I'm only ...

Mr Tanner I know what you are. But I'm here t' get stuff out of mines, not fill in forms. I'm here to do away with bottlenecks.
(*Close up on his revelation.*)
And that's what you are, me lad, a bottleneck.
(*Close up on the unnamed bureaucrat's face, bisected by his neatly coiffured little moustache. He shows outrage followed by resolution.*)

Young man All I ask is that you fill out and return the necessary departmental forms.

Tanner And all I ask is to be left alone to get on with the job I'm here for. So you can go back to Whitehall and tell them to stop pestering me with bits of paper. Or they can take the job and ... give it to somebody else.
(*He jams the young man's hat on and walks away, turning only for the parting shot.*)
And don't have so much starch in your diet!
(*Cut to YOUNG MAN, complete with slim pencil umbrella and hat, which he repositions with a 'humph' before departing, his mission unsuccessful.*)[51]

Young men on the Home Front would have struggled to find positive representation of their role. The lack of any film addressing men as *Millions Like Us* addressed women is significant to the study of gender in war. On the one

FIGURE 5.2 *Confrontational civilian masculinity in* Love Story *(1944)*

hand, the roles performed on the Home Front were not new to men, other than those in civil and home defence, which, as noted, were treated differently in film in any event. On the other hand, the importance of maintaining male civilian morale was not overlooked: propaganda poster campaigns sought to credit the 'Back Room Boys' who 'also serve', and claimed that 'The Attack begins in the Factory'.[52] Yet the interdependence of the civilian and military male did not find specific cinematic representation; the closest we get is perhaps *The Foreman went to France* (1942) in which Fred Carrick (Clifford Evans) travels to France to retrieve machinery before it falls into the hand of the German invaders: he is hindered by wartime red tape, and helped by two soldiers (Gordon Jackson, Tommy Trinder) and the American Anne Stafford (Constance Cummings). Carrick is an unconventional action hero, and was based on the wartime exploits of the Welsh munitions worker Melbourne Johns, who retrieved equipment from the Hispano Suiza works in France.

Gender constructions in wartime were severely challenged by the dual policies of reserved occupations (which kept civilian men on the Home Front) and conscription (which brought women in significant figures into the Auxiliary Forces and industry). Femininities were poised – sometimes torn – between the paradoxes created by the symbolic and the pragmatic mobilization of women for the war effort. While film after film contributes to the discussion of the tensions inherent in wartime femininity, it is all the more striking that the key tension of wartime masculinity was barely touched upon in film: the accommodation of civilian masculinity. There was also a dearth of filmic representations which brought together the collectives of masculinity and femininity in any way other than through individual (romantic) relationships (such as the relationship between factory foreman Charlie Forbes (Eric Portman) and Jennifer Knowles (Anne Crawford) in *Millions Like Us*, an observation of the potential impact of the war on class relations). The answer perhaps lies in the impossibility of reconciling the gendered hierarchy of service with the fluidity of role and status. Uniformed women were clearly auxiliary to uniformed men. Civilian women were dilutees under the watchful eye of male foremen. But how to position women in uniform in relation to young civilian men?

Conclusion

This chapter has argued that wartime cinema offers rich source material for the study of gender and war, and that historical and film methodology can be mutually enriching. As the rich historiography of gender studies and film suggests, these arguments are not contentious. However, as the exploration of some of the different possible dimensions for study has suggested, there are still revelations to be gained from reading within and across the films. This is true of wartime femininities and masculinities; it is also true of gender theory. The absences outlined above suggest perhaps that existing models of gender practices in wartime, which depend on a rigid boundary between the sexes (whether transgressed or negotiated) cannot accommodate all experiences and representations of gender relations in war. Film provides interesting evidence that the boundary might better be understood as a fuzzy not rigid boundary, that is, one that permits a gradual transition between the two zones.[53] As the exploration of the themes and absences in wartime film suggests, it is in the fuzzy area of overlap, in which mobile women go into uniform (as determined by their domestic situations) and civilian men are deemed immobile (as determined by their occupations), where we find the most resounding silences and hence, perhaps, the greatest challenges to the gender order.

Notes

1   I would like to thank Rona Johnston and Kirsten A. Smith for their comments during the writing of this chapter. The classification of a film as British is currently based on a points system based on four areas: Cultural Content (for example the location of the plot, the nationality of the characters, and the language they speak); Cultural Hubs (location of studio or technical support, such as audio post-production); Cultural Contribution (the film demonstrates British creativity, British heritage and/or diversity); and Cultural Practitioners (the nationality of the director, script writer, actors, crew, etc.) The films here all exhibit these traits, albeit to differing degrees. Department for Culture, Media and Sport, 'Cultural Test for British Films; Final Framework' (November 2005, rev. 2015): Available online: http://old.culture.gov.uk/images/publications/CulturalTestFilm.pdf (accessed 22 November 2015) and 'The Cultural Test for Film'. Available online: http://www.bfi.org.uk/film-industry/british-certification-tax-relief/cultural-test-film#cultural-test (accessed 22 November 2015).

2   All films mentioned are listed with full details in the film bibliography at the end of the book.

3   Quoted by S. Aspinall, 'Women, Realism and Reality in British Films, 1943–53', in *British Cinema History*, ed. J. Curran and V. Porter (London: Weidenfeld and Nicolson, 1983), 290, ref. 33.

4   See, for example, A. Kuhn, *An Everyday Magic, Cinema and Cultural Memory* (London and New York: I.B. Tauris Publishers, 2002) or J. Richards, D. Sheridan and Mass-Observation, *Mass-Observation at the Movies* (Cinema and Society) (London and New York: Routledge & Kegan Paul, 1987).

5   For excellent engagements with gender and melodrama see C. Gledhill, *Home Is Where the Heart Is: Essays on Melodrama and the Woman's Film* (London: BFI, 1987) and R. Murphy, *Realism and Tinsel: Cinema and Society in Britain, 1939–48* (London and New York: Routledge, 1989).

6   The shorts of the small independent companies on topics deemed of
    particular interest to women, 'although conforming to the main propaganda
    framework, were more carefully nuanced in their gender address'. S. Harper,
    Women in British Cinema, Mad, Bad and Dangerous to Know (London and
    New York: Continuum, 2000), 32.

7   For a discussion of film policy and gender see Harper, *Women in British
    Cinema*. In 1942, *Kinematograph Weekly* noted that the MoI now only
    wanted films 'which were not nostalgic about the old ways and old days
    ... but realistic films of everyday life'. Cited in Harper, *Women in British
    Cinema*, 32.

8   An exception is J. Richards, 'Film and Television, the Moving Image' in
    *History Beyond the Text: A Student's Guide to Approaching Alternative
    Sources* ed. S. Barber and C. M. Peniston-Bird (London: Routledge, 2009).
    Richards is of course of interest to any reader of this chapter for his multiple
    publications on film in the Second World War, including A. Aldgate and
    J. Richards, *Britain Can Take It: The British Cinema in the Second World
    War* (Edinburgh: Edinburgh University Press, 1994). See also references
    below.

9   J. Chapman, M. Glancy and S. Harper (eds), *The New Film History:
    Sources, Methods, Approaches* (New York: Palgrave Macmillan, 2007).

10 Murphy, *Realism and Tinsel*, 233.

11 There are numerous publications to support the acquisition of appropriate
    knowledge and vocabulary, for example, J. Monaco, *How to Read a Film.
    The Art, Technology, Language, History and Theory of Film and Media*
    (New York and Oxford: Oxford University Press, 2009 [1981]).

12 A. Kuhn, *'Living within the Frame' An Inaugural Lecture delivered at the
    University of Lancaster* (Lancaster: University of Lancaster Pamphlet, 2003).
    1–28, here 4.

13 Such lists are always minefields for glaring omissions, but femininities in the
    films of the Second World War have been insightfully illuminated by authors
    including Aspinall, de Cacqueray, Gledhill, Harper, Lant and Swanson. The
    study of wartime masculinities in film lags somewhat behind, but has caught
    the attention of Elliot, Geraghty, Plain and Spicer among others: all these
    authors are referenced below.

14 For discussion of women's functions in the plots of the first two films, see
    E. de Cacqueray, 'New Slants on Gender and Power Relations in British
    Second World War Films' *Miranda* 2 (2010): 2–14. Available online: https://
    miranda.revues.org/1146 (accessed September 2017).

15 Aspinall, 'Women, Realism and Reality', 279, 280.

16 For Bechdel's discussion of the development of the test, see her blog.
    Available online: http://dykestowatchoutfor.com/testy (accessed December
    2014)

17 Robinson wrote an insightful column on the wasted potential of the 'strong
    female character', carefully introduced and then rapidly and systematically
    undermined in favour of bolstering male characters. T. Robinson (2014)
    'We're losing all our strong Female characters to Trinity syndrome'. Available

online: https://thedissolve.com/features/exposition/618-were-losing-all-our-strong-female-characters-to-tr/ (accessed June 2014).

18   Smith also notes in her study of representations of men and women in espionage fiction and films that the war introduces a new identity to the angel/whore spectrum: that of the Patriot serving her country and taking a professional and pragmatic attitude to her responsibilities. See K. A. Smith, 'Espionage in British Popular Culture of the 20th Century: Gender, Moral Ambiguity and the Inextricability of Fact and Fiction' (Unpublished PhD thesis, Lancaster University, 2016).

19   For the popular allure of the RAF, see M. Francis, *The Flyer: British Culture and the Royal Air Force 1939–1945* (Oxford and New York: Oxford University Press, 2008). Both of the latter films feature jokes about imaginary maiden aunts providing cover for leave. *We Dive at Dawn* (1943) exemplifies unmarried and married heteronormativity with multiple subplots concerning romantic relationships and the film topped and tailed with a reference to the Captain's (John Mills) active social life with the opposite sex:

'By the way, who are you seeing this leave, your Aunt Margaret again?'

'I can't risk it, sir, her husband's on leave.'

And at the end:

'Enjoy your leave this time, you'll be seeing your aunt.'

'Yes, all of them.'

20   G. Plain, *John Mills and British Cinema: Masculinity, Identity and Nation* (Edinburgh: Edinburgh University Press, 2006), 86–7.

21   A. Vickery, 'Golden Age to Separate Spheres? A Review of the Categories and Chronology of English Women's History', *The Historical Journal* 36 (2) (1993): 383–414.

22   E. V. Kealey (1915), *Women of Britain say "Go!"*, London: Parliamentary Recruitment Committee, reproduced at Imperial War Museums. Available online: http://www.iwm.org.uk/collections/item/object/14592 (accessed 1 March 2016).

23   Harper, *Women in British Cinema*, 50.

24   On the rhetoric of antithesis, when an individual or community is ascribed traits, ideas or actions, 'in terms which are in themselves antithetical and in tension', see S. Barber, 'The Formation of Cultural Attitudes: The Example of the Three Kingdoms in the 1650s', in *The Stuart Kingdoms in the Seventeenth Century: Awkward Neighbours*, ed. A. I. Macinnes and J. Ohlmeyer (Dublin: Four Courts Press, 2002), 176. Lant also notes that women had to negotiate contradictory versions of themselves in the war. A. Lant, *Blackout: Reinventing Women for Wartime British Cinema* (Princeton, NJ: Princeton University Press, 1991), 61, 89.

25   A. Lant, *Blackout: Reinventing Women*, 72–3. The scene in which Celia and Fred are observed by the guests as they go up to the room in the bed and breakfast in which they are to lose their virginities marks their awkwardness, although we believe Fred when he says he does not really mind.

26   De Cacqueray 'New Slants', 8.

27 A. Spicer, *Typical Men: The Representation of Masculinity in Popular British Cinema* (London and New York: I.B. Tauris, 2003), 4.

28 Tosh defines hegemonic masculinity 'to stand for those masculine attributes which are most widely subscribed to – and least questioned – in a given social formation: the 'common sense' of gender as acknowledged by all men save those whose masculinity is oppositional or deviant'. J. Tosh, 'Hegemonic Masculinity and the History of Gender', 47. and see also S. O. Rose, 'Temperate Heroes: Concepts of Masculinity in Second World War Britain' in *Masculinities in Politics and War: Gendering Modern History*, ed. S. Dudink, K. Hagemann and J. Tosh (Gender in History; Manchester: Manchester University Press, 2004). See also S. O. Rose *Which People's War* (Oxford: Oxford University Press, 2003).

29 Spicer, *Typical Men*, 7.

30 J. Richards, *Films and British National Identity: From Dickens to Dad's Army* (Studies in Popular Culture; Manchester and New York: Manchester University Press/St. Martin's Press, 1997), 89: 'This was the key: individuality (characteristic difference) as opposed to individualism (a philosophy of the self), and individuality maintained with the collectivity of heroism, the people as hero, learning tolerance of each other and building cooperation, comradeship and community through it'.

31 C. Geraghty, 'Masculinity', in *National Fictions: World War Two in British Films and Television*, ed. G. Hurd (London: British Film Institute, 1984), 63.

32 Ibid.

33 Ibid. 'Waiting at the Church' was a popular music hall song written by Fred Leigh (words) and Henry Pether (music), told from the perspective of a woman jilted at the altar by a married cad. Its use at the end of the film is highly ironic: the full lyrics include the line 'I've lost my husband, the one I never had!' However, it is perhaps the music hall credentials which explain its choice.

34 C. Gledhill and G. Swanson, 'Gender and Sexuality in Second World War Films – A Feminist Approach' in *National Fictions: World War Two in British Films and Television*, ed. G. Hurd (London: British Film Institute, 1984), 62.

35 Harper, *Women in British Cinema*, 49

36 For extensive discussion of the relationship between mobile women and men, see P. Summerfield, *Women Workers in the Second World War: Production and Patriarchy in Conflict* (London and New York: Routledge, 1989).

37 Audiences would have been well-prepared for a comedy turn from Marriott, well-known as Will Hay's toothless sidekick, Harbottle.

38 P. Elliot, 'The Weak and the Wicked: Non-conscripted Masculinities in 1940s Cinema', in *The Home Front in Britain: Images Myths and Forgotten Experiences since 1914*, ed. M. E. Andrews and J. Lomas (Basingstoke: Palgrave Macmillan, 2014), 182.

39 Cartoons did represent both possibilities; contrast, for example, Joseph Lee's depiction of a conversation between a milkman and an abandoned husband

washing up in his kitchen, 'Smiling Through: Left Husbands / "… and as I was saying to the other lady at No 47 …"' *Evening News,* 26 November 1940, British Cartoon Archive, JL3006, and his later cartoon 'Smiling Through / Washing up / "… and soon, after four long years, my darling wife will be in her own dear kitchen again … I saved you the washing up"'. *Evening News,* 16 October 1944, British Cartoon Archive, JL2731.

40 Gledhill and Swanson, 'Gender and Sexuality, 57. See also their edited collection C. Gledhill and G. Swanson, *Nationalising Femininity: Culture, Sexuality, and British Cinema in the Second World War* (Manchester and New York: Manchester University Press, 1996).

41 Aspinall, 'Women, Realism and Reality, 290.

42 De Cacqueray, 'New Slants', 8.

43 M. R. Higonnet and P. Higonnet, 'The Double Helix', in *Behind the Lines, Gender and the Two World Wars,* ed. M. R. Hignnet, J. Jenson, S. Michel and M. Collins (Yale: Yale University Press, 1988), 31–47, here 34.

44 Gledhill and Swanson, 'Gender and Sexuality', 62.

45 Aspinall, 'Women, Realism and Reality', 290.

46 P. Howlett and Great Britain Central Statistical Office (1995), *Fighting with Figures.* London: H.M.S.O. Table 3.3: Distribution of total manpower. Looking at the age distribution of the United Kingdom, in 1945, men under the age of twenty or over the age of forty-four but under sixty were just shy of seven million. Table 1.5: Age distribution of the resident population of the United Kingdom.

47 *Schedule of Reserved Occupations* (Provisional) (1939) (London: His Majesty's Stationery Office). Men were reserved at the ages of twenty-one, twenty-three, twenty-five or thirty.

48 Contrast, for example, the gender of the workers depicted in the image 'Hawker Hurricanes in assembly shops Brooklands, credited to Brooklands Museum archive courtesy of BAE Systems' (1940) reproduced on Exploring Surrey's Past, Airfield and Aircraft Production. Available online: http://www.exploringsurreyspast.org.uk/themes/subjects/military/battle_of_britain/airfield/ (accessed December 2013) with those in the painting by Elsie Dalton Hewland *Assembling a Hawker Hurricane* (1940–7) reproduced on Your Painting. Available online: http://www.bbc.co.uk/arts/yourpaintings/paintings/assembling-a-hawker-hurricane-205190 (accessed December 2013).

49 See Murphy, *Realism and Tinsel,* 149. For a discussion of these 'Heroes on the Home Front', see L. Robb, *Men at Work: The Working Man in British Culture, 1939–1945* (Basingstoke: Palgrave Macmillan, 2015).

50 Employment in National and Local Government rose from 1,386,000 in 1938 to 1,903,000 in 1945. P. Howlett and Great Britain Central Statistical Office, Table 3.3.

51 This segment begins at c. 27.59 minutes into the film.

52 See for example Fred Taylor's series 'They also serve' reproduced on the IWM catalogue PST 3422 to PST 3428, e.g. available online: http://www.iwm.org.uk/collections/item/object/26040 (accessed 1 March 2016) and

Leslie Oliphant's 'The Attack Begins in the Factory'/'Back them up!'; (see
PST 16898, PST 16899, PST 16900 and PST 16901) on the Imperial
War Museums Catalogue, e.g. available online: http://www.iwm.org.uk/
collections/item/object/20594 (accessed 1 March 2016).

53   A good example of a fuzzy boundary is the meaning of the amber
light in traffic lights: see S. Mehan and V. Sharma. 'Development of
traffic light control system based on fuzzy logic', In *Proceedings of the
International Conference on Advances in Computing and Artificial
Intelligence* (ACAI '11). ACM (New York, 2011) 162–5. DOI: http://dx.doi.
org/10.1145/2007052.2007085.

The concepts of 'fuzzy logic'; 'fuzzy boundaries' and 'vagueness' have been
explored in a wide variety of contexts from computer science to biology to
educational theory. My musings on fuzzy boundaries were first triggered by
I. Visser, 'Protoypes of Gender: Conceptions of Feminine and Masculine',
Women's Studies International Forum 25 (5) (September–October 2002): 5,
29–39.

CHAPTER SIX

Screening multicultural Britain: Blair, Britishness and *Bend It Like Beckham*

Sarah Ilott

Introduction

In a letter to director Gurinder Chadha, former Prime Minister Tony Blair proclaimed his love for the film *Bend It Like Beckham* (2002), 'because it represented his Britain, a very diverse, multicultural Britain'.[1] As such, this film (and its enthusiastic mainstream reception) is emblematic of a Blairite political climate that ostentatiously claimed to celebrate multiculturalism. However, this chapter will, using a close reading of Chadha's film, explore what is at stake in constructing Britain as a multicultural utopia. Through an against-the-grain reading of the film, this chapter draws attention to what is repressed in the comedy in order to highlight people and ideals that are, by extension, excluded from both Chadha's and Blair's visions for a multicultural Britain.

Chadha's third feature film, *Bend It Like Beckham*, was an immediate success, breaking UK box office records by earning more than any previous film financed and distributed in Britain, making £2 million in its opening weekend. It went on to achieve international acclaim, setting new records for British film in both the US and India. Beyond its economic success, it received recognition for its considerable cultural impact: the film has been credited with inspiring the first all-girls national football league in India and was selected for inclusion in the UK Film Council's 'Stories we tell ourselves' study (2009) as one of 200 iconic British films of the past sixty years chosen to assess the 'impact ... British cinema [has] had on the way we see ourselves, and the way others see us'.[2]

Bend It Like Beckham was recently relaunched as a musical in London's West End (May 2015) and in interview, director Gurinder Chadha celebrates it as a 'state of the nation piece'.[3] This suggests that the musical, and the film that it was based upon, can be used to interpret the socio-political climate of Britain in its 2001 setting. However, the image of Britain in the film is somewhat at odds with that being constructed in the media and political discourse at the time. In 2002, when the film was released, Britain had recently witnessed race riots in northern towns and cities and a marked rise in Islamophobia following the terrorist attacks of 11 September 2001 and Britain's subsequent entry into a 'war on terror' in Afghanistan. Historically, film has had an important role to play in the construction and reflection of national identity, often functioning as a tool of propaganda in times of national crisis.[4] We can perhaps draw parallels between these earlier periods of crisis and the one Britain was confronted with in 2001 with the onset of unrest at home and abroad, meaning that it would be appropriate to read the film as presenting a politically consumable image of the nation. The historical significance of the film and the impact it had on constructions of Britishness and multiculturalism more broadly are evidenced by the contemporaneous prime minister's enthusiastic avowal and appropriation of its vision, as previously mentioned. This case study considers what *Bend It Like Beckham* can tell historians about the 'state' of multicultural Britain in the early twenty-first century, paying particular attention to New Labour's narrative of British multiculturalism.

Bend It Like Beckham launched the careers of both Parminder Nagra, who played British Asian Jesminder Bhamra (Jess), and Keira Knightley in her role as white British Juliette Paxton (Jules). The film centres on the girls' shared struggle to realize their footballing ambitions against the wishes of their respective parents. While Mrs Paxton dislikes her daughter's sporting hobby on account of concerns about it making Jules less sexually desirable to men, Mrs Bhamra expresses her unease at Jess baring her legs to men and believes that she should spend more time perfecting various domestic duties. In the meantime, the Bhamras are preparing for Jess's sister Pinky's wedding. Jess's ambitions repeatedly conflict with those of her mother and sister, as she does not 'want all this' (the lavish wedding, domestic life and children), but shares with her friend an ambition to make it as a footballer and gain a scholarship to study and train in America. Set in the West London borough of Hounslow within a stone's throw of Heathrow Airport, scenes often end with an upwards panning shot that takes in the planes arriving and departing, foregrounding the film's themes and narrative plot of immigration and emigration. Before embarking on a close reading of the film's representation of multicultural Britain, it is necessary to consider the two terms that we are dealing with in more detail: multiculturalism and Britishness.

'Multiculturalism' is a problematic term. It is sometimes used descriptively to refer to cultural diversity, yet the term can also be used in an ideological sense to denote a way of managing or approaching diversity. For Fortier, 'Multiculturalism is not so much a policy and governing response to the "realities" of cultural and ethno-racial pluralism, as ... an ideal aimed at the achievement of well-managed diversity'.[5] The way that the term can be used to refer to both an existing reality, a set of policies and an ideal state of affairs is clearly challenging; it is not always clear how the term is being employed in different contexts. This becomes important when we consider how the fictional (and largely idealized) version of multi-cultural Britain represented in Chadha's film has been misinterpreted as a description of reality.

'Britishness' is also a difficult term to define, as it means so many different things to so many different people. In a landmark theoretical work on the formation of ideas of nation, Benedict Anderson describes the nation as an 'imagined political community' (see also Chapters 5, 12 and 14).[6] He suggests that nations are imagined because no one will ever meet all of the other members of that community, so the idea of collectivity and common ideals can only ever be constructed via the imagination. Unlike an actual community, such as a group of friends, in which an understanding of the community will be based on face-to-face meetings, this can never be the case for a national community. This suggests that nationhood is more a fictional than factual entity, constructed through the imagination. Commentators such as Anderson and Homi Bhabha remind us that there are similarities between nation and narration, because we can only under-stand the nation in terms of its constructed nature, its imaginative qualities and its modes of expression.[7] This is where things become problematic: if the nation is an imagined community, then how it is imagined will differ from person to person. When an imagined idea of the nation is expressed to others in the form of a story (or film) it allows room for personal or political bias, persuasion, or coercion to creep in. For Bill Ashcroft, Gareth Griffiths and Helen Tiffin, this means that 'Constructions of the nation are ... potent sites of control and domination', potentially allowing for the perpetuation of nationalism.[8] It is therefore important to bear in mind that if *Bend It Like Beckham* is, as Chadha suggests, a 'state of the nation piece', then it is an idea of the nation collaboratively conceived by the writers, director, producers and actors involved, not necessarily a version that is universally shared.

New Labour's election to government in 1997 marked a significant change in attitudes towards British multiculturalism. Under the former Conservative governance, led by John Major, ideas of Britishness were often constructed nostalgically with reference to a historic period that predated mass-migration to Britain in the post-war period. During a speech delivered at the Conservative Party Conference in Blackpool, 1993, the Prime Minister urged people to get 'back to basics':

> Do you know, the truth is, much as things have changed on the surface, underneath we're still the same people. The old values – neighbourliness, decency, courtesy – they're still alive, they're still the best of Britain.

They haven't changed, and yet somehow people feel embarrassed by
them. Madame President, we shouldn't be. It is time to return to those
old core values, time to get back to basics, to self-discipline and respect
for the law, to consideration for others, to accepting a responsibility for
yourself and your family and not shuffling off on other people and the
state.[9]

Major's reference to 'change on the surface' implies that his version of
Britishness is coded in whiteness and through reference to 'old core values'
he harks back to a nostalgic version of Britishness. This attitude changed
dramatically in the rhetoric of New Labour, in which Britain's diversity and
multiculturalism was celebrated. The new government strove to rejuvenate
ideas of Britishness to match the contemporary ideals of the nation and its
future aspirations, rather than returning to the nostalgic past for a source
of identity.

A report commissioned by the Design Council on how we might rethink
our nation's identity was published on the same day in 1997 that the
Labour Party came into power after eighteen years of Conservative rule.
The report, produced by independent think-tank Demos, suggested that
globally 'Britain is seen as a backward-looking has-been, a theme park
world of royal pageantry and rolling green hills, where draughts blow
through people's houses'.[10] A contingency between internal perceptions
and external projections was evidenced, suggesting it would be necessary
to tackle Britain's image at home in order to effect a change in its image
abroad.[11] A generation gap was identified between those for whom ideas of
Britishness were forged during or in the immediate aftermath of the Second
World War and centred upon hostility to foreigners and the exclusion of
non-white ethnicities, and the younger generation, for whom this idea of
national identity was irrelevant.[12] The desire to project a new image of
Britain was reflected in the report, which concluded with six new stories
about Britishness to replace stagnant ones that lacked resonance with the
youth of the day. One of these new stories, entitled 'United colours of
Britain', foregrounded Britain's cultural hybridity, suggesting that Britain
thrives on diversity, both subcultural and ethnic (examples of literary
success, cuisine and music were listed).[13] Reasons for creating a coherent
and positive national identity were clearly identified: it protects against
atomization and community breakdown, while creating happier citizens.
There were also vital economic reasons for projecting a positive national
identity, central to this report's aim to 'rebrand' Britain and enable the
promotion of British industries and products in a global market. As a
zeitgeist of 'Cool Britannia' and the celebration of multiculturalism took
hold, the desire to project a celebratory image of Britain's diverse communities began to be expressed through film.

Analysing the film

The remainder of this chapter will consider the picture of multicultural Britain that is presented in *Bend It Like Beckham*. By reading the film closely, it is possible to identify the desires and fears about multicultural Britain to which it gives voice, as well as the selections and omissions necessary to create the feel-good comedy. To create a happy and politically consumable image of multicultural Britain, I suggest that the film focuses on putatively universal issues that transcend cultural divisions, such as inter-generational discord and the contested roles of women in the family and society, by minimizing subversion and using a gentle and inclusive form of comedy, and by downplaying the effects of racism. Following this, I turn to Tony Blair's wholehearted embrace of the film and his appropriation of its image of multicultural Britain as a means of interpreting New Labour's narrative of multicultural Britain.

Like other films engaging with multicultural Britain in the 1990s and early 2000s, such as Chadha's first film, *Bhaji on the Beach* (1993) and O'Donnell's *East is East* (1999), *Bend It Like Beckham* depicts concerns associated with particular religious or ethnic groups as part of more universal problems of intergenerational strife and discrimination against women. In *Bend It Like Beckham*, much of the conflict is identified as arising from a generation gap. The older generation are conservative in their views on love and matrimony and intolerant or naïve regarding homosexual relationships, the younger generation embark on premarital relationships and are represented as welcoming of a spectrum of sexualities; the older generation wears subcontinental dress and alternates between English and Punjabi speech in a manner that marks an affiliation with a 'home' that is elsewhere, the younger generation adopts Western dress and a regional West London accent that marks their Britishness; the older gener-ation assigns women to the domestic sphere, the younger women dismiss such values as outdated and position themselves in roles and activities traditionally occupied by men; the founder of Sikhism, Guru Nanak, takes centre-stage in the Bhamras' living space, Jess's bedroom represents a shrine to the footballing god of the era: David Beckham.

The experiences and values of the teens and twenty-somethings of Jess and Jules's generation are frequently shown as being at odds with that of their parents, and this disjunction is often reinforced in the film through the use of setting. While Jess and Jules's scenes often take place outside in the open spaces of the football pitch or on the dynamic and bustling streets of London, representing freedom, movement and vitality, the domestic interiors of the Bhamras' and Paxtons' homes are associated with the stifling expectations of the older generation, with the majority of scenes involving Jess's parents, in particular, taking place indoors. A pertinent example of this disjunction between the lives of the girls and their elders is evident in the visual juxtaposition of two sequences. Firstly, viewers are presented with an uplifting exterior montage shot using natural lighting and resplendent with bright colours as Jess buys her football boots, symbolic of the defiance of her parents' wishes and commands. The montage is accompanied by 'Independence Day', an early track by Melanie C, formerly of Sporty Spice fame and associated both with vocal assertions of girl power and with Mrs Paxton's disapproval of her daughter's footballing ambitions (by this point Mrs Paxton has warned 'There is a reason why Sporty Spice is the only one of them without a fella'). Following the city montage that has focused on the Leicester Square environs, redolent of futurist technology and communications, the film cuts to the Bhamras' living room, which is claustrophobic and dull in comparison, with a colour scheme defined by beiges and browns, near-static characters, and walls that serve both to frame and enclose the scene. The juxtaposition of scenes creates an incongruous effect in which the Bhamras' house does not seem to have a place in the dynamism and colour of the world outside.

Jess is not alone in feeling alienated from her parents and a more broadly existing generation gap is frequently shown in the film through the vastly different treatment of similar issues by the younger and older generations. Mrs Paxton is portrayed as feeling awkward in Jess's company, drawing on conversation topics that reveal her assumptions about British Asians, such as references to curry and her hopes that Jess will teach Jules about her culture 'including respect for elders and the like' that later leave the two girls in stitches. Mrs Paxton also voices her (incorrect) assumption that Jess will have an arranged marriage, phrasing her question to Jess in a way intended to demonstrate her cultural knowledge: 'I expect your parents are fixing you up with a handsome young doctor soon, aren't they'. This assumption does not first allow Jess the space to express her own identity and beliefs. Alternatively, Jess's friends on her football team ask questions regarding arranged marriage openly and frankly, allowing Jess the space to express herself. Jess confides that although she will not have an arranged marriage, she would not be able to marry a white, black or Muslim man. This list of off-limits men is delivered as an escalating progression of taboo, designed to encourage her teammates' laughter. When the Captain, Mel (played by Shaznay Lewis, former member of girl band All Saints), says 'I don't know how you Indian girls put up with it', Jess genially replies 'It's just culture, that's all. Better than sleeping around with boys you're not gonna end up marrying. What's the point in that?', to which one of the white girls replies 'that's the best bit', a comment greeted with peals of laughter. Among the younger generation, the subject of marriage is discussed frankly and its potential seriousness is humorously deflated without the awkwardness and assumptions present when the same topic is brought up by Mrs Paxton. In sum, the generation gap is mobilized within the film to distinguish the liberal views of the younger generation from the illiberal or tradition-bound views of the older generation in a manner that favours the former at the expense of the latter.

Though the focus of the film is predominantly on Jess, and the blocks to her footballing ambitions, these are placed in the context of wider issues of sexism, patriarchal values and limited roles available for women in the family and society more broadly. Where a focus solely on Jess might suggest that her choices are limited due to her ethnic and religious affiliations as a British Asian Sikh, parallels made with Jules ensure that viewers are positioned to see the problems Jess encounters as stemming predominantly from her gender, rather than her ethnicity. A conversation set in the changing rooms explicitly shifts attention from ethnicity to gender: when Jess confides that 'Indian girls aren't supposed to play football', Mel replies with 'That's a bit backward innit?' Jules's timely reminder that 'it ain't just an Indian thing is it? How many people come out and support us?' serves to refocus the issue around engrained sexist attitudes that deny women's footballing capabilities. Jess and Jules alike must struggle against the essentialist and heteronormative constructions of femininity – encoded in shopping, physical appearance and dress, and heterosexual relationships – that society projects onto them. By focusing on universal topics like family disputes, patriarchal attitudes and the place of women in society, this film gently undermines stereotypes and questions an inclination to Other according to cultural difference by creating parallels between different cultures.

In order to create a happy image of multicultural society suited to a feel-good comedy, Chadha also provides narrative reparation for experiences of racism, which serves to construct them as individual and surmountable incidents, rather than engrained or institutionalized within British society. The first incident sees Jess fouled on the football pitch then called a 'Paki' by the girl who has fouled her. This triggers Jess's anger and she shoves the other player, meaning that the referee sends her off with a red card.

The camera follows her long walk off the pitch, allowing viewers to dwell on Jess's feelings of anger and injustice. This experience is heightened by the dramatic irony that unbeknown to Jess, her father – who has previously cautioned Jess as to the hopelessness of her footballing ambitions given the racism which he has experienced on the sporting field – is in the crowd and witnesses the whole incident. The seriousness of the event is nevertheless downplayed and diffused through Jess's conversation with her manager, Joe. When Jess feels isolated in her experience and claims that Joe 'wouldn't know what it's like', Joe reassures her: 'I'm Irish, of course I'd understand what it feels like.' This expression of light-hearted solidarity from a white man indicates that prejudice works in a number of ways and suggests that while not ideal, the incident can be shrugged off. Though the abuse goes unpunished officially, Jess does receive narrative retribution. When she is fouled again in the most important match of the film, she is awarded a penalty kick from which she scores the winning goal. The way that the second scene is constructed is made to mirror the first, so that the

FIGURE 6.1 *Jess receives a red card,* Bend It Like Beckham *(2002)*

audience is positioned to feel anxious that events will be repeated. When they are not, it gives the impression that reparations have been made and that Jess has obtained the justice that she should have received in the first place. Jess emerges as the hero and the previous racist incident – and Jess's unfair treatment from the referee – is shown not to have had an effect on the overall plot trajectory.

The film also begins to confront and address the more enduring and institutionalized form of racism that Mr Bhamra has experienced in the past. In an attempt to protect Jess from the same racism that he encountered upon first coming to Britain, he describes to his daughter his sense of dismay at being excluded from English cricket teams despite his former prowess in Uganda: 'the goras [white men] in the club houses made fun of my turban and sent me off packing'. The sense of hurt that Mr Bhamra still carries many years after the event is evident. However, the way that the scene is constructed suggests that Indians are not solely on the receiving end of prejudiced attitudes. When Jess tells her father that 'it's all changing now' and points to Nasser Hussain as captain of the England cricket team as an example, her mother contends that his is a Muslim name, highlighting her own intolerance and desire to create 'others' differentiated against her own ethno-religious self. Nevertheless, the film makes narrative recompense for Mr Bhamra's earlier exclusion by ending with a sunlit and laughter-filled scene of Joe and Mr Bhamra playing cricket together on the green outside the Bhamras' house, in an image of neighbourly harmony. The resolution implies that the deep-seated racism encountered by Mr Bhamra upon his arrival to the UK is a thing of the past, as the two men play the most English, most Indian, of games together. It is significant that the men play cricket – a sport associated with the British colonization of the

Subcontinent – in a manner that serves both to foreground and to subvert former colonial power relationships, 'unveiling the complicity of sport in the colonial domination'.[14] Structurally, the plot suggests a happy resolution to – and overcoming of – past prejudice, downplaying its lingering presence in contemporary society.

An image of a happy multicultural society is further reinforced through the form of the comedy itself. In a chapter on 'Multicultural British Comedy' in *New Postcolonial British Genres: Shifting the Boundaries*, I have considered at length the spectrum of ways in which comedy functions to reinforce or challenge the status quo, to include or exclude, depending on a variety of factors such as implied audience, the butt of the joke, the power dynamics at play, and the specific objects of satirical attack, parody, mimicry or mockery.[15] In regards to *Bend It Like Beckham* in particular, I have suggested that Chadha creates a feel-good comedy through the integration of difference and a form of gentle multidirectional satire that takes many objects of attack, thereby democratizing the laughter and softening the blow(s). Reminiscent of a comedy of errors, much of *Bend It Like Beckham*'s humour derives from cases of mistaken identity, and there is a happy finale in which conflict is resolved. The comedy has a levelling effect, as many characters are duped at different stages, whether it be Tony's parents, who believe their homosexual son to be hopelessly in love with Jess, Mrs Paxton, who mistakenly fears that her daughter is a lesbian, or Mrs Bhamra, who is rarely aware of her daughter's actual activities. I borrow the term 'multidirectional satire' from literary critic John Clement Ball, who asserts that the 'concept of satirical multidirectionality ... works against the binary model of norm and deviation and offers one in which

FIGURE 6.2 *Cricket on the Green,* Bend It Like Beckham *(2002)*

oppositions may be set up without either side being endorsed'.[16] This
satirical multidirectionality is particularly evident during a scene that takes
place at the end of Pinky's wedding, when Jules's mother drops her off at the
celebrations. When Mrs Paxton sees Jess wearing a pair of her own shoes,
she takes this as confirmation of her long-held suspicions that her daughter
has been involved in a lesbian relationship with Jess, demanding that the
latter 'get your lesbian feet out of my shoes!' Rather than causing the
consternation that audiences might expect from the sexually conservative
group of people gathered around, the word 'lesbian' triggers a sequence of
misunderstandings. One of Jess's relatives counters with 'she's not Lebanese,
she's Punjabi', which is then topped with 'I thought she was a Pisces', misin-
terpreting 'lesbian' as a star sign. Audiences are encouraged to laugh at a
number of different characters who all fail to read the situation correctly
(Jess has, in fact, borrowed her friend's mum's shoes in order to save the
money given to her by her own mother and purchase some football boots).
If Mrs Paxton had been isolated in her misreading, then the full force of the
laughter would have been directed at her and she would have been the sole
butt of the joke. As it actually plays out, the laughter is dispersed between
a group of characters, its blow is weakened, and an inclusive situation in
which characters are joined in their shared misunderstanding is produced.

Alongside a gentle form of comedy that has an inclusive and uplifting
function, Chadha makes a number of deft moves to minimize the film's
subversion and guarantee its mainstream appeal. Though it gently critiques
homophobia and challenges the role of women society, Nisha Ganatra,
Chadha's friend, claims that the main romantic plot was intended to be
a lesbian one, but she '"chickened out" at the last minute for fear of
offending and upsetting Indian audiences'.[17] Through such manoeuvres,
Bend It Like Beckham presents an ultimately happy, hopeful and multicultural Britain, successfully designed to maximize mainstream appeal. This
is not problematic in itself, until it is taken as a representation of reality in
a manner that undeniably turns a blind eye to political realities of the day,
as Blair's celebration of the film suggests.

Critiquing the film

Given that the film was likened by Britain's contemporary Prime Minister
to a mirror on the realities of British multiculture, it is necessary to consider
how this representation compares to other sources from the time. The film
was released in 2002, a year after race-riots in northern English towns
and the terrorist attacks of 11 September 2001. These events combined to
produce a shift in multicultural discourse in Britain. Following 'race riots'
in Oldham, Burnley and Bradford in the summer of 2001, political rhetoric
surrounding multiculturalism shifted and was increasingly constructed as

a failed experiment rather than an ideal or aspiration. The Cantle Report, published in December 2001, was commissioned to 'seek the views of local residents and community leaders in affected towns ... on the issues which need to be addressed to bring about social cohesion'.[18] The report laid blame upon the 'parallel lives' lived by communities in the towns affected by the riots.[19] Home Secretary Blunkett's speech reflected this view and heralded the failure 'to produce cohesive communities and common citizenship in the UK'.[20] Shortly following the riots, the 9/11 terrorist attacks and subsequent increase in Islamophobia acted as a further catalyst for constructing multiculturalism as a failure, and British Muslims were increasingly policed, interrogated and suspected as the 'enemy within'.

There was no tipping point that engendered a sudden shift in Britain's multicultural reality, and this was by no means the first time that multiculturalism had been critiqued; it had been for many years prior to 2001, largely by the political right. However, what did occur at this point was a shift in official rhetoric, as the word 'multiculturalism' came to be constructed discursively as a failed ideal by voices from the liberal left as well as the right. By celebrating Chadha's feel-good film as representing 'his multicultural Britain', then, it becomes apparent that Blair is at best myopic, as his own government is simultaneously tolling the death knell of the British multiculturalism project. The tension between hopes and realities playing out in Blair's embrace of the film's representation of multicultural Britain is reflected in the title of this chapter: 'screening multicultural Britain'. To screen means to air a film on the silver screen, and to protect, conceal and divide, which usefully conveys the conflicting impulses present in the film and its reception, both to parade and to delimit multicultural Britain.

Chadha's motivations for making and producing the film were clear: she wanted to 'make the most commercial, mainstream, wide-appealing, multiplex movie [she] possibly could – with an Indian girl in the lead'.[21] Highly critical of film collectives such as Black Audio and Sankofa for making 'films that only academics are going to see and appreciate', Chadha was aiming for mainstream spectatorship and success.[22] This involved avoiding the subject matter and style that Chadha identified as lacking mainstream appeal, such as that of Black Audio Film Collective's critically acclaimed *Handsworth Songs* (1986). This documentary film was recorded during the 1985 riots in the district of Handsworth, Birmingham and in parts of London. The film dealt with a problematic side of multicultural Britain, focusing on conflict, alienation and decline at the hands of a white Britain hostile to a black presence. Alongside the bleak subject matter, the material was presented in an experimental and fragmented way that called on viewers to create their own narratives and interpretations. These elements combined to create a film with little mainstream appeal. Yet appealing to a mainstream audience – as Chadha desired – somewhat limits what can be said on the subject of multicultural Britain, as it limits the capacity for critiquing mainstream viewers. In order to garner *Bend It Like Beckham*'s mainstream success, Chadha has avoided topics that evidence the more problematic aspects of multicultural Britain (economic disparity, institutionalized and endemic racism and/or Islamophobia, unjust policing and relationships between cultures based upon distrust, hostility and violence).

It is possible to discern how the representation of multicultural Britain offered in the film works to exclude factors that would mar its happy ending. The resolution of the film's various conflicts is only possible because ethnic minority characters conform to values that are widely understood to be embodied by the West, above other (conflicting) cultural values such as respect for elders or religious duties, illustrated by the various scenes concerned with Jess covering her legs. Jess expresses unease at having to bare her legs to play football and requests to keep her tracksuit bottoms on, but Joe unquestioningly replies in the negative. However, when she hovers in the spectator stand rather than warming up, Joe comes to see what is wrong, and it is revealed that Jess is embarrassed about a burn that has disfigured her leg. After a short conversation Jess's embarrassment is comically deflated: when Joe says he's sorry (for Jess's misfortune), Jess replies: 'I know; put me off beans on toast for life.' However, Jess's mother had previously expressed concern at her daughter revealing her legs during a daydream at the film's opening, so reasons for keeping her legs covered had been foreshadowed by this stage. The fact that Jess's reasons for covering are different to her mother's does not change the fact that Jess is given no option *but* to wear shorts before Joe has even allowed her to explain. In this manner, the film assumes unquestioning submission to modern Western values, suggesting that traditional cultural or religious concerns are archaic and irrelevant to younger generations.

What audiences are presented with, therefore, is a form of multiculturalism predicated on assimilation. This is reflected by Sonia Friedman, who has co-produced the musical adaptation of the film alongside Chadha. In interview, Friedman describes the story as 'a timeless tale of assimilation … an unashamed celebration of what it is to be British, of diversity and difference and the richness and potential of all being on the same team, kicking the same ball and having the same goals!'[23] The language employed, placing pride in assimilation and a certain level of uniformity comes close to Gove's unveiling of the 'British values' that supposedly unite us as a country and are now required to be taught on school curricula.[24] Models of multiculturalism such as these prioritize sameness over difference and submission to mainstream values over alternative cultural affiliations and values. The assimilatory function of the film is similarly identified in the BFI's 'Stories we tell ourselves' report:

> The past 15 years have seen a growing number of British-Asian films achieving significant cross-over success (*Bhaji on the Beach*, *East is*

East and *Bend It Like Beckham*). The films were made by British Asian directors and writers, and dramatised multi-cultural Britain, helping assimilate it with the wider mix of British youth culture.[25]

This construction implies that the film has a pedagogic function in the assimilation of diverse cultures.

It is also significant to consider what is excluded by the film, as this can indicate what Blair wished to overlook or ignore in his multicultural Britain. Rather than naively celebrating the film for its inclusively multicultural representation of Britain – as critics and politicians alike have been given to doing – it is important to consider what we are actually being offered: a film that wholeheartedly excludes the working classes and implicitly dismisses older generations or serious religious affiliations as outdated. It is necessary to read the nuanced acts of exclusion that films such as *Bend It Like Beckham* make in the process of pandering to a utopian and politically consumable image of multicultural society. This is not to critique the utopian *vision* of a society with no outsiders that films and political agendas ostensibly attempt to create, but rather to draw attention to those who *are*, by necessity, excluded from such a vision. Reading *Bend It Like Beckham* against the grain can tell historians a great deal about New Labour's narrative of multicultural Britain – its selections and omissions, the desires and fears to which it gives voice. Film is an accessible and mainstream medium, bringing political debates into the public domain and shaping the worldview of the audience. Though there is a suspension of disbelief when we watch a film, ideas linger and, in the case of *Bend It Like Beckham*, certain ideas of Britishness are reflected and reinforced. The historical significance of the film and the impact it had on constructions of Britishness and multiculturalism more broadly are evidenced by the prime minister's enthusiastic avowal and appropriation of its vision. When political discourse takes a selective representation of reality and presents it as a complete picture, it is necessary for historians to step in to fill the gaps.

Notes

1   Chadha in B. Korte, and C. Sternberg, *Bidding for the Mainstream: Black an Asian British Film since the 1990s* (Amsterdam: Rodopi, 2004), 246.

2   UK Film Council, 'Stories we tell ourselves', BFI (2009), 4. Available online: http://www.bfi.org.uk/sites/bfi.org.uk/files/downloads/bfi-opening-our-eyes-stories-we-tell-ourselves-report-2006.pdf (accessed 30 April 2015).

3   Chadha in B. Quinn, '*Bend It Like Beckham* to be made into musical', *Guardian*, 31 October 2014. Available online: http://www.theguardian.com/stage/2014/oct/31/bend-it-like-beckham-musical (accessed 5 January 2015).

4   See further R. Howells and R. Matson, *Using Visual Evidence* (Berkshire:

Open University Press, 2009), 128. In particular, when discussing the role of cinema in the early 1930s they argue that 'a positive representation of the nation and empire in the media, and especially in film, was essential for national recovery'.

5   A. Fortier, *Multicultural Horizons: Diversity and the Limits of the Civil Nation* (London: Routledge, 2008), 3.

6   B. Anderson, *Imagined Communities* (London: Verso, 1991), 6.

7   See further H. K. Bhabha, *Nation and Narration* (London: Routledge, 1990).

8   B. Ashcroft, G. Griffiths and H. Tiffin, *Key Concepts in Post-Colonial Studies* (London: Routledge, 1998), 150.

9   J. Major, speech delivered at the Conservative Party Conference in Blackpool, 1993. Available online: http://www.britishpoliticalspeech.org/speech-archive.htm?speech=139 (accessed 13 March 2016).

10   M. Leonard, 'Britain™: Renewing our Identity', *Demos*, 1997, 1. Available online: http://www.demos.co.uk/files/britaintm.pdf (accessed 29 April 2015).

11   Leonard, 'Britain™: Renewing our Identity', 17.

12   Ibid., 26–8.

13   Ibid., 52–3.

14   J. Bale and M. Cronin, 'Introduction: Sport and Postcolonialism', in *Sport and Postcolonialism*, ed. J. Bale and M. Cronin (Oxford: Berg, 2003), 1–24, 8.

15   The following paragraph is paraphrased from the longer work found in chapter on 'Multicultural British Comedy' in S. Ilott, *New Postcolonial British Genres: Shifting the Boundaries* (London: Palgrave Macmillan, 2015).

16   J. C. Ball, *Satire and the Postcolonial Novel: V. S. Naipaul, Chinua Achebe, Salman Rushdie* (London: Routledge, 2003), 21.

17   Ganatra in E. Dengel-Janic and L. Eckstein, 'Bridehood Revisited: Disarming Concepts of Gender and Culture in Recent Asian British Film', in *Multiethnic Britain 2000+: New Perspectives in Literature, Film and the Arts*, ed. L. Eckstein (Amsterdam: Rodopi, 2008), 45–64.

18   CCRT (Community Cohesion Review Team), 'Community Cohesion: A Report of the Independent Review Team, chaired by Ted Cantle', *Cohesion Institute*, 2001, 2. Available online: http://resources.cohesioninstitute.org.uk/Publications/Documents/Document/DownloadDocumentsFile.aspx?recordId=96%26file=PDFversion (accessed 16 December 2014).

19   CCRT, 'Community Cohesion', 10.

20   D. Blunkett, 'The full text of David Blunkett's speech, made in the West Midlands to highlight the publication of reports into inner-city violence this summer', *Guardian*, 11 December 2001. Available online: http://www.theguardian.com/politics/2001/dec/11/immigrationpolicy.race (accessed 17 December 2014).

21   Chadha in Korte and Sternberg, *Bidding for the Mainstream*, 250.

22   Ibid., 251.

23   G. Chadha and S. Freidman, 'Exclusive: A New British Musical About Where We Are Now: Gurinder Chadha and Sonia Friedman on what inspired them to tackle Bend It Like Beckham the musical', Bend It Like Beckham: The Musical, 2015. Available online: http://benditlikebeckhamthemusical. co.uk/?gclid=Cj0KEQiAiamlBRCgj83PiYm6--gBEiQArnojD8OY81uGgNtQ DEKMgO7m0SJ1xzV4U4wR0S-J-Tpx7AYaAqiL8P8HAQ#content (accessed 5 January 2015).

24   R. Adams, P. Wintour and S. Morris, 'All schools must promote "British values", says Michael Gove', *Guardian*, 9 June 2014. Available online: http:// www.theguardian.com/politics/2014/jun/09/michael-gove-says-all-schools-must-promote-british-values-after-trojan-horse-reports (accessed 16 May 2015).

25   UK Film Council, 'Stories we tell ourselves', 4.

CHAPTER SEVEN

Mammy, Mandingo, Django and Solomon: A century of American slavery in cinema from *Uncle Tom's Cabin* to *12 Years a Slave*

Lydia Plath

In 1903, black activist, scholar and intellectual W. E. B. Du Bois declared that 'the problem of the twentieth century is the problem of the color-line'.[1] Writing during a period widely known as the 'nadir' of African-American history, Du Bois knew that the twentieth century would face enormous conflict and struggle over race. However, his words could be equally applied to the history of cinema; the first silent feature film was also produced in 1903, an adaptation of Harriet Beecher Stowe's 1852 anti-slavery novel *Uncle Tom's Cabin*, which marked the beginning of more than a century of conflict over the representation of African Americans in American cinema. Edwin S. Porter's *Uncle Tom's Cabin: Slavery Days* (1903) was a 15 minute film based more on long-running 'Tom Shows' (the hugely popular minstrel shows of the nineteenth century) than on Stowe's novel, and as such starred white actors in blackface happily picking cotton and doing 'very funny dance[ing]' at every opportunity.[2] By the turn of the twenty-first century, representations of African-American slavery on film were much improved, but still highly contested. The furious public debates between historians and filmmakers over Steven Spielberg's *Amistad* (1997) demonstrated that even with a big-budget Hollywood production, a world-renowned director, an African-American producer (Debbie Allen), an all-star cast including Morgan Freeman, and the exciting true story of a slave rebellion, filmmakers could still fail to do the history of slavery justice. Allen hoped that the film would 'create a dialogue about the very nature of history', but eminent historian Eric Foner pointedly declared in the *New York Times* that *Amistad*, despite its claims to be a true story, 'is by no means a work of history'.[3] Similarly, Natalie Zemon Davis implored filmmakers to be less 'cavalier' about historical evidence and to 'tell the truth' about slavery in the future.[4] When historians criticize these such films, they are not complaining about minor inaccuracies in costume or setting, but about the broader 'truth' claims of the filmmakers (see Chapter 2). In recent years, these debates have continued in the wake of *Django Unchained* (2012) and *12 Years a Slave* (2013).

Creating a work of history, whether written or visual, requires creating a coherent narrative. This is difficult for all producers of historical films; documentary evidence is fragmented and contradictory, historians disagree on what is significant, and Hollywood filmmakers favour a clear ending (preferably a happy one), which often doesn't exist. As Robert Brent Toplin notes of *Amistad*, 'its story is a scriptwriter's nightmare'.[5] With a history as complicated, contested and significant to the contemporary United States as that of slavery, the stakes are even higher. The spectre of slavery has continued to haunt race relations in the US since its abolition in 1865, through the terrors of Reconstruction, the violence of segregation, the backlash against civil rights struggles, and, more recently, in the high rates of police brutality towards, and incarceration of, young black men. Slavery has not been resolved; it is not in the past, and therefore it cannot be treated with historical distance. Indeed, the portrayal of slavery in American film *matters* to race relations in the present. The National Association for the Advancement of Colored People (NAACP) staged protests against *The Birth of a Nation* (1915), *Gone with the Wind* (1939) and other movies not just because they were inaccurate in the details, but because the organization rightly believed that the racist way in which these films portrayed African Americans was detrimental to the progress of the race.

Scholarly discussions of films about slavery have tended to focus on one or two films in depth, providing detailed analyses of these films' representations of black life and the 'peculiar institution'.[6] However, this chapter considers a broader range of films and argues that rather than trying to understand the experiences of enslaved people, or to present audiences with accurate or authentic narratives of slavery and slave life, the present looms large in filmic treatments of American slavery. By considering a range of films across a century, it is possible to see how writers, directors and producers have consistently used slavery as a lens through which to comment on American race relations in their own time, and to entertain and inform their audiences about present-day issues. Although most of these films are too concerned with the present to portray historically authentic 'truths' about slavery, they can give us valuable insight into race relations in the period in which they were produced.

Silent slaves: Slavery in early cinema

In the late nineteenth century, one of the most popular forms of enter-tainment was the minstrel show. Minstrelsy involved impersonations of African-Americans by white actors and singers in blackface, which, although intended to be comical, perpetuated negative racial stereotypes of black men and women as lazy, foolish, childlike and unwilling (or unable) to work without white supervision and punishment. As a result of the popularity of such performances, it was natural for early American filmmakers to continue in this tradition and make use of African-American characters and racist stereotypes. As well as the numerous versions of *Uncle Tom's Cabin* that were produced, films such as *For Massa's Sake* (1911), *In Slavery Days* (1913), and *His Trust Fulfilled: The Faithful Devotion and Self-Sacrifice of an Old Negro Servant* (1911), confirmed established stereo-types of African-Americans as stupid, lazy and loyal to their masters during slavery and the Civil War.[7] African-Americans were also frequently depicted as comic 'coons', ravenous for watermelons or chicken, and frequently dancing.[8] For *Uncle Tom's Cabin* in 1903, for example, director Porter hired an existing troupe of minstrel dancers rather than actors, and as a result black characters are seen dancing for around a fifth of the short film.[9]

There are moments in these early films, however, particularly *Uncle Tom's Cabin*, which demonstrate a more complicated approach to slavery.[10] For example, William Robert Daly's 1914 version of *Uncle Tom's Cabin* was the first to employ a black actor to play Tom (Sam Lucas, a Tom stage actor) and includes an extraordinary scene in which a fugitive slave (also played by an uncredited black actor) shoots the white overseer, and the camera angle allows the audience to see this shooting from the slave's point of view. The intertitle tells us that this 'boy' had a 'desire for swift revenge' after he learns that Tom was beaten for refusing to whip him. Although it is still infused with racist language ('boy'), such justified rebelliousness on the part of a slave, and from the viewpoint of a slave, was a rare sight in American cinema before the Second World War.

The following year the first feature length film ever made, D. W. Griffith's racist epic, *The Birth of a Nation* (1915), appeared on American screens. Griffiths' adaptation of Thomas Dixon's *The Clansman* rewrote the history of slavery, the Civil War and Reconstruction as a story of a 'quaintly' white society destroyed by war, black brutes and evil 'mulattoes', and only rescued by the Ku Klux Klan's restoration of white supremacy.[11] In this film, African-Americans are not only depicted in racist stereotypes, but also blamed for the Civil War; as one intertitle explains: 'The bringing of the African to America planted the first seed of disunion.' In the first half of the film, slaves are portrayed as docile, loyal and loving of their owners. Slaves appear in almost every scene set in the South, either dancing or picking cotton, as a nostalgic backdrop to the growing love between the

FIGURE 7.1 Birth of a Nation *(1916)*

white characters Phil Stoneman (Elmer Clifton) and Margaret Cameron (Miriam Cooper).

Slavery is portrayed as entirely benign; for example one intertitle states that slaves are given two hours to have their lunch. Snead notes that these shots have a 'documentary' quality; they are intentionally designed to show viewers 'the way things were'.[12] The NAACP, African-Americans and some liberal whites protested extensively against the film's release, and were successful in getting some material removed, including one early scene in which a woman at an abolitionist meeting was shown to recoil in disgust at the smell of a black child.[13] Despite these protests, however, *Birth of a Nation* set the tone for depictions of plantation slavery for decades to come, not least because it was endorsed by President Wilson, also a historian, who allegedly declared it 'like writing history with lightning'.[14]

By 1927, it was time for another production of *Uncle Tom's Cabin*. However, this version proved controversial. Despite director Harry Pollard's claims that 'the true Southerner was and is ... kindly, considerate, and in short, the Negro's best friend', and his attempts to play down Tom's martyrdom, southerners denounced the film.[15] A number of scenes, including a scene of a slave auction, were cut before opening, and more were removed after initial screenings in the South. However, this did not placate southerners: as confederate veteran General Goodwyn put it, the film was 'an insult to our ancestors'.[16] It is unclear, especially after the inclusion of the slave auction scene and a rebellious slave in earlier productions, exactly what southerners found so offensive. Uncle Tom (James B. Lowe) appears on screen for less than nine minutes of a two-hour long film, and the film is replete with racist dialect and stereotypical characters. Indeed, when it was released for DVD in 1999, some scenes were cut because they were deemed too racially offensive to modern audiences. In particular, a scene in which two children, white Little Eva (Virginia Grey) and enslaved Topsy (Mona Ray), discuss why Topsy is 'bad', originally resulted in a conversation about the 'worthlessless' of black people, which was subsequently removed from the DVD release:

> **Topsy** 'Couldn't be nuthin' but a nigger if I wuz ever so good. If I could be skinned and come out white, I might be good.'
> **Eva** 'Oh, Topsy, people can love you, even if you are black.'
> **Topsy** 'Nobody loves niggers – 'cause niggers ain't worth nuthin', nohow.'

This scene was followed by one featuring Topsy sitting alone at a mirror, attempting to apply white makeup. When questioned by her mistress, she explained: 'Please, Miss Feely, I jes' wanted to make myself white – so I could be good like Missy Eva.' This scene was also cut from the DVD release.[17] By the 1990s, it seems that film distributors considered Topsy's self-denigration too much for audiences to bear.

The contrast between what was acceptable to audiences in 1903, 1914, 1927 and 1999, in various versions of the same story, demonstrates the significance of present-day concerns to filmmakers and distributors. Despite Griffith's claim in his opening intertitle that *Birth of a Nation* was 'an historical presentation ... and is not meant to reflect on any race or people of today', both filmmakers and audiences were aware that the representation of slavery on film was entirely relevant to race relations in the present. The early twentieth century was marked by growing civil rights activism among African Americans in all aspects of their lives, but their particular attention to the depiction of slavery on screen demonstrated growing concerns about whites' domination of this new media, and the damage that it could do to racial progress. On the other hand, white audiences concerned about changes in society, including urbanization and feminism as well as black activism, were unwilling to relinquish their nostalgic view of the Old South as an idyllic time. These concerns, rather than any debate over the accuracy of the depictions of slavery, were at the forefront of filmmakers' minds. By 1946, NAACP protests prevented MGM from producing yet another version of *Uncle Tom's Cabin*, and it has not been produced since for the cinema.[18] However, in 1987, it was remade for television by director Stan Lathan for Showtime. In this version, which claimed to return to the 'original spirit of the novel', the emphasis is on

Tom's religiosity, kindness, loyalty and dignity, values that the filmmakers clearly wanted modern African-Americans to emulate (perhaps instead of the militant Black Power activity of the early 1970s). As the final voiceover explains, 'Tom's spirit rose out of the pages of Harriet Beecher Stowe's novel to agitate the conscience of the nation. A war was fought. The black people were legally freed. Today one hundred and twenty years later, the battle for true freedom still continues'.

Mammies and mistresses: The plantation epic

In the 1930s, in the midst of the Great Depression and the social changes wrought by the New Deal, the nostalgia initially invoked by *The Birth of a Nation* became even more popular among white Americans who wished they had lived in, as they perceived it, simpler and more honourable times. The opening credits of the most famous film about slavery from this period, the plantation epic *Gone with the Wind* (1939), indicate this desire: 'There was a land of cavaliers and cotton fields called the Old South ... Here was the last ever to be seen of knights and their ladies fair, of Master and of Slave ... Look for it only in books, for it is no more than a dream remembered. A Civilisation gone with the wind.' In this imagining of the Old South, slavery was not considered cruel or unjust, simply an example of the way society should be organized.[19] The slavery imagined in *Gone with the Wind*, and in other similar films from the era, such as *So Red the Rose* (1935) and *Jezebel* (1938), was drawn from the plantation stereotypes of *Birth* and emphasized slaves' loyalty to their owners.[20] In contrast, there were also films made in this period that focused on the illegality and the immorality of the Atlantic slave trade. Considered in comparison to the plantation epic, however, films such as *Souls and Sea* (1937) and *Slave Ship* (1937) indicate that it was only a very specific type of slavery – that of the plantation – that evoked white American's nostalgia. White audiences could seemingly abhor the illegal transportation of Africans to the United States and simultaneously wish they lived on a big plantation like *Gone with the Wind*'s 'Tara' or *Jezebel*'s 'Halcyon' surrounded by enslaved people.

So Red the Rose, *Jezebel* and *Gone with the Wind* contain many similarities in their depictions of the Old South. All feature a young white woman left in charge of a plantation during a period of crisis: in *Jezebel*, Julie (Bette Davis) has to face the yellow fever epidemic in New Orleans; for Valette (Margaret Sullavan) and Scarlett (Vivien Leigh) in *So Red the Rose* and *Gone with the Wind* it is the Civil War. The depictions of plantation slavery are broadly similar in each. Slaveholders are paternalistic and benign, slaves are happy and loyal, and often seen dancing, singing, or providing comic relief in moments of crisis. Unlike in earlier films, however, African-Americans were employed to portray all of the black characters and were thus able to use their status on set to progress a civil rights agenda. For example, Hattie McDaniel, who won an Oscar for her role as Mammy in *Gone with the Wind*, and Butterfly McQueen (Prissy) success-fully campaigned to remove the word 'nigger' from the film's dialogue.[21]

Small moments of black resistance to slavery also made their way into the scripts of these films, although they are largely negated and neutralized by white characters. For example, enslaved characters in *So Red the Rose* sing a rendition of the freedom-seeking slave spiritual 'Let My People Go', although the filmmakers appropriated it for the confederate cause, as it is sung while the slaves gather around their master as he departs for war and promise to 'guard and protect' the plantation in his absence. As the war continues, the plantation slaves begin to rally for their freedom, but this is shown as laziness and stupidity as the slaves cry 'no more choppin' cotton … just sittin' in the sun', 'let's go sit around and do nothin'!' and 'we don't work no more'. This minor attempt at rebellion (along with its anti-New Deal overtones), however, is immediately quashed by Valette slapping one of the ringleaders.

Mirroring the white female protagonists, enslaved women also played significant roles in these films. In *Gone with the Wind*, it is Mammy (McDaniel) who takes the leading role in defending southern traditions and keeping Scarlett in line. While the character has rightly been criticized for its stereotypical portrayal of black womanhood, McDaniel's Mammy is more dignified than the equivalent character in *Birth of a Nation*, or of that of the stupid, cowardly, lying Prissy (McQueen) in *Gone with the Wind*. As Malcolm X recalled on seeing the film, 'I was the only negro in the theatre, and when Butterfly McQueen went into her act, I felt like crawling under the rug'.[22] Prissy's most demeaning scene involves her lying about her ability to be a midwife, and her frantic utterance 'I don't know nothin' 'bout birthin' babies!' resulting in a slap from Scarlett.[23] Prissy is similar to Zette (Theresa Harris) in *Jezebel*. When Julie (Davis) causes scandal by buying a red dress, originally meant for a prostitute, to wear to the Olympus Ball (to which she is supposed to be wearing white), Zette is the only one who likes it, which simultaneously shows that she is ignorant of social norms, and codes Julie's wanton behaviour as 'black'.[24] While Mammy belongs to the nostalgia of the Old South, Prissy and Zette seemingly represent a younger generation of African Americans who do not understand or respect society's rules.

Malcolm X was not the only African-American to critique *Gone with the Wind*, which led to widespread protests for its racist depictions of happy and loyal slaves: 'You'd be sweet too under a whip!' read one placard in Washington.[25] The most devastating critique came from Melvin Tolson in in the *Washington Tribune*, who noted that the film's danger lay in its subtlety and its presentation of itself as historical: 'the story of the Old South'. As it did not directly insult African-Americans and did not reproduce the racist depiction of the black brute from *Birth of a Nation*, or show any violence towards slaves, it would be 'swallowed as the truth by millions'. He was clearly concerned that as the film lacked 'the motivation of historical truth' and did not depict slavery as the 'bloody institution' it actually was, it would cause whites watching the film to believe that African-Americans were better off enslaved, hindering racial progress.[26] However the excellent acting by Hattie McDaniel offset the concerns of many African-Americans; as soon as she won her Oscar, criticism of the film almost entirely disappeared among black audiences.[27]

Despite widespread civil rights protests during the Second World War, including the NAACP's successful blocking of a remake of *Uncle Tom's Cabin*, in 1946 Disney produced what Snead has called 'one of the best imaginable elaborations of some deeply revealing and disturbing American fantasies about slavery and blackness'.[28] *Song of the South* (1946), a children's film that combined cartoons and live-action sequences to retell Chandler Harris's 'Uncle Remus' stories, had a plantation setting that clearly resembled the Old South of earlier films, despite filmmakers' claims that it was supposed to be set in the late nineteenth century. As the cartoon Brer Rabbit explained, in racist dialect that would signify his blackness to audiences, "Twas a long time ago. An in dem days, eve'thing was mighty satisfactual'. James Baskett played the Uncle Tom-esque Uncle Remus, devoting all of his time and love to a white child called Johnny, and Hattie McDaniel returned as Mammy. As with *Gone with the Wind*, African-Americans supported James Baskett but were highly critical of the racism of the film.[29] Walter White of the NAACP called it a 'dangerously glorified picture of slavery', and picketers at the film's premiere in New York chanted 'We fought for Uncle Sam, not Uncle Tom!'[30] The context of this film, released just as black soldiers returned from the Second World War ready to fight for civil rights, is key to understanding why it was so controversial. Bosley Crowther, the film critic for the *New York Times*, exclaimed that Disney had 'committed a peculiarly gauche offense in putting out such a story in this troubled day and age. One might almost imagine that you figure Abe Lincoln made a mistake. Put down that mint julep, Mr. Disney!'[31] In later years, it seems that Disney finally took this advice, as the company stopped releasing *Song of the South* on video and television in 1986, and it has never appeared on DVD.[32]

Song of the South marked the end of the depiction of slaves as uniformly happy, docile and loyal. As the Civil Rights Movement gained momentum in the 1950s and 1960s, filmmakers largely turned their attention to contemporary race relations. While Sidney Poitier challenged white audiences to reconsider their racial prejudices in films like *Guess Who's Coming to Dinner* (1967), slavery was largely absent from American filmmaking. One notable exception is *Band of Angels* (1957), also starring Poitier, which tells the story of Amantha (Yvonne de Carlo), a white woman who discovers that she was actually born a slave, and who is thus sold into slavery and purchased by Hamish Bond (Clark Gable, reprising his role as a southern slaveholder from *Gone with the Wind*). As a slave she encounters Rau-Ru

(Poitier) the 'boss negro' on the plantation, who challenges her sense of white supremacy and the idea that their master is kind to them: 'I hate him. For his kindness, that's worse than the rawhide. When a man uses a whip you know what there is to fight against, but this kindness, it's a trap that can hold you in bondage forever!' Rau-Ru seethes with animosity and resentment towards Bond and all white people, and reverses the imagery of white women slapping slaves in *Gone with the Wind* and *So Red the Rose* when he hits Amantha for saying that in freedom, she plans to ignore her racial heritage and pass as white. These scenes demonstrate that by the 1950s, the plantation was no longer merely a setting for racist stereotypes, but could be used to discuss contemporary racial issues. However, by no means are all aspects of the film progressive: Rau-Ru is the only black character fully developed to demonstrate agency and resistance, and scenes meant to demonstrate Bond's kindness as a master could have been taken straight out of *Birth of a Nation*. When he arrives home to his plantation, for example, he is greeted by around a hundred slaves cheering and singing 'Hallelujah'. Black audiences in the 1950s found this ridiculous. As John O. Killens explained,

> white people in the theatre were weeping, some slyly, some unashamedly, at the touching scene, when suddenly my friend and I erupted with laughter, because we thought that surely, in the time of Montgomery and Little Rock, this must have been put into the film for comic relief.'[33]

The filmmakers were indeed cognizant of the changing times in which they worked; when the Civil War begins, Bond placates his slaves by explaining that 'if we can live another hundred years we could probably see white justice for the blacks'.

Sex, violence and slavery: The blaxploitation era

By the 1970s, it was clear that 'justice for blacks' was going to take longer than the 100 years Clark Gable's Hamish Bond had suggested in *Band of Angels*. In 1968, iconic and influential civil rights leader Martin Luther King was assassinated in the midst of his 'poor people's campaign'; a moment that for many marked an end to the mainstream movement for civil rights. The late 1960s and early 1970s saw a rise in Black Power activism, in which young African-Americans, such as those who joined the Black Panther Party, became increasingly frustrated with the slow pace of change and increasingly militant in their demands for equal rights and social justice. This shift, combined with a rising white conservative backlash against the Civil Rights Movement, led to a ready audience for films that depicted violent black revenge against racist whites. Hollywood filmmakers saw an opportunity to make large profits from low budget movies made for black audiences, and hundreds of films were produced on this basis. Several of these films were set in the antebellum period and depicted graphic scenes of violence, interracial sex and slave resistance. It is important to note that these films were not popular among black critics; many felt that films like *Mandingo* (1975) were 'a "rip off" of Black people's past'.[34] B. J. Mason, in *Ebony* magazine, questioned whether these new films were 'Culture or Con Game?' and noted that many critics thought that the old stereotypes of *Birth of a Nation* and *Gone with the Wind* had merely been glamorized.[35] Despite negative reviews, these films were incredibly popular among black audiences because they spoke directly to contemporary concerns about high levels of violence in black communities and the slow pace of change.

Some blaxploitation slavery films spoke directly to the present through their characters' dialogue. For example, in *The Legend of Nigger Charley* (1972), Charley (Fred Williamson) is given his freedom by his dying master, but denied it by the overseer Houston (John Ryan), who tells Charley: 'You got no right to be free, boy. Only a man gets a right to be free, and you ain't a man – you're a nigger!' Charley decides to take his freedom, and along with Joshua (Don Pedro Colley) and Toby (D'Urville Martin), escapes the South and settles in a small western town. Despite having claimed their freedom, they discover, as Joshua puts it, that 'there ain't never going to be an end to black man's troubles' as they still encounter violence and racism from local white people. At the end of the film, after several violent skirmishes, Charley and Toby ride off over the horizon to an uncertain future, as Charley explains that it 'don't make no difference where we go … there's trouble for us everywhere'. These lines spoke directly to black audiences in the early 1970s. As Theophilus Green explained in *Ebony* magazine, noting that *Nigger Charley* 'grossed $1 million in its first two weeks', it was the violence of these new male characters towards whites that was particularly appealing. Whites seeing characters like Charley 'as examples of black America would be frightened out of their skin tans', he explained:

> Many have killed white men, taken their women, stolen their money and had one helluva good time outsmarting them at their own game – the same crimes many white Americans committed with seeming impunity against blacks. Black audiences want their own larger-than-life heroes … They would like to ride off into the sunset with Fred Williamson … after a hard day fighting racism.[36]

While black audiences may have found a hero to cheer for in *Nigger Charley*, the release of *Mandingo* a few years later offered no such relief. Director Richard Fleischer explained that his intention was to 'stop' the romanticized image of slavery perpetuated in earlier films by being 'as brutal as I could possibly be, to show how these people suffered'.[37] Fleischer was successful in depicting brutality, as *Mandingo* tells the story of a violent southern plantation dedicated to slave breeding, where no character escapes the degradation of the system. Mede (Ken Norton), is purchased as a 'mandingo fighter', and as such is required to fight other slaves to the death (and he does so by chewing on the necks of his opponents). The plantation is rife with rape and violent sexual exploitation, both of black women and black men, including Mede who is forced to have sex with his white mistress Blanche (Susan George).

Black and white critics almost universally denounced *Mandingo*'s depiction of slavery, calling it racist, pornographic and exploitative.[38] For example, Ida Peters in the Baltimore *Afro-American* thought it was 'a distorted sick film' that 'makes you want to vomit or just plain walk out'. In particular, she criticized Ken Norton for allowing himself to be degraded by the film: 'That naked rape scene was disgusting', and worried that the film did not show slaves resisting their enslavement.[39] However, her readers disagreed, and African-Americans flocked to watch what they considered to be a truthful account of the brutality of slavery. Gloria Nicholson responded angrily to Peters' review in a long letter to the *Afro-American*, explaining that she thought the film was the 'truth and reality of slavery and its frightening experiences':

> Ken Norton portrayed exactly what he was supposed to be: a stupid, dumb, nigger animal. Right? ... Slavery was exactly what the film let it be known to be. Blacks then were beaten, degraded, killed and oppressed ... Now that Blacks know and have seen some of the things that happened to their ancestors, they will stop and think about what they are doing to themselves today. You say that the fighting scenes of the two Black men disgusted you. Well what about the beating, stabbing, and killing Blacks do to each other today? ... I think that it's time we all learn to accept what happened. Maybe if we do, we'll be able to understand things about ourselves a little better and treat ourselves better and give ourselves the human dignity that we so deserve. Sincerely one who knows my color.[40]

This impassioned response demonstrated how significant the representation of slavery could be to black audiences. Viewers like Nicholson drew clear parallels between the violent scenes depicted in *Mandingo* and current race relations; in her case, black-on-black violent crime. Guerrero notes that *Mandingo* 'expressly mediates the militant thinking, language, and aspirations of the Black Power Movement'.[41] African-Americans in the early 1970s would have recognized Black Power's influence particularly in the character of Cicero (Ji-Ti Cumbuka), who kills his master and attempts to escape, but is caught by the slave patrol. 'You just better know, this is just as much our land as it is yours', Cicero declares, moments before he is hanged, 'and after you hang me, kiss my ass!' This rhetoric speaks of and to the early 1970s far more than it does to the era of slavery; the words 'kiss my ass', demonstrate the desire on the part of the filmmakers to engage the present, rather than to pretend a historically accurate past.

In *Django Unchained* (2012), Quentin Tarantino revived the blaxploitation slavery film with a modern twist. Django (Jamie Foxx) is a twenty-first-century Charley, only this time he returns to the South to rescue his wife, Broomhilda (Kerry Washington) with the help of German bounty hunter Dr King Schultz (Christoph Waltz), before riding off into the sunset. *Django* also draws upon the violence of *Mandingo*, both in the 'mandingo' fights organized by Broomhilda's evil slaveholder Calvin Candie (Leonardo DiCaprio) and in the film's gory revenge fantasy ending. Responding to criticisms about the extensive levels of violence in the film, Tarantino explained that as a movie about slavery, both dialogue and scenes needed to be 'ugly'.[42] While emphasizing that *Django* was fictional, and aimed to be entertaining, Tarantino also explained that one of his motives in making the film was to force Americans to 'look their own past sins directly in the face', rather than to think about slavery with an intellectual distance.[43] The character of Schultz, whom many critics thought was merely another 'white saviour' of oppressed black slaves, acts as a stand-in for this modern perspective.[44] Schultz has no idea of the realities of slavery; he is visibly shocked when he sees scars from whippings on Django's back. A more careful viewing of *Django* (and to a lesser extent, *Nigger Charley* and *Mandingo*) therefore demonstrates that while the stories of blaxploitation movies may be far-fetched and fictional, the fundamental messages of these films – that slavery was a violent institution that negatively affected all who lived under it, and that slaves were willing to do almost anything to free themselves (and their families) from bondage – do have the important ring of historical truth.

Telling 'true' stories: Real slaves and reel slaves

For eight consecutive nights in January 1977, the television network ABC showed *Roots*, the series based on Alex Haley's book *Roots: The Saga of an American Family* (1976) about his African ancestry. The televised *Roots* aired to a record-breaking 130 million viewers (85 per cent of households), with 80 million tuning in for the final episode, making it the most watched programme in television history. Notably, the record that it broke was previously held by *Gone with the Wind*.[45] Roots told the story of Kunta Kinte (LeVar Burton), a young man stolen from his family in Africa and sold into slavery in 1765, and the stories of his descendants throughout the eighteenth and nineteenth centuries. Marketed to both white and black audiences, *Roots* was an American immigrant story that emphasized the significance of family ties.[46] There were some violent scenes, for example when Kunta Kinte is whipped until he accepts his slave name, 'Toby', but nothing that resembled the gore of *Mandingo*. Schickel in *Time* magazine called *Roots* 'Mandingo for middlebrows', as it turned slavery from graphic violence to sanitized family melodrama.[47] Nevertheless, *Roots* was a turning point in the representations of slavery on film; despite its flaws, the series was the first attempt to tell an allegedly 'true' story of the experience of slavery. Instead of using fiction to speak to broader 'truths', as earlier filmmakers had done, *Roots* claimed historical accuracy and authenticity. Much of the commentary upon its release, however, focused on its impact on race relations, rather than on its historical accuracy. One critic called the series 'a potentially important benchmark in US race relations' because it showed Americans, white and black, that they had a shared heritage. This resulted in feelings of anger among some black audiences, and guilt for some whites, because 'for millions of Americans, *Roots* was real – if not necessarily literally true'. However, this would only matter, the commentator claimed, 'if *Roots* turns the anger at yesterday's slavery into anger at today's ghettos'.[48] Just a few months later, however, in May 1977, *Jet* magazine reported 'Even After *Roots*, Whites Don't See Job Bias Against Blacks Today', as the number of whites who did not believe that African-Americans were discriminated against in the workplace rose from 57 per cent in 1976 to 64 per cent in 1977, after *Roots* was shown. This, according to *Jet*, demonstrated that black Americans were 'more aware of the degradation of their past and its effect on the present than whites'.[49] *Jet's* desire that a television show, even one as popular as *Roots*, would affect perceptions about workplace discrimination was perhaps optimistic, but it demonstrates the ways in which depictions of the past of slavery were expected to speak directly to contemporary issues.

Telling the 'truth' about the past, some filmmakers have claimed, is the first step to mending racial tensions. Explaining their motivations for making *Amistad* (1997) producer Debbie Allen and director Spielberg explained that the events upon which the film is based – an 1839 rebellion on board a slave ship and subsequent trials to determine whether the Africans on board should be enslaved or free – were unknown to black Americans. Allen went as far as to claim that this was the fault of professional historians: 'the real history has just been castrated – left out – and great historians have done it. It's beyond racism, I think.'[50] A number of historians pointed out that a great deal of research had been published about American slavery in general and the Amistad affair in particular, and that the film *Amistad* was so full of historical inaccuracies that it did not further understanding of the past.[51] While these inaccuracies and fictionalizations may be acceptable as part of an entertaining movie (see also Chapters 2 and 9), historians were particularly concerned when Spielberg distributed 'learning kits' for the classroom. Eric Foner retorted that 'if the film's producers really want to promote an understanding of slavery, they should direct students to the local library'.[52] *Amistad* attempts to strike a balance between the agency of the rebel Africans and the justice of the American legal system, but the latter overshadows the former. Although there are scenes of the middle passage and of the rebellion, most of the film is a dry legal drama in which Roger Sherman Baldwin (Matthew McConaughey) and John Quincy Adams (Anthony Hopkins) discourse on the injustice of slavery. Even the scenes of rebellion, which are supposed to depict the Africans, led by Cinque (Djimon Hounsou), fighting for their freedom, are brief and graphically violent. In one shot, the audience is placed in the position of the Spanish slaver being drawn through by Cinque's sword, and thus the African is coded as brutish and animalistic.[53] This othering of the Africans is exacerbated by the failure to subtitle their Mende language, so much of their speech is incomprehensible to American audiences. Spielberg explained that this lack of communication was deliberate, because it reflected 'what's happening today in this country'.[54] Reviewers also noted that the film spoke to contemporary debates. Gary Rosen called *Amistad* 'a major artistic offensive in the current debate over race', in particular in the inclusion of the black American character Theodore Joadson (Morgan Freeman), who is entirely fictional. Rosen saw the inclusion of Joadson as an attempt to maintain a 'racial quota'; to ensure that there was 'a strict one-to-one ratio' between black and white characters. He argued that viewed in the context of the 1990s debates over affirmative action – a highly controversial policy of increasing black opportunities in education and employment by giving preferential treatment to African Americans – it was clear which side the film was on.[55] Rich in the *New York Times* disagreed. In a review entitled 'Slavery is Bad', Rich saw *Amistad* as a 'diversion, however worthy, from what ails us now … The whole country can, after all, agree that slavery is bad – and still come to blows over affirmative action'.[56] Writer David Franzoni explained that he had invented Joadson because the 'most important issue for me was that this is a movie about black Americans'.[57] This is significant because in reality the Amistad affair was expressly *not* about black Americans. Cinque and his fellow slaves were Africans, and that the Supreme Court granted them their freedom because their capture in 1839 was illegal (the Atlantic Slave Trade having been abolished in 1808), did nothing to alleviate the enslavement of the four million black American slaves living in the United States. In an attempt to make this film 'about' African Americans, the filmmakers did a disservice to the real history of Cinque and his demand to 'give us free'.

Amistad is not the only film which purports to tell a 'true' story about American slavery but avoids directly addressing the subject of American slaves. In *Glory* (Edward Zwick, 1989) and *Beloved* (1998), filmmakers focus on the memory and trauma of slavery and its effect on those recently freed. It is only in one scene in *Glory*, the story of the courage of the black men of the 54th Massachusetts regiment led by Robert Shaw (Matthew Broderick) during the Civil War, that the scars of slavery (both literal and figurative) are exposed: when Shaw orders the whipping of Trip (Denzel

Washington) for desertion. Trip's back is already heavily scarred by slavery, but it is Shaw, and the audience, who are scarred by the scene as Trip's dignity and strength force viewers into the position of being the one holding the whip.

As whipping was outlawed as a punishment by the Union Army, this scene must have been included for its resonance to audiences: shorthand for the violence of slavery. Similarly, an early scene in the film involves Shaw practicing his swordplay on horseback by slicing through watermelons, which would not have been available in February 1863 when the scene is set. As Gerald Horne noted in his review, 'even one not schooled in deconstruction could readily and verily grasp the cinematic attack by whites on racial stereotypes and racism'.[58] While historians largely praised *Glory* for its emphasis on African-American soldiers' contribution to the fight for freedom, the strongest message of the film for some reviewers was that of 'black manhood and responsibility', which Lance Morrow in *Time* magazine called 'the most profound theme of race in America in 1990'.[59] The former slaves depicted in *Glory*, Morrow argued, had fought for their freedom, and young black men in the 1990s should therefore do the same, as the 'worst problems of the black underclass today' were a 'culture of victimization' and black men's failure to take responsibility.[60] Oprah Winfrey made a similar point (although from a different political perspective) when interviewed by *Ebony* magazine about *Beloved*, a film based on Toni Morrison's 1987 novel of the same name that she both funded and starred in. *Beloved* fictionalizes the traumatic memory of Margaret Garner, who killed her own children in 1856 in order to prevent their enslavement. 'Think of all the Sethes [Garner] in the world whose names aren't in the history books who were able to withstand what they did in a world where they had zero, nothing', Winfrey explains of her character. 'If they were able to stand that,

FIGURE 7.2 Glory *(1988)*

what can we do?'[61] As a film, *Beloved* struggled to convey the complexity of Morrison's novel, especially in the character of Beloved herself (Thandie Newton), but its overall message about the deep wounds of slavery is clear, and the 'tree' of scars on Sethe's (Winfrey) back are as haunting as the ghost of Beloved.[62] Even if it does little to illuminate the lives of the enslaved, by focusing on the trauma of slavery, *Beloved* allows for a subtle, poignant and discomforting understanding of its ongoing effects.

In attempts to find true stories that translate well to a filmic narrative, some filmmakers have drawn upon the true stories of exceptional enslaved people. The stories of Sally Hemings and Solomon Northup have each appeared twice on American screens: Hemings in *Jefferson in Paris* (1995) and *Sally Hemings: An American Scandal* (2000), and Northup in *Solomon Northup's Odyssey* (1984) and *12 Years a Slave* (2013). The passage of time between the two versions of the same life story in each case demonstrates a shift in contemporary concerns, and illuminates the ways in which the present affects the retelling of the past. *Jefferson in Paris*, as the title suggests, focuses on the years that Thomas Jefferson (Nick Nolte) spent in France as US Ambassador in the years before the French Revolution. Mid-way through the film, he is joined in Paris by one of his enslaved women, the fifteen-year-old Sally Hemings (Thandie Newton), who seduces him with her beauty and childish affectations. When she discovers that she is pregnant, her brother James (Seth Gilliam), who has been influenced by the calls for 'liberté, egalité, fraternité' during his time in Paris, tries to convince her to remain in France and claim her freedom, asking her: 'don't you want to see what it's like to own your own body?' She responds that Virginia is her 'home' and returns with Jefferson to Monticello. Such a representation of a founding father caused outrage among both historians and the public. Douglas Egerton explained that he 'doubt[ed] that the master of Monticello would engage in a torrid romance with a "quarteroon" he believed to be his biological inferior', and criticized the depictions of a 'typical lusty Virginian' bedding a 'simple-minded child … with "sho 'nuff" slave dialect'.[63] Egerton was correct about the portrayal of Hemings, as aspects of Newton's performance reflect outdated stereotypes of enslaved people, but any doubts that their relationship existed were disproved when a combination of DNA testing and historical research by Annette Gordon-Reed demonstrated that they had a relationship lasting thirty-eight years and that Jefferson fathered Hemings' children.[64] The exact nature of that relationship is unknown, but in 2000, CBS aired a miniseries called *Sally Hemings: An American Scandal*, which cast it firmly as a love story. In this rendition, Hemings (Carmen Ejogo) is far from child-like. She declares that it is her 'choice' to stay at Monticello, and uses her power and education to help other slaves to resist: teaching them to read and write, and helping them to escape across the river to freedom. She is vocal and defiant towards Jefferson (Sam Neill) and urges him to abolish slavery if he becomes president: 'you cannot come to my bed, then go to your white congress and do nothing about this plague on my people', she remarks scornfully. The pair also have heated arguments about Jefferson's *Notes on the State of Virginia* (1781), but are clearly shown as being in love. By the time the film was released on DVD in 2011, it had been renamed *Sally Hemings: An American Love Story*, reflecting an ongoing shift in public perception.[65] It seems that in the era of a black president, people were now willing to accept a founding father's sexual relationship with a slave as long as it was based on love. Historians, of course, do not know whether the relationship was based on love or on coercion.[66]

Director Steve McQueen explains that he was looking for a story about slavery that would translate to film: 'I had an idea of a free man – a free African American who gets kidnapped into slavery, and that's where I got stuck.'[67] He found the answer in Solomon Northup's 1853 book, *Twelve Years a Slave*.[68] Like Debbie Allen's discovery of the story of the rebellion on the Amistad, McQueen was amazed that 'no one I knew knew this book'.[69] The resulting film, *12 Years a Slave*, starred Chiwetel Ejiofor in the leading role and was incredibly successful: it went on to win three Oscars, including Best Picture, and was hailed by a number of commentators for its authentic depiction of slavery.[70] However, McQueen was very clear that he intended *12 Years a Slave* to speak directly to contemporary issues. 'The whole movie in a way is a call to arms. There's so much that we can do and should do', he told Henry Louis Gates at *The Root*.[71] Similarly, to Nelson George of the *New York Times*, he explained that 'You see the evidence of slavery as you walk down the street ... the prison population, mental illness, poverty, education ... I hope it could be a starting point for [people] to delve into the history and somehow reflect on the position where they are now.'[72] Northup's kidnapping, for McQueen, was evidence of the precarious nature of freedom. Despite being a hardworking, middle-class American, Northup lost twelve years of his life to slavery, and McQueen saw clear parallels between his experience and that of the many other young black men, such as Trayvon Martin, who lost their lives to racism.[73] Valerie Smith agrees, arguing that the film is evidence of the 'proximity of freedom to enslavement and of the fragility of black life' as the 'sudden descent from freedom into captivity recalls the numbers of African Americans wrongfully convicted and incarcerated' in recent years.[74] It is this concern with contemporary issues that makes McQueen's version of Northup's narrative so different from an earlier production, Gordon Parks's *Solomon Northup's Odyssey*, which was made for television and broadcast on PBS in 1984. In this version, there is nothing 'fragile' about Solomon Northup (Avery Brooks). Director Gordon Parks was most famous for *Shaft* (1971), one of the most significant movies of the blaxploitation era, so perhaps it is unsurprising that Brooks spends large amounts of time with his shirt off, revealing a muscular torso, a trope that is reminiscent of the athletes employed during the 1970s to demonstrate the strength of black men.

Paradoxically, while *12 Years a Slave* is arguably the more accurate film, *Solomon Northup's Odyssey* is in many ways the more authentic of the two. John Ridley's screenplay for *12 Years a Slave* follows the detail of Solomon Northup's autobiography far more closely than writers Lou Potter and Samm-Art Williams chose to for *Solomon Northup's Odyssey*, and in doing so, it recreates the abolitionist-inspired critical distance that infuses the original text. For example, aside from their physiques, the most striking difference between Ejiofor's Northup and Brooks's Northup is the extent to which each becomes involved in the enslaved community on the plantation. Whereas Ejiofor's Northup seems to remain remote, and does not appear to spend much time in the company of other slaves, Brooks's Northup becomes entirely immersed with these people, including having a long term intimate relationship with an enslaved woman called Jenny (Rhetta Greene), despite having a wife and children at home in Saratoga Springs. Ejiofor's Northup is isolated, psychologically adrift without his freedom; Brooks's Northup is part of a group of slaves who, by living and working together, are able to resist their enslavement and to survive. One of the most significant (and uncomfortable to watch) scenes in *12 Years a Slave* depicts Northup, after a violent encounter with overseer Tibeats (Paul Dano), hanging from a tree, his toes only just touching the ground. McQueen forces his viewers to watch Northup hang, his life in the balance, for several minutes, while the rest of the slaves on the plantation continue their work in the background. For Smith, this scene is evidence of how slaves' 'survival depended upon their ability to become inured to each other's suffering'.[75] McQueen explained that 'The lynching had to be the best it could be done. Because that happened to hundreds of thousands of people. As someone whose ancestors experienced that, I needed to do that the way that I did it.'[76] Again, McQueen's concerns with slavery's link to the present are clear: in Northup's original book, he does not hang, life in danger, from the tree, but rather he explains that the rope was left 'still dangling from my neck'.[77] But McQueen wanted to include lynching – 'needed' to include lynching – because that violence connects the violence of slavery to the violence of the present; a painful shorthand for the evils of white supremacy. Similarly, Northup's whipping of Patsey (Lupita Nyong'o) in *12 Years a Slave* is so bloody and brutal that reviewer Armond White called the film 'torture porn'.[78] In contrast, Gordon Parks leaves out the near-hanging entirely in *Solomon Northup's Odyssey*, and in twist of resistance, shows Northup pretending to whip Jenny (Patsey is not a character in this version) as they hide in a woodshed and she feigns screams. While this is not true to Northup's book, it is authentic to what many enslaved people surely would have done if they could. This solidarity means that when Brooks's Northup is rescued, he does not leave immediately, as Ejiofor's Northup does, but spends time saying goodbye: 'I wish that I could take everybody.' Brooks's Northup has two families now, one he is to return to in Saratoga Springs, and one left behind on a plantation in Louisiana.[79]

Lessons for the present

Mirroring the work of historians, filmmakers since the 1960s have been keen to reverse the images of happy and loyal slaves seen in films like *Uncle Tom's Cabin*, *The Birth of a Nation* and *Gone with the Wind* by emphasizing African-American solidarity and resistance. The idea that black people during slavery could undermine white supremacy and rise above conditions of degradation is a 'truth' that historians and filmmakers can agree upon. The vast majority of slaves never stopped working together to resist the system of slavery, and this message is clear in a number of films that ask their audiences to do the same. For example, *Nightjohn* (1996), tells the story of an enslaved girl called Sarny (Allison Jones) and her friendship with John (Carl Lumby), a mysterious black man who teaches her how to read. While there is some violence in the film, and a great deal of prejudice exhibited by the white characters, the emphasis is firmly on the solidarity of an enslaved community who seek to resist their enslavement at every opportunity, and continually debate the best method of doing so. John explains that the nature of slavery is not just in the violence of the whip but in the written words of laws, deeds and free passes, so, as the film's tag line states, 'words are freedom'. The film has a clear message to young black viewers about the importance of working together and education for improving their lives. In contrast, Haile Gerima's *Sankofa* (1993) tells the story of Mona (Oyafunmike Ogunlano), an African-American model who, while on a photoshoot at Cape Coast Castle in Ghana, is spiritually transported back in time to become Shola, an enslaved woman. As Shola, she experiences repeated sexual violence and eventually joins a band of rebels led by Nunu (Alexandra Duah) and Shango (Mutabaruka): the message about resistance in *Sankofa* is that only a community-led violent rebellion will suffice because death is better than slavery. 'Rise up!' calls the film in a voiceover at the beginning. 'Stolen Africans, step out of the ocean, from the wounds of the ships ... step out of the acres of cane fields and cotton fields ... those lynched in the magnolias ... claim your story.' *Sankofa* also has a particular message for black women. Enslaved women, as Shola experiences, were raped and brutalized, so Mona, as a model responding to her photographer's calls for 'more sex, Mona!' is betraying her ancestors. Ancestry is collective, for Gerima, as he argues that the descendants of enslaved Africans across the Americas must accept their African heritage: it is Mona's belief that 'I'm not African, I'm an American!' that she must overcome in order to move forward. Gerima argued that African-Americans in the early 1990s were in a present-day 'slavery' because the US was still constructed around a 'plantation arrangement', and like McQueen and Spielberg, he wanted his film to encourage discussion and debate.[80] Reid agreed, noting that *Sankofa*, produced in the aftermath of the assault on Rodney King in 1992 and the nomination of black conservative Clarence

Thomas to the Supreme Court in 1991 despite allegations of sexual harassment, offered 'a moment for self-reflection and healing'.[81]

These opportunities for reflection are what make films about slavery significant as commentaries on the present, rather than as histories of the past. We may not be able to learn much about eighteenth- or nineteenth-century slavery from the majority of these films, but their role in contemporary debates about race, whether they are as racist as *The Birth of a Nation*, as violent as *Mandingo*, or as problematic as *Amistad*, mean that such films shed important light upon the 'color-lines' of the twentieth and twenty-first centuries. Cinematic representations of slavery in the United States have ebbed and flowed with the currents of African-American struggles for civil rights, and an analysis of the changing representations of slavery over time provides a lens through which to view race relations in modern America.

In the early twentieth century, derogatory stereotypes abounded, as filmmakers adopted the racist themes of minstrel shows. By mid-century, nostalgia in the wake of broad societal changes (not least the growing protest culture among African-Americans) led to films that idealized life on the Old South plantation as a 'dream remembered'. By the 1960s and 1970s, the success of black activism shifted filmmakers' focus to the violence of slavery, and there were high hopes that an understanding of the violence faced by African-Americans in the past might still the troubled waters of race relations in the present. In recent years, a search for 'truth' and authenticity has begun to challenge American audiences to confront the history of slavery, but has to some extent been hampered by filmmakers' desire to make their subjects speak to contemporary concerns while telling stories of the struggles of enslaved people. Stereotypes of African-Americans – as well as of other minority groups – still abound, and the battle for fair and unprejudiced representation in American film is far from won. As films about slavery continue to be produced, then, they will likely continue to illuminate the dark corners of American racism, and will therefore enable us to see far beyond the contours of the 'peculiar institution' that was slavery in the antebellum United States.

Notes

1　　W. E. B. Du Bois, *The Souls of Black Folk* (Chicago: A. C. McClurg & Co., 1903), vii. Available online: http://docsouth.unc.edu/church/duboissouls/dubois.html (accessed 28 June 2015).

2　　T. A. Edison, 'Uncle Tom's Cabin Film Catalogue' (New York: Edison Manufacturing Co., 1903), 3. Available online: http://utc.iath.virginia.edu/onstage/films/ficattaeat.html (accessed 28 June 2015).

3　　Cited in J. R. Jeffrey, '*Amistad* (1997): Steven Spielberg's "True Story"',

Historical Journal of Film, Radio and Television 21 (1) (2001): 80; E. Foner, 'Hollywood Invades the Classroom', *New York Times*, 20 December 1997.

4   N. Zemon Davis, *Slaves on Screen: Film and Historical Vision* (Cambridge: Harvard University Press, 2000), 130.

5   R. Brent Toplin, *Reel History: In Defense of Hollywood* (Lawrence: University Press of Kansas, 2002), 71.

6   Examples of such analyses are available in the notes throughout this chapter. For broader overviews of African Americans in film, see D. Bogle, *Toms, Coons, Mulattoes, Mammies, & Bucks: An Interpretive History of Blacks in American Films* (New York: Continuum, 2003); T. Cripps, *Slow Fade to Black: The Negro in American Film, 1900–1942* (New York: Oxford University Press, 1993b); T. Cripps, *Making Movies Black: The Hollywood Message Movie from World War II to the Civil Rights Era* (New York: Oxford University Press, 1993a); E. Guerrero, *Framing Blackness: The African American Image in Film* (Philadelphia: Temple University Press, 1993); V. Rocchio, *Reel Racism: Confronting Hollywood's Construction of Afro-American Culture* (Boulder, CO: Westview Press, 2000); J. Snead, *White Screens, Black Images: Hollywood from the Dark Side*, ed. C. MacCabe and C. West (New York: Routledge, 1994); M. Stokes, *American History through Hollywood Film: From the Revolution to the 1960s* (London: Bloomsbury Academic, 2013).

7   R. Jackson, 'The Celluloid War before *The Birth*: Race and History in Early American Film', in *American Cinema and the Southern Imaginary*, ed. D. E. Barker and K. McKee (Athens, GA: University of Georgia Press, 2011), 38.

8   Ibid., 29–31.

9   See S. Railton, 'Uncle Tom's Cabin on Film 1: The Silent Era' (2007). Available online: http://utc.iath.virginia.edu/interpret/exhibits/utconfilm/utconfilm.html (accessed 28 June 2015); J. W. Frick, *Uncle Tom's Cabin on the American Stage and Screen* (Basingstoke: Palgrave MacMillan, 2012), 190.

10   There is some debate over how 'racist' depictions of African Americans in this era were. See T. Cripps, 'The Unformed Image: The Negro in the Movies before *Birth of a Nation*', *Maryland Historian* 2 (1) (1971): 13–26; C. J. Robinson, 'In the Year 1915: D. W. Griffith and the Whitening of America', *Social Identities: Journal for the Study of Race, Nation and Culture* 3 (2) (1997): 161–92.

11   Stokes notes that Dixon deliberately attempted to 'challenge and replace' *Uncle Tom's Cabin* as the 'master narrative of Southern history and race relations.' M. Stokes, *D. W. Griffith's The Birth of a Nation: A History of 'the Most Controversial Motion Picture of all Time'* (New York: Oxford University Press, 2007), 54. *Birth* has received a great deal of scholarly attention, but largely for its depictions of Reconstruction and the portrayals of former slave Gus (Walter Long) and northern 'mulatto' Silas Lynch (George Siegmann) who both attempt to 'marry' (read: rape) white women. See especially M. Rogin, '"The Sword Became a Flashing Vision": D. W. Griffith's *The Birth of a Nation*', *Representations* 9 (1985): 150–95.

12   Snead, *White Screens, Black Images*, 43.

13   Stokes, *D. W. Griffith's The Birth of a Nation*, 104.

14   Ibid., 111.

15   Frick, *Uncle Tom's Cabin*, 215.

16   Railton, 'Uncle Tom's Cabin'.

17   See *Uncle Tom's Cabin* (1927) [DVD], dir. H. A. Pollard, USA, Kino Video; 'Illustrated "Text" of Pollard's Film', available online: http://utc.iath.virginia. edu/onstage/films/1927/27titleshp.html (accessed 28 June 2015).

18   'Uncle Tom's Cabin in Hollywood: 1929–1956'. Available online: http://utc. iath.virginia.edu/onstage/films/cameos/hollywood.html (accessed 28 June 2015).

19   Bogle argues that 'the black servants provided a down-hearted Depression age with buoyancy and jocularity … a marvellous relief from the harsh financial realities of the day'. Bogle, *Toms, Coons, Mulattoes, Mammies and Bucks*, 36.

20   For a discussion of the similarities between *Birth* and *Gone with the Wind*, see R. Ellen Burks, '*Gone with the Wind*: Black and White in Technicolor', *Quarterly Review of Film Video* 21 (1) (2004): 53–73.

21   L. J. Leff, '*Gone with the Wind* and Hollywood's Racial Politics', *Atlantic Monthly* 284 (6) (1999): 109.

22   Cited in Cripps, *Making Movies Black*, 3.

23   Offscreen, though, McQueen had far more dignity, and she refused to continue acting until Vivien Leigh stopped slapping her so hard. See Burks, '*Gone with the Wind*', 71.

24   For a longer analysis of race in *Jezebel*, see M. Bibler, 'Always the Tragic Jezebel: New Orleans, Katrina, and the Layered Discourse of a Doomed Southern City', *Southern Cultures* 14 (2) (2008): 6–27.

25   Cited in Leff, '*Gone with the Wind*', 114. Also see J. D. Stevens, 'The Black Reaction to *Gone with the Wind*', *Journal of Popular Film* 2 (4) (1973): 366–72.

26   M. Tolson, '*Gone with the Wind* is more Dangerous than *Birth of a Nation*', in *American Movie Critics: An Anthology from the Silents until Now*, ed. P. Lopate (New York: Library of America, 2008), 140–2.

27   See J. F. Tracy, 'Revisiting a Polysemic Text: The African American Press's Reception of *Gone with the Wind*', *Mass Communication Society* 4 (4) (2001): 419–36.

28   Snead, *White Screens, Black Images*, 86.

29   M. Bernstein, 'Nostalgia, Ambivalence, Irony: *Song of the South* and Race Relations in 1946 Atlanta', *Film History* 8 (1996): 219–36.

30   M. T. Inge, 'Walt Disney's *Song of the South* and the Politics of Animation', *Journal of American Culture* 35 (3) (2012): 223; Snead, *White Screens, Black Images*, 93.

31   Cited in Cripps, *Making Movies Black*, 190.

32 This decision was not uncontroversial. See J. Sperb, 'Reassuring Convergence: Online Fandom, Race, and Disney's Notorious *Song of the South*', *Cinema Journal* 49 (4) (2010): 25–45; J. J. Weinman, 'Zip-a-dee-doo-don't mention it', *Maclean's*, 14 May 2007, 63–4.

33 Cited in E. Mapp, *Blacks in American Films: Today and Yesterday* (Metuchen, NJ: Scarecrow Press, 1972), 44–5.

34 'New York Beat', *Jet*, 1 May 1975, 62.

35 B. J. Mason, 'The New Films: Culture or Con Game? Rash of "Black" Movies Draws both Condemnation and Praise', *Ebony*, December 1972, 60–9.

36 T. Green, 'The Black Man as Movie Hero: New Films Offer a Different Male Image', *Ebony*, August 1972, 145.

37 Cited in R. Keser, 'The Greatest Film About Race Ever Filmed in Hollywood: Richard Fleischer's *Mandingo*', *Bright Lights Film Journal* (30 July 2014). Available online: http://brightlightsfilm.com/greatestfilmraceeverfilmedhollyw oodrichardfleischersmandingo (accessed 28 June 2015).

38 See A. DeVos, '"Expect the Truth": Exploiting History with *Mandingo*', *American Studies* 52 (2) (2013): 127–33.

39 I. Peters, 'What's Happening: "Mandingo" ... Sick, Brutal!' *Baltimore Afro-American*, 31 May 1975.

40 Letter from reader Gloria A. Nicholson (Richmond, VA) to Ida Peters, 'What's Happening: A Reader's View... of "Mandingo"', *Baltimore Afro-American*, 17 June 1975.

41 Guerrero, *Framing Blackness*, 33.

42 In H. L. Gates, 'An Unfathomable Place: A Conversation with Quentin Tarantino about *Django Unchained* (2012)', *Transition* 112 (2013): 54.

43 Ibid., 61.

44 For more on the idea of the 'white saviour', see H. Vera and A. M. Gordon, *Screen Saviors: Hollywood Fictions of Whiteness* (New York: Roman and Littlefield, 2003).

45 'Why "Roots" Hit Home', *Time*, 14 February 1977.

46 L. Fishbein, '*Roots*: Docudrama and the Interpretation of History', in *Why Docudrama? Fact-Fiction on Film and TV*, ed. A. Rosenthal (Carbondale, IL: Southern Illinois University Press, 1999), 271–95.

47 R. Schickel, 'Television: Viewpoint: Middlebrow Mandingo', *Time*, 24 January 1977.

48 'Why "Roots" Hit Home', *Time*, 14 February 1977.

49 'Even After *Roots*, Whites Don't See Job Bias Against Blacks Today: Poll', *Jet*, 19 May 1977, 29.

50 Cited in Jeffrey, '*Amistad*' (1997), 80.

51 See, for example Foner, 'History Invades the Classroom'; S. Hadden, 'How Accurate is the Film?' *The History Teacher* 31 (3) (1998): 374–79.

52 Foner, 'History Invades the Classroom'.

53 Eckstein argues that the film uses the violence of slavery as catharsis for
     white audiences. See L. Eckstein, 'The Pitfalls of Picturing Atlantic Slavery:
     Steven Spielberg's *Amistad* vs Guy Deslaurier's *The Middle Passage*', *Cultural
     Studies Review* 14 (1) (2008): 72–84. Similarly, Caryl Phillips described
     Amistad as 'a black gay porno flick' due to the 'obscene' way that Spielberg
     'exoticises the black male form'. See C. Phillips, 'Slaves in Spielberg's
     manacles', *The Times*, 28 February 1998. There have been numerous
     scholarly analyses of *Amistad*. See especially Jeffrey, '*Amistad*' (1997); N.
     Zemon Davis, 'Slaves on Screen; "*Amistad*: Controversy about the Film and
     Its Use"', *The History Teacher* 31 (3) (1988b), Special Section: 369–402.

54 Cited in Jeffrey, '*Amistad*' (1997), 87.

55 G. Rosen, '"Amistad" and the Abuse of History', *Commentary* 105 (2)
     (1998): 46–51.

56 F. Rich, 'Journal; Slavery Is Bad', *New York Times*, 6 December 1997.

57 Cited in Jeffrey, '*Amistad*' (1997), 82.

58 G. Horne, 'Glory', *American Historical Review* 95 (4) (1990): 1142.

59 L. Morrow, 'Cinema: Manhood and The Power of GLORY', *Time*, 26
     February 1990. For historians' reviews of *Glory*, see especially I. Berlin,
     'Glory Be', *Radical History Review* 53 (1992): 141–8; P. Finkelman, 'Glory',
     Journal of American History 77 (3) (1990): 1108; Horne, 'Glory'.

60 Ibid.

61 Cited in L. B. Randolph, 'Oprah and Danny Sizzle in Her First Love Scenes
     in the Powerful Film "BELOVED"', *Ebony*, November 1998, 42.

62 For scholarly analyses of *Beloved* see especially E. C. Scott, 'The Horrors of
     Remembrance: The Altered Visual Aesthetic of Horror in Jonathan Demme's
     Beloved', *Genders* 40 (2004). Available online: http://www.iiav.nl/ezines/
     web/GendersPresenting/2005/No41/genders/g40_scott.html (accessed 10
     June 2015); A. J. Wardi, 'Freak Shows, Spectacles, and Carnivals: Reading
     Jonathan Demme's *Beloved*', *African American Review* 39 (4) (2005):
     513–26; Zemon Davis, 'Slaves on Screen'.

63 D. R. Egerton, 'Jefferson in Paris', *American Historical Review* 100 (4)
     (1995): 1203.

64 A. Gordon-Reed, *Thomas Jefferson and Sally Hemings: An American
     Controversy* (Charlottesville: University of Virginia Press, 1997); A.
     Gordon-Reed, *The Hemingses of Monticello* (New York: W. W. Norton,
     2008b); D. Smith and N. Wade, 'DNA Test Finds Evidence of Jefferson Child
     by Slave', *New York Times*, 1 November 1998.

65 *Sally Hemings: An American Love Story* (2000), [DVD] Dir. C. Haid, USA,
     Inspired Studio.

66 See A. Gordon-Reed, 'Did Sally Hemings and Thomas Jefferson Love Each
     Other?' *American Heritage* 58 (5) (2008a). Available online: http://www.
     americanheritage.com/content/didsallyhemingsandthomasjeffersonloveeachother?
     (accessed 18 June 2015). For more discussion of representations of Hemings
     see S. Monteith, 'Sally Hemings in Visual Culture: A Radical Act of the
     Imagination?' *Slavery & Abolition* 29 (2) (2008): 233–46.

67 In H. L. Gates, 'Steve McQueen and Henry Louis Gates Jr. Talk *12 Years a Slave*' (Part 1), *The Root*, 24 December 2013. Available online: http://www.theroot.com/articles/culture/2013/12/_12_years_a_slave_henry_louis_gates_jr_interviews_director_steve_mcqueen.1.html (accessed 21 June 2015).

68 S. Northup, *Twelve Years a Slave: Narrative of Solomon Northup, a Citizen of New-York, Kidnapped in Washington City in 1841 and Rescued in 1853, from a Cotton Plantation near the Red River in Louisiana* (Auburn, NY: Derby and Miller, 1853). Available online: http://docsouth.unc.edu/fpn/northup/northup.html (accessed 28 June 2015).

69 In Gates, 'Steve McQueen' (Part 1).

70 See, for example, '*12 Years a Slave: An ALH Forum*', *American Literary History* 26 (2) (2014): 317–84.

71 In H. L. Gates, 'Steve McQueen and Henry Louis Gates Jr. Talk *12 Years a Slave*' (Part 3), *The Root*, 26 December 2013. Available online: http://www.theroot.com/articles/culture/2013/12/_12_years_a_slave_director_steve_mcqueen_interviewed_by_henry_louis_gates_1.html (accessed 21 June 2015).

72 In N. George, 'An Essentially American Narrative: A Discussion of Steve McQueen's Film "12 Years a Slave"', *New York Times*, 11 October 2013.

73 Gates, 'Steve McQueen' (Part 3).

74 V. Smith, 'Black Life in the Balance: *12 Years a Slave*', *American Literary History* 26 (2) (2014): 365.

75 Ibid., 363.

76 Cited in D. P. Lee, 'Where It Hurts: Steve McQueen on Why *12 Years a Slave* isn't just about Slavery', *Vulture*, 8 December 2013. Available online: http://www.vulture.com/2013/12/stevemcqueentalks12yearsaslave.html (accessed 21 June 2015).

77 Northup, *Twelve Years a Slave*, 118.

78 A. White, 'Can't Trust It', *City Arts: New York's Review of Culture*, 16 October 2013. Available online: http://cityarts.info/2013/10/16/canttrustit/ (accessed 21 June 2015).

79 For a longer comparison of these two films see D. Kellner, 'The Horrors of Slavery and Modes of Representation in *Amistad* and *12 Years a Slave*', *Jump Cut: A Review of Contemporary Media* 56 (2014). Available online: http://ejumpcut.org/currentissue/Kellner12YearsSlave/text.html (accessed 10 June 2015).

80 H. Gerima and P. Woolford, 'Filming Slavery', *Transition* 64 (1994): 101.

81 M. A. Reid, 'Haile Gerima: "Sacred Shield of Culture"', *Contemporary American Independent Film: From the Margins to the Mainstream*, ed. C. Holmlund and J. Wyatt (Athens, GA: University of Georgia Press, 2011), 107.

CHAPTER EIGHT

The Empire at the movies: India in newsreels, c. 1911 to 1947

Tilman Frasch

Newsreels are still a relatively neglected source for the study of history despite their undoubted importance as vehicles of information for cinema audiences during the first half of the twentieth century. The new genre was born in 1909/10, when the Pathé brothers embarked upon filming events from around the country (and soon from around the world) and screened these in special shows, called *Pathé's Animated Gazette*. The first purpose-designed newsreel cinemas opened soon after. Combining the power of the moving image with forceful music (from the cinema organ) and later off-voiced sonorous comments, the newsreels became a crucial source of information-cum-entertainment to the ever-growing cinema audiences, both in dedicated newsreel cinemas and as starters before the main feature film in 'normal' cinemas.[1]

To explore these newsreels and assess their value for historical teaching and research, this chapter will pose a rather simple question: How did they portray India and Indian affairs? In other words, what did average cinemagoers in Britain see and hear about India? India, taken here in a slightly wider sense including Burma (a province of British India until 1937), Ceylon, and other British possessions in the East, has been selected because of the prominent position it occupied in the Empire: often styled the 'brightest jewel in the crown of Britain', one should expect that events taking place in India would receive greater attention than events happening elsewhere. Not last, people such as Gandhi, who made headlines on global scale from the 1920s, should have secured India affairs wide attention.

In looking at the representations and perceptions of the Empire and its parts at home, this chapter feeds into what may simplistically be called the 'Porter-Mackenzie debate'. This debate revolves around the question of whether the British were 'absent-minded imperialists' (Porter) or whether the multiple ways by which the Empire was propagated to society in

Britain resulted in more proactive and conscious forms of participation in and engagement with the Empire (Mackenzie).[2] Newsreels or even films in general did not play a prominent role in that debate, but do provide fresh insights and therefore pose new questions. The debate as such seems to elude an easy answer; it not only requires definitions to be agreed upon,[3] but is also open to a host of aspects that can (and will have to) be studied in relation to the propagation and perception of the Empire by the British public. As perceptions, which are by nature individual and periphrastic, are hard to trace (and even harder to trace for the historian),[4] research has focussed on other mediums of communication – newspapers, telegraphy, radio, picture postcards and, more recently, film.[5] Studies of the latter have shown that newsreels picked up pivotal events, often involving a member of the royal family – in the case of India, the Delhi coronation *durbars* of 1903 and 1911 – and wars.[6] As will be shown, the Second World War became a catalyst for securing India and more precisely the Burma-China-India theatre of operations, a fixed place on British cinema screens.[7] Subsequently, the independence and partition of India continued to receive newsreel coverage, though they tended to emphasize imperial ceremonies while neglecting the human suffering and massacres resulting from partition. This was to a degree due to Mountbatten's handling of the 'transfer of power' and his directing of the camera teams present in India.[8]

This chapter will analyse the portrayal of Indian affairs and events between 1903 and 1947 in three chronologically organized blocks, covering the years before the First World War (i.e. the Delhi *durbars* of 1903 and 1911), the interwar period, and the years from the Second World War through to independence. A brief reflection on the nature of newsreels and their potency for shaping public opinion will introduce these three sections. It should also be emphasized that this survey is preliminary, based primarily on the archive of the Pathé company, and aims to highlight the *potential* of studying such films.

Newsreels and their audiences

According to the standard definition, newsreels are a specialized form of film, consisting of a loose variety of short cuts, sometimes taken from (and also turned into) more purpose-made films. They are normally seen as forming a contrast to both fictional, scripted films and documentaries, but were once a common part of cinematic shows screening a main feature film. They presented visual news that tended to be entertaining and non-controversial.[9] This definition makes clear that, despite their name, newsreels did not necessarily present news, at least not in the modern sense of the word. Newsreels were about curiosities, spectacle and sensation but hardly selected their topics according to political importance. In fact, political information and news was more likely to be omitted intentionally.

It is not possible to distinguish newsreels as 'factual films' from the fictional, scripted ones, by claiming that the former presented a plain, unfiltered and undirected 'reality' (see Chapter 2).[10] It is obvious that filming right from its earliest forms involved the creating, performing and staging of the images to be recorded, even in cases where simple street scenes or other parts of urban life were portrayed. The films produced by Mitchell & Kenyon on the streets of Manchester in the early 1900s attest this amply; they show how people in front of the camera responded to the directives of the cameraman or his aide. A similar blurred boundary exists between the newsreels and documentaries, which became a popular genre after the First World War.[11] Though pretending to document reality at greater length than the newsreels, documentaries possessed a script and often a storyline as well, but more importantly, they also provided the raw material from which the short films to be shown in newsreels could be cut. Moreover, the documentary movement owed much of its production to the fact that two major companies, the Empire Marketing Board and the General Post Office, had put their weight and resources behind it.[12]

With regard to content, newsreels displayed a preference for members of the royal family and representatives of royalty – the contemporary form of gossip before the Second World War – and curiosities such as primitive people, wild animals, and other strange phenomena of the Empire and the world beyond.[13] Sports, entertainment and other events compatible to filming made up another part of the coverage. The coincidence of the new medium of film with the occurrence of a major imperial war, the Boer War, around the turn of the century determined the third thematic focus of the newsreels. This link was further strengthened in the First and Second World Wars when newsreels (and not to forget the new genre: the war film – see also Chapters 1 and 11) became major propaganda instruments on all sides.[14] General political news in contrast played only a minor role, the more so if they concerned places as far afield as India or China; and above all tight censorship imposed upon the film companies further limited the amount and contents of topics put on display, as news and pictures deemed politically sensitive would have been swiftly banned.[15]

However, the interwar period also witnessed a degree of thematic expansion by way of documentaries. Often educational in nature, documentaries attempted ethnographic, geographic and economic portraits of the world to the cinema audiences at home. Although often scripted and with a storyline at their core, they retained an aura of truthfulness by claiming to present the world 'as it is'. This made them perfect instruments in the hands of the companies which produced them to drive home certain messages – 'buy Empire products', 'drink more tea' and 'come to know the country by using the railways'.

The screening of newsreels coincided with the rise of the cinema as the most popular place of entertainment for British society, which eventually replaced the music halls and theatres. From 1905, when the first purpose-built movie houses opened, to the 1930s, cinemas not only grew massively in numbers – there were some 4,500 of them – but also in size, with the largest theatres seating more than 1,000 visitors.[16] Audiences increased accordingly. No serious figures are available until the mid-1930s, but credible estimates suggest that the number of tickets sold every week rose from around 7 million in 1914 to somewhere around 17 million in the early 1930s.[17] The seminal survey conducted by Simon Rowson in 1934 put the numbers of cinema audiences on safer footing for the first time. He showed that ticket sales averaged 18.5 million that year, which meant that every Briton above the age of fifteen went to the movies approximately once every two weeks.[18] There were regional variations, too, which e.g. highlight a strong link between the working classes in the Northwest and cinema-going. A separate survey for Liverpool revealed that 40 per cent of its population went to the movies twice per week.[19] The number of cinema-goers continued to grow until 1940, when attendance figures peaked at more than 20 million per week, even though cinemas had begun to close down by then due to damage done by the Blitz or lack of operators who had joined the army.

Of course, attendance does not necessarily leave a spectator with lasting impressions, even when exposed to a medium which combines vision and sound (by the end of the 1920s, talkies had conquered the cinema screens) in a uniquely effective way. It is clear, however, that spectators do not consciously perceive and actively remember the 'spectacle of actuality', the scenes and stories put before them. This effect results either from multiple exposures to the same scene – that is, they had to watch a newsreels three times or more – or through an existing, personal link to it, which may be momentary. In other words, the film watched has to remind the spectator of something or send a message that is meaningful to their current life (see also Chapter 3).[20] It is obvious that such a message and its meaning to an individual cannot be examined by a historian, who is interested in how, for example, news relating to India was understood as 'imperial propaganda'. What can be examined are the figures for the frequency of cinema-going – less than once a week, as calculated above. This rhythm has to be set against the frequency by which fresh newsreels went on show, which was once to twice per week. This means that an average British cinema-goer would usually see a piece of news, no matter whether concerning Britain, India or any other part of the Empire, only once or exceptionally twice. This was hardly often enough for a piece of news to become recognized or remembered, let alone enough to produce a lasting impression.

However, before the possibility of a piece of news from India making an impact upon a British cinema audience can be ruled out, another aspect has to be taken into account. Mass observations in cinemas conducted during the 1940s have shown that audiences did in fact watch the films and newsreels put before them consciously and to a degree critically.[21] Cinema-goers thus complained that a feature film contained too much propaganda

– 'there's enough of it in the newsreels',[22] while the overall survey suggested that even such 'bad' feature films never received the level of dislike newsreels did.[23] These and similar such remarks suggest that audiences were well aware of the topics and ideologies brought before them, even if they had only a single opportunity to watch them.

Film and the *durbars*

India's life in the newsreels began with the *durbar*, which Viceroy Lord Curzon staged at Delhi in 1903 to celebrate the accession of King-Emperor Edward VII. Staging an imperial assemblage, on which the Indian princes could honour the new Emperor, was not an innovation, as the site at Delhi and the proceedings had already been determined by Lord Lytton, who celebrated Queen Victoria's official assumption of the Crown of India in 1877 with great pomp and circumstance.[24] However, Curzon did everything he could to display the power, splendour and progressiveness of the *raj*. His vehicles were the latest symbols of modernity: electric lights and electrically driven fans in the tents, telephones and toilets, a tramway and, for more distinguished guests, motor cars to take the visitors from the city to the *durbar* site, and film teams to put the proceedings on record. British film pioneer Robert W. Paul and the Gaumont Film Company were among those to whom the latter task had been entrusted. In 1903, filming was still a delicate technology, the more so under tropical conditions, so only a short reel of less than two minutes survived. It shows a host of troops on parade, various maharajas on elephants, and of course the arrival of the Viceroy, who took the place of the absent King-Emperor.[25]

It is not known how the films from the 1903 Delhi *durbar* were received back in Britain, but bearing all the hallmarks that normally appealed to cinema audiences – featuring a member of the royal family, exotic animals, oriental pomp and spectacle – they will almost certainly have become an instant success. This can be seen more clearly from the fact that the procedures of the subsequent coronation *durbar* of King George V in 1911 were completely recorded in film. On this occasion, the King-Emperor was present in person, and consequently the procedures of the *durbar* became even more lavish, magnificent and elaborate. Some 60,000 spectators from around the world watched a ceremony involving almost 150,000 participants (besides the royal couple, virtually all Indian princes and about 55,000 troops), which lasted from 10 a.m. to 5 p.m.[26] No less than eight film companies were handed the opportunity to record the proceedings.[27] The newsreels were speedily developed to be rushed to the cinemas in Europe and elsewhere. The royal couple attended a show at Calcutta shortly before their departure from India in January 1912,[28] just before the first newsreels from the *durbar* were shown in Britain and the United States.[29] The short

FIGURE 8.1 *King George V and Queen Mary in India, 1911*

interval between the event and its screening represented the quickest means of transfer at a time when a journey from India to Britain on a steamboat would still take at least three weeks.

Except for the sheer scale of the ceremony, the 1911 *durbar* hardly outshone its 1903 predecessor. Its only innovative element of displaying cutting-edge technology was coloured film. This was the recently patented invention of Charles Urban, an American entrepreneur, who had set up a film company in London. Urban successfully used coloured filters for both the camera and the projector to produce 'natural' colours; a technique he trademarked as 'Kinemacolor'.[30] In India, Urban and his team recorded not only the ceremonies of day but also followed the royal couple on their tour through India. Their efforts produced hours of film, which went onscreen in spectacular fashion from February 1912. *With our King and Queen through India* (1912) was screened at London's *Scala* cinema, which had been fitted out in the style of the Taj Mahal, and the shows (which lasted 2.5 hours in average) were accompanied by a forty-eight-piece orchestra, twenty-four singers and an electrical lightshow.[31] The final triumph came when the royal family attended a show in May 1912,[32] but even without the royal blessing, the shows became a spectacular success and earned Urban a small fortune.[33] What caught the imagination of the audience, apart from being presented in colour and showcasing a perfect blend of celebrities (the royal family) and the exotic, was one scene which had by then already made headlines in press. The maharaja (or 'Gaekwar') of Baroda, one of the leading native rulers of India, had dared to break with the protocol, variably described as only nodding the Emperor when formally paying obeisance, swinging his walking stick and even turning his back to the King when leaving the elevated canopy which served as a throne hall. The news of the alleged insolence had been spread by observers present on the occasion and picked up by British newspapers, and cinemagoers were eager to respond to the scene with hissing.[34]

The interwar period

The First World War not only provided the defining topic for the newsreel companies (besides Pathé, Gaumont had entered the market just before war), the war also stopped the production of films in faraway places almost completely, as necessary materials were rationed and maritime transport connections became restricted. Above all, tightening censorship turned the companies into crucial allies of the state at its home front. The end of the war brought further changes. First of all, further competitors appeared on the scene: by 1922, five companies – besides Pathé and Gaumont, these were Paramount, Movietone and Universal – sought to bring their films before the audiences.[35] Secondly, American influence in the market grew considerably, as three of these companies were American-owned and moreover American investors had acquired a substantial share in Pathé.[36] However, the companies soon found it more practical and economic to pool their resources and share the films they were producing. What looked like a competition between five companies was in fact a joint business, particularly when it came to filming in places outside Europe and the US.[37]

Coverage of Indian and Far Eastern affairs remained therefore limited even though one of the companies, Pathé, claimed worldwide presence including a 'Far Eastern Office'.[38] More commonly, a company would send a film team to the East, often to accompany a member of the royal family or some other celebrity on an official tour. The topical mix from the pre-war days, consisting of royalty/celebrity news and the curiosities of the Orient including primitive people and exotic animals, remained mostly unaltered, as a cursory survey of the Pathé archive shows. The Duke of Connaught's (Prince Arthur) visit to India in January–February 1921 provided an opportunity to send a film team along, which covered the Duke's activities in a lengthy documentary, but also threw an eye on Indian people, life and religion.[39] Interestingly, political news in the narrow sense were rarely touched upon, even though they constituted the actual reason for the tour of the Duke. In 1920, a major constitutional reform, the Montagu-Chelmsford reform, had been introduced in India, which enfranchised a slightly larger part of the Indian population and enabled Indians to take executive responsibilities in the provincial governments under the 'dyarchy' scheme. The opening of the Legislative Assemblies and Chamber of Princes at Calcutta and Delhi on behalf of the King-Emperor were the central duties of the Duke and occupied most of his time,[40] but were hardly recorded on film save for very brief references in connection with the Duke's opening of the Chamber of Princes and the Bombay Legislative Councils.[41]

The same year, 1921, witnessed another royal tour through India, this time by the Prince of Wales (the future King Edward VIII). It received even more coverage, as the accompanying film team produced a full bi-colour documentary entitled *Through India and Burma with H.R.H. The Prince of Wales* (1922) that was shown in cinemas across Britain during 1922. The Cinechrome company had been experimenting with colour films for about a decade, but despite the promotion gained through the royal tour the company seems to have abandoned the film business a few years later.[42]

For the rest of the 1920s, the already mentioned focus of the newsreel films continued to rest on the curious and exotic side of India on the one hand and the personalities of British India. The former include reports of festivals at Benares (1924 and 1926), a Hindu festival at Hardwar (1927) and a portrait of Indian temples (1929), while the latter chronicle events such as the arrival of the new Viceroy, Lord Irwin (1926) and his wife (undated, probably the same year), his trip to Lahore (1926) or the inauguration of the new governor of Bombay.[43] The Viceroy's visit to Burma provided an opportunity for filming there. Pictures produced include a day at the Rangoon races, *Burma's Ascot* (1924), the funeral of a monk and very likely general scenes from life in Rangoon and Burma, *Life in Rangoon* (undated), as well. This rather narrow thematic focus was rarely abandoned, notably when modern achievements required it, for instance the opening of the Imperial Airways services to India (1923) or the commencement of a daily flight connection between London and Delhi in 1927.[44]

Political news from India was mostly suppressed save for a cursory mention of Gandhi addressing a rally of the Indian National Congress in 1922. Having been sentenced to imprisonment in the aftermath of his first campaign and again in 1929–31, Gandhi was seen as a criminal and a corrupter of the masses, who had to be kept away from the cinema audiences in Britain, let alone in India.[45] However, Gandhi's moment on the screen came in 1931 in the context of another constitutional reform to be introduced in India. In 1929, the Simon Commission toured India to assess whether a larger part of the Indian people, especially those living in rural areas, could be enfranchised. The work of the commission and the response of the INC, which demanded *purna swaraj* or 'full independence', was duly reported in a rather long newsreel, aptly entitled *India Today – the Empire's Greatest Problem* (1929). To emphasize the INC's demand, Gandhi staged his second campaign of 'civil disobedience', which began in 1930 with the famous twenty-four-day Salt March. As Gandhi became the champion of the Indian peasants, who began to feel the impact of the Great Depression, Viceroy Lord Irwin, fearing their rebelliousness, persuaded Gandhi to travel to London and participate in the upcoming second meetings of the Round Table Conference. This official recognition by the Viceroy and Gandhi's subsequent journey to England made it impossible to keep him out of the news any longer. A set of newsreels from 1931 show Gandhi's Salt March, his arrival in London and even his subsequent conflict with B. R. Ambedkar

FIGURE 8.2 *Gandhi in London, 1931*

over the question of whether India's Untouchables should be given the right to vote as separate electorates.[46]

After this brief interlude, the coverage of India in the newsreels returned to the usual mixture of important people, oriental splendour, curiosities and sports (for instance a cricket match between an English and an Indian side in 1936). Technological advances such as the opening of an international telephone connection between London and Delhi, *Hello India* (1933), were still deemed important news, but the bulk of the reports were about a maharaja's wedding party (Mysore 1935; Patandi 1939) or diamond jubilee (Kapurthala 1938), the Viceroy at the Calcutta Races and the like. Possibly, the new transport link to India by plane made it easier to send a film team over without a member of the royal family determining the time and route.[47] Gaumont, for instance, produced two series of films named the *Secrets of India* (1934) and *Indian Town Studies* (1937), which were essentially documentary in nature but could also be used for news coverage.[48]

The elimination of politically sensitive information at this time becomes even more obvious when one looks at wider Asia. In 1931, Japan invaded and annexed Manchuria, in what was to form a prelude for the Second World War in Asia. This event, however, found hardly any mention in newsreels, as the American-made panoramic Pathé reel entitled *World Troubles 1914–1934* (1934) illustrates. It throws brief spotlights on both Gandhi and Manchuria, to conclude (with much pro-American bias) that in this world of madness and chaos only the US stood firm and properly armed.[49]

The war, partition and independence

This situation changed completely with the outbreak of war in 1939 and its possible spread to the East. As Lant has observed, companies producing newsreels and documentaries benefitted from the war as their pictures became critical vehicles of propaganda for the home front.[50] The war necessitated a shift in the official perception of India, which supplied troops, money, raw materials and manufacture for Britain's war effort, besides providing a training ground and deployment zone for the re-conquest of the lost territories of Burma, Malaya and Singapore. Any attempt to communicate to the cinema audiences in Britain that the war could be won required an appreciation of the sacrifices and contributions made by people in the colonies. Initially, this was no easy task as the Asian theatres of war produced only news of defeat and retreat. Rather than boosting morale at home, newsreels reporting Asian affairs were disheartening.[51] Only India seemed to be capable of producing positive headlines, serving as a bulwark against the Japanese tide, sheltering refugees from Burma, reorganizing the remnants of an army originally meant to defend the Empire, supplying China through its eastern airfields, and not least providing the recruits for what would become the world's largest volunteer army.[52] Filming these events was at first restricted to India – though some cameramen seem to have stayed in Burma up to its fall, as will be shown below – but when the Allied forces opened the China-Burma-India (CBI) theater of operations, several film teams followed their trail. Lord Mountbatten, Supreme Commander of that theatre, in particular was eager to give the cameramen access to the action on the battlefields. One street through his headquarters at Peradeniya (Ceylon) was dubbed 'Hollywood Lane' for all the film teams, which had their offices there.[53]

As the newsreels produced in and about India and those subsequently in the course of the Burma campaign have been examined already in detail and under various aspects, this need not be repeated here.[54] But what should not be overlooked is that a good survey of war correspondents, photographers and cameramen especially for the Second World War theatres in the East is still wanting.[55] A few prominent examples such as John Hersey, Darrell Berrigan or Harold Guard notwithstanding, who are known for their publications during and after the war,[56] these reporters often remain hidden behind their pictures. Filming war action from close to the frontline is more usually associated with wars from the second half of the twentieth century, notably the Vietnam War. But it had already happened in Burma: when George Rodger, photographer for the American *Life Magazine*, flew into Rangoon in January 1942, he met there two cameramen, Alec Tozer from Movietone News and Maurice Ford from Paramount.[57] Ford produced a number of newsreels from Burma including one shot from air, when he accompanied a small RAF squadron on a reconnaissance flight to

Martaban in Lower Burma, and one recording Chiang-Kai-shek's visit to Burma.[58] Tozer and Rodger together went on a trip along the Burma Road to the Chinese border and back to Rangoon,[59] and all three presumably left for India before the Japanese finally conquered Burma.

The relative safety of India and Ceylon, where the reorganization and training of the Allied Forces were planned and realized, gave film companies an opportunity to send their own film teams there. These film teams then followed troops into the battlefields of the CBI. Their work was much facilitated through Lord Mountbatten, the Supreme Commander of the Allied Forces in Southeast Asia, who had invited film companies to set up offices at his headquarters in Peradeniya (Ceylon) and often provided transportation for the film teams. Portraits of and references to Mountbatten were accordingly plentiful in these films.[60] The role of propaganda being undisputed – and the CBI now finally providing positive news for the audiences back in Britain – the Indian government felt obliged to contribute to this aspect of the war through sponsoring another newsreel company, Indian News Parade, which supplied mainly the home market.[61]

In view of the wide coverage given to warfare in the CBI, the victory parades and even the trials of Japanese officers accused of crimes against humanity, interest in Indian affairs seems to have shrunk considerably after the war, despite the crucial developments taking place there. The focus was back on Britain and Europe, while the preparations for the transfer of power in India only appeared when they involved British politics and decision-making, with Mountbatten once again taking centre-stage after becoming Viceroy of India.[62] This was as much a return to the former imperial reporting of the interwar period as it satisfied Mountbatten's lust for publicity. The lack of coverage of general affairs becomes most apparent in respect of the partition of India and the amount of population movements and violence it triggered. In relation to the scope of the event – partition caused some 12–15 million refugees and more than one million casualties – an amazingly small number of newsreels were produced. This might seem to lend support to the theory that the unfolding of events caught the outgoing British and incoming Indian/Pakistani governments alike by surprise.

It is however also clear that not only were there a mere three film companies working in India when the tragedy unfolded, the film teams based at Delhi also found it difficult to get through to the hotspots of communal violence in the worst affected Punjab province.[63] After all, a near-to complete collapse of public order put the lives of the cameramen at risk, too. Much of the available film material was therefore filmed on the outskirts of Delhi, and very little of it recorded the clashes and massacres that marked the partition during the weeks from mid-August 1947.[64]

Concluding reflections

This chapter has explored how India (plus a few other parts of the British Empire in Asia) was presented to the British public by way of newsreels screened in cinemas. Newsreels were potentially influential sources of information and opinion-making as they combined the power of the image (and later sound) with an extremely wide outreach – even the smallest of the newsreel companies had a larger audience than Britain's biggest daily newspaper, the *Daily Mail*. Like all films, newsreels were subject to strict censorship that would prevent the display of any kind of news deemed politically sensitive. The coverage of India in these newsreels was therefore limited to 'people news', usually related to members of the royal family or Viceroys, and portrayals of the 'exotic' – maharajas (and other strange people) and their splendour, religious festivals and natural beauty. This came to its height at the Delhi *durbar* of 1911, which headlined the newsreels in British cinemas from January 1912 and became a major cinematic event in the subsequent months.

Even a figure as prominent as Gandhi remained outside the news, though his case was special insofar as he had been discretely embargoed due to his conviction for sedition. The sole 'Gandhi moment' of the newsreels came in 1931 when he toured Britain after being rehabilitated (half-heartedly, but nevertheless) by the Viceroy, so his absence from the news could neither be hidden nor justified. The screening of Gandhi's political activism, however, remained an episode, and not only did he disappear from the scene again, but also the portrayal of India returned to its scope of the 1920s, with its focus on maharajas, vice regal tours, sports and nature. The coverage did not change until the outbreak of the Second World War in the East, which turned India into a powerhouse of Allied war production and recruitment and thus pushed it into the limelight of propaganda on the home front. The re-conquest of the territories lost to Japan in 1941–2 was closely observed and recorded by several newsreel companies, with the Supreme Commander of the Allied Forces in the Southeast Asian theatre, Lord Mountbatten, supporting their work as far as possible.

While the changing image of India on British cinema screens can be examined rather easily and concisely (though again, this survey is by no means comprehensive), the further question of how effective newsreels were in impressing people and shaping their perception of India is less conclusive. The outreach of newsreels was undoubtedly very wide, as cinema-going became the preferred pastime of the interwar period and audiences grew consistently. At the end of the 1930s, newsreels reached on average a much larger audience than any national newspaper. The conclusion that cinema-goers would therefore be more conscious of affairs concerning India or the Empire more generally will however have to be set against the 'default function' of the human brain, which tends to ignore those bits of information that are irrelevant for a person's current life and condition. Alternatively, such pieces of information may be admitted to the memory if people are exposed to them repeatedly. Even if growing attendance rates and regional variations are factored in, the exposure of cinema audiences to news from and about India (or again, the Empire more generally) may have been too infrequent to provide for a memory effect. This will have to be set against the results stemming from the mass observation of cinema audiences in the 1930s, which revealed that they were actively engaging with the news put before them – a phenomenon also seen in their responses to the Gaekwar incident on the Delhi *durbar*. On the other hand, their often wholesale rejection of the propagandistic content of newsreels indicates that audiences may have paid little interest to the newsreels put before them.

These findings add an – albeit small – piece of evidence to the debate about the presentation and perception of the Empire in British society. As mentioned above, Mackenzie, the leading advocate of a highly propagated Empire has referred to films, though in a rather vague manner, and has not mentioned newsreels at all. If nothing else, this may indicate the author's uneasiness with the way cinema screenings of films and newsreels fit into his argument. The opposite voice, Porter, did not refer to films at all, though paradoxically they might have substantiated his standpoint better than that of Mackenzie, if one accepts that audiences in 1930s Britain had much too little exposure to affairs of even such a crucial part of the Empire as India, and that they may not have paid too much attention to the newsreels for their alleged propagandistic tweaking of reality. This hypothesis, however, requires further investigation to move beyond a single case study (India) and medium (newsreels). It will be required to examine films more broadly and compare the evidence from films to that of other media, notably newspapers.

Notes

1   The following articles and overviews have been seminal for the writing of the paper: R. Low, *History of the British Cinema*, vols 5/6 (London: Routledge, 1971); S. L. Althaus, 'The Forgotten Role of the Global Newsreel Industry in the Long Transition from Text to Television', *The International Journal of Press/Politics* 15 (2) (2010): 193–218; *'The Story of the Century': An International Newsfilm Conference* (London: National Film Theatre, 1996); N. Pronay, 'The Newsreels: The Illusion of Actuality' in *The Historian and Film*, ed. P. Smith (Cambridge University Press, 1976), 95–120; L. McKernan (ed.), *Yesterday's News: British Cinema Newsreel Reader* (London: BUFVC, 2002b); J. Hammerton, 'The Spice of the Perfect Programme. The Weekly Magazine Film during the Silent Era', in *Young and Innocent? The Cinema in Britain, 1896–1930*, ed. Andrew Higson (Exeter: University Press, 2002), 162–78.

2   J. Mackenzie, *Propaganda and Empire: The Manipulation of Public Opinion, 1880–1960* (Manchester: University Press, 1984); B. Porter, *The Absent-minded Imperialists. Empire, Society and Culture in Britain* (Oxford: Oxford University Press, 2004). An investigation of how the Empire has been presented to and perceived by British society – including its media, channels and addressees – has of course wider implications which cannot be adequately tackled in an article. Besides the two works mentioned above, see e.g. C. Hall, *Cultures of Empire. A Reader* (Manchester: Manchester University Press, 2000) and numerous other volumes in MUP's 'Studies in Imperialism' series; F. Cooper and A. L. Stoler, *Tensions of Empire: Colonial Cultures in a Bourgeois World* (Berkeley: University of California Press, 1997); and now A. Thompson, *Britain's Experience of Empire in the Twentieth Century* (Oxford: Oxford University Press, 2011).

3   Both Porter's category of 'participation' and Mackenzie's term 'propaganda' have quantitative and qualitative properties, which are not easily distilled from the sources.

4   An exception is James Burns, who explores how cinema-going shaped debates about the Empire and imperial identities both at home and in the colonies. The focus of his work is however on colonial people, and newsreels occur only occasionally. J. Burns, *Cinema and Society in the British Empire, 1895–1940* (New York: Palgrave Macmillan, 2013).

5   See e.g. C. Kaul, *Reporting the Raj: The British Press and India, c. 1888–1922* (Manchester: Manchester University Press, 2003), and C. Kaul, *Communications, Media and the Imperial Experience. Britain and India in the Twentieth Century* (London: Palgrave Macmillan, 2014); E. Milne, *Letters, Postcards, Email. Technologies of Presence* (London: Routledge, 2010), esp. Ch. 2 'The Postcard', 93–135.

6   For the topics of the newsreels, see Mackenzie, *Propaganda*, 71–2. For the *durbars*, see S. Bottomore, '"An Amazing Quarter Mile of Moving Gold, Gems and Genealogy": Filming India's 1902/03 Delhi Durbar', *Historical Journal of Film, Radio and Television* 15 (4) (1995): 495–515; Bottomore, '"Have You Seen the Gaekwar, Bob?": Filming the 1911 Delhi Durbar', *Historical Journal of Film, Radio and Television* 17 (3) (1997): 309–45. L. McKernan, '"The Modern Elixir of Life": Kinemacolor, Royalty and the Delhi Durbar', *Film History: An International Journal* 21 (2) (2009): 122–36.

7   I. Jarvie, 'The Burma Campaign on Film', *Historical Journal of Film, Radio and Television* 8 (1) (1988): 55–73; P. Woods, 'Filming the Retreat from Burma, 1942: British Newsreel Coverage', *Historical Journal of Film, Radio and Television* 35 (3) (2015): 438–53. S. Higashi, 'Melodrama, Realism, and Race: WW2 Newsreels and Propaganda Films', *Cinema Journal* 37 (3) (1998): 38–61.

8   P. Woods, '"Business as Usual"?: British Newsreel Coverage of Indian Independence and Partition, 1947–1948', in *Media and the British Empire*, ed. C. Kaul (London: Palgrave Macmillan, 2006), 145–59; C. Kaul, *Indian Independence, the British Media and Lord Mountbatten* (Delhi: IIC Occasional Paper no. 26 [2011]), 12–13.

9   B. McFarlane and A. Slide, *Encyclopedia of British Film*, 3rd edn
     (Manchester: Manchester University Press, 2013), s.v. 'Newsreels' (511).

10   This has already been pointed out by Pronay in his initial analysis of the
     relationship between films and history, 'The Moving Picture and Historical
     Research: The State of the Art', *Journal of Contemporary History* 18 (3)
     (1983): 365–9, here 369. Also see P. Taylor, 'Introduction', in *Britain and the
     Cinema in the Second World War*, ed. S. Taylor (Basingstoke: Macmillan,
     1988), 5, who specified that there is no intrinsic difference between 'factual'
     and 'fiction' film as far as they represent mass communication.

11   R. Low, *History of British Film*, vol. 4 (London: Routledge, 1971), 285;
     P. Swann, *The British Documentary Film Movement* (Cambridge: Cambridge
     University Press, 1989); I. Aitken, *Film and Reform. John Grierson and the
     Documentary Film Movement* (London: Routledge, 2013)

12   It should not be forgotten here that a similar structure of companies
     sponsoring film units to advertise their products was found in India and
     Ceylon, see N. Majumdar, 'Film Fragments, Documentary History, and
     Colonial Indian Cinema', *Canadian Journal of Film Studies* 16 (1) (2007):
     63–79 (on films produced by the Indian Railways), and the Ceylon Tea
     Board, which had the EMB produce *The Song of Ceylon* (1934): available
     online: http://www.colonialfilm.org.uk/node/486 (accessed 4 May 2016).

13   See Mackenzie, *Propaganda*, 71–2.

14   For the Boer War see Low, *History of British Cinema*, vol. 5, 47. For later
     wars, see e.g. R. Manvell, *Films and the Second World War* (London:
     Dent, 1974); S. Taylor, *Britain and the Cinema in the Second World War*
     (Basingstoke: Macmillan, 1988). For India, see now S. Bhattacharya,
     *Propaganda and Information in Eastern India, 1939–45: A Necessary
     Weapon of War* (London: Routledge, 2001), and for Japan D. Desser, 'From
     the Opium War to the Pacific War: Japanese propaganda films of WW2',
     Film History 7 (1995): 32–48.

15   Low, *History of British Cinema*, vol. 6, 17.

16   Low, *History of British Cinema*, vol. 5, 47, and S. Rowson, 'A Statistical
     Survey of the Cinema Industry in Great Britain in 1934', *Journal of the
     Royal Statistical Society* 99 (2) (1936): 76.

17   N. Pronay, 'British Newsreels in the 1930s, pt. 1: Audience and Producers',
     History 56 (3) (1971): 412–13; Low, *History of British Film*, vol. 4, 47.

18   Rowson, 'Statistical Survey', 70. Also see N. Hiley, 'Audiences in the
     Newsreel Period', in *'The Story of the Century': An International Newsfilm
     Conference* (London: BUFVC, 1996), 60.

19   S. Jones, *The British Labour Movement and Film* (London: Routledge and
     Kegan Paul, 1987), 7; and Pronay, 'British Newsreels in the 1930s' 413–14.

20   L. Anderson, 'The Porous Boundaries of Newsreel Memory Research',
     in *Cathedrals of the Movies: A History of British Cinemas and Their
     Audiences*, ed. D. Atwell (London: Architectural Press, 1980), 71–86.

21   T. Harrisson, 'Films and the Home Front. The Evaluation of their
     Effectiveness by Mass-observation', in *Propaganda, Politics and Film*,

1918–1945, ed. N. Pronay and D. W. Spring (London: Macmillan, 1982), 234–45.

22   Ibid., 237.

23   Ibid., 241.

24   A. Trevithick, 'Some Structural and Sequential Aspects of the British Imperial Assemblages at Delhi, 1877–1911', *Modern Asian Studies* (1990): 561–78.

25   Four of Paul's films survive, which are available online: https://www.youtube.com/watch?v=oKF_lie2Wc8 (accessed 31 March 2016). The first part, filmed from ground level, is also available online: http://www.colonialfilm.org.uk/node/1956 (accessed 31 March 2016).

26   See R. E. Frykenberg, 'The Coronation Durbar of 1911: Some Implications' in *Delhi through the Ages: Selected Essays in Urban History, Culture and Society*, ed. R. E. Frykenberg (Delhi: Open University Press, 1993), 369–90. The manual containing the list of official guests ran up to more than 200 pages: *Coronation Durbar, Delhi 1911. Official Directory with Maps* (Calcutta: Government Printing, 1911).

27   Bottomore, 'Have you seen the Geakwar', Bob, 312–16.

28   McKernan, 'Modern Elixir of Life', 130.

29   Ibid.; *New York Times*, 23 February 1912, 7, and ibid., 17 March 1912, 5 (Urban's visit to New York).

30   L. McKernan, 'Putting the World before You: The Charles Urban Story', in A. Higson (ed.), *Young and Innocent? The Cinema in Britain, 1896–1930* (Exeter: University Press, 2002a), 65–76. McKernan's research on Urban is now available as a monograph (*Charles Urban. Pioneering the Non-fiction Film in Britain and America, 1897–1925* [Exeter: Exeter University Press, 2014]).

31   McKernan, 'Putting the World before You', 73. A breakdown of the film's contents, curated by Luke McKernan is available online: http://www.charlesurban.com/documents_durbar.html (accessed 31 March 2016).

32   *Observer*, 12 May 1912, 9.

33   McKernan, 'Putting the world before you', 73. The splendour of the *durbar* and the success of the cinema shows seems to have inspired further *durbar*-themed performances: In January 1912, Oswald Stoll, owner of the Coliseum theatre, contracted Edward Elgar to compose a musical play (or 'masque') entitled 'The Crown of India'. First rehearsals began in late February, and the show ran between 11 March and the end of April – parallel to Urban's film screenings. See N. Ghuman, *Resonances of the Raj. India and the English Musical Imagination, 1897–1947* (Oxford: Oxford University Press, 2014), Ch. 2, 53–104.

34   Bottomore, 'Have you seen the Gaekwar, Bob?', 334–5. As Bottomore has pointed out, there were several similarly clad Indian princes behaving unusually, and it is neither clear who did what nor which of their actions constituted the *lèse-majesté*.

35   Low, *History of British Film*, vol. 6, 13; Pronay, 'Illusion of Actuality', 112.

36   Ibid. Elsewhere, Pronay has drawn attention to the fact that, when the war

broke out in 1939, the British government were dependent on American goodwill in producing propaganda films: N. Pronay, 'The Newsmedia at War' in *Propaganda, Politics and Film,* ed. N. Pronay and D. W. Spring (London: Macmillan, 1982), 186.

37   Low, *History of British Film,* vol. 6, 13, 17.

38   I haven't been able to establish where this office was located, with Hong Kong or Shanghai being probable places.

39   Newsreels such as *The Duke of Connaught in India* and *The Duke of Connaught Hunting* were all part of the film *With the Duke of Connaught in India* (1921). Other episodes were screened under titles such as *An Indian Carnival* and the *Maharaja of Jhalawar.* These and all the other films referred to here (unless otherwise stated) are available online: www. britishpathe.com (accessed 31 March 2016).

40   See *His Royal Highness The Duke of Connaught in India 1921. Being a collection of the speeches delivered by His Royal Highness* (Calcutta: Superintendent Government Printing, 1921).

41   Available online: http://www.britishpathe.com/video/with-the-duke-of-connaught-in-india-reel-1 (Bombay LC), and http://www.britishpathe.com/video/with-the-duke-of-connaught-in-india-reel-2 (Chamber of Princes) (both accessed 31 March 2016). Also see Mackenzie, *Propaganda,* 82.

42   There is little information on this company even in the BFI's website. For a brief note, see H. Mario Raimondo-Souto, *Motion Picture Photography – A History, 1891–1960* (Jefferson: MacFarlane, 2007), 48.

43   Another short newsreel from 1923, produced by Gaumont, shows the new Governor of Burma (Spencer Harcourt Butler) taking up office. Available online: www.itnsource.com/en~BurmaFootage (accessed 3 February 2016).

44   See also Mackenzie, *Propaganda,* 82.

45   Mackenzie, *Propaganda,* 82, and C. Deprez, 'India', in *The Concise Routledge Encyclopedia of the Documentary Film,* ed. I. Aitken (London: Routledge, 2013), 400.

46   'Gandhi Fast brings new India Crisis'. Available online: http://www.britishpathe.com/video/gandhi-fast-brings-new-india-crisis-aka-ghandi-fas/query/gandhi [*sic*]; (accessed 3 February 2016). The film is dated to 1930, though Gandhi's fast against the Communal Award, which would have given separate electorates to India's Untouchables, was first announced in London in early 1932 and did not start until September 1932. As the film's intermediate slide says, the statement by Frederick Sykes, Governor of Bombay, was recorded during the world cruise of the 'Empress of Britain', which took place between December 1931 and March 1932. The newsreel was therefore compiled in 1932.

47   A film showing the unveiling of a statue of Lord Irwin in 1934 was declared to have been shot 'by our cameraman now travelling the East'.

48   Available online: http://www.colonialfilm.org.uk/node/1774 (accessed 31 March 2016). The main purpose of that series seems to have been to film

Mt. Everest from a plane. The 43-min documentary was screened as *Wings over Everest*.

49 https://www.britishpathe.com/video/world-troubles-1914-1934 (accessed 31 March 2016).

50 A. Lant, 'Britain and the End of the Empire', in *The Oxford History of World Cinema,* ed. G. Novell-Smith (Oxford: Oxford University Press, 1966), 369.

51 Pronay, 'The Illusion of Actuality', 116.

52 J. Voigt, *India in the Second World War* (Delhi: Arnold-Heinemann, 1988), esp. Ch. 2.

53 A. Jackson, *The Colonial Film Archive and the British Empire at War, 1939–1945* (London: Defence Studies Dept., King's College, 2010) [= Research Papers 1].

54 See Jackson, *The Colonial Film Archive*; Jarvie, 'The Burma Campaign on Film'; Woods, 'Filming the Retreat from Burma, 1942'. The 'colonialfilm' website gives 350 and 798 hits respectively for the search terms 'India' and 'Burma'. For the rise of film and newsreels ('March of Time') in US cinemas, see R. Manvell, *Films and the Second World War* (London: Dent, 1974).

55 B. Best, *Reporting the Second World War* (Barnsley: Pen & Sword, 2015), has two brief sections on the events in Asia. While this volume was in the making, the war correspondents working in Burma during 1941/42 have become the subject of a detailed study: Philip Woods, Reporting the Retreat. War Correspondents in Burma (London: Hurst, 2017).

56 J. Hersey, *Hiroshima* (Harmondsworth: Penguin, 1946); H. Guard, *The Pacific War Uncensored* (Havertown: Casemate, 2011). Berrigan stayed on in Southeast Asia after the war and eventually became the editor and publisher of his own magazine, the *Bangkok World*. He was killed in 1952 under uncertain circumstances, his killer never being caught.

57 G. Rodger, *Red Moon Rising* (London: Cresset Press, 1943), 11.

58 The Imperial War Museum has a series of reels from Burma in its collection, all shot in February to April 1942. Available online: http://film. iwmcollections.org.uk (accessed 31 March 2016). I've noted the *RAF Raid of Mataban*, dated April 1942, not only for its misspelling of 'Mataban' (for Martaban) in the title as well as the somewhat boisterous claim of a 'raid' on that city (which was in British hands until mid-February 1942), but also for showing the visit of Chiang Kai-shek to Burma on 5 April of that year. According to Chiang's biographer, he should have been accompanied by Stilwell and the American publisher Henry Luce on that occasion, who are both absent in the film. Probably the reel shows his earlier stop-over at Lashio on 27 February, when only his wife and son were with him. See J. Taylor, *The Generalissimo* (Cambridge: Harvard University Press, 2009), 196, 202.

59 Rodger, *Red Moon Rising*, 60.

60 Jackson, *The Colonial Film Archive*, 16–17, 19. On Mountbatten's attitude towards filming, see also Kaul, *Communications*, Ch. 5, 172–218.

61   P. Sargent, 'Indian News Parade', in *The Story of the Century*, 90; B. D. Garga, *From Raj to Swaraj: The Non-fiction Film in India* (Delhi: Penguin, 2007), 62. Also see S. Roy, 'Moving Pictures: The Post-colonial State and Visual Representations of India' *Contributions to Indian Sociology* 36 (1–2) (2002): 233–63, who perceives a continuation between wartime and post-war film production and screening, which she discusses in context of post-war attempts of nation building.

62   Kaul, *Communications*, Ch. 5; Woods, 'Business as Usual', 148–9.

63   Woods, 'Business as Usual', 147–52. The teams originally consisted of those working for Paramount and Movietone, with a third team, led by John Turner, arriving just days before independence. The local enterprise, Indian News Parade, had its operations temporarily suspended due to the uncertainty of its role and perspective in the partition process.

64   Films produced by Pathe only display the transfer of power and the celebrations. Much of the existing film material has been included in the BBC documentary *The Day India Burned* (2007).

CHAPTER NINE

'Truth' and 'interiority': Screening and interpreting the early modern era

Jonathan Spangler

Filmmakers have had a long love affair with the early modern period (roughly 1500 to 1800), an era full of compelling narratives, dramatic conflicts and opportunities for lavish sets and beautiful costumes. 1930s cinema is remembered for its epic swashbuckler adventures of buccaneers and pirates starring Errol Flynn and Douglas Fairbanks, Jr, while leading ladies of Hollywood made their mark playing famous (or infamous) queens of the age: Katharine Hepburn, Greta Garbo, Bette Davis. The culmination of this pre-war interest is Flynn and Davis together, in *The Private Lives of Elizabeth and Essex* (1939), swashbuckling and romance rolled into one. Films set in the early modern period are enriched by the brilliant colours of the Renaissance, the spiritual drama of the Reformation, the opulence of the Baroque, and the optimism mixed with anxiety and even terror in the age of Revolution.

But are films set in these times more than entertainment? Can they be viewed and analysed as part of a serious study of history? On the one hand, they can be used to convey a sense of the views of the filmmaker and his or her contemporary audience. To use once again the example of *Elizabeth and Essex*, viewers in 1939 were expecting a woman to be 'ruled by her heart, not her head', and were duly pleased when the steely Davis ultimately fell for the charms of Flynn, even though their romance was doomed in the end. Contemporaries retained a somewhat Victorian view of women, and were uncomfortable with the idea of Elizabeth I acting in a manly, authoritative manner. Lytton Strachey's biography of her (1928), the basis for the film, is gratifying in that Elizabeth's firm resolve for duty clashes strongly with her womanly desires for love and romance.[1] Society in the late 1930s was already changing, however, and historical figures could become national champions, reflecting the fears of an impending global conflict and attempts by filmmakers to rally patriotic fervour (Flora Robson plays a heroic Elizabeth in *Fire Over England* [1937]). To examine the trajectory of Elizabeth I in film, we can follow the sequence of: Glenda Jackson's portrayal of the Queen in *Elizabeth R* (BBC 1971) as a burgeoning feminist, a working woman of her times; a silly, flirtatious monarch for a more frivolous decade in Miranda's Richardson's 'Queenie' in *Blackadder II* (BBC2 1985); a postmodernist view of Elizabeth as a drag-queen, all myth and little reality, provided by Quentin Crisp in Sally Potter's *Orlando* (1992); a New Labour 'Great Britons' resurgence portrayal starring Cate Blanchett (1998, 2007); and a revisionist, realistic, more world-weary version of the Queen for the post-9/11 world, in Helen Mirren's portrayal in the television miniseries *Elizabeth I* (HBO/Channel 4 2005; see below).[2] This aspect of the use of historical films in academic study has been analysed thoroughly by experts in cinema history and cultural studies.[3] But it is also possible to examine films set in specific historical periods for other didactic reasons, to study the period itself, rather than just focus on the cultural and political environment in which the film was made. This chapter will offer some useful case studies for accessing the history itself, using films from recent decades that are set in the early modern period.

In addition to helping students, especially those unfamiliar with the period, to see and feel the atmosphere of this period (settings, costumes, furniture, artwork, and sometimes dialogue, music), some films lend themselves well to the study of the early modern period due to their usage of primary source material, from private letters to published speeches, plays and novels. One theme to emerge is the importance of 'interiority' – Queen Elizabeth I is often said to have pronounced that she did not want to 'open windows into men's souls', but by looking at well-made films set in earlier times, we can at least glimpse (or debate) how people from an earlier era felt differently, or the same, from us.

The historiography of the historical film

As Robert Rosenstone pointed out in the 1990s, the debate over what kinds of history should be put onto film is not new.[4] In a later article, Rosenstone warned of the dangers of making history trivialized, romanticized, distorted or even falsified in the name of drama and immediacy of emotional connection (see also Chapter 2).[5] Starting with Sergei Eisenstein in the 1920s–30s, some history films were meant to be deliberately informative, didactic, at least in emotional content if not in fact – most usually cited for Eisenstein is *Battleship Potemkin* (1925), but for earlier periods we could equally cite *Alexander Nevsky* (1938) (thirteenth century) and *Ivan the Terrible* (1944) (sixteenth century). At the other end of the spectrum, removing the emotion from a film entirely in an effort to achieve 'realism' in a historical event, is Roberto Rossellini's *The Taking of Power by Louis XIV* (*Le Prise de Pouvoir de Louis XIV*, 1966), which Rosenstone categorizes as 'historical film as experiment' (in this case history that is 'de-dramatized'), in his tripartite division of historical films (the other two being historical film as drama or as document).[6] This film may be considered by specialists of the period as an accurate portrayal of the coming of age and surprising assumption of full power by the young Louis XIV in 1660, but is mostly devoid of anything that could be described as 'entertainment'. At yet another extreme, we can see experimental films that present the viewer with almost pure emotion to produce shock, such as *The Devils* (1971) by Ken Russell, based on a 1952 book, *The Devils of Loudun* by Aldous Huxley, which fictionalized a real set of events in western France in the 1630s in which a priest was accused of seducing a convent of nuns with the assistance of a satanic pact and demonic possession. The fascinating historical context (the priest was really a victim of political rivalries at the highest levels) is unimportant in Russell's film, merely the expression of the horrors of a period of such intense religious devotion as the early seventeenth century.[7]

In the later 1970s, a new style of historical film making began to emerge, in a sense parallel to the new type of historical scholarship now known as 'revisionism'. These films sought to achieve both historical accuracy and emotionality while also hoping for enough drama to create a hit with audiences. They sought to tell stories of people previously unpresented: fewer kings and queens, more ordinary people, both male and female. The now classic example of this is *The Return of Martin Guerre* (*Le Retour de Martin Guerre*, 1982), directed by Daniel Vigne, which featured a well-known film star, Gérard Depardieu, and a genuine historian as an advisor, Natalie Zemon Davis, then of Princeton University. This film, and the accompanying book by Davis,[8] was based on actual events in the south of the France in the 1560s, much of which could be documented through court records found in archives of several southern French départements. The film transports audiences to a small village in rural France, Artigat, and is visually rich in costume and settings appropriate for peasant life in the sixteenth century – you can practically feel the warmth of the southern sun and smell the pungency of living in the same space as your livestock. The trial scenes are set in the Parlement of Toulouse, conforming as much as possible to historical records to provide an accurate look and feel of early modern judiciary settings. The story itself is a truly riveting tale of identity theft: Martin Guerre, married as a teenager, abandons his wife after a family dispute, returns after eight years to reclaim his wife and child, and his family inheritance, and is gradually revealed not to be Martin Guerre. But the revelation comes only after a lengthy lawsuit, the details of which are provided in a published account by one of the magistrates involved, Jean de Coras.[9] There is much for students to see and learn from in this film and from Zemon Davis's book: rural marriage practices and folk traditions surrounding couples who, for reasons unknown but deemed suspect, were infertile ('Charivari' or 'rough music'); growing tensions between Catholics and Protestants, and between urban and rural societies; and judiciary practices in the pre-modern world (notably the custom of 'Confrontation', between defendant and witnesses, before the latter's statements are known to the former).[10]

The key person in upholding the false Martin's story, is surprisingly (spoiler alert!), his wife, Bertrande de Rols, and this becomes a main feature of the film, and of Davis's book: an attempt to give a voice to a woman in a period which is notably devoid of women's voices. The fascinating question that intrigues audiences and makes this film a dramatic success is: why would a woman knowingly lie to support an imposter's claims? Was it simply the security of having a healthy male which an early modern peasant woman needed to survive in a harsh world, or was it something more compelling to modern audiences: love and a woman's right to choose? These are very human questions, often absent in theoretical debate. It was these questions, however, which led to the sharpest criticism of Davis's work on this film, in an article by Robert Finlay published in *The American Historical Review*.[11] Finlay accused Davis of interpolating modern values more appropriate to the feminist age onto the character of Bertrande. What was portrayed as a wicked and devious deed in the sixteenth-century texts (Coras and the other court documents), became an act of devotion and collaboration between a man and woman; Bertrande and the 'false Martin' become heroes, rather than dupe and villain. Davis said she had striven to 'fill in the gaps' of the historical record by giving Bertrande's side of the story when the court records were silent or biased, as she contends Coras's *Arrest Memorable* is. The published debate between Davis and Finlay provides a compelling starting point for students of history in film for the early modern period, asking the fundamental question: how much is it the right or the responsibility of the historian to 'fill in the gaps' in our knowledge through informed invention?

Another film from this period worth mentioning in this context of informed invention is the classic film on the dangers of revolutionary idealism that has turned to unquestionable dogma: *Danton* (1983) by Polish director, Andrzej Wajda (again starring Gérard Depardieu). Set in the year of the Terror (1794), it closely examines the unravelling of the friendship and political relationship of the two giants of the French Revolution, Maximilien Robespierre and Georges Danton (Depardieu). The film is loosely associated with debates then going on in Poland about the virtues of freedom of expression versus the security of government authority, but it is useful to students of the early modern period for its use of 'imagined history', as in *The Return of Martin Guerre*. The speeches of Danton and Robespierre can be found in published document collections of the French Revolution.[12] But this film also allows us to imagine the undocumented conversations these men must have had, in private, which ultimately led to the break-down of their relationship and the guillotine for Danton.[13] These conversations were 'imagined' several decades before this film was made, by Stanley Loomis, in a process French cultural historian Marc Ferro defined as 'historical reconstitution'.[14]

This sort of 'scenic invention' can be found in other well-known historical narratives, most famously, the completely fabricated 'interview' between Elizabeth I and Mary, Queen of Scots – who never met in reality – as reconstituted by Friedrich Schiller in his play, 'Maria Stuart' (1800), which was subsequently imported into retellings of this story in opera (by Donizetti, 1835) and in film, from *Mary of Scotland* (1936) starring Katharine Hepburn; to *Mary, Queen of Scots* (1971) starring Vanessa Redgrave and Glenda Jackson (again as Elizabeth); to the 2005 Helen Mirren television version, where, in a clever nod to the audience, the Queen says to Dudley: 'If I were to visit her, it would have to be in secret, for all of court would argue against it, but it could be done, I imagine.' The scene begins with Mary Queen of Scots: 'You were not announced', and Elizabeth's response: 'I am not here.' Such scenes make for great drama, and allow professional historians a bit of fun, but also stimulate useful classroom discussion about how much we can assume of historical figures' actions or thoughts in the absence of historical records.

Twentieth-century myths and legends

With the coming of a flashier period in filmmaking, the later 1980s and early 1990s, Hollywood filmmakers turned to more obviously blockbuster historical films, where storytelling took premier place, and 'serious' representation was pushed aside. Most of the bigger budget films were made based on accepted semi-mythical nationalist narratives rather than facts (such as *Braveheart*, 1995), and more art-house films sought to present 'revisionist' views at that time dominant in historical scholarship, reflecting an interest in postcolonialist re-evaluations of Europeans' presence in the New World (*The Mission*, 1986), or post-nationalist views of events such as the English Reformation (*Lady Jane*, 1986). Other films from this era, while excellent films, reinforce national myths and stereotypes rather than reveal 'true' history. A good example of this is *La Reine Margot* (1994) by Patrice Chéreau, which reinforces the long-standing image of wicked Catholics slaughtering innocent Protestants in the St Bartholomew's Day Massacre (23–24 August 1572), the bloodiest episode of the French Wars of Religion, and in particular the wicked, foreign-born queen, Catherine de Medici, who masterminded the blood-soaked event. Scenes set within the Valois court draw a portrait of a decadent and sexually deviant royal family, in strong contrast with the moral and honest Protestant prince,

Henry of Navarre. This is compelling viewing, but it is based on a novel by Alexandre Dumas (1845), and reveals more about the feelings of nineteenth-century Frenchmen about the resurgence of Catholic fanaticism and bigotry in their own time, and a rise in devotion to the memory of a morally upright royal dynasty, the Bourbons in the 1840s represented by the 'people's king', Louis-Philippe (one of Dumas's early patrons). But as a study of historiographical change and national myth, *La Reine Margot* is useful for its depiction of the 'black legend' of Catherine de Medici (and it helps that the role is played so artfully by an Italian actress, Virna Lisi): Catherine here is truly the 'black widow', lurking in corners, shuffling along corridors as a spider, barely human at all. This image can feature centrally in a classroom discussion, making usage of an excellent article on the evolution of Catherine's image across the centuries, by an eminent scholar of the period, Nicola Sutherland.[15]

There are other films based on Dumas novels, most famously the series of books focusing on the Three Musketeers, which have been made into numerous films and television series, from the first silent films to the present: a blockbuster Hollywood film of 1993 was outdone by an even more blockbuster version in 2011, followed by a fairly lacklustre, and strangely ahistorical, BBC television series in Britain in 2014. The most famous recent film of this type is probably *The Man in the Iron Mask* (1998) starring Leonardo DiCaprio, which is not very useful for use in class as it is full of anachronisms and is based on a clearly fictional story of the young Louis XIV having a secret twin. This is in contrast to *La Reine Margot* which although it too has anachronisms, portrays events with enough uncertainties of fact that it allows students to engage with the ongoing academic debates over the causes and meanings of the Massacre of St Bartholomew's Day.[16]

But fictional accounts can be useful for the basis of a historical film, many of which were written in the early modern period itself. The first true 'novel' is usually considered to be the *Princess of Cleves* by Madame de La Fayette, published in 1678, and although it was made into a French art-house film in 1961 (with dialogue 'adjusted' by Jean Cocteau), it has thus far never made it onto the big Hollywood screen. A more useful example therefore is *Dangerous Liaisons* (1988), based on the novel by Pierre Choderlos de Laclos, *Les Liaisons dangereuses* (1782). Aside from beautiful costumes and elegant settings, the film conveys an important aspect of the French Enlightenment: the importance of wit and the careful usage of language as a mark of 'civilization' – though of course in the end, it is revealed that this shallow pursuit is not a mark of civilization, rather of brutal barbarity. As such, the story can be set in any period, and indeed it has been (the 1959 French version is set in the 1950s, the two 1980s versions *Dangerous Liaisons* [1988] and *Valmont* [1989] are set as the novel in the 1780s, while *Cruel Intentions* [1999] is famously set amid the modern Manhattan jet set). Students can compare the language used in the original novel with the way text is turned into dialogue in the more recent films.[17] Another film which conveys a similar message, but is entirely based on new material, is the delightful *Ridicule* (1996). Both stories reconstruct a past quite different from ours, but also reinforce deeply held notions (certainly in France) that pre-Revolutionary French aristocrats were vicious, decadent, and got what they deserved once the Revolution came (and the guillotine). This allows for stimulating classroom discussion about the truths over who was or was not in fact leading the earliest stages of the Revolution of 1789.[18] Other fictional accounts of this period allow students to get into the look and feel of the early modern world without attempting to look for 'fact', for example, those based on works of theatre like *Cyrano de Bergerac* (1990) (yet again starring Depardieu), based on a play by Edmond Rostand, 1897; *Amadeus* (1984), based on the play from 1979 by Peter Shaffer; or *The Madness of King George* (1994), based on a play from 1991 by Alan Bennett. These examples are useful for allowing students to consider those things that were of concern to different sorts of people in seventeenth-century France, eighteenth-century Vienna or eighteenth-century England.

Source and scene: Integrating the history

Some films from this period can be useful in the classroom because they are based on actual letters or memoirs that have survived from the period. Once again looking at seventeenth-century France and the age of Louis XIV, the 'Sun King', *Vatel* (2000) is based on a tale recounted in a letter by the famous epistolary author, Madame de Sévigné, on 24 and 26 April 1671.[19] In her letter to her daughter, the Marquise de Sévigné provides descriptive colour and dramatic narrative about a weekend party thrown by the Prince of Condé for his cousin, the King, and, crucially, provides the ultimate anecdote about early modern 'honour' when the famous chef, François Vatel, commits suicide rather than dishonour his master (Condé) when the fish do not arrive on the final day of the royal visit:

> The King arrived on Thursday evening. Hunting, lanterns, moonlight, a gentle walk, supper served in a spot carpeted with daffodils – everything was perfect ... Night falls. The fireworks are a failure owing to fog, and they cost 16,000 francs. By four in the morning Vatel was rushing round everywhere and finding everything wrapped in slumber. He found a small supplier who only had two loads of fish. 'Is that all?' he asked. 'Yes, sir.' He did not know that Vatel had sent round to all the seaports. Vatel waited a short time, the other suppliers did not turn up, he lost his head and thought there would be no more fish. He went and found Gourville [Condé's chief steward] and said, 'Sir, I shall never survive

this disgrace, my honour and my reputation are at stake.' Gourville laughed at him. Vatel went to his room, put his sword up against the door and ran it through his heart ... Meanwhile the fish was coming in from all quarters ... Monsieur le Prince [of Condé] told the King very sadly, explaining that it was a matter of honour as he saw it. His courage was both praised and blamed. The King said that he had been putting off his visit to Chantilly for five years because he realized what an extreme embarrassment it would be ... He swore that he would not allow Monsieur le Prince to take all this trouble, but it was too late for poor Vatel. However, Gourville tried to make up for the loss of Vatel. He did so, and there was a very good dinner, light refreshments later, and then supper, a walk, cards, hunting, everything scented with daffodils, everything magical.

The film, directed by Roland Joffé, and yet again starring Depardieu (this time in English), is wonderful at evoking the atmosphere conjured by Sévigné, with lavish period costume, beautiful sets, and especially noteworthy reconstructions of the mechanical wonders of late seventeenth-century court entertainments: the astonishing array of pulleys and levers, the fetish for orientalism (*Turkerie*) in decoration and entertainment (and development of court ballet), early forms of fireworks, and the lavish outlay of food (see figure 9.1). Less effective is the love story added in the film for Vatel, but it is fun for students studying this period to see well-drawn portraits of the most prominent personages who feature in historical literature about the court of the Sun King: a stiff and unfeeling Louis XIV, a slightly befuddled Queen Marie-Thérèse (she never properly learned to speak French), an impish and playful Philippe d'Orléans (a fop who can wield a sword with deadly accuracy when needed – a welcome revised view of the homosexual brother of the Sun King), the notorious rake Lauzun (played wonderfully by Tim Roth, who steals nearly every scene), and a pompous royal mistress (Montespan) greeting her rival (La Vallière), weeping, on the stairs, with the quip: 'Are you going down, Madame? I am going up!'[20]

Using Madame de Sévigné's text in conjunction with this film suggests how a fairly short contemporary letter can truly bring a period to life, allowing students to 'see' and 'experience' the past, not simply read about it. Analytical discussions can be centred around reactions to the film by social and cultural historians.[21] However, attention should also be drawn to the fact that, as with other films examined in this chapter, the Joffé film reasserts some holdovers from the Romantic (nineteenth-century) past, notably that Vatel killed himself for the love of a woman, and that he prized talent over birth as the measure of a man's worth, neither of which is mentioned in the Sévigné story, and is not in keeping with the aristocratic values she espoused, but derives instead from later nineteenth-century views of the events described.[22]

A second good example of a film based on correspondence is the television miniseries *Aristocrats* (1999), co-produced by the BBC, Irish

FIGURE 9.1 *Lavish set design in* Vatel *(2000)*

Screen and American PBS. Based on a book of the same title by historian Stella Tillyard,[23] the four-episode series is based around the thousands of surviving letters written by the four Lennox sisters, spanning from the 1740s to the early 1800s. These four women, daughters of one of the highest ranking peers in Georgian England, the Duke of Richmond (and great-grand-daughters of King Charles II, via his mistress Louise de Keroualle, Duchess of Portsmouth), provide an epistolary record of a variety of life experiences, and reveal a great deal about choices available to women of this rank – highly educated, but given little chance to use their education. Instead, at least in two cases, they passed their aspirations on to their sons: Lady Caroline was the mother of Charles James Fox, the leader of the liberal Whig party at the end of the eighteenth century; Lady Emily was mother of Lord Edward Fitzgerald, a prominent leader of the Irish rebellion of 1798. Is it contradictory to consider how two of the most highly born women in eighteenth-century Britain – an era in which women, especially in the upper classes, were considered, and indeed treated, like little more than a man's property[24] – gave birth and oversaw the education of two of the most reform-minded men of the age? The exploration of these women's lives provides a useful antidote to the generalization that all women were powerless, and that all aristocrats were conservative and hell-bent on exploiting the peasants. In conjunction with Tillyard's book exploring the letters, students can explore a myriad of social issues facing upper class women from the period: family and kinship (especially the importance of matrilineal connections in a mostly patrilineal society); administration of a large aristocratic household; romance and marriage, duty and choice; women's roles as daughters, sisters, wives and mothers to prominent politicians; death and inheritance; and so on. The text and the miniseries are both especially rich in these areas, as the four sisters each dealt with these issues in varying ways, successfully and, in some cases, spectacularly unsuccessfully (Sarah's story includes adultery, divorce and illegitimacy). They can be studied as models of their era and their class, but the human element as individuals is abundantly evident as well in the sisters' correspondence, as they struggle with issues of love, marriage and betrayal, such as would be found in any Jane Austen novel.

The letters drawn upon by Tillyard and transformed into dialogue or narration in the series help to humanize historical people; some of their words and phrases are quite modern, while others are unusual and distant. Letter writing was an art, in fact the sisters refer to their mutual love of the letters of Madame de Sévigné, to them 'the quintessential, rational woman of feeling'.[25] For example, Caroline wrote to Emily to compliment her daughter: 'She is a delightful correspondent, her style quite formed.' And Emily wrote: 'When one receives a letter, sitting down immediately to answer it is like carrying on a conversation.'[26] And the same, to scold her brother-in-law Henry Fox (Caroline's husband) for flouting the convention of publicly read letters: 'What a creature you are! I receive your letter before a thousand people. "A letter from Mr. Fox, oh we shall have some news." Everybody waits with impatience till I have read it. I open it with an important face and then behold it's full of nonsense and indeed such stuff as is not decent to shew to any creature.' Students may also find it useful and interesting to read Caroline's letters as a traveller, a point of view normally reserved for men in this period – unusually for a woman, she travelled to Italy as her 'Grand Tour' in 1766–7.[27] Students can go further and supplement Tillyard's written word with the film's carefully researched period costumes, hairstyles, modes of transportation, or architecture.

Using historical films to look at styles and settings are thus also useful, but are often full of pitfalls. The classic *Three Musketeers* film trilogy by Richard Lester (1973, 1974, 1989) certainly convey the zest of life on horseback for a cavalier in the seventeenth century, but racing cross-country in dry and treeless central Spain is hardly evocative of lush, green northern France. The above-cited *Vatel* does allow us to see appropriate settings (much was filmed at the Château of Chantilly, the actual setting of the story), but uses English music from a half-century later: instead of Lully or Charpentier (perfectly acceptable for French dramatic music from the 1670s), we hear Handel's 'Music for Royal Fireworks' written for George II in 1749.[28] Appropriate period music seems to be the poor step-sister to costume and interior decoration when it comes to historical film making. The Kapur version of the Elizabeth I story (1998) relies on outrageously anachronistic music for emotional effect: Mozart's *Requiem* (from eighteenth-century Austria) to evoke sorrow, and Elgar's 'Nimrod' (from late nineteenth-century Britain) to stir the nationalist sentiments of British audiences – in an ironically imperialist view of English history given the director's origins.[29] The blockbuster version of *Marie-Antoinette* (2006) uses Vivaldi (who died in 1741) to convey the energetic frenzy of court life, rather than equally frenetic music more likely to have been played at the French court in the 1770s (for example, the 'Dance of the Furies' from Gluck's opera 'Orfée'). This film has other problems: the budget spent on costume and hair must have been vast – but historians versed in the literature and culture of this period may wonder if the producers therefore ran out of funds when it came to constructing dialogue. Louis XVI, Marie-Antoinette and their courtiers come across sounding more like modern-day California teenagers than eighteenth-century aristocrats. But then again, this is the stated aim of the director, Coppola, an impression of the emotions of a lost teenager, not a factual representation of the period.[30] Historian Caroline Weber criticizes Coppola for creating a far too simplistic character, mostly a victim of her surroundings;[31] in contrast, Weber's own book on the subject explores the young Queen's adroitness at using fashion to control her environment and her self-representation.[32]

But Coppola's *Marie-Antoinette* is useful in the use of historical sources in a few of its key scenes. Take, for example, the complex ceremony in which the young Austrian archduchess is completely undressed – even her Austrian dog is removed – and she is re-dressed as a French princess; scenes like this can be read in vivid detail in the excellent biography by Antonia Fraser, Coppola's inspiration for the film.[33] Students can go a step further to examine the primary source relating to a scene evoking the complicated court ceremonial surrounding the process of getting out of bed and getting dressed each morning at Versailles. The scene in the film is humorous (as each lady of higher rank enters the room, the ceremony is restarted, leaving the young, startled Marie-Antoinette naked and shivering), but is in fact based on a well-known passage from the memoirs of one of the Queen's ladies in waiting, Madame Campan.[34]

[Marie Antoinette's] *toilette* was a masterpiece of etiquette; everything was done in a prescribed form. Both the *dame d'honneur* and the *dame d'atours* usually attended and officiated, assisted by the first *femme de chambre* and two ordinary women. The *dame d'atours* put on the petticoat, and handed the gown to the Queen. The *dame d'honneur* poured out the water for her hands and put on her linen. When a princess of the royal family happened to be present while the Queen was dressing, the *dame d'honneur* yielded to her the latter act of office, but still did not yield it directly to the Princesses of the blood; in such a case the *dame d'honneur* was accustomed to present the linen to the first *femme de chambre*, who, in her turn, handed it to the Princess of the blood. Each of these ladies observed these rules scrupulously as affecting her rights.

One winter's day it happened that the Queen, who was entirely undressed, was just going to put on her shift; I held it ready unfolded for her; the *dame d'honneur* came in, slipped off her gloves, and took it. A scratching was heard at the door; it was opened, and in came the

Duchesse d'Orleans: her gloves were taken off, and she came forward to take the garment; but as it would have been wrong in the *dame d'honneur* to hand it to her she gave it to me, and I handed it to the Princess. More scratching it was Madame la Comtesse de Provence [the Queen's sister-in-law]; the Duchesse d'Orleans handed her the linen. All this while the Queen kept her arms crossed upon her bosom, and appeared to feel cold; Madame observed her uncomfortable situation, and, merely laying down her handkerchief without taking off her gloves, she put on the linen, and in doing so knocked the Queen's cap off.

The Queen laughed to conceal her impatience, but not until she had muttered several times, "How disagreeable! how tiresome!"

A filmed scene like this can be used to supplement a primary source text to prompt discussion of a historical topic: if French monarchs were supposedly deemed 'absolute', why were they so imprisoned by the rituals of their daily lives? After comparing a primary source anecdote and its filmic counterpart, students can examine such an issue as debated by historians, in this case, the debate over absolutism in France.[35]

Televisual Tudors: Historical narrative on the small screen

It is not only big-screen historical films that can be used in conjunction with primary sources and historical analysis. Recently there has been a spate of very popular television serials, most with large budgets and subsequently lavish outlays on costume, sets and on-location shooting. Some have been terrible, but others have been quite good, and, in addition to being good entertainment, can be employed like the above examples to help students engage with the early modern period. Some of these have been analysed in a recent volume geared especially towards this aspect of the topic of historical film.[36]

By far the most popular has been *The Tudors*, produced by Showtime (2007–10), in which a handsome actor portrays (rightly, by the standards of 'revisionist' scholarship) a young Henry VIII as a healthy and vigorous prince rather than the bloated monster we are familiar with in popular narratives.[37] But the series has many anachronisms, twists of historical facts (notably blending together Henry's two sisters into one character) and wooden engagement with the important movements of the time (humanism, church reform) which make it clear that this series is mostly about entertainment.[38] But *The Tudors* attracted a vast new audience to the early modern world, and was emulated by *The Borgias* (Showtime 2011–13), *The White Queen* (BBC 2013), *Wolf Hall* (BBC 2015), and several others. As a study of 'interiority', the latter of these is excellent, as author Hilary

Mantel painstakingly researched her subject and artfully constructed the inner world of Henry VIII's chief minister and reformer, Thomas Cromwell. Non-English-language production companies followed in the wake of such programmes, for example, another version of *The Borgias* (a French-German-Czech-Italian co-production 2011–14); *Isabel* (Spain 2012–14); and *Magnificent Century* ('Muhtesem Yüzyi') about the Ottomans in the sixteenth century (Turkey 2011–14), cited as one of the most popular programmes ever in the Muslim world, which is unfortunately (so far) not released with English subtitles.[39] Most of these are very entertaining, but are of limited use in the classroom as they are riddled with anachronisms, often projecting twenty-first-century values and emotions onto late medieval or early modern situations.

For an exception, we can once again turn to the 2005 miniseries *Elizabeth I*, starring Helen Mirren. While it has flaws, there are certain elements which suggest its value and usefulness as a secondary source: digitally reconstructed settings; historically informed themes; and dialogue based in some places on written primary sources. The first of these, the digitally reconstructed sets, make watching the action more compelling for a student of history. Instead of setting Elizabeth's court in a vast, dark medieval space as is often done (the Kapur 1998 version of Elizabeth seems to be set entirely within Gothic cathedrals), the producers opted to recreate (as much as we are able based on sparse and sometimes contradictory evidence) the English royal palace at Whitehall, either on a set (in Vilnius, Lithuania), or digitally, with its small courtyards, narrow corridors, wooden interiors, and, most interestingly, its waterfront landing on the Thames, where Elizabeth receives and sends away her important guests (see figure 9.2).[40] One of these guests leads us to the second point: historically informed debates, notably about Elizabeth's relationships with her French marital suitors. Again the Channel 4 version is in contrast with the Kapur version of Elizabeth's story, which merely reinforces national stereotypes: all Spaniards are wicked and swarthy, all Frenchmen are homosexual, or at least cross-dressers. In fact, as we have seen with *La Reine Margot*, much of this notion of the Valois court as a nest of transvestism, sodomy and incest came originally from writers of histories of post-Valois France (that is, by Bourbon historians), or by contemporary Protestant writers. These views were then reaffirmed in the writings of men like Alexandre Dumas, whose version of the Valois court is filled with all three vices.[41] Mirren's Elizabeth is more nuanced, showing her pain in having to reject a suitor she actually likes due to the demands of 'public opinion', a fairly new phenomenon in the history of the English monarchy, and one which is corroborated in the academic literature. For example, Susan Doran argues that Elizabeth was not ultimately able to choose whether to marry or whom to marry, but was constrained by the pressures of her position, her advisors, her people.[42] This is depicted well across the series, notably in repeated scenes in the Council Chamber where the Queen bemoans her lack of freedom in such matters.

Finally, the third element: the use of actual letters and speeches by Elizabeth, delivered by a first-class actor. Several short selections are drawn upon to create the dialogue for the series, from the very well known, such as the speech before her troops at Tilbury, 9 August 1588, or the so-called 'Golden Speech' before Parliament on 30 November 1601, to the relatively unknown.[43] An example of the latter reinforces the point made above about Elizabeth's true feelings for her French suitor, the duc d'Anjou (unlike what is often portrayed in popular films). A letter she wrote to him (about December 1579 or January 1580) concludes in a rather melancholy yet affectionate tone, with Elizabeth noting that their marriage cannot proceed since 'the public exercise of the Roman religion sticks so much in their hearts', and signing off with 'my commendations to my very dear Frog'.[44]

Conclusion

Overall, the question is not just about students seeing and 'experiencing' the period – through settings, costumes and music – but also about exploring how the early modern mind differs from our own. This can be challenging – attaining 'interiority' – but using film in conjunction with historical documents can allow students a chance to get closer to historical experience.

This chapter has focused mostly on a type of historical film that has been especially popular in recent years: based on upper class, European lives. These are easy sells for film and television producers, as they feature great costumes and dramatic narratives. It is also usually easier for historians to find primary sources to analyse these stories, or to accompany classroom discussions. Nevertheless, we should certainly be aware of other geographical and social contexts. American history in the early modern period can be examined through large-scale films ranging from the discovery of the New World, such as *1492: Conquest of Paradise* (1992) (starring yet again Gérard Depardieu!) or *The New World* (2005), to the struggles for independence of the American Colonies, such as *The Patriot* (2000). But, as we have seen above, it is often the small-screen efforts that are more useful in terms of their historical narrative, and their engagement with contemporary historiography. *John Adams* (HBO 2008) is based on a Pulitzer-prize winning biography of one of the United States' founding fathers by David McCulloch, and was directed by Tom Hooper, the same director of the Helen Mirren television version of *Elizabeth I*. The seven-part series, starring Paul Giamatti, was filmed in some genuine historic sites, such as Bruton Parish Church, in Williamsburg, Virginia, though these were meant to represent Boston. Much of the dialogue is derived from actual letters and speeches, though the series is not without its critics within the historical community.[45] Such criticisms are of course excellent stimulators of classroom discussion and debate.

FIGURE 9.2 *Elizabeth I (Helen Mirren) sits on the Thames,* Elizabeth I *(2005)*

Other broad early modern topics not covered here include the Reformation or the Renaissance: there are numerous films based on the life of Martin Luther (recently one starring Joseph Fiennes, 2003), but surprisingly few depicting fifteenth-century Italy, Florence in its golden age, its ruling Medici family, or the artists they patronized such as Michelangelo or Da Vinci. Some of the emotionality and sensuality of the later Baroque age of the fine arts can be examined through the film *Caravaggio* by Derek Jarman (1986), but for a more critically aware examination of the contexts (political, intellectual, cultural) in which these artists (including Caravaggio) operated, it would be better to use the docu-drama series by historian Simon Schama, *Power of Art* (BBC 2006). Schama, famous for his *History of Britain* (BBC 2000–2), also authored the series *Rough Crossings: Britain, the Slaves and the American Revolution* (2005) (for more on Schama, see Chapter 14). Finally, we should mention a sub-genre of historical films that has become increasingly popular in recent years, partly due to the expansive popularity of video games that are based in historical settings (most notably 'Assassin's Creed', Ubisoft 2000–15), which is the 'epic battle film'. Examples include *Henri 4* (Germany, 2010), called *Henry of Navarre* for the English-subtitled version, marketed cleverly, if deceptively, with the tag line 'Ridley Scott Styled Battle Scenes' (Scott was not affiliated with the film); or *1612* (2007), a Russian film about the 'Time of Troubles' when Russia had no tsar and fought a bloody succession war versus Poland, which is essentially two hours of non-stop bloodletting. Are films like these worthy of inclusion in a course about early modern history? Such films are a useful resource through which to explore the pivotal role played by warfare in the early modern world, and the sense of relentless violence that led to the rise of modern diplomacy and the first pacifist movements. Moreover, they also call attention to an issue often ignored by the historical record: the extent to which the lives of the 'ordinary' were, in a pithy summary offered by contemporary philosopher Thomas Hobbes, 'nasty, brutish, and short'.[46]

In conclusion, we can see that the early modern era presents its own sets of issues for filmmakers and historians, notably the distance between the world of the viewers and that of the periods being portrayed. People in the more distant past dressed differently, their surroundings looked different, their music sounded different, and, most critically, they spoke and thought differently. This 'interiority' of historical characters has been the focus of much debate ever since the 'Martin Guerre' exchange between Natalie Zemon Davis and Robert Finlay over the 'imagined' speech and thoughts of early modern protagonists. Most big-budget popular historical films for the cinema or for the small screen do not, however, have even this pretence at what is conventionally understood to be 'historical authenticity' (see Chapter 2). Nonetheless, such 'popular' forms of history should not be rejected outright. Carefully selected, and interrogated next to more traditional forms of historical narrative, such films and television programmes offer an invaluable means through which to explore the politics, performance, and 'interiority' of the early modern age. Moreover, the very discussions and disputes that many of these productions have caused – over their worth, value, accuracy and authenticity – are themselves powerfully suggestive of the fluid nature of historical debate.

Notes

1   See E. H. Ford and D. C. Mitchell, *Royal Portraits in Hollywood: Filming the Lives of Queens* (Lexington, KY: University Press of Kentucky, 2009).

2   There have been several fascinating studies of the evolution of the image and portrayal of Elizabeth I, all of which are useful for examining this issue as part of a history class, from M. Dobson and N. J. Watson's *England's Elizabeth: An Afterlife in Fame and Fantasy* (Oxford: Oxford University Press, 2002); to S. Doran and T. Freeman's *The Myth of Elizabeth* (Basingstoke: Palgrave Macmillan, 2003), especially the final chapter, by T. Betteridge, 'A Queen for All Seasons: Elizabeth I on Film'. Doran and Freeman also co-edited a follow-up volume, *Tudors and Stuarts on Film: Historical Perspectives* (Basingstoke: Palgrave Macmillan, 2009). See also B. Latham, *Elizabeth I in Film and Television. A Study of Major Portrayals* (Jefferson: McFarland, 2011).

3   For example, P. Sorlin, *The Film in History: Restaging the Past* (Totowa, NJ Barnes & Noble Books, 1980); or more recently, M. Chopra-Gant, *Cinema and History: The Telling of Stories* (London: Wallflower Press, 2008).

4   R. A. Rosenstone, 'Introduction', in *Visions of the Past: The Challenge of Film to Our Idea of History* (Cambridge: Harvard University Press, 1995).

5   Rosenstone, R. A. 'The Historical Film: Looking at the Past in a Postliterate Age', in *The Historical Film: History and Memory in Media*, ed. M. Landy. (New Brunswick, NJ: Rutgers University Press, 2001), 50–66.

6   Rosenstone, *Visions of the Past*, 50.

7   The film was so incendiary it was given an X rating in the United States and the United Kingdom, and banned by several British localities. For a recent analysis of this incredible story within its historical context, see M. de Certeau, *The Possession at Loudun*, trans. M. B. Smith (Chicago: University of Chicago Press, 2000).

8   With the same title (Cambridge: Harvard University Press, 1983).

9   Published as 'Arrest Memorable du Parlement de Toulouse' in 1561.

10   'Charivari' is discussed briefly in N. Zemon Davis, *Return of Martin Guerre* (Cambridge, MA: Harvard Univerity Press, 1983), 29; as is 'Confrontation', 63–6.

11   R. Finlay, 'The Refashioning of Martin Guerre', *The American Historical Review* 93 (3) (1988): 553–71. This is followed in the same issue by a riposte by N. Zemon Davis, 'On the Lame' *The American Historical Review* 93 (3) (1988a): 572–603.

12   For example, L. Mason and T. Rizzo, *The French Revolution: A Document Collection* (Boston: Houghton-Mifflin, 1999).

13   See J. Falkowska and A. Wajda, *History, Politics and Nostalgia in Polish Cinema* (Oxford and New York: Berg, 2008); and H. A. Garrity, 'The French Revolution and the Seventh Art', *The French Review* 62 (6) (May 1989): 1041–51.

14   S. Loomis, *Paris in the Terror* (Philadelphia: Lippincott, 1964), 298–9; M. Ferro, *Cinema and History*, trans. N. Greene (Detroit: Wayne State University Press, 1988), 29, 162.

15   N. M. Sutherland, 'Catherine de Medici: The Legend of the Wicked Italian Queen', in Sutherland, *Princes, Politics and Religion, 1547–1589* (London: Hambledon, 1984) [previously an article in *Sixteenth Century Journal* 9 (2) (1978): 45–56].

16   B. B. Diefendorf, *The St. Bartholomew's Day Massacre: A Brief History with Documents* (Boston and New York: Bedford/St. Martin's, 2008); A. Jouanna, *The Saint Bartholomew's Day Massacre: The Mysteries of a Crime of State*, trans. J. Bergin (Manchester: Manchester University Press, 2013).

17   There is a new translation of the novel by H. Constantine, published by Penguin Classics (London and New York: Penguin Classics, 2007).

18   For a recent examination of this debate, see W. Doyle, *Aristocracy and its Enemies in the Age of Revolution* (Oxford: Oxford University Press, 2009).

19   These letters can be read in the Penguin version, *Selected Letters*, trans. L. Tancock (London: Penguin, 1982), 95–9 (specifically 97–9).

20   Though it is tempting to think this anecdote also comes from a contemporary source, it does in fact derive from the witty pen of N. Mitford, *The Sun King* (London: Vintage Classics, 2011 [1966]), 94, which is often more fiction than fact. Nevertheless, there are ample published contemporary sources in

translation from this period that can be used in conjunction with a viewing of *Vatel* to gain understanding of court life and aristocratic values: the letters of Liselotte von der Pfalz (the Duchess of Orléans), the Duc de Saint-Simon, La Grande Mademoiselle (the Duchess of Montpensier) and so on.

21   For example, M. Longino Farrell, 'Writing Letters, Telling Tales, Making History: Vatel's Death Told and Retold', *The French Review* 66 (2) (1992): 229–42; S. Shapiro, 'Roland Joffé's *Vatel*: Refashioning the History of the *Ancien Régime*', in *Studies in Early Modern France*, vol. 10 ed. A. L. Birberick and R. Ganim (Charlottesville: Rockwood Press, 2005), 77–88.

22   This is discussed in the conclusion ('Inventing Traditions of Honor in Post-Revolutionary France') of the study by J. J. Davis, *Defining Culinary Authority: The Transformation of Cooking in France, 1650–1830* (Baton Rouge: Louisiana State University Press, 2013).

23   S. K. Tillyard, *Aristocrats: Caroline, Emily, Louisa and Sarah Lennox, 1740–1832* (London: Chatto & Windus, 1994), with several reprints.

24   The subject of a recent BBC television drama, *The Scandalous Lady W* (August 2015), based on a true story of Sir Richard and Lady Seymour Worsley, whose marital problems scandalised Georgian Britain when they were unveiled in a public trial where she revealed that she had not committed adultery with one man, but with twenty-seven, and that this was mostly done to satisfy the kinky sexual practices of her husband (her accuser). Nevertheless, though Lady Worsley won a moral and emotional victory over her husband, without his granting her a divorce, she remained his 'property' and had to continue to submit to his wishes.

25   See the discussion in Tillyard, *Aristocrats* 93–100.

26   Both quoted on 96.

27   Her letters are happily available online for use in the classroom. J. T. Boulton and T. O. McLoughlin (eds), *News from Abroad: Letters Written by British Travellers on the Grand Tour, 1728–1771* (Eighteenth Century Worlds, no. 3; Liverpool: Liverpool University Press, 2012), 213–59. Available online: universitypublishingonline.org (accessed 26 August 2015).

28   Students wishing to explore the music of the early modern period can instead be directed to *Farinelli* (1994), about the castrato superstar from Naples; or *Le Roi Danse* (2000), about the French composer Lully and the invention of French court ballet. Both films are by Belgian filmmaker Gérard Corbiau and are scrupulously researched and performed by leading interpreters of early music.

29   See G. Kaufman, 'Royal Flush', *New Statesman* 11 (524) (2 October 1998): 36–7.

30   R. Murray, 'Writer/Director Sofia Coppola Talks About "Marie Antoinette"', *About.Entertainment*. Available online: http://movies.about.com/od/marieantoinette/a/mariesc101006.htm (accessed 25 August 2015).

31   C. Weber, 'Queen of the Zeitgeist', *New York Times*, 21 October 2006.

32   C. Weber, *Queen of Fashion: What Marie-Antoinette wore to the Revolution* (New York: Henry Holt, 2006).

33 A. Fraser, *Marie Antoinette: The Journey* (London: Weidenfeld & Nicolson, 2001). The 'handover' is described on the pages following 59.

34 The memoirs of Madame Campan have been variously translated into English, and are easily available in paperback or online, for example J. L. H. Campan, *The Private Life of Marie Antoinette. A Confidante's Account* (New York: 1500 Books, 2006), in which this passage is on 73.

35 See the classic statement of the argument by N. Henshall, 'The Myth of Absolutism', *History Today* 42 (6) (June 1992): 40–7; or a more recent analysis by W. Beik, 'The Absolutism of Louis XIV as Social Collaboration', *Past and Present* 188 (2005): 195–224.

36 G. R. Edgerton and P. C. Rollins (eds), *Television Histories: Shaping Collective Memory in the Media Age* (Lexington: University of Kentucky, 2003).

37 The healthy virile prince is presented, for example, in D. Starkey, *Henry: Virtuous Prince* (London: Harper Press, 2008).

38 By the end of the series, historians can certainly criticise the producers' choices to leave Henry as a slender attractive man (he limps a bit by the end), or to portray perceived ugliness in 'Hollywood style' as only slightly less beautiful, as in the character of Anne of Cleves, played by the completely attractive Joss Stone.

39 See E. Batuman, 'Ottomania: A Hit TV Show Reimagines Turkey's imperial Past', *New Yorker*, 17 February 2014.

40 See 'Behind the Scenes', 'Sets', Eve Stewart, production design, and David Bowman, vfx supervisor, on the HBO website for the series. Available online: http://www.hbo.com/html/movies/elizabeth/behind-the-scenes/index.html (accessed 25 August 2015).

41 For recent historical analysis, see K. Crawford, 'Love, Sodomy and Scandal: Controlling the Sexual Reputation of Henri III', *Journal of the History of Sexuality* 12 (X) (2003) 153–42.

42 S. Doran, *Monarchy and Matrimony: The Courtships of Elizabeth I* (London: Routledge, 1995); or N. Mears, 'Love-making and Diplomacy: Elizabeth I and the Anjou Marriage Negotiations, c. 1578–1582', *History* 86 (284) (2001): 442–66.

43 These can be found in multiple sources online, but a good printed collection that gathers them all into one place is L. S. Marcus, J. Mueller and M. B. Rose (eds), *Elizabeth I. Collected Works* (Chicago: University of Chicago Press, 2000). The Tilbury speech is 325–6; the Golden Speech is 335–44 (in three versions).

44 Printed in Marcus, Mueller and Rose, *Elizabeth I*, 243–4.

45 J. Stern, 'What's Wrong with HBO's Dramatization of John Adams's Story' (October 2008). Available online: http://historynewsnetwork.org/article/56155 (accessed 4 April 2016). For further academic analysis of this topic, see B. Osterberg, *Colonial America on Film and Television* (London: McFarland, 2001). The series was also compared to an earlier television series that focused on Adams (and his descendants), which relied heavily on

actual letters and speeches for dialogue, and thus comes across as quite stiff and lacking in drama: 'The Adams Chronicles' (PBS, 1976).

46 Hobbes, *Leviathan* (1651), from Chapter XIII, 'Of the Natural Condition of Mankind As Concerning Their Felicity, and Misery'. Available online: http://www.bartleby.com/34/5/13.html (accessed 25 August 2015).

CHAPTER TEN

Hollywood musicals make history

Nicholas Gebhardt

Introduction

Towards the end of *The Wizard of Oz*, Metro-Goldwyn-Mayer's (MGM) iconic 1939 film musical, the central character, Dorothy (Judy Garland), sadly declares to the recently unmasked Wizard that, while Scarecrow has discovered his brain, Lion his courage, and Tin Man a heart, there is nothing in his magical black bag for her. How will she ever get home? Her new friends agree. 'What about Dorothy?' they implore. Taken aback, the Wizard famously replies: 'You force me into a cataclysmic decision. The only way to get Dorothy back to Kansas is for me to take her there myself.' He then goes on to tell the story of how he arrived in the land of Oz:

> I'm an old Kansas man myself, born and bred in the heart of the western wilderness. Premier balloonist par excellence to the Miracle Wonderland Carnival Company, until one day, while performing a spectacular piece of stratospheric skill, never before attempted by civilized man, an unfortunate phenomenon occurred. The balloon failed to return to the Fair ... Then suddenly the wind changed, and the balloon floated down into the heart of this noble city where I was instantly acclaimed Oz, the first Wizard De-Lux ... Times being what they were I accepted the job, retaining my balloon against the advent of a quick getaway. Ha ha! And in that balloon, my dear Dorothy, you and I will return to the land of e pluribus unum.

But what kind of land does the Wizard imagine they are going to go back to? Does the film offer us a coherent way of making sense of Dorothy's adventures in the Wonderful World of Oz, all of which appear to be motivated by her desire to return to the desolate monochrome Kansas prairies? Does it serve as a parable of American Populism, as some historians have claimed?[1] Or is the film instead referring to universal themes of displacement and homecoming to which we can all relate?

Answering such questions highlights a number of difficult issues regarding how we approach Hollywood musicals as historical documents. When considering studying history on film, we are more likely to turn to the great Westerns such as *Red River* (1948) or *The Searchers* (1956), or renowned war films such as *Apocalypse Now* (1979) or *Saving Private Ryan* (1998), or those profound dramas of the human condition such as *The Grapes of Wrath* (1940) or *On the Waterfront* (1954). In comparison, musicals seem less concerned with revealing something essential about the way human societies lived in another time or their attitudes to their world. Part of the problem is that they frequently play fast and loose with the facts, often skimming over issues of truth and accuracy that govern the claims professional historians make about their approach to reconstructing the past (see also Chapter 2). Musicals do not seem to be guided by conventional ideas of cause and effect; nor do they appear overly committed to exploring the psychological motivations of their characters in any meaningful way. All of which presents a difficult question: what do these films have to do with the qualities we identify with historical understanding?

This chapter explores what Hollywood musicals can tell us about that past, as well as considering some of the ways in which they enable us to ask important questions about the object of historical analysis. Because this raises such a large and complicated set of questions, only four of the most influential Hollywood musicals will be focused upon: Victor Fleming's *The Wizard of Oz* (1939), Vincente Minnelli's *Meet Me in St. Louis* (1944), Stanley Donen and Gene Kelly's *Singin' in the Rain* (1953), and Robert Wise's *The Sound of Music* (1965). In each, the problem of the past is posed in a very specific sense, but in ways that are very different from those we have come to expect from written or oral histories. Why they are so interesting as films, I want to suggest, is also why we find it so difficult to incorporate them into conventional historical account in any but the most superficial way.

Before discussing these examples in detail, a brief overview of the genre will help provide a clear sense of the sources we are examining. This will also help us to understand how Hollywood musicals relate to those other major cinematic genres such as the Western, which seem to be much more directly engaged with, and relevant to, debates about the past. We can start with the musical's central themes. 'In a musical,' according to Leo Braudy, 'there is no need for Shane [in the 1953 Western of the same name] to wander off, left out of the world he has united by his actions; instead the energy of the central character or couple can potentially bring the community together in an array around them'.[2] Whereas Westerns look back nostalgically to a lost world, in order to explore the mythic significance of the closing of the American frontier and its impact on Americans' core values and ideals, musicals elaborate the utopian potential for individual and collective transformation through song and dance.[3] Typically, they achieve this by celebrating spontaneity and naturalness, mocking pretensions and high culture, reconciling art and everyday life, and continuously reflecting on the forms of entertainment that they provide. Musicals not only entertain, but are self-consciously about the value and meaning of Hollywood entertainment.[4]

An example of this self-consciousness appears in a pivotal scene in Judy Garland's last film for MGM, *The Summer Stock* (1950). Big-city director, Joe Ross (Gene Kelly), describes to country girl, Jane Falbury (Garland), what the essence of a musical is. 'Now we're trying to tell a story with music and song and dance,' he explains, 'well, not just with words. For instance, if the boy tells the girl that he loves her, he just doesn't say it, he sings it.' Garland then asks the question that is central to all musicals: 'Why doesn't he just say it?' 'I don't know', Kelly replies. 'But it's kind of nice. Look, let me show you. The curtain goes up. I'm in love, and I tell you ...' He then proceeds to sing the song, 'You Wonderful You', to which she responds, dreamily, but in words: 'I like that.' 'And then they dance', he continues, starting on a very delicate tap routine. 'A nice easy dance, it's a nice easy song', he observes, still dancing. He brings her into the dance and they start dancing together, as he continues with the song. 'You're like a breath of spring, a whole new thing ...'. The song and the dance finish with them singing to each other and in unison: 'You're my love, you wonderful you.'

According to Rick Altman, this kind of sequence epitomizes the genre. Whether set backstage on a Hollywood movie lot, a Caribbean island, or the streets of New York City, film musicals are organized around a basic duality of parallel stars of the opposite sex (Garland and Kelly or Rogers and Astaire are the archetypal couples), and the different values they each symbolize. 'This dual-focus structure', he claims, 'requires the viewer to be sensitive not so much to chronology and progression – for the outcome of the male/female match is entirely conventional and thus quite predictable – but simultaneity and comparison.'[5] Few scenes actually advance the plot; and when they do, they leave little room for human complexity or variation. Musicals thus require a different kind of theoretical approach in order to understand them, one that recognizes that their structure derives not from their plot, but from the repeated confrontations or parallels between their characters that arise from, and continuously reflect on, the deeper opposition in American culture between art and entertainment, immediacy and artifice, and nature and culture.[6] When Fred Astaire effortlessly follows his speech into a song along a railway platform in Minnelli's *The Band Wagon* (1953), and his walk gracefully stretches into a dance, what he sings, and how he sings it, and with whom he dances, are not incidental to the story unfolding, but the very essence of what we have come to see.

The discussion that follows will highlight several instances that explicitly concern the temporal structure of historical experience. In the first film under discussion, *The Wizard of Oz*, I want to concentrate on the key moment at the beginning of the film when Dorothy pauses to reflect on her place in the world. That her reflection takes the form of a song seems to open up important issues about how we come to understand ourselves as historical subjects and to reflect upon the past. Likewise, in *Meet Me in St. Louis* (1944), singing is at the centre of the discussion. By focusing on the film's title song, I explore the way in which its public performance creates a particular relation to time, an experience that Alfred Shütz describes as 'growing old together while the music lasts'.[7] The final two examples consider the possibility that Hollywood musicals might have something important to say about the politics of historical consciousness. Both films engage with contemporary political conflicts, but only by removing them from the present to the past, as if the immediacy of those conflicts was too much for their audiences to bear. Let us begin, though, with dreams of escape.

Kansas ... the early 1900s

Victor Fleming's *The Wizard of Oz* has proven to be one of the most celebrated films ever produced by a Hollywood studio. Released in the same year as *Gone with The Wind*, which Fleming also directed, the story is based on L. Frank Baum's classic 1903 children's story. Living on a farm on the dusty Kansas plains in the early 1900s with her hardworking Uncle Henry and Auntie Em, Dorothy Gale finds farm life harsh, while her friendly companions, the farmhands, are likely to lose their jobs. Worst of all, because the local landowner Elvira Gulch dislikes Toto, Dorothy's dog, she is likely to lose him too. She decides to run away from home, and this is when she encounters Professor Marvel, a travelling showman, who offers to find out what the future holds for her in his crystal ball. Marvel manages to conjure an image of the girl's very worried aunt, and realizing she has made a terrible mistake, Dorothy sets off back to the farm. When the storm arrives, Dorothy is hit on the head, and awakens to find that she and Toto have been transported to the Land of Oz. Wearing ruby red slippers, she ventures down the yellow brick road seeking the Wonderful Wizard of Oz, gathering several new friends, Tin Man, Scarecrow and the Cowardly Lion, as well as having to engage in almost constant battle with the Wicked Witch of the West.

The opening credits make explicit reference to our sense of the past and how as we grow older we come to understand our relationship to it. Over a sepia-drenched image of the Kansas sky we read: 'For nearly forty years this story has given faithful service to the Young in Heart; and Time has been powerless to put its kindly philosophy out of fashion ... To those of you who have been faithful to it in return ... and to the Young in Heart ...

FIGURE 10.1 *Judy Garland in* The Wizard of Oz *(1939)*

we dedicate this picture'. The film begins as Dorothy and Toto are running along an isolated road with fields on both sides and a small farmhouse close by. Something or someone has scared them, and they are desperately trying to get back to the farmhouse. 'She isn't coming yet Toto', Dorothy comforts the dog. 'Did she hurt you? She tried to, didn't she? Come on. We'll go tell Uncle Henry and Aunty Em. Come on'. Once there, she runs up to an older woman, who turns out to be her aunt, and says to her: 'Aunt Em, Aunt Em. Just listen to what Miss Gulch ...' Distracted, Aunt Em interrupts her niece: 'Dorothy, please, we're trying to count.'

The exchange that follows, firstly between the girl, her aunt and uncle, and then, between the girl and the farm hands, highlights one of the film's central themes: the inadequacy of adults.[8] A major problem for Dorothy is that no one wants listen to her story about Miss Gulch. And when they finally do begin to take notice, they don't take her seriously. Aunty Em and Uncle Henry are too busy with their chickens, while the farm hands tease her and suggest that she avoid their neighbour by taking a different route home. The scene culminates with Aunty Em telling Dorothy that she always gets into a fret over nothing and that if she really wants to help them out, she should find a place where she won't get into any trouble. Bemused, the girl stops short and stares straight ahead, thinking, leaving her aunt to rush off towards the house. 'Some place where there isn't any trouble', she muses, partly to herself and partly to her dog. 'Do you suppose there is such a place Toto? There must be. It's not a place you can get to by boat or a train. It's far, far away … behind the moon, beyond the rain'. At which point she starts to sing 'Over The Rainbow', and the whole register of the film shifts.

Garland's performance of the song is a decisive moment within the structure of the film. Not only does the song break the frenetic pace of the narrative, but it also opens up a space for her to meditate on the possibilities available to her that terrifyingly bleak place.[9] The camera tracks her in semi-close-up, excluding everyone but Toto, as she wanders through the farmyard, leaning against a stack of hay, and then swinging on the wheel of a hay cutter, all the while continuing to sing about that other place and how she might get there. She ends her song with another question: 'Why, oh why, can't I?' There follows a brief pause, the sky darkens, the frightening figure of Miss Gulch appears riding towards the farm on her bicycle, a look of determination on her face, and the strange and wonderful events of the film begin to unfold.

Can a song that refers, among other things, to rainbows, lullabies, dreams, clouds, lemon-drops, chimney tops and flying bluebirds, tell us anything meaningful about our awareness of the past? To begin with, 'Over the Rainbow' slows the film down. Up until that moment, when Dorothy stops to ask herself whether a place without trouble exists, the pace of the movie has been relentless, pushing the first part of the narrative toward the confrontation that is about to take place with Miss Gulch. The choice of a ballad so early on, just prior to this crucial event, dramatically forces our attention on to Dorothy's predicament, as well as emphasizing that the decisions she will go on to make (running away, returning home, journeying to Oz, returning to Kansas) arise from, and remain in dialogue with, the song's powerful vision of escape. Yip Harburg, the song's lyricist, seems to have understood this very clearly. 'The function of song is to simplify everything,' he explained, 'to take the clutter out of too much plot and too many characters to telescope everything into one emotional idea.'[10] By opening up a different temporality, one in which Dorothy is free to imagine another world, the song transforms her situation from one in which she must accept things as they are, to one in which the world she imagines becomes the reality to which she must return.[11] 'It wasn't a dream,' she insists, when she is finally back in Kansas, 'it was a place. A real, truly live place. Doesn't anyone believe me?' There are at least two issues here relating to our awareness of the past that deserve more detailed exploration. But before elucidating further, I want to shift our focus from Dorothy's dreams of escaping the desolate Kansas plains to the opulent world of St. Louis in the same period.

St Louis ... summer 1903

One of the notable things about Vincente Minnelli's *Meet Me in St. Louis* is how little actually happens in the film. The narrative centres on the Smith family, and follows the up and downs of their daily lives over the course of four seasons in a small corner of St. Louis, Missouri, as they await the opening of the 1904 Louisiana Purchase Exposition or 'World's Fair', which each family member is certain will bring to their city the attention of the whole world. Alonzo Smith and his wife Ann live a comfortable middle class life in a large house on a picturesque street in the Kensington suburb of St. Louis. They have four daughters: Rose, Esther (Garland), Agnes and Tootie; and a son, Lon (short for Alonzo Jr.). Grandpa Smith lives with them too. The film is about the sisters' education in the ways of the world, and most especially about love and the potential for heartbreak. Esther, the second eldest daughter, is besotted with her neighbour, John Truitt, who has just moved in to the house next door. Rose too is in love, with someone called Warren Sheffield. Although he is away studying in the east, at Princeton University, she believes that he is going to ask her to marry him (which he eventually does).

The major event of the film is Alonzo's announcement to the whole family just before Christmas that he has taken a job in New York, and that they will be moving there with him. The family is devastated and upset at the news, especially Rose and Esther whose romances, friendships, and educational plans are threatened. Esther is also deeply disappointed because they will miss the opening of the Exposition. On Christmas Eve, even more upset at the imminent move, Tootsie destroys the snowmen the family has made, and so Mr. Smith changes his mind and declares that they will all stay in St. Louis. The film ends with the family taking two horse drawn buggies to the 'World's Fair' and the entire family (including the girls' new beaux, John Truitt and Warren Sheffield) overlooking the Grand Lagoon at the centre of the Exposition site just as thousands of lights illuminate the grand pavilions.

The opening sequence sets up the key themes of the film. 'In half a dozen shots,' James Naremore notes, 'all of them joined together so smoothly that they seem like one continuous movement of the camera, we are introduced to six characters and taken on a tour of the house where most of the story will take place. The sequence begins and ends in the Smith family kitchen – a locus of female work, providing communal activity, nourishment, and maternal care – and is unified by a 'pass along' version of the title song'.[12] The sequence is vivid and meticulous in the way in which each element that we see and hear reproduces the historical period in which the film takes place, from the characters passing around 'Meet Me in St. Louis' (it was a hit in the year the film is set), to the focus on women as representatives of an emerging consumer society.[13] It is important to note, however, that

Minnelli was not particularly interested in what St. Louis was actually like in this period, but rather, in recreating an imagined reality within which the events of the film unfolded. For example, while he was very attentive to the smallest details in each shot, including period furniture, clothing, cars and so on, he also based the sets he had built on the paintings of Thomas Eakins, as a way of enhancing the film's visual coherence and authenticity.[14] 'You have to have great discipline in what you do', he once remarked.[15] 'I spent a great deal of time in research, and finding the rights things for it. I feel that a picture that stays with you is made up of a hundred or more hidden things'.[16]

More than any other element, the communal singing of 'Meet Me in St. Louis' establishes our sense of the world that Minnelli recreates.[17] How is this achieved? To begin with, we hear it sung by a choir over the film's titles, and will do so again at the end of the film. Returning in the opening sequence, it starts as an inaudible refrain when Lon enters the kitchen, tasting his mother's ketchup on the stove, looking through his mail, and absent-mindedly humming 'De-la-da-dee dee dee ...' The tune is then picked up by the third sister, Agnes, as she leaves the kitchen and goes upstairs, and quickly taken up in another key by Grandpa as he finishes shaving. He exits the bathroom still singing (but getting the words slightly wrong), waltzes down the hallway and into his room, where he substitutes 'la-la-las' and humming when he can't remember the words. He, too, is interrupted by Esther and her friends, who are singing the song together as they pull up outside in a carriage. The young people finish the song as Esther gets out of the carriage, gathers her things, and runs inside to the kitchen. Two scenes later, Esther re-enters the kitchen half-singing and half-humming the tune, and then, later, we watch as she and Rose sing two choruses of the song at the family piano (Rose is the pianist and Esther dances around her). At this point their father arrives home from work, hears the song coming out of the house, walks in the front door and heads straight towards the source of the sound. 'For heaven's sake, stop that screeching', he demands, interrupting the girls before they can complete the song's final line. 'That song. The fair won't open for seven months. That's all everybody sings about or talks about. I wish everybody would meet at the fair and leave me alone.'[18]

When Shütz talks of 'growing old together while the music lasts', he is making a claim about our temporal experience of a song and the way in which it includes within it, and in fact imaginatively shapes, the histories of which we are a part.[19] When we compose or perform or listen to music, he argues, 'the social relationship between performers and listener is founded upon the common experience of living simultaneously in several dimensions of time'.[20] 'Meet Me in St. Louis' substantiates the past to which the movie refers by encompassing each of its characters within the specific temporality of the song, and thus the community it calls in to being. At the same time, the song facilitates the expression of individual differences (of singing style, pitch, ability and interest) through their collective participation in it. This mutual 'tuning in', as Shütz calls it, creates in the space of a song the sense of rediscovering in the past the possibilities for the future, even as it reminds its audience that that such a past can no longer exist.[21]

Hollywood ... 1927

What is the difference between what we see and what we hear? The question is raised in very first scene of Stanley Donen and Gene Kelly's *Singin' In the Rain* (1951). In the scene, movie star Don Lockwood (Kelly) has just arrived with his co-star, Lina Lamont (Jean Hagen), at the opening night of their new film, *The Royal Rascal*, at Grauman's Chinese Theatre in Los Angeles (a theatre which is still in use). As the couple step out of their limousine onto the red carpet leading into the theatre, a gossip columnist, Dora Bailey (Madge Black), stops Lockwood, and asks him to describe to the assembled audience how it all happened. 'The story of your success is an inspiration to young people all over the world', she graciously declares, to which the crowd ecstatically agrees. After a moment of mock humility, in which he appears to have nothing especially interesting to say, Lockwood replies to her (and the cheering crowd) with not just one, but two parallel stories about his life. The first one follows what we might think of as a classic narrative of dedicated study and high-artistic achievement:

> Well, any story of my career would have to include my lifelong friend, Cosmo Brown [Donald O'Connor]. We were kids together, grew up together, worked together ... I've had one motto I've always lived by: dignity, always dignity. This was instilled in me by Mom and Dad from the very beginning. They sent me to the finest schools, including dancing school – that's where I first met Cosmo – and with him I used to perform for Mom and Dad's society friends. They used to make such a fuss over me. Then, if I was very good, I was allowed to accompany Mom and Dad to the theatre. They brought me up on Shaw, Molière, the finest of the classics. To this was added rigorous musical training at the conservatory of fine arts. Then we rounded out apprenticeship at the most exclusive dramatics academy. At all times, the motto remained: dignity, always dignity. In a few years, Cosmo and I were ready to embark on a dance concert tour. We played the finest symphonic halls in the country. Audiences everywhere adored us. Finally we decided to come to sunny California. We were stranded here ... I mean ... staying here when the offers from the movie studio started pouring in.

The second, parallel story unfolds in counterpoint to Lockwood's first account; yet this second narrative is visible and audible only to us, the audience. For example, when Lockwood proudly announces that he and Cosmo attended the finest schools, including dancing schools, what the movie audience see is a cut-away image of the two of them as kids, performing for money in a dingy pool hall. His parent's 'society friends' are in fact the other players around the pool tables, who throw the boys some spare change for their efforts. Eventually, we see Lockwood's father carting them out of the hall. Accompanying his comments about being exposed to Bernard Shaw, Molière and the classical theatre, we watch the two boys sneaking into a Nickelodeon movie house to see B-grade monster movies. When Lockwood describes his rigorous musical training to the adoring crowd, we see him on violin and Cosmo on piano playing with a ragtime band in a beer hall. Their apprenticeship at 'the most exclusive dramatics academy' is in reality time spent at amateur nights in vaudeville, where they perform a comic dance routine to the popular song 'Fit as a Fiddle and Ready for Love' (only to be 'gonged' off the stage); while his description of touring the 'finest symphonic halls' refers not to Steinway Hall in New York, or Symphony Hall in Boston, but to the vaudeville circuits, where the two are regularly booed of stage by audiences. The two performers finally get a job playing music for silent films, and by chance, Lockwood offers to stand in for an injured stunt man. The director likes him and offers him more stunt work, which he pursues with a crazy single-mindedness that almost kills him. Eventually the head of the studio spots him, tells Lockwood that 'he's got something' (looks, charisma, talent, perseverance, a winning smile, a wonderful way with words ... or maybe just a great imagination?), and he lands a leading role. The two stories – one told by voice-over, the other through a series of images – converge when the camera returns to the ever-smiling Lockwood, standing in front of the microphone, reciting his motto once again, but this time for both audiences: 'Dignity,' he announces, 'always dignity'. From our perspective, the joke seems to be on that *other* audience, the one inside the film; nonetheless, by the end of the film it is clear that the joke might also be on us; for nothing we know about art, entertainment, singing, dancing, love and life it seems, can be taken for granted.

By admitting that when we go to the movies, hear a song, listen to someone speak, go to a Broadway show, or fall in love, we are some way deceived by our senses, the scene raises a number of important questions about our knowledge of the world, our place within it, and our relationships with those around us. Kelly and Donen are asking us to evaluate the power that images, speech, voice and text have on us, to assess our reasons for believing, or not believing, in what someone says, or does. They are also asking us to think about the kinds of stories we tell ourselves about who we are: how we tell them – that is, in what form, or with what accent, or with what tone, we try to say what we mean – and, what happens to those stories once they are no longer ours to tell.

The film raises a number of interpretative issues that are essential to understanding the claims that musicals make about the past. I want to focus on just one in this instance, to assess its implications for thinking about historical consciousness. The early 1950s was a difficult time in Hollywood. For several years following the end of the Second World War the United States Congress House Un-American Activities Committee (HUAC), led by Senator McCarthy, had been waging a largely successful fight against American communists, ex-communists, communist-sympathizers, and the socialist and liberal Left more broadly. In 1947, HUAC had already indicted the group known as the 'Hollywood Ten' for refusing to answer the committee's question, 'Are you now or have you ever been a member of the Communist Party?' In 1951, HUAC launched its second wave of hearings focused on 'the communist threat' in Hollywood, which led to the long period of blacklisting, informing, denouncing and refusals to testify.[22] It was in this context that Kelly decided to leave for Europe where he and his wife, the actress Betsy Blair (who was eventually blacklisted), were able to continue working. It eventually took him nineteen months to negotiate an acceptable clearance with the powerful International Alliance of Theatrical Stage Employees (IATSE) union and HUAC in order to return to the United States without the possibility of further persecution and finally see the film released.[23]

Although not directly about the political struggles over anti-communism, *Singin' in the Rain* does explicitly highlight the problem of knowing oneself and of finding one's true voice, in a context in which no one is sure what anyone means to say, or why and how things are being said in the first place. The question of belief thus structures the narrative in such a way as to imply that the fundamental questions of political commitment and truth that defined the early 1950s in Hollywood were inseparable from the conflicts that took place in the 1920s over the coming of sound to film. This temporal ambiguity or sliding seems to go to the heart of what Hollywood musicals are about. For while it is common to see such films as offering audiences an escape from life, as a fantasy that either simplifies or distorts reality, I want to propose something like the opposite view. To quote Stanley Cavell: 'It is a poor idea of fantasy which takes it to be a world apart from reality, a world clearly showing us unreality. Fantasy is precisely what reality can be confused with.'[24] *Singin' in the Rain* wants us to understand that it is exactly this kind of confusion which connects cinema's past so powerfully to the politics of the present.

Austria ... the 'Last Golden Days' of the 1930s

No recent Hollywood musical has had anything like the impact of *The Sound of Music*. Along with *Gone with The Wind* (1939) and *Star Wars* (1977), it is still one of the highest grossing films in American cinema history.[25] Directed by Robert Wise, and based on the 1959 stage show of

FIGURE 10.2 *Julie Andrews in* The Sound of Music *(1965)*

the same name by Richard Rogers and Oscar Hammerstein, the film tells
the story of a novice nun, Maria (Julie Andrews), who leaves her abbey
to become the governess of the von Trapp family. It takes place mostly
in and around Salzburg on the eve of the Second World War, and focuses
on the rising tensions in Austrian society brought about by the threat of
Nazism. The film's central theme is the freedom and joy to be found in
music, set in opposition to the conformity and restrictions of the abbey,
the silence and discipline of the von Trapp household, the pretensions of
aristocratic privilege, the limitations of marriage, and the totalitarian power
of the Nazis. According to Richard Dyer, 'the film sets up human (but also
specifically female) problems, and solutions to them, that by implication,
run contrary to the interest, hence ideology, of the dominant groups'.[26] It
takes as its point of departure class relationships, sexual ambivalence, and,
most importantly, the contradictions between personal freedom and the
repressive institutions of the bourgeois social order, including the church,
home, military, big business, and marriage.[27] 'The film tries to offer easy
ways out through the ideologies of nationalism and marriage,' Dyer goes on
to argue, 'yet they are not brushed aside so lightly and the film ends rather
with a celebration of human endurance.'[28]

While Dyer focuses primarily on universal struggles for liberation,
especially the socialist struggle, another way of understanding the film's
appeal to themes of personal freedom and human endurance is to see
it in the context of the political struggles of the 1960s, in particular the
African-American civil rights movement. In 1964, the year the film was
in production, the United States Congress passed the Civil Rights Act
to end discrimination based on race, colour, religion, sex, or national
origin. The Act was the culmination of a century-long struggle among

African-Americans to obtain fundamental rights that had been codified in the Reconstruction Amendments after the Civil War. The following year, when the film was released, Congress also passed the Voting Rights Act. The passage of the Act revolutionized the access African-Americans had to the ballot throughout most of the southern states, forever altering the politics of those states.[29] While the film does not directly question the realities of power and control in the United States in this period, what is striking about its thematic content, as Dyer points out, is how effectively it conveys the way the opposition between freedom and social control looks and feels for its characters.[30]

   This same opposition is also evident in an earlier film based on a Rogers and Hammerstein stage show, *The King and I* (1956). Directed by Walter Lang, the film famously tells the story of an English woman who became schoolteacher to the children of the King of Siam in the 1860s. As with the story of Maria and the von Trapp family, *The King and I* highlights the contradictions of personal liberation at a crucial moment in the struggle for civil rights in the United States. In this case, the film's release coincided with the national debate over the United States Supreme Court's 1954 decision in the case of *Brown versus the Board of Education of Topeka*. This landmark decision argued that the public education doctrine of 'separate but equal' was inherently unequal and violated the Fourteenth Amendment to the United States Constitution.[31] Both films thus displace their immediate political concerns onto other historical times and places, but in order to convey with greater immediacy and emotional intensity the experiences and feelings about the present they want to explore. On the surface, they may appear to be either grossly nostalgic or heavily romanticized, as critics are often quick to point out, but *The King and I* and *The Sound of Music* bring us to a renewed understanding of our awareness of the past by transforming how we view the present.

   In *The Sound of Music*, the space opened up by each of the songs includes the possibility of personal and collective liberation, and not just for the characters singing them. The film's audiences can also experience this possibility. An important example of this process is when Maria sings 'My Favorite Things' for the children so as to calm their fears about a thunder-storm outside. The scene begins, however, with an exchange between Frau Schmidt (Norma Varden), Captain von Trapp's housekeeper, and Maria, in her room. 'The von Trapp children don't play,' says the housekeeper, 'they march.' 'Surely you don't approve of that?' asks Maria. 'Ever since the Captain lost his poor wife,' Frau Schmidt explains, 'he runs this house as if he were on one of his ships again. Whistles, orders, no more music, no more laughing. Nothing that reminds him of her ... even the children.' 'It's so wrong', Maria observes. 'Oh well', the housekeeper replies, sighing and shrugging her shoulders as she leaves. Left in her room alone, Maria starts to pray, when Liesl (Charmian Carr) appears at the window, soaking wet from the storm outside. While Liesl changes her clothes, Maria contemplates going to bed, when suddenly the youngest von Trapp child, Gretel (Kym Karath) appears at her door as well, scared by the storm, and soon to be followed by the rest of the children. Once they're all gathered on her bed, Maria tells the children: 'Well now, when anything bothers me and I'm feeling unhappy, I just try and think of nice things'. Listing some of those things, Maria starts to sing. For Dyer, 'My Favorite Things' '… is the occasion for the demonstration of music's power to banish the fears of the real world. The children have run to Maria's room, terrified by the thunderstorm. To cheer them up, she asks them to think of nice things like kittens, rainbows, snow, and out of the list develops the song. But it is essentially the *music* that cheers, not thinking of the nice things, for when, later in the film (after Maria has temporarily left the von Trapps), the children attempt to reprise the song, the result is lugubrious, dispirited. It is only when Maria returns during the attempted reprise, and in her singing recovers the song's bounce, that it is effective'.[32]

The film's immense popularity in the United States – the soundtrack reached the number one spot on the *Billboard* charts in 1965, it remained in the top ten for a record breaking 109 weeks, and stayed on the charts until 1968 – becomes explicable once we begin to understand how powerfully it speaks to themes of freedom and control.[33] Evidence of this can be found in the response to 'My Favorite Things' by the influential jazz saxophonist, John Coltrane, who recorded a version of it in 1961.[34] Although he first heard it in 1960, performed by Mary Martin in the Broadway production of the musical, Coltrane's decision to record this song (and to continue performing it frequently up until his death in 1967) tells us a lot about the way in which its affirmation of music as a means of overcoming one's fears connected it to its immediate political context. Most jazz critics (and many scholars) credit Coltrane with rescuing the song, praising the superiority of his interpretation over the original, which they accuse of being sentimental, vacuous, and nostalgic.[35] This kind of criticism, however, misses something important about the way in which film's thematic contents and its attempt to mediate the past was continuous with the saxophonist's own musical project. 'Lots of people imagine wrongly that 'My Favorite Things' is one of my compositions', he told a reporter. 'I would love to have written it, but it's by Rogers and Hammerstein'.[36] This generous acknowledgement suggests a more complex relationship between the reality of the past imagined by the film and the way its songs summon its audiences to reflect on their potential for transforming the present.

Conclusion

My original question was: what can Hollywood musicals tell us about our relationship to the past? One answer is to consider how the medium has come to affect our sense of what counts as the past. Within three years of being invented, according to Geoffrey Nowell-Smith, 'the cinema was already inserting itself into the problematic of the historical record and re-marking the boundaries between fact and fiction, truth and falsehood, in history'.[37] This is the defining feature of each of the above examples; they augment the reality to which they refer by enfolding the past into a present that is inseparable from the images they create. 'One of [cinema's] operations', Nowell-Smith goes on to argue, 'is to confer a certain status of reality on what it shows.'[38] Films achieve this by opening onto 'the imaginary ... not a timeless and unhistorical imaginary, but a specific twentieth-century imaginary which the cinema itself has formed'.[39] All of which is to say that if we are to understand the past within a film, we may in fact require something other than a 'historical' knowledge of history.

Robert Rosenstone, too, believes that films propose new ways of thinking about the past. 'These ways are unsettling', he claims, 'because they escape the confines of words and provide elements – visual, aural, emotional, subconscious – that we don't know how to admit into our knowledge. There is something about the moving image and the way it means that seems to escape the confines of words ... To mean more and to mean differently than the words can say'.[40] Hollywood musicals are doubly unsettling because of the centrality of song and dance routines to our experience of these films. What we remember when we leave the theatre are the great songs and dance routines and not the accuracy of the setting or the verisimilitude of the story it tells. 'Of all the elements that make up a historical film,' observes Rosenstone, 'fiction, or invention, has to be the most problematic (for historians). To accept invention is, of course, to change significantly the way we think about history. It is to alter one of written history's basic elements: its documentary or empirical aspect. To take history on film seriously is to accept the notion that the empirical is but one way of thinking about the meaning of the past'[41] (see also Chapters 2 and 9).

Throughout this chapter, I have claimed that Hollywood musicals are not just entertainment and nor do they exist independently of the past. Because of their status as mass-cultural events, with huge global audiences, they frequently take up many of the same historical and theoretical themes that we find in other art forms. In order to understand how Hollywood musicals develop these themes, and why we would want to take their historical meaning seriously, my point is that these films enable us to conceptualize the historical imagination in ways that factual or literal accounts of the past can't always do. They speak to, and are part of, our changing experiences of the past, as well as envisaging and redefining our relationship to the possibilities of present. In other words, Hollywood musicals do more than just reflect our sense of the past, or distract us from the reality of historical events; they challenge us to rethink what we imagine the past to be about, and to reconsider what we think it will come to mean for us in the future.

Notes

1   For example see Hugh Rockoff, 'The "Wizard of Oz" as a Monetary Allegory', *Journal of Political Economy* 98 (4) (1990): 739–60; Henry M. Littlefield, 'The Wizard of Oz: Parable on Populism', *American Quarterly* 16 (1) (1964): 47–58.

2   L. Braudy, *The World in a Frame: What We See in Films* (Chicago: University of Chicago Press, 2002), 140.

3   Ibid., 140.

4   J. Feuer, 'The Self-Reflexive Musical and the Myth of Entertainment', in *The Film Genre Reader II*, ed. B. Keith Grant (Austin: University of Texas Press, 1995), 441–55.

5   R. Altman, *The American Film Musical* (Bloomington: Indiana University Press, 1987), 19.

6   Ibid., 21.

7   A. Schütz, 'Making Music Together: A Study in Social Relationship', *Social Research* 18 (1) (1951): 76–97.

8   S. Rushdie, *The Wizard of Oz* (London: Palgrave Macmillan, 2012), 10.

9   R. Dyer, *In the Space of a Song: The Uses of Song In Film* (London: Routledge, 2012), 1–56.

10 A. Harmetz, *The Making of the Wizard of Oz* (Chicago: Chicago Review Press, 2013), 87.

11 Rushdie, *The Wizard of Oz*, 58.

12 J. Naremore, *The Films of Vincente Minnelli* (Cambridge: Cambridge University Press, 1993), 76.

13 R. Ohmann, *Selling Culture: Magazines, Markets and Class at the Turn of the Century* (New York: Verso, 1996).

14 Naremore, *The Films of Vincente Minnelli*, 75.

15 G. Kaufman, *Meet Me in St. Louis* (London: BFI, 1994), 40.

16 Ibid.

17 Dyer, *In the Space of a Song*; R. Knapp, *The American Musical and the Formation of American Identity* (Princeton: Princeton University Press, 2006); Naremore, *The Films of Vincente Minnelli*.

18 See Dyer, *In the Space of a Song*, 58–9; Knapp, *The American Musical*, 95

19 Schütz, 'Making Music Together', 93.

20 Ibid., 94.

21 Ibid., 96; and; Dyer, op. cit. 80.

22 L. May, *The Big Tomorrow: Hollywood and the Politics of the American Way* (Chicago: University of Chicago Press, 2002), 196–211; P. Wollen, *Singin' In the Rain* (London: BFI, 1992), 45–6.

23 Wollen, *Singin' In the Rain*, 50–1.

24   S. Cavell, *The World Viewed: Reflections on the Ontology of Film* (Cambridge: Harvard University Press, 1979), 85.

25   C. Flinn, *The Sound of Music* (London: Palgrave Macmillan, 2015), 10.

26   R. Dyer, *Only Entertainment* (London: Routledge, 1992), 46.

27   Ibid., 58.

28   Ibid. In *The Politics of Hollywood Cinema*, Richard Rushton also makes a compelling case for the claim that *The Sound of Music* presents '... complex problems that can be said to be of a political nature'. R. Rushton, *The Politics of Hollywood Cinema* (London: Palgrave Macmillan, 2013), 78.

29   G. May, *Bending Toward Justice: The Voting Rights Act and the Transformation of American Democracy* (New York: Basic Books, 2013).

30   Dyer, *Only Entertainment*, 58.

31   Ibid.

32   Ibid., 51.

33   Keith Caufield, '50 Years Ago: "The Sound of Music" Soundtrack Hit No. 1 on the Billboard 200', *Billboard*, 13 November (2015). Available online: http://www.billboard.com/articles/columns/chart-beat/6762397/sound-of-music-soundtrack-no-1-anniversary (accessed 18 August 2016).

34   John Coltrane, *My Favorite Things* (Atlantic, 1961)

35   See for example I. Monson, 'Doubleness and Jazz Improvisation: Irony, Parody and Ethnomusicology', *Critical Inquiry* 20 (2) (1994): 283–313; L. Kramer, *Musical Meaning: Towards A Critical History* (Berkeley: University of California Press, 2002), 242–57.

36   Coltrane quoted in L. Porter, *Coltrane: His Life and Music* (Ann Arbor: University of Michigan Press, 1998), 182.

37   G. Nowell-Smith, 'On History and the Cinema', *Screen* 31 (2) (1990): 162.

38   Ibid., 163.

39   Ibid.

40   R. Rosenstone, *Visions of the Past: The Challenge of Film to Our Idea of History* (Cambridge: Harvard University Press, 1995), 235.

41   R. Rosenstone, 'The Historical Film: Looking at the Past in a Postliterate Age', in *The Historical Film: History and Memory in Media*, ed. M. Landy (New Brunswick, NJ: Rutgers University Press, 2001), 65.

CHAPTER ELEVEN

'Moving' images: Educational uses of D-Day imagery

Michael R. Dolski[1]

Modern society's engagement with warfare is often mediated by a fixation on spectacle. Visual imagery tends to prevail as the primary means for understanding the nature, experience, costs, and consequences of war. There is an element of pageantry and propaganda at play as well, suggesting caution is warranted when handling such material.[2] Nevertheless, people often use imagery, particularly moving images, as a vehicle for understanding warfare. This bears particular relevance when considering the frenetic American society characterized by the ephemerality of its own culture. In that context, war on film presents a quick and relatively easy way to engage with the past, just as it is a more entertaining means by which to 'learn' history.

War as spectacle connotes two ideas worth consideration. First, wars of the past century are often captured or represented on film (see also Chapters 3 and 8). Second, people are generally familiar with filmic representation of warfare. Describing the Second World War, one author ventured that 'the documentary footage and Hollywood films of the war years – compiled, reedited, remade, replayed endlessly – are a vivid cultural heritage and a vital historical link ... to a past that no longer recedes before the eye'.[3] He further identified these sources as offering 'a way of seeing America during the Second World War', which constitutes 'a second sight into the most dramatic and decisive moments of the century'.[4] War offers viewers drama, emotion, action, and the fate of the world hinging upon the acts of a few brave or industrious souls. Film presents an opportunity to distill warfare to a few moments of high tension or hyperkinetic activity with momentous result.

The Second World War has proven consistently popular for filmmakers and viewers alike, on both big and small screens. Americans in particular have devoted near-continuous attention to selected components of that lengthy, worldwide experience. The Allied invasion of north-western France in June 1944, D-Day, is one aspect of the war singled out for scrutiny. One recent history of the battle described it as a 'vast, complicated, multilayered saga'.[5] The one day of battle that traditionally draws attention encapsulates many themes popular with filmmakers and audiences: the fate of the war and the world turning on the actions of a relatively small group of people, the thrill of frenzied military action and destructiveness of modern warfare, and clearly demarcated ethical boundaries. The salability of this overall characterization has endured. Despite social, political, and cultural upheavals of the past seventy years, Americans have continued to consume avidly audio-visual productions dedicated to D-Day; English-language depictions have included at least thirteen major films and fifty-six documentary films or significant television specials, not including widespread broadcast anniversary event coverage, in 1994, 2004 and 2014.[6]

To sift through this material requires time and patience. Any attempt to employ these moving image sources for instructional purposes brings forth additional concerns. For instance, the thematic constructs suggested in the preceding paragraph deserve some attention. In addition, no matter how insightful or engaging, Second World War veteran and filmmaker Sam Fuller rightly cautioned that films are *not* actual war.[7] Even film stock captured at the time of the event risks decontextualization or often requires some sort of editorial oversight to ascribe meaning to the images.

Despite these caveats, it is hard to deny the power of moving images to shape our understandings of the past. Such engaging imagery often assumes a level of veracity or authenticity that is hard to attribute to the written word; this applies to the vast majority of individuals that did not participate in the events depicted and even for many of those that did. Moreover, when it comes to D-Day moving imagery, the sheer scale of overall effort indicates a collective social fascination. For all of these reasons, educators and students alike may be tempted to dive in headfirst, select a few more popular sources, and get on with the task of learning the past through these materials. This chapter, however, seeks to elucidate a deliberate course of action, one that pushes for engagement with D-Day moving imagery as *historical* source material. That thought connotes a critical engagement with these records as a means to better understand the details of the past as well as the processes of historical thinking.

D-Day and the movies

June 6, 1944, was a momentous day in the Second World War. The Allies overwhelmed defences along a seventy-mile zone in the Normandy region of German-occupied France with the use of astounding firepower, impressive logistical capability, sheer grit and determination, as well as deft exploitation of happenstance.[8] It was a grueling day, which cost Allied forces more than 4,000 dead.[9] The intense fighting leveled entire French towns and resulted in the deaths of thousands of their citizens.[10] At the day's end, however, more than 150,000 Allied soldiers stood on French soil.

The magnetism of the moment quite naturally attracted widespread attention to the events then and ever since. *News of the Day* newsreels played in American theatres as early as 15 June 1944. These sources conveyed a patchwork of images filmed on inbound landing craft and material captured from German film stock.[11] The battle drew sporadic interest throughout the rest of the war, as seen in other newsreels or major documentary productions, such as *The True Glory* (1945).[12]

The first decade following the conclusion of the war in 1945 saw a number of uneven treatments of D-Day on both big and small screens. Hollywood only sporadically addressed battle events until the 1950s. The global Cold War confrontation, with its moments of intense crisis and danger, pulled attention away from the past. Television, still in its infancy, also proved slow to focus on the Second World War. D-Day, as a result, appeared infrequently until the late 1950s. Lack of market saturation, however, does not imply complete absence, as indicated by subpar films like *D-Day, The Sixth of June* (1956), or trite television programming such as the D-Day episode of the popular programme *You Are There* (1955).[13]

The end of the 1950s saw a growing fusion between Cold War concerns, popular culture, and depictions of the recent past. Themes ascribed to the Allies in the Second World War and its major battles like D-Day proved instructive and useful during the new world confrontation. With major anniversary events, widespread publishing efforts, and other commemorative activities connected to D-Day, so came a renewed round of television fare and major films. It is hard to exaggerate the lasting impact and importance of *The Longest Day* (1962) (see also Chapter 3).[14] This epic war film epitomizes the way an entire international generation (primarily American and Western European) viewed the events of D-Day. Yet even so, this round of popular activity was not strong enough to withstand the anti-militarist turn provoked by the divisive Vietnam War, resulting in the limited creation or distribution of D-Day imagery for the following two decades.

There were a few halting half-steps in the intervening years, such as with the box-office flop (though now critically acclaimed) *The Big Red One* (1980).[15] The immense outpouring of affective sentimentality that defined D-Day's fortieth anniversary events provoked a major return of moving imagery content. The widely televised performance of US President Reagan as he waxed poetically about the 'boys of Pointe du Hoc' tugged the heartstrings of a nation.[16] The year 1984 serves as a major turning point that brought D-Day back to the public consciousness. Major television specials and documentary features soon followed. Hardly an anniversary would pass from that period to the present without some new major offering on the D-Day battles or their importance.

Popular culture proved fixated on D-Day and entertainment media took note. The blockbuster *Saving Private Ryan* (1998) shocked with carnage just as it conveyed a romanticized militarist message that struck a chord.[17] Afterwards, D-Day specials abounded on television, major documentaries became available in many venues, and made-for-television movies even participated, such as the 2004 film, *Ike: Countdown to D-Day*.[18] D-Day now appears in video games, online content, in dedicated special features, even as an implicit reference, as seen with *Edge of Tomorrow* (2014) about a futuristic air-sea-land assault along the beaches of Normandy.[19]

The brief outline here serves merely to provide a general context for evaluation of the entire body of D-Day moving imagery. To disaggregate one work from this whole raises the risk of missing ways in which it contributed to a larger conversation. Contextual awareness is an integral element of source analysis, and that truth holds for moving image sources. With a rough grounding in the evolution of D-Day film image, we can move into specific examples of the manner in which film sources can assist historical understanding.

Grand spectacle

Famous war correspondent Cornelius Ryan purportedly devoted more than a decade to researching and writing the immensely popular book, *The Longest Day* (1959).[20] The book's success attracted the attention of several individuals interested in silver screen glory. The most prominent was Darryl F. Zanuck, then head of the Hollywood film studio Twentieth Century Fox. Zanuck liked the book's focus on common soldiers in extreme adversity as they fought to victory despite the odds. After a series of unsuccessful ventures, Zanuck also hoped to boost the studio's flagging fortunes by latching onto a popular topic. A promotional sheet on the movie declared that 'Zanuck looks to "The Longest Day" as the crowning achievement of his long and distinguished career. He fully expects it to be the most important war film ever made'.[21]

Translation to the big screen demanded herculean efforts. Historian Stephen Ambrose once indicated that this film 'powerfully re-created on a *grand scale* the largest amphibious invasion in history'.[22] He further suggested that '*The Longest Day* remains one of Hollywood's most remarkable logistical achievements'.[23] The process of creating this significant and influential film deserves attention. The 1962 film version of *The Longest Day* borrowed heavily from the book, yet it also deviated. The film involved thousands of people, several governments and their military forces, nearly a year of shooting, and an equally oversized publicity campaign.[24] There were many inputs into this product and to describe it as dependent upon the vision of Ryan or Zanuck alone would vastly oversimplify that reality.

In fact, this film formed part of a Hollywood pattern in the 1960s and 1970s to focus on large-scale or epic re-creation of events. Often billed as 'filmed on location', which was true for *The Longest Day*, these films claimed an authentic realness while conveying the enormity of grand events.[25] Zanuck, in fact, wrote early in the process that 'It is the most expensive and difficult undertaking I have ever attempted in my life'.[26] The expense accrued, in large part, from the absence of viable moving imagery from the actual battle that could be incorporated into the production. Thus, *The Longest Day* required a re-creation of the landings and, in step with the penchant for epic scale, Zanuck and crew went large. To evoke the vast Allied panoply of battle, the filmmakers convinced several militaries to lend soldiers or equipment, but that alone was not sufficient. Zanuck's people scoured Europe for cast-off Second World War material.[27] The film succeeds in conveying the enormity of battle because of the superb attention paid to the big picture and scale of the events. With a 'galaxy of historical figures played by stars appearing in cameo roles', the film portrays the immensity (almost anonymizing impact) of modern, industrial warfare.[28] Shockingly, *The Longest Day* filmmakers led the ninth largest military force in the world during production.[29] The scale came at cost; with a total production outlay of nearly $10 million *The Longest Day* was 'the most expensive black and white film ever made'.[30]

The Longest Day depicts the chaotic uncertainty of D-Day and its alleged moral implications. The story abruptly begins on 5 June, one day before the 'longest day'. A staccato of drum music before the title sets the pace, while on screen an upended helmet resting alone on the beach symbolizes the losses soon-to-be witnessed. The camera shifts to the pursuit and cold blooded murder of a French resistance agent by German occupiers. In ways such as this, the film displays a tension between showing the skillfulness of German soldiers (by the 1960s, allies in the Cold War) and the immorality of their cause. As the plot develops, German leaders prepare for battle while Allied troops worry over the impending action. The difference is revealing: the film perpetuates the Prussian militarist image while humanizing the Allies. A series of vignettes that increase in intensity last the entire 3 hours (pared from 66 hours of captured imagery). These glimpses intersperse actions of high-level leadership with the gritty clash of arms experienced by the junior ranks. All the landing beaches receive some treatment, yet Canadian forces do not figure in the story. Although seeking a realistic depiction of warfare, a jaunty musical score and stirring combat scenes carry a glamorized tint. As Colonel Vandervoort (John Wayne) proudly declares to his troops, they were on the 'threshold of the most crucial day of our times'. This is an adventure tale of one glorious day. Even at Omaha Beach, the Allies surge forward to victory.

The impact of *The Longest Day* was so immediate, and turned out to be so long lasting, that it became the main historical primer on D-Day for millions of people. According to film historian Lawrence Suid, the movie

FIGURE 11.1 The Longest Day *(1962)*

'leaves a lasting impression of the human element of war' even without the meaningful development of any of the countless characters.[31] *The Longest Day* exposed young people to D-Day, while reaping enormous financial rewards for Zanuck and Twentieth Century Fox. It earned approximately $17 million in domestic markets, a huge windfall for the struggling studio. '*The Longest Day*', Suid further explained, 'succeeded at the box office because it drew its story from a popular book and attained a unique visual and dramatic authenticity.'[32]

What, then, does *The Longest Day* provide to the student of history? *The Longest Day* offers the opportunity to assess the nature of historical knowledge production and its collective impact. This film was a massive project that involved many individuals. Some were more important than others, such as author Ryan or producer Zanuck. Nevertheless, other scriptwriters, like famed author James Jones, influenced the final product.[33] The work included five major directors and thousands of actors (to varying degrees).[34] Zanuck's need for assistance with securing equipment and personnel led to a degree of military review and oversight of the film. More direct censorship appeared with the intervention of the Production Code Administration (PCA), Hollywood's vehicle for self-censorship that remained in effect until the late 1960s. Correspondence between Zanuck and head of the PCA, Geoffrey Shurlock, displays the latter's sensitivity to harsh language and what seemed 'an excessive amount of slaughter'.[35] Students must remember that film histories are mediated realities that pass a variety of tests prior to distribution.

More importantly, this film provides an excellent window through which viewers can assess the enormity of mass warfare in battles like D-Day.

Although dismayed by some of the artistic licence exhibited in the film, Ryan praised it as 'probably … the most accurate and comprehensive historical representation of a battle ever made in a film [which] probably will never be surpassed simply because of the logistics involved'.[36] Additional revelatory points include the nature of allied or coalitional warfare and its impact on the D-Day battlefield as well as the universal experience of soldiers facing combat. *The Longest Day* serves as spectacular history on an epic scale. While exploring the nature of D-Day through this version of the past, the viewer can also ponder what this film's creation and popularity demonstrate about the time in which it was created.[37]

Technologies of destruction

War and film are both technologically dependent enterprises. To illustrate the impact of these technologies of destruction, we will jump to *Saving Private Ryan* (1998). Its D-Day landing scene exhibits a special effects bonanza of gore and destruction. This film also takes viewers away from the macro level of *The Longest Day* down to the micro level of a few, highly developed characters and their stories.

As with *The Longest Day*, *Saving Private Ryan* derived from another popular book on D-Day: Stephen Ambrose's 1994 bestseller, *D-Day, June 6, 1944*.[38] Scriptwriter Robert Rodat drew on the captivating book's combat descriptions as framework for a new war film.[39] As later recounted, the second scene of the film – the D-Day landings – provided the emotional power to carry the rest of the storyline through to completion.[40] Rodat pitched the project and Paramount signed him to write a script in June 1995.[41] Spielberg brought in his friend, Tom Hanks, to help shape and then star in the production.[42] As Spielberg explained, 'I was trying to put chaos upon the screen as close to as what [veterans] told me'.[43] In effect, Spielberg, Hanks and Ambrose (who consulted for the film), all sought to convey a reverential regard for the young Americans that suffered through that awful day. An odd sanctification extended throughout the production process. At one point Spielberg claimed – in a reversal from *The Longest Day* – that he dare not profane the sacred landing sites by shooting on location. Instead, they used beaches in Ireland.[44] Instructing audiences how to react to this new, supposedly more 'real' war film, Spielberg indicated that 'this isn't the kind of movie you see and then go to a bistro and break bread talking about it – you have to go home and deal with it privately'.[45]

Promotional efforts aside, the way that Paramount executives, Spielberg, and Hanks really sought to convey their lesson was through extremely graphic displays of military destruction, a response to the claims of verisimilitude offered by earlier generations of filmmakers such as Zanuck. Spielberg wanted to rub the violence in viewers' faces to make them

FIGURE 11.2 Saving Private Ryan *(1998)*

appreciate the horrendous nature of war and the extreme sacrifices it demands. Without the PCA dictating content boundaries, and in light of astounding advances in film production technologies, it was easier to act upon this desire than in the past. To stamp their own authority on the film, Hanks pushed Spielberg to enlist the aid of a retired US Marine and his company. Dale Dye formed Warriors Incorporated in 1985 to help promote in the mass media what he felt was a more accurate depiction of the US military's past and present.[46] For *Saving Private Ryan*, Dye focused on recreating the historical conditions, attitudes, and actions of the characters, rigorously training the main actors in an intensive miniature boot camp.[47] Dye also worked on the minutiae that bring life to the screen: uniforms, weapons, equipment. Once more evoking scale, Spielberg employed a cast of thousands that again included many military personnel (this time Irish). To evoke a sense of pastness, the director filmed without camera lens filters to produce grainy imagery. The real emotive power, however, emanated from the shocking displays of technological skill in transmitting the sounds and sights of combat. Explosions dominate the screen and computer generated imagery adds to the unremitting destruction in combat scenes. Audiences see soldiers blown to pieces or eviscerated in excruciating detail. Nearly half of the film shoot (twenty-four of fifty-nine days) focused on this one scene alone, which shows the emotional power accorded to it by the producers.[48]

Saving Private Ryan's D-Day scene almost risks overwhelming the senses and emotions.[49] Viewers receive no orientation, suddenly finding themselves 'on board' a landing craft on its way into shore. The ominous overcast sky helps set the mood as the camera displays a host of nervous men engaging in final prayers or vomiting profusely. Last-minute instructions impart tactical guidance in a cold, clinical way: this is serious business. Despite these preparations, the ensuing chaos seems to suggest that chance is just as responsible as skill and planning for determining battlefield results. In the final approach to the beach, the transition to danger zone becomes apparent with the shoreline breaking through the gloom while the audio track now includes small arms fire and thunderous explosions. When the ramp descends on the landing craft, the world plummets into a hellish nightmare of confusion, terror, and death. The next 20 minutes of viewing time demonstrates Spielberg and crew's technical virtuosity in depicting war. Explosions disorient, small arms fire from points unseen kill and maim at random, dismemberments and gory wounds shock (and titillate), and the audio track muffles at points to evoke the disorientation of nearby blasts. Plans seem hopelessly foiled until Captain Miller (Hanks) begins to rally troops to relative safety further up the beach. He and his men landed on the westernmost portion of Omaha Beach, alone and isolated, facing deadly defences and enemies tenaciously clinging onto them.[50] Somehow this depleted force maintains the wherewithal to gather needed equipment, blast an egress route through obstacles, and advance inland. The final few minutes of the scene focus on the fight to surmount the local beach defences, showing that callous hatred of enemy can lead to atrocious acts by even American soldiers. The final glimpse back at the liberated beach seems to vindicate the bloodletting just depicted.

This was only the second scene of a lengthy film. The start and end of the movie take place in the Normandy American Cemetery to showcase the enormity of losses exacted by the so-called 'good war' (see Chapter 3). The plot centres on the effort by a small group of D-Day survivors to rescue under fire another soldier who lost several brothers in the war. The fictional Private Ryan earned a ticket home to mitigate, in some small way, the family's tragedy. There are other combat scenes and extended, absurdly unrealistic, moments of character development in between. Throughout the message remains one of conflicted impulses: honor the men that went through so much, but be wary of the violence that defines warfare. These thematic elements will appear for more detailed consideration below. It suffices to say here that most reviewers fixate on the D-Day scene when discussing the movie; many mistakenly characterize it as the first scene of the film, which shows the magnetic draw of the horrific screen violence.[51]

The destructive slaughter on the beaches set this film apart from previous depictions of D-Day combat. Film historian Basinger argued that 'the violence of *Saving Private Ryan*'s opening sequence [*sic*] (the D-Day landing on Omaha Beach) is overwhelming' and described it as a 'nightmare'.[52] Most reviews of the film highlighted its shocking spectacle of violence. Lawrence Suid suggested that through this display of 'unrelenting violence of torn bodies, blood, gore, and vomit [it] perfectly captured the reality of combat'.[53] He further noted that 'Spielberg made brilliant use of his handheld cameras to create images of men in battle trying to survive in a hostile environment'.[54] *Saving Private Ryan*'s blend of visual imagery and sound assails the senses of the audience as Captain Miller and his comrades struggle to survive. 'Throughout all of this,' Thomas Doherty argued, 'the guilty secret is that far from being horrifying and repulsive, the stunning spectacle of sight and sound is a joy to behold and h[e]arken to from a theater seat, pure cinema at its most hypnotic and intense'.[55] The violence seemed so intense at the time that some questioned the morality of exposing people, particularly veterans of the battle, to its horrors.[56]

Some level of public concern stemmed from the media blitz Spielberg, Hanks and Ambrose engaged in prior to the film's release. They collectively inscribed *Saving Private Ryan* with significant authenticity because of its unblinking fixation on battlefield carnage. Ambrose declared, 'There's no other World War II movie like this. The only things missing are the smell of battle and the smoke of battle'.[57] Spielberg claimed, 'I wanted the audience to realize what it was like to be in a real war rather than a Hollywood war' and that he was 'not making another "movie", but rather *the* American war movie'.[58] Yet not everyone was as impressed; some pointed out a number of flaws in the film's depiction of equipment, battle tactics, small unit dynamics and leadership, the casualty accounting process, or even the basic premise of rescuing one man under fire.[59] Despite claims to uniqueness, this movie also fit well within the conventions of the traditional combat film genre. The gory destruction at the centre of *Saving Private Ryan*'s authenticity thus becomes more a function of technological change and erosion of censorship constraints.[60] It is also a reflection of the cultural atmosphere of the 1990s, which likely pushed Spielberg and Paramount to 'outdo his fellow filmmakers' by throwing 'more arms, legs, heads, guts, and vomit all over the screen and then justif[ying] the images as necessary to capture the realism of battle'.[61]

These thoughts aside, *Saving Private Ryan* was a major success, grossing more than $400 million in domestic and international markets during the initial run.[62] 'A popular and critical success of epic proportions', as described by Doherty, 'it was not just a motion picture but a cultural milestone, an occasion for another solemn encounter with the meaning of World War II and perhaps the last chance for a face-to-face salute to the surviving warriors'.[63] *Saving Private Ryan* offers students of history the chance to see ways in which historical entertainment has transformed into big business in the past two decades. Television stations devoted to historical content, especially military history, now coexist with historical publications directed at general audiences and the seemingly ceaseless offerings of historically themed motion pictures. This mixture of opportunities to engage with the past offers consumers newer experiences that blend historical reality and fiction.[64] One scholar highlighted what he described as *Saving Private Ryan*'s 'faction', which used the historical 'facts' of D-Day with fictitious storyline and characters. In this manner, the past becomes just another commodified form of entertainment.[65] This fact, together with the film's intense, gruesome, and affecting qualities, ensure that *Saving Private Ryan* presents something of interest to the student concerned with D-Day and the Second World War.

Hierarchy and perspective

Modern militaries are essentially hierarchical organizations. Structure funnels responsibility for decisions and actions of greater importance to ever-higher levels of authority. In reflection of the chaos and chances that materialize on the battlefield, at times great results stem from the acts of those on the lowest rungs of power. This characteristic of warfare brings to light the question of focus. At what level of experience and action should one look when attempting to understand an event such as D-Day?

One manner of accessing this past is through an examination of the top-level leadership and the key decisions made in regard to the battle. American General Dwight D. Eisenhower was the Supreme Allied Commander in charge of Operation Overlord (code name for the invasion). Eisenhower bore responsibility for an enormously significant military operation that involved hundreds of thousands of personnel, immeasurable hours of planning and preparation, and the incorporation of vital types and quantities of materiel. Victory or defeat would depend in large measure upon the decisions and actions of this one individual. Despite the enormous burden of responsibility, Eisenhower routinely acknowledged the tremendous importance of the soldiers, sailors, airmen, and civilians underneath him. In one iconic statement, he commended all for embarking on a 'great crusade' to liberate Europe from Nazi tyranny.[66] These sensible leadership actions, however, did not efface the obligations of authority imposed on this one man. For instance, after delaying the invasion in May 1944 to acquire more shipping, Operation Overlord had to commence soon to leave a sufficient campaign window afterwards. The weather took a drastic turn for the worse late on 4 June, threatening one of the two acceptable invasion periods that month. Eisenhower had to choose between launching despite the inclement weather – and risking disaster in an already challenging action – or stalling in the hope of clear weather. Eisenhower opted to go ahead, setting the sixth of June as D-Day.[67] Popular conceptions of D-Day have latched onto Eisenhower's leadership role in preparing for victory.[68] For Eisenhower, D-Day represented an amalgam of positive meanings as the defining moment of his career and the beginning of Europe's liberation.[69]

In reflection of the public association between the man and the event, CBS aired a special programme on the invasion to commemorate the twentieth anniversary in 1964. This programme was tellingly titled *D-Day Plus 20*

Years: Eisenhower Returns to Normandy. It consisted of CBS anchorman Walter Cronkite accompanying Eisenhower on location in southern England and Normandy as the two discussed the decisions, key moments, and moral significance of D-Day.[70] Plans for the venture took shape through a series of meetings and communications in mid-1963 in which CBS production officials, such as Fred Friendly, defined the intent of the programme. Friendly felt that a focus on Eisenhower and his decisions relating to this event was only natural, as people should know more about 'the greatest day in American history'. These interactions elicited an ambivalent response from Eisenhower. He readily acknowledged the world-saving significance of Allied victory, while concluding that 'he had lived more hours between the time of decision and the time that the lodgment was secure ... than in any other moment in public life'. As befitting a leader of Allied forces in the Second World War and after, Eisenhower also stressed the coalition's role in achieving victory.[71] All concerned felt such a programme was worthwhile and they arranged to film it during late summer 1963.

D-Day Plus 20 Years, which aired on the anniversary, 6 June 1964, displays a compelling mixture of static imagery with voiceover narration alongside filmed interactions between Eisenhower and others, such as Cronkite or Normandy locals. The narrator at the outset establishes the immense stakes at hand with D-Day, intoning that 'a battle was joined between the world of freedom and the world of tyranny', to thrust off the 'Nazi jackboot' crushing Europe. The programme emphasizes the enormity of the events as a way to impress upon viewers the great burden of responsibility shouldered by Eisenhower. For the remainder of the show, Cronkite prompts Eisenhower with questions or stands alongside while Eisenhower reminisces with people touched by D-Day. Moments such as these further reinforce the human costs and consequences of the battle, but also allow Eisenhower to focus on the junior ranks and his deep appreciation for their sacrifices. In Normandy, Eisenhower and Cronkite tour famous battle zones such as Omaha Beach, Pointe du Hoc, and Sainte-Mère-Église. One repeated refrain from Eisenhower is that the junior ranks determined success that day, as everything that could have did go wrong. The continuous focus on his preparations for the battle, his decisions that shaped the battle, and his reactions at news of the unfolding battle, all perforce emphasize the top-level perspective. The production juxtaposes bathers on Norman beaches in the then-present with archival pictures or grainy film stock from the invasion, as if to demonstrate the freedoms these soldiers fought to protect and preserve. The theme of gratuitous liberation is also prevalent, as one would expect from the man that termed the invasion a 'crusade' against despotic tyranny. One closing thought aired by Eisenhower maintains that American forces fought 'not to gain anything for ourselves, not to fulfill any ambitions that America had for conquest, but just to preserve freedom ... in the world'.

D-Day Plus 20 Years was one of many commemorative activities linked to the battle's twentieth anniversary.[72] But while CBS's programme

FIGURE 11.3 *'Ike' returns to Normandy, 1964*

extolled the leadership of one man, other productions provided Americans
a different glimpse into D-Day. In fact, Walter Cronkite, who would show
up repeatedly in D-Day related programming, served as a guide once more,
hosting the popular television programme *You Are There*. This series
featured re-enactments of historical events that would introduce viewers to
a fictional character/participant. In the process of acting through the events,
characters often turned to converse with the narrator or directly address the
camera in the guise of educating audiences. The series included a D-Day
episode that aired on 6 March 1955.[73]

The episode begins as a newscast, which draws upon Cronkite's iconic
status. Cronkite broadcasts a warning to French citizens that the invasion
was nigh and they should seek safe shelter. Such a warning was not
transmitted for the actual invasion lest the German defenders prepare
accordingly (with concomitant suffering of the civilian population as a
result).[74] The depiction of the invasion relies heavily on footage of film
stock created at the time, along with several still pictures and a 'embedded
reporter' voiceover serving as the narrator, focusing on one American unit,
C Company, 116th Infantry Regiment, 29th Infantry Division. This unit
rides the landing craft into the beach, while one junior officer presents a
map to discuss ingress routes and the gathered soldiers hear Eisenhower's
'great crusade' order of the day. Once on land, the unit pauses to gather

forces then surmounts beach defences and natural obstacles. There is some indication of confusion with misplaced landings, wounded leaders, and hesitation to advance in the face of fire. The programme shows several soldiers dying (clean deaths). Nevertheless, the unit advances inland after only a brief halt. The end displays the soldiers marching off in the midst of notable destruction. Although there were other 'embedded reporters' with Allied units, the focus remains with this American force. Cronkite concludes the episode by reading from President Franklin Roosevelt's famous D-Day prayer, transmitted across radios in the US on the night of 6 June 1944. Roosevelt beseeched 'Almighty God' while he instructed Americans on the morality of D-Day since their forces were liberating others from oppression.[75] After demonstrating the carnage and confusion of the battle, this *You are There* episode was clear in showing the reason for such sacrifice.

The 1950s, in fact, witnessed multiple commemorative celebrations of D-Day. The tenth anniversary attracted attention, as did the opening of the Normandy American Cemetery that overlooks the Omaha Beach landing area. Despite this, one other project – another Hollywood film depiction of the invasion – failed to gather steam. Sam Fuller, himself a D-Day veteran, sought to pay homage to the soldiers of his 1st Infantry Division, nicknamed the Big Red One due to the division insignia of a large red number one. Fuller, by that time an accomplished scriptwriter, director, and producer, experienced difficulty in advancing his project. The first issue centred on censorship, as Geoffrey Shurlock, from the Production Code Authority, felt the draft script had 'scenes of vicious fighting in hand to hand combat which appear to us to contain elements of brutality and gruesomeness'.[76] The gruesome depiction of violence was central to Fuller's attempt to show war in its unvarnished reality. He intended to focus on the junior ranks – the soldiers that fought through the war. Nevertheless, a second issue arose that derailed the project: major studio executives at Warner Bros. insisted on using John Wayne for the role of the Sergeant at the centre of the story. Fuller balked because 'Wayne would succeed in shrinking my story from a dark story for survival and sanity into a patriotic adventure movie'.[77] The obvious point about multiple inputs into filmmaking aside, the significance here is that despite a favourable climate, it took Fuller another two decades to push this project to conclusion.

By the 1970s, Fuller decided to return to his favoured project.[78] He convinced Lee Marvin to sign up as the Sergeant, and the actor helped to convince Lorimar Pictures to back the film. Fuller also acknowledged the tremendous role played by famed director, critic, and film connoisseur Peter Bogdanovich, who secured initial funding for the production.[79] Shot in Israel because of budgetary constraints, the production displayed all of Fuller's usual cost-conscious features: limited technological excess and active improvisation by the crew. As he later wrote, 'The frills of larger budget productions were completely absent from *The Big Red One*.

My crew needed to be innovative in every scene, relying many times on close-ups rather than on crane shots to convey the scope of the conflict'.[80] That filming technique lent itself to strengthening his inclination to focus on a few junior rankers. Production notes indicated 'the film's central concern is the characters who are fighting men surviving in a nightmare in which time and life moves only from battle to battle'.[81] The 'men' were portrayed by young actors to evoke the youthfulness of actual soldiers; 'the vast majority of them were kids, boys still in their teens', according to Fuller.[82] In many ways, the film was viewed as homage to this noble youth. Evincing a sharp post-Vietnam rebuttal of venerated leadership, Fuller argued that he was 'interested in the irony that the lower you are on the ladder of humanity ... if you go all the way back to whether it's [General Omar] Bradley, Eisenhower, or [General George] Marshall, they're depending on those kids ... but depending on their dying.'[83] The production company was not as enamored as Fuller was with these figures and this story. The first cut resulted in a 6-hour movie, which he helped pare to four and a half hours. When the studio insisted on further excisions, Fuller walked away, allowing Lorimar to reduce it to just under two hours for the 1980 theatrical release.[84]

Difficulties aside, Fuller scripted and directed a movie that includes a riveting depiction of the D-Day combat in which he had personally participated. As one scholar asserted, 'Fuller wants us to *feel* what it is like to be a footsoldier', which he does by centring on a few characters, point-of-view shots, and close-up reactions to the events.[85] These aspects all carry through with the D-Day scene, the central combat sequence of the film. In barely nine minutes of screen time, The Big Red One explicates the horrors of Omaha Beach by focusing on the efforts of five men to survive. Viewers bear a jarring transition from placid discussions about impending battle to explosions and death on the beaches. To avoid costly filming sequences, Fuller eschewed the landing process or the inclusion of the many ships and other large equipment that would require. Instead, our group faces unseen foes that seem well prepared to mow down the American soldiers. In one affecting scene, men advance one after another, with each new man stepping up after his predecessor dies, in an effort to blast a hole in the defences. Indication of time passage appears through close-up shots of a wristwatch on a lifeless arm floating in the surf. Hours of effort, isolated on the beach, finally lead to a fortuitous stroke that allows the soldiers to push inward past the key danger zone. In this tense scene, The Big Red One 'condenses the entire D-day invasion into the experience of one small squad, and ultimately the paralyzing fears of one soldier'.[86] As film scholar Lisa Dombrowski wrote, 'only fifty yards of the beach are seen, and no more than thirty men at a time. No sense of the larger battle is presented, and no sign exists of any Allies or even a discrete enemy. The grand scope of The Longest Day has been massively reduced in scale, allowing for an intimate vision of war that emphasizes what each man must do to survive'.[87]

FIGURE 11.4 *Lee Marvin in* The Big Red One *(1980)*

The Big Red One, as Fuller explained, was part of a larger conversation with other depictions of the war, such as *The Longest Day*. Fuller chose to focus on the emotions of combatants rather than provide strategic overview, show senior leaders, or rely upon a dizzying array of star actors.[88] This allowed audiences to identify with the characters.[89] As one journalist conveyed, 'Wars, believe Fuller and Marvin ... are fought by the privates, not by the generals. Documenting the small world of a squad, they agree, is probably the best way of telling what war is really about'.[90] Taking a different tack from *D-Day Plus 20 Years*, this movie thus sought to focus on the ground level combatants to relay a small slice of what that battle was like.

The discussion of these three sources serves to highlight the different ways in which moving imagery may demonstrate perspective of experience in warfare. As elite-driven enterprises, militaries are bound by the decisions and capabilities of their leaders. Eisenhower set the stage for the victory that followed and his key choices in personnel, deployments, thrust of operations, and even call to launch all contributed to success. Nevertheless, as several historians have demonstrated, the overall plans of people like Eisenhower did not survive contact with the enemy. Confusion reigned supreme whether from airborne misdrops, tidal shifts of landing craft, or the disarray that real combat produces as people die and friction wears away cohesion of effort. The manner of Allied success depended in large part on junior level initiative of the officers and men in the midst of carnage and confusion.[91] Deeper understanding of what happened and why it happened necessarily depends upon a mixture of these perspectives. This truism explains the bifurcated focus that has endured in popular conceptions of the battle as people focus on leaders like Eisenhower *and* the common soldiers, sailors, and airmen that fought the D-Day battles.

The 'authentic' image

While apposition offers much for the student interested in film and history, the preceding example suffices as an indicator of how to approach that endeavour.[92] The majority of examples discussed thus far have included Hollywood films, of varying quality and impact. At this point, one final category of sources deserves attention: documentary films. This material is often accorded an authority that viewers refrain from attaching to even the best researched or most 'realistic' entertainment products. Despite willingness to concede greater factual accuracy, however, documentary films are also mediated versions of the past that warrant the same level of scrutiny (perhaps even more) than any other source.

During the war, Americans encountered a variety of news media sources: traditional print, radio broadcasts, film reels. The latter played along with feature films at movie theatres (see also Chapter 8). About a week after the D-Day invasion, *News of the Day* clips depicting the landings played in theatres across America. The first of these, which appeared on 15 June 1944, was a special D-Day reel that replaced that day's intended information.[93] Only 10 minutes in duration, this clip presents a variety of themes and images that have linked to the invasion ever since. The thematic thrust focuses on the extensive obstacles Allied forces confronted, and overcame. The democratic nature of these forces forms a constant point of reference, which the film extols as a source of strength as well as the motivating impetus behind the invasion. Coverage is broad, including consideration of the Allied forces as well as airborne, amphibious, and naval elements. The film – as a piece of wartime propaganda – welds home front and fighting front together in professed unity of wartime purpose. Despite the proximity of the events, this clip incorporates aerial gun camera images, footage generated on inbound landing craft, and captured German film. The kinetic presentation serves to emphasize the action of battle.

Lengthier D-Day documentary films also appeared in 1944. Famed director Frank Capra served with the US Army's Signal Corps during the war and was responsible for many powerful propaganda pieces, such as the *Why We Fight* (1942–5) series. In 1944, his D-Day film appeared in American theatres. The film begins several days after the landings and displays invasion beaches still cluttered with the detritus of battle (minus dead bodies). Upon establishing the outcome, *D-Day: The Normandy Invasion* flashes back to American units conducting amphibious training and aerial bombing of the area prior to the operation.[94] The context is explained via a series of monthly updates from January through June of 1944. Starting in June, the film provides a daily recap up until D-Day on the sixth. The focus remains on US forces and once the fighting begins, the camera stays with them. Viewers see landing craft approaching the beaches and repeated shots of larger naval vessels firing their guns (especially the few battleships present that day). Capra's film countenances some of the costs of battle, yet quickly elides the terrible realities of mass warfare. Progress on the beaches appears a steady endeavour without any real stalling imposed by entrenched enemies. The narrator concludes 'silent evidence of the fierce battle is apparent everywhere' as the screen, once more, displays equipment and vehicles strewn everywhere. The film ends with Allied forces marching away from the beaches inland towards victory. These soldiers have no time to pause, to look back, to reflect on what they just survived. They have a war to win.

War requirements influenced the presentation of these documentaries. Interpretation and thrust focused viewers' attention on the ultimate victory on D-Day and the nobility of Allied sacrifice. Actual footage content selection was limited by material produced under trying combat conditions: stock shots of landing craft headed to the beach, airplanes flying over the invasion zone, or the huge naval battlewagons firing their main guns often dominated these sources. These features become especially pronounced in one of the last major propaganda pieces of the war, *The True Glory* (1945).[95] This documentary film represented the combined efforts of the British Ministry of Information and the American Office of War Information. It constituted the last theatre-focused documentary prior to the dominance of home television viewing.[96] Eisenhower launched the show with an on-screen introduction that purports to focus on the 'really important men of this campaign', the enlisted soldiers, sailors and airmen. That focus carries through as one lead scriptwriter, Paddy Chayefsky, had intensively sought out and interviewed veterans from the events covered.[97] As Eisenhower explained, the 'teamwork' of the free, democratic troops was able to overcome the worst the enemy had prepared for them. The implicit suggestion hinted that this model also assured victory in the Pacific, which still roiled in war at the time of this film's release.

In 24 minutes of screen time devoted to the preparations for and execution of the invasion, *The True Glory* conveys the enormity of events and the dangers encountered by the combatants. Of the sources covered thus far, *The True Glory* probably presents the most compelling and comprehensive coverage of pre-battle requirements, including logistical build-up, control of the sea, and aerial bombing of occupied countries. This documentary also includes re-enacted scenes for some of the iconic moments of D-Day that were not filmed at the time, the first documentary to use such an approach. Employing the technique that *D-Day Plus 20 Years* would artfully emulate, this film skips back and forth between the awful moments of combat with depictions of placid London, almost oblivious to the distant carnage. The message: soldierly sacrifice makes such scenes possible. During the combat scenes, rousing music keeps the pace and is interrupted only by sounds of explosion or veterans off screen relaying their experiences. After displaying intense combat, with relentless advance by Allied forces, the film moves on to the remainder of the European campaign.

Many documentary films on D-Day would follow in the years after the conclusion of the Second World War. Most of them were largely derivative of the images, themes, and approaches employed by these wartime pieces. For any student investigating D-Day through film, and perhaps those interested in film through D-Day, this is of significance. Those interested can assess other early documentary features like the D-Day episodes for the *Crusade in Europe* (1949) or *Victory at Sea* (1953) series.[98]

The World at War was an enormous, and enormously expensive, British documentary series that aired in 1973–4 (see also Chapter 14).[99] This costly and probing account of the war years consisted of twenty-six episodes with the seventeenth primarily devoted to the D-Day invasion. The episode title, 'Morning', bespoke the creators' intention of using the amphibious assault as the key turning point – the awakening point after a long nightmare.

This episode starts with wartime Prime Minister Winston Churchill arguing, in 1940, that a dawn will break and British fortunes will be restored. D-Day is the act of restoration. Between those two points, this episode is at pains to present the strategic overview of the war, often absent in the pieces covered above. Meanwhile, rather than purely martial music, the Thames Television production company incorporates period pieces that provide a cultural and historical atmosphere. Jazzy music accompanies the flood of American men and material coming to English shores in preparation for the invasion. Cultural accommodations shift to political ones, as British leaders accept and then ultimately defer to their more powerful American Allies. Despite the high-level framing, *The World at War* is consistent in its emphasis on the horror of warfare. Viewers see the debilitating effect of the rough weather and hear unidentified veterans describe their struggle with nature and man alike. The overwhelming impact is to drive home the utter misery of those that fought on D-Day, although the German opponents are notably absent. The concluding thoughts to this 37-minute film ordeal centre on the ghastly toll of the supposed quest for liberty: nine thousand Allied casualties mentioned and a devastated French countryside. This unflinching assessment of war has proven consistently popular; *The World at War* series plays on airwaves to this day.[100]

Echoes of this presentation have lingered for decades later and are notable in even the recent major production by famed documentarian Ken Burns (see also Chapter 1). Burns's Second World War piece, *The War*, first aired in 2007.[101] The fourth of seven episodes, 'Pride of Our Nation', depicts a major swing in the momentum of the war with D-Day (about half of the episode) taking centre stage. While stressing the enormity of the plans, preparations, and world-historical significance of the moment, the episode evokes *The World at War*'s more sombre assessment by focusing on the soldiers and civilians caught in the path of war. Burns insisted that every person shown on screen for this production had to be a veteran and that intent helps create an air of intensity and anguish as these old soldiers recount their stories. As typical for American productions, this documentary fixated on 'Bloody Omaha' in the effort to display the American sacrifice required for French/European liberation. In the end, however, the repeated flashed of France, destroyed in part through liberation, spoke to dark wartime realities for all involved – both during the Second World War and the then-ongoing wars in Iraq and Afghanistan.

While historians may display a general unease with documentary films, or indeed any moving image source, the public readily embraces these versions of the past (see Chapter 2). As such, we would do well to pay serious attention to their presentation of history. That point aside, we must treat all such sources with a great degree of caution. Documentary sources, despite the pretension to document 'reality', have a tenuous dual-nature in that they show actual imagery, but in a mediated or constructed manner.[102] The preceding discussion, however, has hopefully demonstrated some of the insights offered by these sources, as well as some of the ways in which they present artificial renderings of the past.

D-Day film as source

The eminent historian Peter Novick argued that even the most ardent proponents of objective historical truth succumb to their own inherent biases and false assumptions.[103] If true, then what makes a visual image source any different from other possible materials to use when exploring the past? Not that much. The films and other resources described or mentioned above provide a group of possibilities for any student interested in D-Day. As is hopefully apparent, none of them is free from reproach (as with any other source), just as each has something worthwhile to offer. Perhaps now it is best to discuss the most promising ways to employ these sources.

No historian purports to understand the past through accessing one single resource. To base comprehension on one source, or even one category of sources, risks missing a wealth of uncovered detail or the points of disagreement that arise when informed people review complex matters. The most convincing approach is to start with a plan of action. Rather than jump into the mix with a binge of film watching, an interested student would be better served by considering what questions to ask of the material, what answers to seek, and what pitfalls to avoid. In order to accomplish that assessment successfully, preparatory work is required.

An action plan should begin with a problem statement and some sense of what you hope to achieve. Then, list steps to take towards achieving that objective in a way that will frame analysis as the project proceeds. A sequential approach *could* consist of the following steps:

1   read reputable secondary sources to understand the general scope of the topic and points of scholarly debate

2 conduct research with primary sources to facilitate deeper understanding of the topic

3 select a few moving image sources for additional analyses and insights

4 investigate or research those sources

5 watch, assess, think about them as sources

The endnotes suggest potential starting points for secondary source research. Some of the more popular, more accessible, or more respected authors include Stephen Ambrose, Gordon Harrison, Flint Whitlock or John McManus.[104] As with film sources, each has a particular thrust, advantages and disadvantages. Book reviews and review essays in academic journals, such as *The Journal of Military History*, may assist in selecting worthwhile secondary sources. These will generally guide readers to significant primary source material, which is anything produced at or nearly at the time of the events by a participant or eyewitness. Historians tend to work with documents stored in archival facilities, such as war diaries or after action reports created by combat units. Still, there are plenty of resources available for the intrepid student, including oral history collections or websites full of digitized content.[105] Concerns about reliability, accuracy, and representativeness magnify when dealing with online content, so caution is necessary.

After establishing a firm base, the moving image source selection process can take place in an informed manner. Depending on the topic and questions, certain sources are more useful than others. Interested in the big picture view of a major amphibious invasion? *The Longest Day* is a good starting point. If the questions centre on the nature of leadership and decision making in complex circumstances, *D-Day Plus 20 Years* serves as a better resource. In the process of selecting sources, the student should conduct a study of the sources. When were they made, by whom, why, what was the reception? These questions can lead towards better understanding of their content and guide selection of those most likely to assist.

With a series of film sources in hand, the work begins. Simply watching once and moving on is clearly not the most fruitful approach. Nuances, gaps, even significant events sometime pass by without catching the eye (these are often frenetic films). Assess these as historical sources, rather than act as a passive recipient of information an active engagement with the content should occur. What exactly does the film show, and what does it avoid? Were the producers fair or clearly biased in presentation? How does this material help or hinder understanding of the topic?

Moving image sources appear in all manner of format. Entertainment or educational, feature film or short clip, live broadcast or lengthy filmed production, are just some of the variations in format or approach to moving image sources. Film can be critical and interrogative; it can be numbing fluff that glosses over the past. As one historian recently indicated, 'history is fertile as source, backdrop, inspiration, setting or motif' for a wide array of television and film pieces.[106] The variety can be intimidating and the discussion above only scratched the surface of D-Day moving imagery content. Nevertheless, with sound preparation serving as a foundation, there is much to be gained by incorporating D-Day film sources into a comprehensive study of the battle. To borrow from Eisenhower, as he reportedly ordered the invasion to commence: 'Ok, let's go.'

Notes

1	The author acknowledges Sam Edwards and Emily Wilson for offering comments on earlier drafts of this chapter. Further thanks are due to attendees at conferences in Bedford, Virginia (2009), London (2014) and New Orleans (2014), which afforded opportunities to test some of the assertions advanced herein. Finally, Rob Shafer was instrumental in securing key source material.

2	For more on the notion of spectacle, see J. Crary, 'Spectacle, Attention, Counter-Memory', *October* 50 (1989): 96–107; S. Weber, 'War, Terrorism, and Spectacle, or: On Towers and Caves', *Grey Room* 7 (2002): 14–23.

3	T. Doherty, *Projections of War: Hollywood, American Culture, and World War II*, rev. edn (New York: Columbia University Press, 1999), 2.

4	Doherty, *Projections of War*, 2. For more on the relationship between war and film in American culture see especially as applied to D-Day, see M. Dolski, *D-Day Remembered: The Normandy Landings in American Collective Memory* (Knoxville: University of Tennessee Press, 2016).

5	J. C. McManus, *The Dead and Those About to Die: D-Day; The Big Red One at Omaha Beach* (New York: New American Library, 2014), 2.

6	The entertainment film sources include the following titles: *Fighter Squadron* (1948); *Breakthrough* (1950); *D-Day, the Sixth of June* (1956); *The Longest Day* (1962); *The Americanization of Emily* (1964); *Overlord* (1975); *The Big Red One* (1980); *A Foreign Field* (1993, made-for-television); *Saving Private Ryan* (1998); *Band of Brothers* (2001, made-for-television); *D-Day 6.6.1944* (2004, made-for-television); *Ike: Countdown to D-Day* (2004, made-for-television); *Ten Days to D-Day* (2004, made-for-television).

7	S. Fuller, C. Lang Fuller and J. H. Rudes, *A Third Face: My Tale of Writing, Fighting, and Filmmaking* (New York: Knopf, 2002), 122–3.

8	G. A. Harrison, *Cross-Channel Attack, U.S. Army in World War II: European Theater of Operations* (1951; repr., New York: BDD, 1993), offers readers a thorough assessment of the invasion area and many excellent, highly detailed maps.

9	'Sol [Standards of Learning] Education Packet', National D-Day Memorial Foundation, 2002; 'D-Day Plaque Project', National D-Day Memorial website, 2013. Available online: http://www.dday.org/component/content/article/42–the-memorial/programs/75–d-day-programs (accessed 3 October

2014). The figures for the dead of Germany and its allied powers have proven far more difficult to calculate.

10   See, O. Wieviorka, *Normandy: The Landings to the Liberation of Paris*, trans. M. B. DeBevoise (Cambridge: Harvard University Press, 2008); W. I. Hitchcock, *The Bitter Road to Freedom: A New History of the Liberation of Europe* (New York: Free Press, 2008), 19–59; K. C. Lemay, 'Gratitude, Trauma, and Repression: D-Day in French Memory', in ed. M. Dolski, S. Edwards, and J. Buckley, *D-Day in History and Memory: The Normandy Landings in International Remembrance and Commemoration* (Denton: University of North Texas Press, 2014), 159–88.

11   T. Doherty, *Projections of War: Hollywood, American Culture, and World War II*, rev. edn (New York: Columbia University Press, 1999), 243–4.

12   *The True Glory*, dir. G. Kanin, Ministry of Information (UK) and US Office of War Information, 1945 (distributed by E1 Entertainment, 2009, DVD).

13   *D-Day, the Sixth of June*, dir. H. Koster, Twentieth Century–Fox, 1956 (Twentieth Century–Fox Home Entertainment, 2002, DVD); 'D-Day', *You Are There*, CB-Television Network Production, 1955 (6 March), VHS, accessed at the UCLA Film and Television Archive, Los Angeles, CA.

14   *The Longest Day*, dir. K. Annakin, A. Marton, B. Wicki and D. F. Zanuck, Darryl F. Zanuck Productions and Twentieth Century–Fox Film Corporation, 1962 (Twentieth Century–Fox Home Entertainment, 2002, DVD); L. Suid, *Guts & Glory: The Making of the American Military Image in Film*, rev. edn (Lexington: University Press of Kentucky, 2002), 185–8.

15   *The Big Red One*, dir. S. Fuller, United Artists, 1980 (Warner Home Video, 1999, DVD). The film cost $9.5 million to produce, market, and release, but only earned $2.3 million in rentals in 1980. See, L. Dombrowski, *The Films of Samuel Fuller: If You Die, I'll Kill You!* (Middletown, CT: Wesleyan University Press, 2008), 190–1.

16   For more on the key 1984 speeches by Ronald Reagan, see D. Brinkley, *The Boys of Pointe du Hoc: Ronald Reagan, D-Day, and the U.S. Army 2nd Rangers Battalion* (New York: HarperPerennial, 2005).

17   *Saving Private Ryan*, dir. S. Spielberg, DreamWorks Pictures and Paramount Pictures, 1998.

18   *Ike: Countdown to D-Day*, dir. R. Harmon, A&E Television Networks, 2004, DVD.

19   *Edge of Tomorrow*, dir. D. Liman, Warner Bros., 2014.

20   Letter, Cornelius Ryan to Peter Schwed, 24 February 1959, Folder – The Longest Day Correspondence Release Sheet etc, 'The Longest Day' records, Robert E. and Jean R. Mahn Center for Archives and Special Collections, Ohio University Library, Athens, OH. Hereafter referred to as CRC. C. Ryan, *The Longest Day* (New York: Simon & Schuster, 1959).

21   Advanced Fact Sheet on 'The Longest Day', n.d., Folder Ryan, Cornelius Printed Matter The Last Battle #3, Miscellaneous Supplementary Material records, CRC.

22   S. Ambrose, '*The Longest Day* (US, 1962): "Blockbuster" History', in *World*

War II, Film, and History, ed. J. Whiteclay Chambers II and D. Culbert (New York: Oxford University Press, 1996), 97.

23   Ambrose, '*The Longest Day* (US, 1962)', 97. Emphasis added.

24   Suid provides an excellent description of the filming process for *The Longest Day* in *Guts & Glory*, 168–87.

25   J. Basinger, *The World War II Combat Film: Anatomy of a Genre*, with an updated filmography by J. Arnold (New York: Columbia University Press, 1986; Middletown, CT: Wesleyan University Press, 2003), 170.

26   Letter, Darryl F. Zanuck to Hedda Hopper, 16 January 1961, Folder 62 Zanuck, Darryl F. 1939–65, Darryl F. Zanuck papers, Special Collections, Margaret Herrick Library, Academy of Motion Picture Arts and Sciences, Beverly Hills, CA. Hereafter referred to as MHL.

27   Suid, *Guts & Glory*, 170–84.

28   Ibid., 184. See also, Letter, Darryl F. Zanuck to Hedda Hopper, 23 February 1961, Folder 62 Zanuck, Darryl F. 1939–1965, Darryl F. Zanuck papers, Special Collections, MHL.

29   'Operation Overblown', *Time*, 19 October 1962. Available online: http://www.time.com/time/magazine/article/0,9171,827910,00.html (accessed 28 May 2009).

30   Suid, *Guts & Glory*, 184. Adjusted for inflation, the amount would represent approximately $80 million in 2015.

31   Ibid., 185.

32   Ibid., 188.

33   Scriptwriters, like famed author James Jones, also influenced the final product.

34   See, P. K. Scheuer, '"Gen." Darryl Zanuck Takes Normandy, Reviews Battle', *L.A. Times*, 1 April 1962, Suid, *Guts & Glory*, 170–1.

35   Letter, Geoffrey Shurlock (Production Code Administration) to Frank McCarthy (Twentieth Century–Fox), 6 October 1961, Folder – The Longest Day, Film year: 1962 (20th Century–Fox, 1962), Production Code Administration records, Special Collections, MHL.

36   Letter, Cornelius Ryan to Kenneth E. Crouch, 20 August 1963, Folder Ryan, Cornelius, Letters and Correspondence, Zanuck, Darryl F., 'The Longest Day' records, CRC. Advanced Fact Sheet on 'The Longest Day', n.d., Folder Ryan, Cornelius Printed Matter The Last Battle #3, Miscellaneous Supplementary Material records, CRC.

37   For more in-depth assessment of the film and American society in the early 1960s, see M. R. Dolski, *D-Day Remembered: The Normandy Landings in American Collective Memory* (Knoxville: University of Tennessee Press, 2016), 68–73.

38   S. E. Ambrose, *D-Day, June 6, 1944: The Climactic Battle of World War II* (New York: Simon & Schuster, 1994).

39   Rodat's story hinged upon a re-imagining of Sergeant Fritz Niland's experience, as recounted in Ambrose's *D-Day*. Here the small slips in

Ambrose's version of history came to have a profound impact. Ambrose falsely stated that after all of Niland's brothers had perished in battle, military leaders pulled the sergeant from the line. This fabricated tale of a rescue under fire offered a thrilling plot device.

40 Suid, *Guts & Glory*, 625–37.

41 R. Rodat, '"Saving Private Ryan" Production Notes & Synopsis', n.d., Folder Saving Private Ryan DreamWorks 1998 (Credits, Synopsis, Productions Notes) (Music Cue Sheet), Core Collections, MHL.

42 'Saving Private Ryan Nomination Sheet for the 1998 Academy Awards', Core Collections, MHL.

43 'Steven Spielberg', *Inside the Actors Studio*, dir. J. Wurtz, Bravo Channel, 1999, VHS, accessed at the UCLA Film and Television Archive, Los Angeles, CA. Hereafter referred to as UFTA.

44 Ibid.

45 B. Higgins, '"Ryan" Leaves Them Speechless', *Los Angeles Times*, 23 July 1998, Folder SAVING PRIVATE RYAN DreamWorks 1998 (July 1–23, 1998), Core Collections, MHL.

46 J. Meroney and S. Coons, 'The Man Who Brought War to Hollywood', theAtlantic.com, 27 August 2010. Available online: http://www.theatlantic.com/culture/archive/2010/08/the-man-who-brought-war-to-hollywood/62070/1/# (accessed 18 January 2011); J. Lippman, 'Hollywood's Drill Sergeant to the Stars is a Busy Man', *Wall Street Journal*, 10 July 1998, Folder SAVING PRIVATE RYAN DreamWorks 1998 (July 1–23, 1998), Core Collections, MHL.

47 D. Ansen, 'Celluloid Soldiers', *Newsweek*, 13 July 1998. Available online: http://www.newsweek.com/id/93119 (accessed 27 July 2008).

48 'Saving Private Ryan Nomination Sheet for the 1998 Academy Awards'.

49 The film generated sustained scholarly interest. The following articles represent several of the more insightful sources available: P. Ehrenhaus, 'Why We Fought: Holocaust Memory in Spielberg's *Saving Private Ryan*', *Critical Studies in Media Communication* 18 (2001): 321–37; A. S. Owen, 'Memory, War and American Identity: *Saving Private Ryan* as Cinematic Jeremiad', *Critical Studies in Media Communication* 19 (2002): 259–65; J. D. Slocum, 'Cinema and the Civilizing Process: Rethinking Violence in the World War II Combat Film', *Cinema Journal* 44 (Spring 2005): 35–63; and R. J. Spiller, 'War in the Dark', *American Heritage* (February/March 1999). Available online: http://www.americanheritage.com/articles/magazine/ah/1999/1/1999_1_41.shtml (accessed 2 September 2009).

50 A. Kershaw, *The Bedford Boys: One American Town's Ultimate D-Day Sacrifice* (Cambridge, MA: Da Capo Press, 2003).

51 See, for instance, T. Infield, 'Rating "Private Ryan"', *Philadelphia Inquirer*, 26 July 1998.

52 Basinger, *World War II Combat Film*, 254–5.

53 Suid, *Guts & Glory*, 626.

54 Ibid.

55   Doherty, *Projections of War*, 306.

56   L. McCrary, 'Watching "Private Ryan", Veterans Relive the Horrors Years
     from Omaha Beach, Pain Lingers', *Philadelphia Inquirer*, 6 August 1998,
     T. Childers, *Soldier from the War Returning: The Greatest Generation's
     Troubled Homecoming from World War II* (Boston: Houghton Mifflin
     Harcourt, 2009), 272.

57   M. Dolski '"Portal of Liberation" D-Day Myth as American
     Self-Affirmation', in ed. M. Dolski, S. Edwards and J. Buckley, *D-Day in
     History and Memory*, 65.

58   C. Rickey, 'Spielberg's Private Battle In "Saving Private Ryan"',
     Philadelphia Inquirer, 19 July 1998, Suid, *Guts & Glory*, 636. Emphasis in
     original.

59   Suid, *Guts & Glory*, 627–37; Doherty, *Projections of War*, 308–10;
     Spiller, 'War in the Dark', *American Heritage*. Available online: http://
     www.americanheritage.com/articles/magazine/ah/1999/1/1999_1_41.shtml
     (accessed 2 September 2009); P. Fussell, 'Hell and High Water', *London
     Observer*, 2 August 1998.

60   Basinger, *World War II Combat Film*, 257; Doherty, *Projections of War*,
     304.

61   Suid, *Guts & Glory*, 628; Dolski, *D-Day Remembered*, 170–6. Spielberg,
     Hanks and Ambrose would all collaborate on another expensive, techno-
     fetish depiction of D-Day in one episode of the popular HBO series, *Band
     of Brothers*. *Band of Brothers*, dir. D. Frankel, M. Salomon, T. Hanks,
     D. Leland, R. Loncraine, D. Nutter, P. Alden Robinson and T. To, 705 min.,
     HBO in association with DreamWorks Pictures, 2001.

62   For box-office figures, see 'Box office/business for Saving Private Ryan
     (1998)', Internet Movie Database (IMDb), n.d. Available online: http://
     www.imdb.com/title/tt0120815/business (accessed 18 March 2007). The
     movie grossed an estimated $216 million domestically and $224 million
     internationally, while winning five Academy Awards.

63   Doherty, *Projections of War*, 301.

64   J. de Groot, *Consuming History: Historians and Heritage in Contemporary
     Popular Culture* (New York: Routledge, 2009).

65   R. B. Toplin, 'Hollywood's D-Day from the Perspective of the 1960s and
     1990s: *The Longest Day* and *Saving Private Ryan*', in *Why We Fought:
     America's Wars in Film and History* ed. P. C. Rollins and J. E. O'Connor
     (Lexington: University Press of Kentucky, 2008), 312.

66   Dwight D. Eisenhower, 'Order of the Day', n.d. [6 June 1944], Folder
     335.18, Supreme Headquarters Allied Expeditionary Forces (SHAEF) Special
     Staff Adjutant General's Division Executive Section, Record Group 331,
     National Archives and Records Administration in College Park, Maryland.

67   D. Howarth, *Dawn of D-Day: These Men Were There, 6 June 1944* (1959;
     repr., Mechanicsburg, PA: Stackpole Books, 2001), 30.

68   See Transcript of CBS News Special 'Some Friends of General Eisenhower',
     29 March 1969, Folder – Eisenhower, President, Death of, Robert S.

Anderson Papers, Dwight D. Eisenhower Presidential Library, Abilene, KS. Hereafter referred to as DDEL.

69   See, D. D. Eisenhower, *Crusade in Europe* (New York: Doubleday, 1997 [1948]); and W. Cronkite's interview of Eisenhower, recorded in 1963 for a documentary to celebrate the upcoming twentieth anniversary of D-Day. 'D-day Plus 20 Years: Eisenhower Returns to Normandy', CBS Reports, Columbia Broadcasting Systems, 1964 (Ambrose Video Publishing, 1990, VHS), CRC.

70   *D-Day Plus 20 Years: Eisenhower Returns to Normandy*, 123 min., CBS Reports, Columbia Broadcasting Systems, Inc., 1964 (filmed August 1963); Ambrose Video Publishing, 1990, VHS, Robert R. McCormick Research Center, Cantigny First Division Museum, Wheaton, IL. Hereafter referred to as CFDM.

71   Memorandum of Conference with Former President Eisenhower, CBS Productions, 27 May 1963, Folder TR Trips – Europe, July 30–August 15 1963 (1), Principal Files, DDEL.

72   See, Dolski, *D-Day Remembered*, 74–6.

73   'D-Day', *You are There*, CBS Television Network Production, 6 March 1955, VHS, UFTA.

74   Hitchcock, *The Bitter Road*, 19–59.

75   Franklin D. Roosevelt, 'D-Day Prayer', 6 June 1944. Available online: http://www.historyplace.com/speeches/fdr-prayer.htm (accessed 19 November 2009).

76   Letter, Geoffrey Shurlock to J. L. Warner, 28 March 1958, Folder – THE BIG RED ONE (Warner Bros., 1958) unproduced, Special Collections, MHL.

77   Fuller, *A Third Face*, 382–3.

78   Fuller wrote notices and gave interviews regarding the movie for the *Bridgehead Sentinel* in various issues through 1977–8. Copies of these reside in Box Bridgehead Sentinel 1953–78 Smith 1996.113, CFDM.

79   L. Cohn, 'Long Roundabout to "Big Red," Fuller's First Major Pic in 16 Yrs', *Variety*, 8 July 1980, accessed at MHL.

80   Fuller, *A Third Face*, 479.

81   'The Big Red One', Final Production Notes, Lorimar Pictures, undated, Folder – Samuel Fuller's The Big Red One, Lorimar, Core Collections, MHL

82   'The Big Red One', Production Notes, Lorimar Pictures, undated, Folder – Samuel Fuller's The Big Red One, Lorimar, Core Collections, MHL

83   R. M. M. Wiener, 'Ex-soldier Fuller's Dreams Realized in "Big Red One"', *Boxoffice*, 21 July 1980, Folder – The Big Red One, Lorimar/United Artists, 1980, Warner Bros., 2005, Also known as: THE BIG RED ONE: THE RECONSTRUCTION (1979–99), Core Collections, MHL.

84   Fuller, *A Third Face*, 481.

85   Dombrowski, *The Films of Samuel Fuller*, 189.

86   Ibid.

87 Ibid., 189–91.

88 R. M. M. Wiener, 'Ex-soldier Fuller's dreams realized in "Big Red One"', *Boxoffice*, 21 July 1980, Folder – The Big Red One Lorimar/United Artists 1980 Warner Bros. 2005 Also Known As: THE BIG RED ONE: THE RECONSTRUCTION (1979–99), Core Collections, MHL; V. Canby, 'Film: "The Big Red One," 5 G.I.'s in World War II', *New York Times*, 18 July 1980, ProQuest (accessed 28 May 2009).

89 Suid, *Guts & Glory*, 425–7; Basinger, *The World War II Combat Film*, 197. Basinger claimed that this film represented a shift away from the epic (*The Longest Day*) to the personal.

90 J. Borsten, 'A D-Day Landing by "Big Red One" in Israel', *L.A. Times*, 13 August 1978, Folder – The Big Red One Lorimar/United Artists 1980 Warner Bros. 2005 Also Known As: THE BIG RED ONE: THE RECONSTRUCTION (1979–99), Core Collections, MHL. See also, D. Ansen, 'An Unblinking View of War', *Newsweek*, 28 July 1980, Folder – The Big Red One Lorimar/United Artists 1980 Warner Bros. 2005 Also Known As: THE BIG RED ONE: THE RECONSTRUCTION (REVIEWS & MAGAZINE ARTICLES), Core Collections, MHL. Ansen wrote 'His theme is survival and his method is to put us in the shoes of a squad of teen-age soldiers and their sergeant.'

91 For the junior-level initiative argument, see Ambrose, *D-Day*; and J. A. Lewis, *Omaha Beach: A Flawed Victory* (Chapel Hill, NC: University of North Carloina Press), 2001).

92 One other possible course of action linked to D-Day moving imagery would be for a comparison and contrast between sentimental or romantic nationalism presented in films like *Saving Private Ryan* and the critical rejection of glorified militarism evident in the far less popular movie, *The Americanization of Emily*, dir. A. Hiller, Metro-Goldwyn-Mayer, 1964; Warner Home Video, 2006, DVD. For some consideration of the latter, see Dolski, *D-Day Remembered*, 76–9.

93 *News of the Day, Invasion Extra!* (Vol. 15, no. 280), Metro-Goldwyn-Mayer, 1944, VHS, accessed at the UFTA.

94 *D-Day: The Normandy Invasion*, dir. Frank Capra, US Coast Guard, 1944; distr. by Madacy Entertainment Group, Inc., 1998, VHS, accessed at the UFTA.

95 *The True Glory*, dir. G. Kanin, Ministry of Information (UK) and US Office of War Information, 1945; distr. by E1 Entertainment, 2009, DVD.

96 M. Paris, 'Reconstructing D-Day: 6 June 1944 and British Documentary Films', in *The Normandy Campaign 1944: Sixty Years On*, ed. J. Buckley, (New York: Routledge, 2006), 207–9.

97 S. Considine, *Mad as Hell: The Life and Work of Paddy Chayefsky* (New York: Random House, 1994), 22.

98 *Crusade in Europe*, March of Time and Twentieth Century Fox, 1949; New Line Home Video, 1998, DVD; 'D-Day', *Victory at Sea*, dir. M. Clay Adams, 27 min., National Broadcasting Company, 1953; distr. by A&E Home Video, DVD, 2003. The D-Day episode originally aired on 15 February 1953.

99   *The World at War*, dir. J. Pett, Thames Television and the Imperial War Museum, 1973–4; A&E Home Video, 2004, DVD. For more on the series, see the official website: http://www.theworldatwar.com/ (accessed 18 February 2016).

100 T. Downing, 'History on Television: The Making of *Cold War*, 1998', in *The Historical Film: History and Memory in Media*, ed. M. Landy (New Brunswick, NJ: Rutgers University Press, 2001), 295.

101 *The War*, dir. Ken Burns and Lynn Novick, 900 min., Florentine Films and Public Broadcasting Service, 2007.

102 De Groot, *Consuming History*, 112–13, 149–52.

103 P. Novick, *That Noble Dream: The 'Objectivity Question' and the American Historical Profession* (New York: Cambridge University Press, 1988).

104 Ambrose, *D-Day*; Harrison, *Cross-Channel Attack*; F. Whitlock, *The Fighting First*; J. C. McManus, *The Dead*, or *The Americans at D-Day: The American Experience at the Normandy Invasion* (New York: Forge, 2004).

105 For oral history collections, see R. Miller, *Nothing Less Than Victory: The Oral History of D-Day* (New York: William Morrow, 1993); E. F. Prados and US Navy Memorial Foundation (ed.) *Neptunus Rex: Naval Stories of the Normandy Invasion, June 6, 1944* (Novato, CA: Presidio Press, 1998); and S. Terkel, *'The Good War': An Oral History of World War II* (New York: New Press, 1984). Websites on D-Day abound, but a few of the more reputable ones include: http://www.americandday.org/, http://www. nationalww2museum.org/, https://www.dday.org/ (all accessed 18 February 2016), or other sites for any of the museums, libraries, monuments, or memorial associations dedicated fully or in part to D-Day.

106 De Groot, *Consuming History*, 183, 210.

Making memory and identity: The politics and purpose of film and TV: Case studies

CHAPTER TWELVE

Superhero films and American national identity

Michael Goodrum

The concepts of both 'nation' and 'identity' are far from straightforward; the relation of culture to both is an equally vexed question.[1] Partial answers to this complex conundrum, however, can be found in careful consideration of superhero narratives. This is due to the fact that superheroes have often stood in as proxies for the United States of America and its foreign policy. This is most obvious through the literal embodiment of the nation: Captain America (first appearance 1940). The contested terrain occupied by the nation and the character who bears its name, and the way that the latter can help us to understand the former, has been explored by Jason Dittmer.[2] However, it is not only characters bearing the name of the nation who operate as lenses through which audiences can come to a greater understanding of current debates on the US. For instance, the connection between superhero and nation received its most famous formulation in 1952 in the opening credits of the *Adventures of Superman* (1952–8) television series, where it was first stated that Superman fights for 'truth, justice, and the American way'. Such examples offer the brute simplicity with which superhero narratives are all too often associated. 'Truth' and 'justice' are posited as universal categories in a time where there were very different attitudes to such values, embedded in the Cold War ideological battle between the Communist East and the Capitalist West. Superman therefore shows how even apparently innocuous statements are capable of making very clear pronouncements about national identity. Superman, and through association with him the US, was on the side of truth and justice, so the Soviet Union must represent the forces of lies and injustice. Such instances demonstrate clear cut representations of American identity through superhero narratives. In order to further develop and explore these ideas, this chapter will demonstrate how superheroes, and particularly Spider-Man in the trilogy of films directed by Sam Raimi (2002–7), can be used as a means of contributing to and contesting dominant political constructions of the nation and what it means to belong to it. Similar to the ideas outlined in Chapter 1, therefore, this chapter approaches films as cultural artefacts indicative of the dynamic relationship between filmmakers, audiences, and contemporary socio-political conditions, positioning films and their creators as capable of commenting on contemporary events as well as being shaped by them.

Spider-Man

Spider-Man first appeared in a comic-book, *Amazing Fantasy* #15, in 1962: Peter Parker, a physically weak high school student who excels in science, is bitten by a radioactive spider and subsequently gains 'spider powers', such as increased strength and agility. Parker initially seeks to use these newfound powers for financial gain, even going so far as to refuse to help someone being robbed as he feels the victim has denied him money that is rightfully his; the robber goes on to kill Parker's Uncle Ben, teaching him the now famous lesson that 'with great power comes – great responsi-bility!'[3] This maxim has dominated subsequent Spider-Man narratives and stands as a defining tension at the heart of the character: the consequences of action and inaction, and the psychological impact of the struggle and its consequences on Spider-Man/Parker. Spider-Man's origin story is often interpreted as a coming-of-age story, unsurprisingly given Parker's physical and moral maturation, and indeed Parker has been consistently reinserted into this framework in new versions of the Spider-Man story since 1962. In the trilogy of Spider-Man films made by Sam Raimi that followed the terrorist attacks in New York of 11 September 2001, the retelling of the origin story demonstrated how the US could not ignore the world around it, but must use its 'great power' in a more responsible fashion.

Superhero narratives

Superhero narratives have responded to war and violence throughout their history. The genre began with the first appearance of Superman in *Action Comics* #1 in 1938 as the world hovered on the brink of war; the enormous success of Superman ensured that imitators soon followed: Batman and Captain Marvel in 1939, Captain America in 1940, and Wonder Woman in 1941, among a legion of others. After the Japanese attack on the US naval base at Pearl Harbor, Hawaii, on 7 December 1941, even those superheroes who had not already become involved in the Second World War rushed to do so. Throughout the conflict, superheroes fought the Axis in comic-books, animated shorts (such as the *Superman* series produced from 1941–3), in movie serials (such as *Captain Marvel* from 1941, *Batman* from 1943 and *Captain America* from 1944) and on the radio (such as the *Adventures of Superman*, which ran from 1940–51). A decline in superhero popularity followed the war; by the 1950s only Batman, Superman, and Wonder Woman remained in print. However, an explosion of new characters from the publisher Marvel in the early/mid-1960s took the superhero narrative in new directions, introducing characters such as Spider-Man, Iron Man, the Hulk, the X-Men, and the Black Panther. Adaptations from comic-books continued, though despite the growing popularity of Marvel the most notable examples of the 1960s and 1970s were of DC characters: the *Batman* (1966–8) television series and film (1966), starring Adam West and Burt Ward, and the *Wonder Woman* (1975–9) television series, starring Lynda Carter and Lyle Waggoner. The appearance of *Superman* (1978) marked the first full-length cinematic appearance of the most iconic of all superheroes in a film that is still well-regarded, even if the second half of the franchise it spawned (1978–87) is not. *Batman* (1989) ran almost exactly parallel, with the first two films enjoying some degree of critical acclaim before the third and fourth instalments of the franchise undid much of the earlier positivity. What might now be seen as the mature period of superhero film began with *Blade* (1998) and *X-Men* (1999), films that treated their characters and stories seriously and as something capable of contemporary commentary. Grossing $131,183,530 and $296,339,527 respectively, these were commercially successful, but not in the same league that superhero films would occupy after the terrorist attacks on New York of 11 September 2001.[4] The enduring popularity of the genre in the wake of these attacks requires consideration.

Historical context of *Spider-Man* trilogy

Raimi's Spider-Man trilogy did not appear in a vacuum. In fact, its appearance was initially delayed, then redefined, through its political context. On 11 September 2001, terrorists from the Al-Qaeda group hijacked four planes, crashed two into the World Trade Center in New York, a hub of global commerce, a third into the Pentagon, the headquarters of American national defence, and attempted to crash a fourth, Flight 93, into the White House; Flight 93 was brought down through the actions of its passengers before this could happen. The attacks met with considerable shock in the US, and indeed globally. The national mood was best summarized by Charles Krupa, writing in *Time* the day after the events: 'Morning came, and everything was changed'.[5] 9/11, as these attacks came to be known, represents far more than just the terrorist attacks. While still referring to a specific historical event, the term 9/11 is unable to represent the enormity of both that day and what it has subsequently come to mean.

As a term, 9/11 both raises questions and offers answers, the latter of which are generally based on reductive ideas of national unity and a simplification of international politics. Part of this process means that certain elements of 9/11 have been either repressed or privileged throughout US culture. Such a process of 'editing' suggests that 9/11 was, and still is, being constructed through the efforts of the mass media and political elites. This was evident even from the media coverage of the attacks; the destruction of the World Trade Center had to be mediated in order to reach audiences and any process of mediation has an impact on perception. Decisions have to be made about which images to use, how they are to be combined, and the commentary that accompanies them, all of which determine how images are received by audiences. Cultural constructions of rhetoric around 9/11 after the event were also no accident. As James Castonguay notes, 'the film divisions of the major media conglomerates expressed their eagerness to become part of the war effort from the outset', a strategy that ensured, like 9/11, that the War on Terror would also be seen by some onlookers as 'like a movie'.[6]

The post-9/11 period marked a resurgence of interest in the superhero genre, thanks largely in part to the tremendous success of *Spider-Man* (2002). Sam Raimi's cinematic adaptation of the comic-book superhero was already in production prior to 9/11 and early trailers and promotional materials made much of a set piece confrontation around the Twin Towers of the World Trade Center. After the attacks, those materials were withdrawn and the film underwent substantial revisions; the first act of superhero films in the wake of 9/11 was therefore to repeat the erasure of the Twin Towers. This is in contrast to music: Ryan Adams released the single 'New York, New York' in November 2001, featuring him playing in front of the Twin Towers. The single's cover has Adams standing in front of an American flag, fists raised, and profits from the single were donated to a 9/11 charity. Both the single and *Spider-Man* dwell on the geography of New York, and both are effectively a love letter to the city, but the difference lies in the representation of violence: *Spider-Man* and 'New York, New York' are both defiant texts, but the repetition of threats to the Twin Towers in the first version of *Spider-Man* so soon after their destruction is clearly problematic. Images of New York in these two texts demonstrate how representations can be mobilized, but also in turn how they mobilize audiences. *Spider-Man* certainly mobilized people into cinemas – it grossed $821,708,551 worldwide and can be seen as the first of the films that sparked the explosion of interest in superheroes that continues to the present day.[7]

Studios will obviously continue to invest in a popular genre, but this in itself does not make a genre popular; the relevance of superheroes to the socio-political climate must therefore be investigated. Part of the appeal, in the immediate aftermath of 9/11, was the dependence on the origin story. Through the retelling of familiar origin stories, all of which are traumatic, superhero films positioned themselves as uniquely able to respond to the trauma of terrorist attacks, taking a disabling event and transforming it into something profoundly enabling. In this, the films mediated the swift ascent to military mobilization in the wake of the attacks, while also reproducing 9/11 as a moment of historical rupture, a moment when 'everything was changed'; problems came later as the films, like parts of their audiences, began to consider themselves and their historical context more closely and began to question the idea of 9/11 as divorced from previous American policy. In the early stages of the superhero film boom, roughly 2002–4, superheroes contributed to a project of defining and defending the US largely as it was, and as political elites hoped it would remain. As time passed, and conditions changed, faith faltered and superheroes, while continuing to 'fight the good fight', did so in such a way that they could be seen to prompt criticism rather than consensus. This is abundantly clear in the early Marvel Studios films, such as *Iron Man* (2008), where its arms-dealing protagonist abandons weapons manufacture for more peaceful endeavours and *The Incredible Hulk* (2008), where the army are positioned as overreaching themselves to further their own ends, endangering civilians and the nation in the process. While 9/11, or at least the reductive version of it that circulated in the media, was easy to represent, the War on Terror proved more problematic. With 9/11, there were 'good guys' and 'bad guys', a binary that mapped perfectly on to superhero films; the War on Terror asked more questions about the past, present and future conduct of the US, both at home and abroad. As with other arguments about superheroes, this is too broad, and there are clear exceptions – *Avengers Assemble* (2012) does little to recalibrate our understanding of what it is to be American beyond reasserting their apparently innate ability to save the world. But it does demonstrate how superhero films, and the Spider-Man trilogy in particular, are capable of helping historians understand how popular culture draws on and contributes to processes of narrating the nation.

The War on Terror, the foreign policy decisions pursued by the US in the wake of the terrorist attacks, proved problematic, both in terms of reality and superhero representation. The October 2001 invasion of Afghanistan to tackle the sources of the plot against the US – the Taliban who ruled the country and Al Qaeda, who were allowed to use the country as a base – had broad international support, though as with so many superheroic interventions there seemed to be little or nothing prepared in terms of an 'exit strategy', a plan beyond the punching. The Afghanistan operation enjoyed spectacular initial success, and this momentum seemed to encourage elements of the US government to pursue a sequel – the 2003 invasion of Iraq, based on the premise that Saddam Hussein, its then military leader, harboured weapons of mass destruction that could be utilized against the West. However, it is likely that the decision to attack Iraq had been taken far earlier, as demonstrated by Secretary of Defense Donald Rumsfeld's claim in the immediate aftermath of 9/11 that 'there were no decent targets for bombing in Afghanistan … [and as such the US] should consider bombing Iraq'.[8] The Iraq War has remained controversial, and this is no place to enter into its intricacies.[9]

Raimi's trilogy emerged as American identity was being challenged through first external and then internal factors. First, the terrorist attacks on New York in 2001 represented a startlingly violent moment of opposition to the idea that the world welcomed US influence and interference. American confusion as to this point is best summed up by the question 'why do they hate us?' which was asked with such frequency in the wake of the attacks that it found its way into a speech by President Bush.[10] Second, the conduct of the US in the War on Terror; this military response was declared in the aftermath of the attacks and was underpinned by the logic of the Bush Doctrine. The ideological approach argued for pre-emptive self-defence, unilateral action if no support could be found, and the extension of freedom and democracy to those who do not possess it. The conduct of the US in the name of this doctrine, however, began to call into question the very democratic freedoms Bush had cited as cornerstones of American identity and, as such, as reasons for the 9/11 attacks – the reasons 'they' hated the US War on Terror, according to David Holloway, was 'a rhetorical construction, a series of stories about 9/11 and about America's place in the world' that amounted to a means of obscuring the basis of the conflict.[11] At the heart of this construction was the 'representation of 9/11 as the moment when everything changed', a moment of such magnitude that it justified embarking on a lengthy and expensive war.[12] Cultural representations of 9/11 therefore had to fit a certain pattern in order to solicit support, first for the war in Afghanistan and subsequently for the war in Iraq. Cultural engagement with the contemporary socio-political situation had to emphasize the US, rather than individuals, as the victim, and position terrorism as an assault on values such as freedom and democracy. Superheroes fit neatly into this project through Jason Dittmer's argument that they are 'co-constitutive elements of both American identity and the US government's foreign policy practices ... [and that] superheroes serve as a crucial resource for legitimating, contesting, and reworking states' foreign policies', an approach that prompts careful and sustained attention to superhero narratives in their many forms and the ways in which they relate to national identity and national policy.[13] Through the three Raimi Spider-Man films, then, we shall assess how national identity can be both represented and renegotiated through popular culture.

National identity

In order to discuss the negotiation of national identity through popular culture, we must first consider how a nation is defined. Benedict Anderson grapples with this problematic principle and offers the idea that nations, and the sense of nationality that one derives from 'belonging' to such an abstract concept, are 'cultural artefacts of a particular kind' whose existence is emotional as much as it is concrete (see also Chapters 5, 6, 8 and 13).[14] That one belongs to a nation is therefore not just a result of citizenship, but also a process of emotional and ideological investment – one chooses to identify with a narrative of the nation, such as that on offer in superhero stories. Anderson rightly states that the idea that individuals belong to a collective national whole is now so taken for granted that 'everyone can, should, will "have" a nationality', and this has become a foundational point of modern life.[15] The loss of nationhood, in fact, became the central drama of a film made after 9/11, *The Terminal* (2004), where Victor Navorski (Tom Hanks) finds himself stranded on the international soil of JFK airport; after a coup in his home country while he is in the air, Navorski is left without citizenship and unable to gain access to the United States, despite the fact that the purpose of his visit is to get the autograph of a jazz saxophonist, a quest that pays homage to America's greatest musical invention. *The Terminal* therefore demonstrates the problematic nature of the nation; it is an assumed, quantifiable, entity which is like the philosophical idealism of George Berkeley: the nation as a concrete fact is held in existence only as long as it is perceived, or diplomatically acknowledged, by others. The nation as a cultural construct can prove more durable.

If the USA is a cultural construct rather than a monolithic object existing outside the vicissitudes of historical change, Dittmer's argument that superhero films have a role in constructing an American identity becomes increasingly persuasive. Much of the political rhetoric after the 2001 attacks drew on American history: the language of the Wild West was mobilized, through phrases such as 'Wanted: Dead or Alive' on posters for Osama bin Laden, and there were also frequent references to the Japanese attack on Pearl Harbor of 1941 and the 'Golden Generation' of Americans who fought in the Second World War. Such references not only provided a sense of continuity at a moment of profound historical change, they also repositioned those references and sought to mobilize them in a new context that also constructed new histories.[16] These new histories of the American Frontier – famously codified by Frederick Jackson Turner in 1893 as the product of the interaction between European settlers and the 'wilderness' which created 'a new product that is American', show how interaction between 'Western civilization' and the barbarity of the East would create a new society dedicated to the freedom and democracy espoused by the Bush Doctrine.[17] In order to privilege a dynamic history of the US as a guiding force for good in the world, the Frontier Thesis, together with simplistic accounts of the Second World War, overlooked complexities such as the treatment of Native Americans and acquisition of territory in the former and the suppression and containment of ethnic and linguistic minorities in the latter. Such simplistic structures were clearly evident in initial superhero responses to 9/11.

Spider-Man

The United States was not the only thing to be re-created in the wake of 9/11; Spider-Man was also rewritten. The man to do this was director Sam Raimi, who first rose to prominence as the director of the *Evil Dead* trilogy (1981–92), a comic-horror hybrid; *The Evil Dead* (1981) attained wide notoriety, at least in Britain, as part of the 'video nasty' culture of the early 1980s and was banned by the Department of Public Prosecutions. Raimi's later film, *Darkman* (1990), while not enjoying the same level of success as *Evil Dead*, confirmed Raimi's love of superheroes and distinctive visual style that was used to such good effect in his *Spider-Man* trilogy. After 9/11 forced the revision of the film, thanks to the prominent role of the Twin Towers in its action, the film joined broader processes of historical reconstruction and rediscovery. In the version released to cinemas in 2002, *Spider-Man* engages with a recovery of earlier narratives of American purity, a simplification of complex geopolitical realities that allowed national identity to be mapped through a costumed character, his interactions with the general public, and his enemies. At the heart of this interpretation is Spider-Man's 1962 maxim that 'with great power comes – great responsibility'. Like the US more generally, the founding principle of Spider-Man is reinterpreted and repositioned by the new context in which it is presented. The core elements of the origin story remain the same: Parker is bitten by a radioactive spider while on a school trip and is subsequently endowed with the speed, strength, and abilities of a spider. His first thought is to flaunt this power, to use it to raise money to impress the long-term object of his affections, Mary-Jane Watson; this selfishness indirectly results in the death of his uncle, whose incorporeal presence becomes a source of moral guidance throughout the rest of the trilogy. The nation's present is haunted by its past. This is as it happens in the comic-book of the 1960s (albeit without Mary-Jane, who did not make her first full appearance until 1966), so the origin story was not substantially rewritten – but contemporary audiences could potentially reinterpret it in the light of contemporary developments, seeing Spider-Man's loss and re-education as resonant with 9/11 and the failure of the US to meet the requirements of its great power.

A reading privileging Spider-Man's re-education and newfound dedication to altruistic action, however, does not take into account the oft-asked question, 'why do they hate us?', and is less convincing because of it. Spider-Man is all too aware that wrongdoings in his past have led to his current position, whereas the narrative under construction in the immediate aftermath of the attacks overlooked decades of US foreign policy to argue that the terrorists had acted without provocation. We must therefore look deeper. Niall Richardson offers a reading based in Christian theology, where '*Spider-Man* is a metaphor for Christian shame, shame for longings of the flesh and an attempt to transcribe this shame into more manageable guilt', an approach that stresses humility and the flawed nature of the human body.[18] Richardson is correct to stress the number of Biblically derived scenes in the film, most notably the Green Goblin's 'temptation' when he takes Spider-Man above the city and offers him the chance to rule it alongside him, but Richardson is too quick to write off the relationship between Spider-Man and the nation. In stating that 'Spidey swinging past the United States flag is a crude conflation of American citizenship with a Christian-mythologized version of crime', in short a modern morality play, is to overlook the more complex relationship engendered by the strong association between Spider-Man, the US and Christ – and the relationship that this implies between the US and the world.[19] If Spider-Man is being tempted by the Green Goblin, then he is standing in for Christ, an interpretation supported by Spider-Man's adoption of cruciform position during the battle with the Green Goblin by the 59th Street Bridge and Roosevelt Island Tramway when it looks as if Spider-Man may have to sacrifice himself to save those he is defending. If Spider-Man is being positioned this way, he is either the saviour – not just of the people in the cable cars but of the whole world, past, present and future – or someone sufficiently immersed in His teaching to be the latest in a long tradition of American Christian heroes. Given the close association between Spider-Man and the American flag, some of this muscular Christianity rubs off on the country being embodied by the superhero; this has other connotations in the War on Terror, a contest constructed as between the Christian West and a distinctly non-Christian Other in the East. *Spider-Man* therefore draws on Christianity to construct a sense of moral nationhood and of the US as saviour, based on a clear 'good vs. evil' binary opposition. The idea of the US as a Christian exemplar in this way also draws on the idea of John Winthrop's reference in 1630 (via Matthew 5.14) to the New England colony as a 'City upon a Hill' that would be seen by the world and had to act accordingly.

Spider-Man, however, is not the only hero of the 59th Street Bridge scene; he is saved from the Green Goblin's assault by a crowd of ordinary New Yorkers who hurl debris at the Green Goblin, preventing him from killing Spider-Man as he tries to save both a tram car full of children and Mary-Jane. The message of this scene is not so much reinforced as rammed home when one of the crowd shouts to the Green Goblin that if 'you mess with one of us, you mess with all of us', a clear statement that terrorism will not intimidate or defeat the US, and that terrorist actions have resulted in the forging of a newly assertive national identity. This new identity also resonated with contemporary politico-cultural rhetoric, most notably the idea that 'we are all New Yorkers', and that the attacks on the World Trade Center had created an exclusive/inclusive bond that defined those belonging to it through the trauma of 9/11. Ideas of inclusion and exclusion were also referenced by President Bush's claim that in the War on Terror, 'you are either with us, or with the terrorists', terms that made neutrality, or

FIGURE 12.1 *Spider-Man as Christ,* Spider-Man 2 *(2004)*

any kind of critical position, impossible.[20] Spider-Man's support from the crowd, on top of the forceful biblical allusions throughout the film, creates a similarly narrow definition of belonging. It is hard to side with the Green Goblin: one is either with Spider-Man, who is trying to save people, or with the Green Goblin, who is trying to kill them. Such simplistic divisions do not map easily on to a concept as complex as nationality. Unless, that is, it is construed in its simplest, most reductive terms, as in the phrase 'British by birth, English by the grace of God'; or, indeed, of much of President Bush's rhetoric after 9/11, such as his definition of Iran, Iraq and North Korea as the 'axis of evil'. Here, nationality is an immutable concept worthy of considerable emotional and ideological investment and to be defended at all costs: if the enemy is *evil*, all resistance is entirely justifiable. *Spider-Man*, to some extent, reinforced that by positioning the Green Goblin as a surrogate Lucifer, but such narratives uncomfortably involve the US in complex geopolitical discussions they might have preferred to avoid; Lucifer fell from grace and to understand his campaign against righteousness one has to appreciate his former relationship to it, exemplified in Norman Osborn's pre-Green Goblin career as a holder of contracts to supply the US military. Implicit perspectives such as this are largely overwhelmed by flag-waving nationalism which proved tremendously popular and, in turn, became a model for emulation for other superhero films. Spider-Man was popular with crowds both inside and outside the film.

The fact that the Green Goblin was, prior to his transformation, an American working with the American military could be seen as a further complicating factor, but ultimately it resonates with the representation of the character as Lucifer. It is pride and ambition that bring about Norman Osborn's downfall. There are, of course, other readings of Norman Osborn and his transformation into the Green Goblin. Richard L. Kaplan argues that villains of this type mediate 'pervasive American cultural beliefs about masculinity', in particular that of the bad father of Oedipal fantasy.[21] Norman Osborn is the head of a large company, while Spider-Man's Uncle

Ben is old and unemployed – Ben is laid off as his employer is 'downsizing people and upsizing their profits', raising the possibility that the film will become an assault on modern capitalism.[22] Unsurprisingly, this avenue is not pursued; moments such as 9/11 present the opportunity to reconfigure society, but they are moments when conservative forces of retrenchment are also active, and an attempt to criticize capitalism as practiced in the US runs uncomfortably close to the project of the terrorists.

Although continuities in the portrayal of the villain in *Spider-Man 2* (2004) exist, there are also points of divergence that lead to a more nuanced character. Whereas the Green Goblin is an almost entirely unsympathetic character (his only potential source of goodwill being the fact that the Goblin persona could be seen to manifest itself as a mental illness, reducing Osborn's moral and legal responsibility for his actions), Dr Octopus is a different matter. The two characters share many things – Otto Octavius, as he is before the accident that transforms him into Dr Octopus, is a scientist in pursuit of power, although in Octavius' case this is quite literal: he is developing a new power source that will bring cheap, clean energy to everybody. Octavius also works for Oscorp, Norman Osborn's company, now being run by his son, Harry, Peter Parker's best friend. Like Osborn, Octavius is also a father figure to Parker, though whereas Osborn was cruel to his son, Octavius is a kind patriarch, although one without children of his own, who lives with his wife in apparently idyllic circumstances. This all changes after Octavius' experiment explodes, kills his wife, and fuses four metal arms with embedded artificial intelligence to his body. Like Osborn, he now demonstrates symptoms of mental illness as he hears voices in his head, but a clear external factor is given for this, the arms, and the audience is already sympathetic to him because of his earlier treatment of Parker and more peaceful use of science. The biblical imagery so apparent in *Spider-Man* is also greatly reduced in *Spider-Man 2*, which leads to a blurring of the line between good and evil; where present, it is less effective in terms of the internal logic of the film. As with the first film, Spider-Man adopts cruciform position while saving citizens of New York from the villain of the film, this time on a subway train. Spider-Man successfully stops the train from crashing, eliciting the support of those on it as they first take his body down from the cross, as it were, and pass it overhead in hallowed silence before standing up to Dr Octopus when he comes to claim Spider-Man's body, refusing to let him pass. Unlike the actions of the crowd in *Spider-Man*, which were pivotal in Spider-Man's success, the passengers on the train are easily swept aside by their adversary, offering a very different story to that of the first film.

Spider-Man offers a message of unity in the face of adversity, of a nationhood that, although narrowly exclusive (the idea of everyone being a New Yorker is broad, but insists that everyone accept a nationhood based on trauma and in line with government policy), cannot be overcome by external factors. *Spider-Man 2* complicates that by introducing internal

FIGURE 12.2 *Spider-Man and the American flag,* Spider-Man *(2002)*

factors, the idea that the nation must look within itself as well as outside for threats. The fact that the enemy is formerly sympathetic, and that he ultimately attains redemption by destroying his experiment when he realizes that it threatens the safety of New York, means that *Spider-Man 2* provides a different kind of villain and a different kind of threat. In terms of narrating the nation, the second instalment in the trilogy is more cautious and less quick to celebrate the narrative being constructed by the political elite. There are good reasons for this. By 2004, when *Spider-Man 2* was released, the global political situation had changed. Afghanistan had been invaded and occupied; Iraq shared the same fate following allegations that it possessed weapons of mass destruction. The inability of forces occupying Iraq to locate these weapons, plus reports of torture and even murder at Abu Ghraib prison that emerged in late 2003, coloured perceptions of the US making it increasingly difficult to position the enemy as solely external. Some, though not all, observers began to think along lines advanced by Walt Kelly's comic-strip, *Pogo*: 'We have met the enemy and he is us'.[23]

   Spider-Man 3 (2007) further advances this view, calling into question not only the villain but the hero, as Spider-Man becomes an increasingly problematic character. In the third film, Spider-Man begins from a position of mass acceptance, even being presented with the key to the city in tribute to his many heroic acts. What follows mediates the unravelling of the initial broad consensus behind the War on Terror, which can also be tracked through the decline in President Bush's approval rating from a high of 90 per cent in September 2001 to 34 per cent by the time of the release of *Spider-Man 3* in late April 2007.[24] In the film, Spider-Man is infected with an alien symbiote that magnifies his power but also his negative qualities, making him arrogant, self-centred and short-tempered. While in this frame of mind Parker discovers that Flint Marko, the man who murdered his uncle, has escaped from prison; Spider-Man sets out for revenge rather than justice, attempting to kill Marko rather than return him to prison. This could be seen to mediate American refusals to submit Osama bin Laden to trial in an international court for his terrorist activities, and of their failure to solicit international support for the invasion of Iraq in the United Nations. While escaping from prison, Marko becomes trapped inside a huge physics experiment that transforms his body into sand, allowing Marko to alter the density of his body at will. Spider-Man's attempts to drown Marko, or Sandman as he is eventually known, are therefore unsuccessful. Marko, like bin Laden, slips through the fingers of the attacker.

As the seriousness of his attack on Marko dawns on him, Spider-Man attempts to disengage himself from the symbiote, a potential reference to the US' attempt to extricate itself from Bush's politics through the rising popularity of Barack Obama, who announced his candidacy for the presidency in February 2007. Spider-Man proves able to detach from the symbiote, but this is not the end of his problems: in doing so, he only manages to create another enemy as the symbiote bonds with Eddie Brock, a photographer who had falsified pictures of Spider-Man for the *Daily Bugle* in order to secure a job. While still under the influence of the symbiote, Parker had exposed Brock as a fraud, ruining his career. Brock is subsequently fired from the *Bugle* and unable to work in photojournalism again due to the well-publicized retraction the *Bugle* is forced to run. Consumed by rage, Brock and the symbiote become the villain known as Venom. Effectively, the film is suggesting that the US can distance itself from this problem, but that does not mean it is over. In this, it mediates Chalmers Johnson's notion of 'blowback', or the unintended consequences of US foreign policy.[25] Venom seeks an alliance to defeat Spider-Man and joins forces with Marko. Together they kidnap Mary-Jane and force Spider-Man into fighting them, something he reluctantly does after acknowledging that he will not be able to defeat both villains alone. *Spider-Man 3* therefore draws on the idea that the lack of international support for the war in Iraq is detrimental to its long-term success.

As Spider-Man thought, he is unable to defeat both villains alone, something that implicitly criticizes the Bush Doctrine's policy to act unilaterally if necessary. With Spider-Man on the verge of death, Peter's best friend Harry Osborn, using his father Norman's Green Goblin equipment, saves Spider-Man's life. Rather than the triumphant ending audiences might have expected, Osborn is killed, as is Brock. Spider-Man is therefore left to face Marko alone but, instead of fighting, the two of them talk. Both subsequently admit to having done 'terrible things', and Spider-Man forgives Marko for his role in the death of his Uncle Ben.[26] Marko then fragments into sand, drifting away in the breeze. The sand that constitutes Marko's body comes into contact with skyscrapers as he drifts away but glides over their surface rather than destroying them. After a process of negotiation and forgiveness, Marko no longer manifests a desire for destruction, a conclusion from which the audience can infer that the most effective way of dealing with enemies is through dialogue rather than physical confrontation. Through Brock, however, *Spider-Man 3* demonstrates that some enemies can only be defeated through force and sacrifice. Moreover, as Brock owes his career as a villain to Parker's arrogance, the implication could also be that the enemies 'created' by the US are the most difficult to defeat (the group who later became the Taliban had been trained and funded by the US during the Soviet war in Afghanistan [1979–89]). Ultimately, this creates a nuanced ending that suggests how the US should advance in its War on Terror, combining force and diplomacy in alliance with other nations.

Spider-Man 3's critique stems from the representation of social fragmentation rather than outright political commentary. The film is never expressly critical of US policy and it is possible to interpret *Spider-Man 3* in a rather more celebratory way than presented here. After all, Spider-Man 'wins' and New York is made safe again, surely everything else is incidental? An approach of this kind is hopelessly reductive, though, as it fails to take into account the crushingly depressing nature of those incidental factors. Even the conclusion that offers the potential for healing, an embrace between Parker and Mary-Jane, is far from upbeat. Neither participant in the embrace looks particularly pleased to be there, while the choice of music for the scene is hardly uplifting: a halting version of the jazz standard, 'I'm Through With Love', sung by Mary-Jane, which segues into muted strings and synthesizers as Parker and Mary-Jane hesitantly embrace. The camera subsequently reveals a pensive Parker staring straight ahead as Mary-Jane cries on his shoulder. Like the US in the wake of the immensely divisive Bush administration, much work still needed to be done to repair relationships.

Given that the previous scene, the battle between Spider-Man, Marko and Venom had ended with Parker and Mary-Jane crying over the dead body of Harry Osborn, *Spider-Man 3* seems to be deliberately resisting the triumphant endings of superhero narratives that are often used to limit earlier criticism. It uses the conclusion to call into question whether, given that the previous two films have led to this point, the actions of the hero, and by extension the US with which Spider-Man has been closely associated throughout the trilogy, have been worthwhile. Harry is dead; New York is confused by the way Spider-Man has been acting and it appears that, much like the US, the hero has squandered the consensus he had constructed; Mary-Jane and Parker's relationship is potentially damaged beyond repair; and Spider-Man has jeopardized his position as moral guardian rather than lawless vigilante through his failure to live up to his mantra that 'with great power comes great responsibility'. Ideological ties that bound the earlier films together, and indeed bound them to dominant constructions of the nation, have worn through and where there was order and clarity there is now confusion and disappointment. The consensus forged in response to 9/11 has fragmented under the strain of the War on Terror; even though the embrace between Parker and Mary-Jane that concludes the film signals a coming together, it is a downbeat ending that encourages its audience to reflect on what they have seen, to take a critical approach rather than to glory in the violent resolution of violent conflict.

Conclusion

The Sam Raimi *Spider-Man* trilogy, and superhero films more generally, offer a complex means of engaging with the ongoing construction of an American nationality.[27] The use of superheroes to make debates more accessible has the potential to reduce critical engagement with politics, as in *Spider-Man*, encouraging emotional ties to fictional characters who advocate support for real-world policies without appearing to do so while simplifying complicated geopolitical issues into opposing binaries that draw on historical constructions of the nation. While superhero narratives have the potential to open debates to wider audiences, they do so in a way that certain elements of these debates can be obscured, overlooked, or omitted entirely. However, *Spider-Man 3* demonstrates that, even without expressly addressing US foreign policy, superhero narratives can still operate as means of 'contesting and reworking' narratives of the American nation. When Spider-Man gratuitously swings past the American flag in the first film, it is celebratory, an affirmation of American military might; by the third film, Spider-Man's journey past the flag is undertaken on the way to his near death and the ultimate realization that violence is not always the answer. The visible role of the American flag changes as the trilogy progresses and the historical context into which it emerges undergoes profound changes. The Spider-Man trilogy therefore offers an excellent means of investigating the multifaceted role of superhero films in the construction and contestation of an American nationality.

Notes

1   It is explored at length in M. Goodrum, *Superheroes and American Self Image: From War to Watergate* (London: Ashgate, 2016).

2   J. Dittmer, *Captain America and the Nationalist Superhero: Metaphors, Narratives, and Geopolitics* (Philadelphia: Temple University Press, 2013).

3   S. Lee and S. Ditko et al., *Amazing Fantasy* #15 (Marvel Comics: New York, 1962).

4   Box office data from *Box Office Mojo*. Available online: http://www.

boxofficemojo.com/movies/?id=blade.htm and http://www.boxofficemojo.com/movies/?id=xmen.htm (both accessed 20 January 2016).

5   C. Krupa, 'Day of Infamy', *Time,* 12 September 2001. Available online: http://www.time.com/time/nation/article/0,8599,174502,00.html (accessed 20 January 2016).

6   J. Castonguay, 'Conglomeration, New Media and the Cultural Production of the "War on Terror"', *Cinema Journal* 43 (4) (2004): 103.

7   Box office data from *Box Office Mojo.* Available online: http://www.boxofficemojo.com/movies/?id=spiderman.htm (accessed 20 January 2016).

8   R. Clarke, *Against All Enemies: Inside America's War on Terror* (New York: Free Press, 2004), 31.

9   There is a considerable amount of material on this topic. See, for instance, D. H. Dunn, 'Myths, Motivations and "Misunderestimations": The Bush Administration and Iraq', *International Affairs* 79 (2) (2003), Hans Blix, *Disarming Iraq: The Search for Weapons of Mass Destruction* (London: Bloomsbury, 2005), S. Ritter, *Iraq Confidential: The Untold Story of America's Intelligence Conspiracy* (London: I.B. Tauris, 2005), Paul Pillar 'Intelligence, Policy and the War in Iraq', *Foreign Affairs* (March/April 2006), and S. Lucas, 'Recognising Politicization: The CIA and the Path to the 2003 War in Iraq', *Intelligence and National Security* 26 (2–3) (2011).

10   President George W. Bush, 'Address to Joint Session of Congress and the Nation', 20 September 2001. Available online http://www.washingtonpost.com/wp-srv/nation/specials/attacked/transcripts/bushaddress_092001.html (accessed 30 December 2014).

11   D. Holloway, *9/11 and the War on Terror* (Edinburgh: Edinburgh University Press, 2008), 4.

12   Ibid.

13   Dittmer, *Captain America and the Nationalist Superhero,* 3.

14   B. Anderson, *Imagined Communities: Reflections on the Origin and Spread of Nationalism* (London: Verso, 2003), 4.

15   Ibid., 5.

16   Krupa, 'Day of Infamy'.

17   F. J. Turner, 'The Significance of the Frontier in American History', in *The Frontier in American History* (New York: Henry Holt and Company, 1921), Ch. 1.

18   N. Richardson, 'The Gospel According to Spider-Man', *The Journal of Popular Culture* 37 (4) (2004): 696.

19   Richardson, 'The Gospel According to Spider-Man', 702.

20   President G. W. Bush, Address to Joint Session of Congress and the Nation, 20 September 2001. Available online: http://www.washingtonpost.com/wp-srv/nation/specials/attacked/transcripts/bushaddress_092001.html (accessed 30 December 2014). For a further discussion of this, see J. Butler, *Precarious Life: The Power of Mourning and Violence* (London: Verso, 2006).

21   R L. Kaplan, 'Spider-Man in Love: A Psychoanalytic Interpretation', *The Journal of Popular Culture* 44 (2) (2011): 294.

22   *Spider-Man* (2002), dir. Raimi.

23   The line was first used on a poster for Earth Day in 1970 and is based on an earlier quotation from Oliver Hazard Perry at the Battle of Lake Erie in 1813, 'We have met the enemy, and they are ours'. Another instance of the reinterpretation of American history as contemporary commentary.

24   'Presidential Approval Ratings – George W. Bush', Gallup Poll. Available online: http://www.gallup.com/poll/116500/presidential-approval-ratings-george-bush.aspx (accessed 31 December 2014).

25   C. Johnson, *Blowback: The Costs and Consequences of American Empire* (New York: Holt Paperbacks, 2001).

26   *Spider-Man 3* (2007), dir. Raimi.

27   The question of gender within this construction is explored in M. Emad, 'Reading Wonder Woman's Body: Mythologies of Gender and Nation', *The Journal of Popular Culture* 39 (6) (2006): 954–84. Wonder Woman remains a complicated, and complicating, presence thanks to her gender, *Wonder Woman*. Possible reasons for this are explored in C. Howell, '"Tricky" Connotations: Wonder Woman as DC's Brand Disruptor', *Cinema Journal* 55 (1) (2015): 141–9. A more complete history of Wonder Woman can be found in T. Hanley, *Wonder Woman Unbound: The Curious History of the World's Most Famous Heroine* (Chicago: Chicago Review Press, 2014), and an investigation of her creator, William Moulton Marston, and the politics that informed the character's origins can be found in J. Lepore, *The Secret History of Wonder Woman* (London: Scribe Publications, 2015).

CHAPTER THIRTEEN

'We will remember them': Television and British memory of the First World War, 1964–2014

Sam Edwards

'Our understanding of the [First World] war', declared Michael Gove in a widely publicized *Daily Mail* article published on 2 January 2014, 'has been overlaid by misunderstandings, and misrepresentations which reflect an, at best, ambiguous attitude to this country and, at worst, an unhappy compulsion on the part of some to denigrate virtues such as patriotism, honour and courage'.[1] Here was the opening salvo in what duly became a highly public confrontation concerning British memory of the 'war to end all wars'. For Gove, the Education Secretary who had driven a return to explicitly 'British' history in the school curriculum, the Centennial of the war's outbreak demanded a suitably reverential homage to those who gave their lives in a 'plainly just war'. In turn, continued Gove, this demanded a concerted assault on the 'myths' of the war so-long pedalled by left-wing academics and, most worryingly of all, disseminated in popular culture. As Gove explained:

> The conflict has, for many, been seen through the fictional prism of dramas such as *Oh! What a Lovely War*, *The Monocled Mutineer* and *Blackadder*, as a misbegotten shambles – a series of catastrophic mistakes perpetrated by an out-of-touch elite.[2]

To be sure, this outburst contained more than a hint of the familiar Right-wing critique of the role and power of the media, and especially of the BBC. But Gove's article also represented a purposefully timed intervention into the Centennial preparations; an attempt to frame the terms upon which the war was to be remembered. Unsurprisingly, given that these terms have been vigorously debated since the end of the war, the article provoked an engaged response. Sir Tony Robinson, who played Baldrick in *Blackadder*, was reported as saying that Gove's comments were 'particularly unhelpful and irresponsible' as they essentially amounted to 'just another example of slagging off teachers',[3] while Ben Elton, one of *Blackadder*'s writers, remarked that Gove's thinking was 'very silly'.[4] In due course, another wave followed up the counter-attack. With characteristic aplomb, Jeremy Paxman, himself the author of a popular history of the war, dismissively implied that Gove was both a 'moron' and a 'charlatan',[5] while the comedian David Mitchell, writing in the *Guardian* (among Gove's most consistent antagonists), playfully dismantled the Education's Secretary's 'all over the place' arguments.[6] But the most devastating counter-battery retort was provided by Richard Evans, Regius Professor of Modern History at the University of Cambridge, published expert on twentieth-century Europe, and the one historian deliberately (and, perhaps, foolishly) singled out by Gove for criticism. Evans, no stranger to historical debate conducted in full glare of the public and press,[7] carefully unpicked Secretary Gove's assumptions, revealing them for what they were: poorly conceived, poorly argued, and poorly evidenced.[8]

For all the politically motivated inaccuracy, hyperbole and bombast, Gove's assault did at least offer a revealing éxpose regarding an important assumption: his assertion that the 'true' history of the war had been lost amid the 'myths' produced and perpetrated by film and television. It was this assumption that constituted the fatal flaw in his argument. Gove – intent on exercising his historical intellect – had failed to do his history; he had not grasped that the Great War – its causes, consequences and commemoration – had been debated and disputed since at least 1918. He had not grasped that British 'memory' of the war had been the subject of intense debate for a century. Rather than offering what he understood to be a historical 'corrective' of Left-wing myths, he had instead merely revealed his own commitment to a particular memory of the conflict.

This chapter traces the role played by various different 'sites' and 'resources' in shaping British memory of the First World War. The chapter shows how British views of the conflict have been shaped and reshaped by a changing political and cultural context, and by the construction of new memorial forms – from monumental sculpture, to a 'monumental' television series, to 'new memory' and new audio-visual memorials. It concludes by exploring what recent television shows reveal about contemporary British memory of the First World War. In particular, I examine the extent to which several innovative First World War focused productions have now begun to self-consciously and purposefully interrogate the very process of making memory.

Old or new? First World War memory in the post-war period

Already before the Armistice was signed, agencies of the British government had commenced the work of commemoration. In 1917, the Imperial War Museum was founded as an institution of memory intended to display the relics and remains of the still on-going 'Great War'. The same year also saw the creation of the Imperial (now Commonwealth) War Graves Commission, tasked with restoring order to the battlefield landscape, and indeed to the British – and imperial – state. [9] From the chaos of conflict would come the order of commemoration; from blood soaked battlefields would come the massed ranks of marble headstones. From one perspective, this was the rightful duty of a state which had conscripted its sons and demanded their sacrifice; from another, this was just another expression of what the war itself had produced: an all-powerful state intent on retaining the right to determine how the dead would be buried and remembered. Here was fought among the very first of the 'memory battles' connected to the experiences of 1914–18.

In towns and villages throughout Britain, those bereft – the loved ones of the fallen – discovered that their 'loss' was permanent; the body that had been conscripted into the service of the nation – their son, husband, father – now belonged to the nation forevermore. Government policy declared that none of the dead were to be returned home, regardless of rank or status. In Britain, the public debate this decision produced never reached the fevered pitch of France, where families of the fallen descended on battlefields and cemeteries in the darkness of the night in order to reclaim the corporeal remains of their loved ones. But even so, discursive battle was joined, protests offered in Parliament, and anger articulated in the Press. Regardless, legislation was enacted, and national – and imperial – cemeteries were duly established throughout northern France and Flanders (and beyond). In many respects, these memorial landscapes were an attempt to realize the vision articulated by poet Rupert Brooke in 1914; they were to be 'corners' of a 'foreign field' which, due to the blood spilt, would 'remain forever England'.[10] Indeed, their very design and form, which had been partly defined by the likes of Sir Edwin Lutyens (among the great architects of Edwardian Britain) and Rudyard Kipling (poet of Empire, and himself a grieving father) was an attempt to capture this Brookian idea: the architecture and horticultural were carefully chosen in order to cultivate the idea of an 'English garden'. Shrubbery, roses and Portland stone were used in an attempt to fulfil this landscape vision so that when relatives visited they would at least feel that the lost resided amid the familiar.[11]

As the imperial state designed and dedicated vast memorials to the massed ranks of the fallen in France, back home in Britain the sheer scale of death, and the fact that no bodies returned, duly produced what would

become the largest programme of public architecture Britain has ever seen.
As Alex King has shown, these local and municipal efforts to commemorate
the dead had first emerged during the war itself, in the form of street
shrines.[12] Once the Armistice was signed, such efforts were redoubled
and expanded. Throughout the 1920s, and in the town halls, churches,
workplaces, schools, colleges, hospitals and universities, the dead of the
conflict were memorialized and re-memorialized; the structures built –
monuments, plaques, stained glass windows, public buildings – defined the
dead in multiple ways: as family, as friends, as parishioners, as employees,
as Britons. By the start of the next war, around 45,000 memorials had been
erected.[13] In Whitehall, too, and in response to the public outpouring which
had accompanied the presence of a temporary commemorative obelisk in
1919, a new, permanent national memorial was dedicated on Armistice
Day in 1920. Its form was innovative and unusual – a *Cenotaph* (an empty
tomb), upon which the dedication 'To Our Glorious Dead' was inscribed.
Not too far away, in Westminster Abbey, a counterpart to this monument
was unveiled on the same day: the Tomb of the Unknown Warrior. Here,
an 'unknown' of the Western Front was 'buried with the kings', an idea
suggestive of the distance travelled since the days of Victoria: in his sacrifice,
the ordinary soldier was now the equal of the titled Noble.[14]

By the eve of the Second World War, a landscape of memory had
been established in Britain. This landscape had certain consistencies, but
also expressed difference and divergence. In overseas cemeteries, and at
the centre of power in London, the dead were remembered as military
servants of the state who had 'given' for their country. Here too were
inscribed the 'big words' – honour, duty, sacrifice – so famously critiqued
by Wilfred Owen in his poem 'Dulce Et Decorum Est'.[15] But together with
these explicitly 'national' expressions of remembrance, linked, but also
subtly different, activities abounded. In the regions and municipalities,
veterans, next of kin, local notables, civic and religious leaders combined
to commemorate. Unsurprisingly, given the sheer extent of these efforts,
the numbers involved, and the issues at stake, the structures duly dedicated
took various forms. For some, 'secular' or non-denominational form was
deemed most fitting – memorials which declared faith not in redemption,
but in the war's cause and purpose: for liberty, for freedom, for peace. For
others, religious iconography came to the fore, most obviously the cross, a
form that enabled the sacrifice of the dead to be equated with the Passion
of Christ. For others still, the monumental was eschewed in favour of the
'practical' and 'utilitarian' – civic buildings, community centres, hospitals
and schools. And for some, the tropes of Classical and Medieval history
were trawled for suitable style and sentiment.[16]

It is these differences which, especially since the 1980s, have generated
intense scholarly debate. For some historians, the First World War is significant because the cultural and commemorative response was demonstrably
new: new forms, new words and new ideas. The extent to which the war led

to the 'democratization' of memory is often identified as crucial: no longer was it sufficient to commemorate conflict with a monument to a Nelson or Wellington; after 1918, the ordinary and even unknown were worthy of national remembrance.[17] By implication and emphasis, this school of thought is connected to a broader historiography: the more general idea that the war – the deluge – severed the present from the past, and in doing so called forth the 'modern' age. Paul Fussell famously argued that the carnage of industrial conflict called forth a new idiom, and a new mode of ironic expression. After the devastation of the Somme and Passchendaele, says Fussell, the old ideas, the old words, the old idealizations – especially, for instance, the literary conventions of English pastoralism – were no longer fit for purpose.[18] Hence the cultural work of those writers and poets who drew attention to the war's destruction via ironic (or bitter) inversions of the old conventions.[19]

For other scholars, the 'modernity' of size, scale and commemorative symbolism should not be allowed to overshadow the 'oldness' of idea and iconography. In this view, the significance of post-war memorials lies in the extent to which they worked to return disrupted British society to something akin to turn-of-the-century 'normality'. Post-war commemoration was thus the last gasp of Victorian tradition, an attempt by the great, the good and the powerful – at both national and local level – to reassert the very values for which Battle was joined: God, King, Country.[20] Central to this view is, once again, the importance of 'landscape' in the memorializing process, long crucial to British conceptions of national identity (think Blake's Green and Pleasant Land). But, contrary to Fussell, this view suggests that a key activity of the post-1918 period was the resuscitation and resurrection of old conventions (rather than their ironic destabilization), hence the English 'gardens' established by the Imperial War Graves Commission. How better to make right what Samuel Hynes has referred to as the First World War's 'death of landscape' than by turning the scarred fields of northern France into pastoral, sacred ground?[21]

Regardless of the extent to which post-1918 memorials were 'modern' or 'traditional' there was at least one consistency – the importance of *names*. Whether the memorial took the form of a Christian cross, a sculptural vision of Classical 'Peace', a Tommy standing sentinel, or a medieval warrior slaying the dragon of Teutonic tyranny, the vast majority of the structures dedicated carried the names of those commemorated. Hence why they produced such engaged discussion: these structures, now often invisible in their sheer ubiquity, carried the names of the loved and lost; and to be realized, therefore, they were the product of grief, tears, outrage, anger, and ultimate agreement (or acquiescence). The very permanence of their form denies this fluid, political and emotional process through which they came to be.

These memorials, in all their varied forms, constitute the first purposefully designed 'sites of memory' connected to the Great War. As Chapter 3 outlined, these were the commemorative 'resources' dedicated in the interwar period and which both constructed and communicated the 'collective memory' of the group responsible. They remained important in the post-1945 period, and they remain important today, a point attested by their continued role in Remembrance Day ceremonies. But, as time has passed, and as the living connection to the conflict has frayed and broken, the role played by memorial *sites* in contemporary British understandings of the First World War has declined. In their place, but continuing the arguments they started, have come *sights* of memory. This is the History of Memory that the Education Secretary might have consulted before offering his ahistorical assault on so-called televisual 'myths'.

Monumental television: The Great War in the Cold War

In the aftermath of the Second World War, the agencies and organizations established in Britain to commemorate the earlier conflict were extended and expanded. In Europe, the Imperial War Graves Commission commenced work to repair the damage inflicted on their post-1918 memorial landscapes, and then embarked upon a new round of commemorative activity. In London, the Imperial War Museum began collecting the machines and materiel of the recent conflict. Remembrance Day – 11 November – became the national day of memory and mourning for all Britain's twentieth-century war dead. In time, the result of these decisions and activities was that the First World War became increasingly overshadowed by the Second: in the post-1945 period, the earlier conflict now appeared just a bloody and brutal prelude to the latter. The Somme remained a trauma and tragedy, but even the bloodiest day in British military history paled before the slaughter perpetrated at Auschwitz, Dachau, and Bergen-Belsen. By the 1950s, the continued 'presence' of the Second World War in contemporary culture was also asserted by film (see also Chapters 4 and 5). For Americans, the battles of 1941–5 provided moral clarity and political purpose (see Chapter 11): freedom versus tyranny (a useful binary opposition during the Cold War confrontation). For the British, stories of Dunkirk, the Blitz and the Battle of Britain were a sop to imperial retreat and national decline: powerful evocations of Britannia's former might and resilience. By the 1960s, Anglo-American interest in the Second World War remained strong: the Eichmann Trial of 1961 drew public attention back to the horrors of the Holocaust and Hollywood epics like *The Longest Day* (1962), asserted the continued importance of the Western alliance formed to liberate Europe. But while British interest in the Second World War remained vital in the 1960s, other contemporary events also turned attention back to the *First* bloodletting. A key cause and consequence of this resurgent interest was a landmark television series, *The Great War* (1964), which aired over twenty-six episodes.

The origins – and politics – of this production have been well-examined by historian Emma Hanna (see also Chapter 14). As Hanna explains, the series was originally conceived by producers Tony Essex and Gordon Watkins, with the former retaining firm control of the project throughout. For Essex, the war was to be 'encoded' as 'epic tragedy', and the structure, script, narration, visual effects, and source material were all mobilized to this end. Ideas first explored in the war poetry of Wilfred Owen, Siegfried Sassoon, John McGrae and Edmund Blunden were all invoked, and at one point Essex even intended that Sassoon be involved in the production process.[22] Crucially, contemporary audiences were already primed for just such a take on the war: the tragic qualities of the war were revisited by, among other things, conservative politician Alan Clark's now infamous history of the First World War era high command. This history – *The Donkeys* (1961) – castigated the first commander of the British Expeditionary Force, General Sir John French, for incompetence and lack of strategic imagination.[23] Widely read, and oft quoted, Clark revitalized dormant debates about the skill and ability of those who ran Britain's war effort.

Much like its stone predecessors, the polished features of this first 'screen memorial of Britain's involvement in the First World War' similarly veiled the politics, argument, and rancour through which it was ultimately produced.[24] For instance, Essex had on-going arguments with his script-writers and historical consultants, while two of the latter – John Terraine and Basil Liddell-Hart – had a public spat over the interpretation of various aspects of the war, particularly the Battle of the Somme. The result was the resignation of Liddell-Hart, who complained in an open letter to *The Times* that his advice and requests had been ignored (Liddell-Hart was particularly aggrieved by the inattention given to the inadequacies of Haig and the General Staff).[25] Nonetheless, the series – which explored everything from the war's origins, to the economics, to the war at sea, to the great battles of the Somme and Verdun – proved a powerful success. The skilful use of ideas and images drawn from the poetry, literature and art of the post-war period ensured it resonated with already established public ideas of the conflict. The decision to incorporate the testimony of veterans themselves returned the voice of the witness to the fore at just that moment when the conflict was both drifting into legend *and* had become increasingly overshadowed by its bloodier and more destructive sequel. And careful attention to the score made the tone and tenor serious, and sombre.

Perhaps most importantly of all, the series made full use of the previously unrealized potential of television to be a memory 'resource'. If, as Chapter 3 explains, collective memory is a 'set of images and impressions' then television provided the perfect means through which to recover, construct, and disseminate such impressions, particularly because the First World War had bequeathed an evocative cinematic legacy. Indeed, long before the dedication of Edwin Lutyens's Memorial to the Missing at Theipval in 1932, the carnage of July 1916 had already been memorialized with a piece of landmark cinema: *The Battle of the Somme* (1916).[26] Moreover, in the post-war period the Imperial War Museum devoted as much energy to the acquisition of visual artefacts of the war as they did to collecting tanks, artillery, and guns. Subsequent years would see the war experience revisited and replayed via the moving image: from Abel Gance's powerful *J'Accuse* (1919)[27] – which concludes with a disturbing scene of the 'return of the dead' – to Lewis Milestone's anti-war *All Quiet on the Western Front* (1930) (famously later banned by the Nazis), to Stanley Kubrick's *Paths of Glory* (1957). The very contemporaneity of the conflict and of cinema – the latter was just then overtaking vaudeville and the music hall as the pre-eminent forum for popular culture – has led David Williams to persuasively suggest that what Fussell defined as 'modern' memory might be better understood as *mediated* memory.[28] Williams points to the fact that significant elements of the literary response to the war betray the extent to which Edwardian perceptions of past and present had been profoundly altered by cinema. As Williams explains, even the poetry of Wilfred Owen is suggestive of this influence, with such 'classics' as 'Dulce et Decorum Est' possessing a 'filmic sense of the invasive power of the moving image'.[29] In this sense, long before 1964, the meaning of the war had already been constructed, shaped and communicated with the moving image (or by literature which was itself 'filmic' in tone and image), a fact that *The Great War* was able to exploit, and accentuate.

The other crucial reason for the success of *The Great War* was its synergy – its connection – to *contemporary* cultural and political context. For if, during the 1950s, Britons were happy to watch stories of the Second World War as a means to help negotiate imperial decline and rising Cold War tensions, a decade later visions of victory were no longer quite so reassuring. By the 1960s, many people had become increasingly concerned that the power of nuclear weapons had produced a world that offered only mutual annihilation. In 1955, the Warsaw Pact of Soviet controlled countries was created as a counter-balance to NATO; in 1958, growing European concerns about nuclear proliferation led to the foundation of the Campaign for Nuclear Disarmament; in 1961, the construction of the Berlin Wall stoked East-West tensions; in 1962, the Cold War came worryingly close to turning 'hot' due to the American discovery of Soviet missiles in Cuba; and in 1964 American perceptions regarding Communist expansion led to increasing American military presence in Vietnam. In this cultural climate, the 'tragedy' of the First World War had renewed currency, particularly since the living link with that tragedy was just then beginning to fray. To be sure, the 'last Tommy' – Harry Patch – would not die until 2009; but already by the 1960s some of those who had defined the war's purpose and politics were starting to pass on (Winston Churchill in 1965; Siegfried Sasson in 1967; Erich Maria Remarque in 1970; Edmund

Blunden in 1974).[30] In terms of international politics *and* human life-cycle, the 1960s was thus a good moment to revisit the catastrophe of the Great War, and television – just then becoming the dominant form of media communication in Britain – was the perfect vehicle through which to undertake this commemorative act.[31] The contemporary emergence of new ways of understanding the past, especially the idea of 'social history' (which placed a premium on the importance of the ordinary, everyday, and lived *experience*, and which was often drawn to the 'victims' of history) only added further to this synergy. Hence the series' intensive use of veterans' testimony. Hence, too, the other prominent audio-visual artefact of 1960s First World War memory: Richard Attenborough's *Oh! What a Lovely War* (1969), a film adaption of the earlier play. Here, the tragedy of the Great War is explored not via testimony, nor by irony, but by satire (another of those 'new' idioms identified by Fussell[32]). In one famous scene, Sassoon's idea of old, detached, distant armchair generals sending young boys to their deaths in the fields of Flanders is visually equated with a cricket match. Red-tabbed general staff officers sit watching the score (death toll) rise as their 'team' 'plays the game'. This obviously critiques Victorian conceptions of war as sport,[33] and it perhaps too owes something to the BBC production, *The War Game* (1965), which offered a bitter take on the threat of nuclear holocaust.[34] But the scene also hints at contemporary links between Great War and Cold War. Indeed, Attenborough's comedic assault on the historical madness of the Western Front might be profitably compared to Kubrick's similar attack on the contemporary madness of Cold War rivalry, *Dr Strangelove* (1964).

After an apparent hiatus during the 1970s (the era of significant domestic economic problems in Britain, and of international détente) a similar synergy between past and present returned during the 1980s, as did a similar British memory of the First World War. This was the decade shaped by President Ronald Reagan's 'new cold war', and by Margaret Thatcher's attack on miners and trade unions. For some in the Pit villages of South Wales and Yorkshire, the destruction of their way of life was a communal trauma surpassed only by the experience of the Great War, an event that had similarly seen their men bloodied, bruised and broken. As the British Left reeled from political (and physical) assault, as CND once again intensified their protests in and around British and American nuclear facilities, as the Reagan administration triggered a new arms race (and explored the means to militarize space), and as the Conservative government initiated a critical review of the resourcing (and 'Liberal' agenda) of the BBC, television writers and producers returned to the events of the First World War. In doing so, they reworked and reconstructed ideas first created in the 1920s, and revisited in the 1960s. The result was, among other things, two powerful and controversial screen memorials: *The Monocled Mutineer* (BBC 1986) and *Blackadder Goes Forth* (BBC 1989), both singled out in the Gove attack cited at the start of this chapter.

That producing and screening *The Moncoled Mutineer* would provoke a furore was almost guaranteed. The lead character – a working-class rogue shot and killed by Police during an attempted arrest in 1920 – was already controversial; the book upon which the film was based – John Fairley and William Allinson's *Toplis: The Monocled Mutineer* – had caused consternation and historiographical argument when first published in 1978. The general subject matter similarly promised an 'engaged' response from press, public and politicians: the ordinary 'Tommy's experience of the First World War; military abuse and command indifference; rape, murder and mutiny at a British Army training camp in Étaples, northern France. The four-part series was authored by John Bleasdale and broadcast – for the one and only time – in September 1986.[35]

The series charts the life of Percy Toplis a working-class orphan abandoned by his parents and raised by his Aunt and Uncle. We see Toplis as a cheeky child and a disobedient youth. He misbehaves, makes mistakes, challenges authority, gets arrested and exhausts the well-meaning intentions of his adopted family. Then comes the war. After initial reluctance, Toplis sees in the military a route to 'escape'. He enlists, and is sent to the Front. What follows is his gradual alienation and disillusionment by the fighting, and the system. His friends are killed; he is forced to take part in the execution of a deserter (a particularly harrowing sequence); and then he is debased and abused in a training facility run by a disciplinarian who administers the camp as though the trainees were Prisoners of War. In retaliation to this persistent degradation, Toplis rebels, and devotes his energy to finding loop-holes in the system. Indeed, rather than simply questioning authority, he impersonates it, and takes a perverse enjoyment from assuming the role and rank of his superiors. When after weeks of insult and injury his fellow trainees at the Étaples Camp mutiny, Toplis' character and charisma results in his quickly assuming command of the rebels. We should be wary, however, of assuming that this story is simply depicted as politically motivated class war; Toplis the revolutionary versus the aristocratic officer class. On more than one occasion, Toplis is vocal in dismissing ideological objectives (especially the ideals of 'socialism'), while one of the characters representative of aristocratic privilege – played by Penelope Wilton (more recently of *Downton Abbey* fame) – is portrayed as very much concerned with the conditions endured by the soldiers at the camp. In one scene, she uses her status and position to secure an audience with the camp commandant in order to deliver a formal protest regarding his regime.

While the story cannot be reduced to a simple 'Left versus Right' narrative, there nonetheless remains a clear politics at work. Two years after the Miners' Strike, and six years into the Thatcher premiership, *The Monocled Mutineer* revisits some of the already established tropes of British war memory – the Home Front/Battle Front distinction; the brutalization and victimization of the ordinary soldier; the detachment of the Officer

Class – and *intensifies* them. For in the hands of John Bleasdale, the real enemy of Toplis throughout is the state. It is the states which arrests and imprisons him as a child; it is the states which recruits him into Total War; it is the state which demands he execute a fellow solder (who of course has also been tried and convicted by that state); it is the states which authorizes and accepts the brutality administered at Étaples; it is the states which kidnaps and kills his more ideologically motivated friend; and it is the state – led by a dedicated MI5 agent – which ultimately pursues him to his death. Here is the perfect example of a historically specific televisual 'screen memory'; a story from the past was reworked and retold, and the result was an image of the First World War powerfully inflected by the politics of the present. Tellingly, this provocative series secured very good ratings (8.8 million viewers), but it also secured critical condemnation.[36]

Three years later, the concerns of the moment were similarly apparent in another controversial BBC production: *Blackadder Goes Forth* (1989). This series, the fourth outing for Rowan Atkinson's cynical and scheming Blackadder character, was a risky proposition. If *The Monocled Mutineer* outraged elements of the press and public because it morphed the heroic and valorous Tommy into a violent mutineer (even seen involved in the gang rape of British nurses), then *Blackadder Goes Forth*, like *Oh! What a Lovely War* (1969) before it, turned their suffering into comedy. Fortunately, by this point in the character's career the series' writers and actors had already secured the affections of the British public. Even so, Ben Elton and Richard Curtis still took care to generate their comedy from playful reworking of the ideas, images and tropes established over the previous eighty years. Herein lay the skill: the ordinary soldiers were honoured by placing Blackadder and Co. among them, and the key characters were used to explore the 'levelling' effect of the trenches. Lieutenant George, played by Hugh Laurie (reprising something of his Prince George character from *Blackadder III*) is the aristocratic, enthusiastic, university-educated but cerebrally challenged subaltern. Baldrick, meanwhile, is the ordinary and oppressed representative of the down-trodden working class: used, abused, beaten, exploited, but resilient throughout. In the middle sits Blackadder – a professional soldier of the late imperial age with all the skills that such a veteran might possess: the ability to avoid duties, outflank responsibilities, moan, complain and survive. In opposition to them all are not the Germans (who feature in just one episode, and then merely as a means to air all the various *Fawlty Towers* and *Dad's Army* clichés), but – once again – the General Staff in the form of Stephen Fry's incompetent and insane General Melchett and Tim McInnery's 'pen-pushing' Captain Darling.

Via these characters the six episodes that constitute the series put a comic twist on well-worn themes: the nature and purpose of British propaganda, memorably equated with toilet paper (soft, strong and thoroughly absorbent); military discipline and punishment (with Blackadder condemned to death by Melchett for shooting his favourite carrier pigeon, and only saved from execution by firing squad at the last moment); the absurdities of Edwardian vaudeville and contemporary popular culture; the daring-do of the Flying Corps (led by a sexually crazed Lord Flashheart, played with relish and mischief by Rik Mayall); Espionage and hospital care; and, most famously, the 'big push' of 1917, ordered by Field Marshal Haig (Geoffrey Palmer), who is seen planning the attack with toy soldiers, dustpan and brush (for clearing away the casualties).

Elton has explained that in writing the series he and Curtis did not set out to deliver a 'truthful' historical account of the Western Front experience.[37] Instead, they drew upon half-remembered school history, of ideas and images picked up in literature, poetry, film and television. In doing so, and because of the comedic format, the series marks an important intervention in British memory of the conflict. Old ideas were revitalized, drawing out a comedic potential offered by scenario and setting which had often been overlooked (or avoided) due to the conflict's essential tragedy. But the humour was acceptable because on the one hand the event was increasingly distant and fading from living memory, and on the other hand it remained frighteningly contemporary.

This latter fact became particularly apparent in the final episode, which dealt with the most difficult subject: an assault 'over the top' which will take the characters to their doom. The episode begins like the others: a situation develops – the order to attack – which Blackadder must strive to avoid. We know that he has done it before (episode one sees Blackadder, George and Baldrick 'miss' a scheduled advance because they have infiltrated HQ, pretending to be a group of wandering Italian Chefs). This time, Blackadder's plan is to avoid partaking in the attack by exploiting a pre-existing connection to Field Marshal Haig, who we learn was saved by Blackadder during a pre-war imperial battle against essentially defenceless 'pygmies'. Blackadder makes the call to Haig, requesting a different assignment; Haig responds by telling Blackadder that if he wants to avoid going over the top he should pretend to be mad. This, he is told, will lead to being invalided back home to Blighty. Unfortunately, Blackadder has already attempted this ruse, and Melchett is wise to his machinations. And so, with no other options remaining, Blackadder must go. It is in and around this moment at which the tone and tenor of the episode shifts: humour remains, and jokes are still told, but the underlying quality becomes pathos as the audience is invited to witness the inescapable sacrifice asked of those in the trenches. As this sacrifice approaches, the audience also learns of the road taken towards this doom.

The key scene is set in the dugout in the hours before the attack is to be launched (as Blackadder sits, pretending to be mad). Baldrick, confused as to the point and purpose of the war, and of the forthcoming assault, asks George and Blackadder about the origins of the conflict. George responds that it is the product of the 'vile Hun and his villainous empire building ways'. Blackadder crushes this line of argument, pointing out that Britain,

FIGURE 13.1 *Field Marshal Haig (Geoffrey Palmer) clears up the casualties following an 'attack'*, Blackadder Goes Forth *(Episode 6, BBC, 1989)*

too, bears responsibility, as it possesses the largest Empire in the world. Blackadder then elucidates further the war's causes, causes which he traces to the development of two rival military blocks, each of which was intended to function as the others 'deterrent'. Baldrick interjects and asks why this system did not stop the war starting. Blackadder's response is cutting: 'because', he explains, the system had one 'tiny flaw' – it was 'bollocks'.

Such an interpretation of the origins of the First World War does have historiographical merit; the role played by the 'Alliance System' in encouraging the escalation of the conflict in the summer of 1914 is well-established. But, in so many respects, the interpretation offered by Blackadder is as much about 1989 as it is about 1914; put differently, it is also about the *contemporary* system of Cold War deterrence just then starting to fracture and fragment, but which had defined international politics since 1945. It is this fact which enabled Elton and Curtis to make the First World War funny, and it is this fact which enabled an audience in 1989 to laugh. To laugh at the sacrificial slaughter of forebears is surely insensitive; but to laugh at a slaughter which might also be *yours* is to laugh at oneself, and in doing so confront catastrophe with comedy. *Blackadder*

Goes Forth, in short, is most certainly about the tragedy of 1914–18; but it is also a comedic caution to the tragedy that, fortunately, did not in the end come to be – the tragedy of a nuclear holocaust. *Blackadder Goes Forth* is a story of the First World War, but like *The Great War* (BBC 1964), and *Oh! What a Lovely War*, it is told from deep within the Cold War.

The centennial on screen: Re-enactment and reflection

The Great War, *The Monocled Mutineer*, and *Blackadder Goes Forth* all clearly betray the mark of their moment, and in doing so offer a profitable way of exploring changing, and historically specific, televisual representations of the First World War. But what does this imply for more recent televisual representations of the First World War? What do the audio-visual artefacts of the turn of the twenty-first century tell us about contemporary memory of the conflict, and of the ways in which the war is currently being commemorated on screen during the Centennial? Here, a brief survey of some of the notable productions of the last decade suggests two key themes: Re-enactment and Re-imagining; and Reflection and Remembrance.[38]

Re-enact and re-imagine

As noted, a key result of *The Great War* was to revitalize dormant ideas and images of the conflict, and the central technique employed to achieve this involved image, sound, and veterans' testimony. The result was a powerful audio-visual text which, in the words of Williams, enabled the past to invade the present while at the same time sign-posting its historical credentials.[39] A similar objective persists in more recent First World War connected television, but, significantly, the means through which to achieve this 'invasion' has altered; this is the age of dramatic re-enactment (see also Chapter 14). Four series are particularly suggestive of this format. The first is *The Trench* (BBC 2002), already well examined by Emma Hanna.[40]

As Hanna has explained, *The Trench* saw twenty-five men from Hull 'recruited' into Kitchener's New Army and sent to the (recreated) Somme. There, minus actual scenes of death and dismemberment, they wear the uniforms, eat the food, carry the rifles, and generally encounter the sights and sounds of the trenches. Predictably, while praised in some quarters, the series came in for scathing criticism, with more than one commentator decrying the way in which it must inevitably sanitize and simplify the trauma of the trenches.[41] In all fairness, as a concept, it does call to mind the wonderful putdown offered by Blackadder to Lieutenant George during the final episode, when the latter suggests something similar: that when the fighting is done they should gather on his family Estate and 'relive' the old times. 'Do you mean', replies Blackadder, '[that we should] dig a hole in your garden, fill it with water, and get your gamekeeper to shoot at us all day?'. A similar, and even more provocative challenge to this idea, has been offered by writer Jasper Ford in his novel *The Fourth Bear* (2006). Published just four years after *The Trench*, Ford imagines a future in which the horrors of the First World War are – literally – revisited: his invented world features a theme park (near Reading) named 'Somme World'. Here, tourists can visit, explore and, just as Blackadder cynically envisages, get shot at.[42] Despite the implicit absurdity of seeking to 'relive' the trench experience, Hanna has nonetheless persuasively argued that the series should not be dismissed as an exploitative assault on the memory of the war; rather, it should be read and understood as a powerful televisual memorial. As Hanna explains, '*The Trench* demonstrated that the animated elements of the television medium can recall the past for the majority of viewers in a more effective and accessible way than more traditional or static forms of history such as war memorials or published books'.[43]

This fact has been powerfully reaffirmed in three more recent productions. In *37 Days* (BBC 2014) an idea previously explored in connection with the Second World War is used to good effect (see *10 Days to D-Day* [Channel 4 2004], and *The Gathering Storm* [BBC/HBO 2002]): the three part mini-series recreates and reimagines the thirty-seven days preceding the outbreak of war in August 1914. From multiple perspectives, and through dramatic reconstruction, the viewer witnesses the inexorable road to war; we see the efforts of politicians and diplomats to avert the crisis; and we see their flaws, failings, and mistakes. Most importantly of all, we see the 'bollocks' of the Alliance System turn regional dispute into continental conflagration.

Connected in general approach, but also in marked contrast in terms of style, is BBC 3's three-part series, *Our World War* (BBC 2014). Inspired by the critical and popular response to *Our War* (BBC 2011), which offered three stories of contemporary conflict via the helmet-cams of soldiers serving in Afghanistan, *Our World War* is very much suggestive of how the present can 'invade' the past. Each episode stands alone, but all are implicitly tied in form and style. The first focuses on the 1914 Battle of Mons, a catastrophic defeat for the British Army that decimated the ranks of the old, regular, pre-war force. The second explores the difficult subject matter of cowardice, desertion and execution (a recurring theme in televisual treatments of the war, as we shall see below). The third – remarkably similar in tone and narrative to another audio-visual product of the very same year, Brad Pitt's *Fury* (2014) – is centred on the claustrophobic and cloistered experiences of a First World War tank crew. Each story is engaging and, at times, provocative. But of most interest here is the way in which the stories are told: slang, swearing, a contemporary sound track and various dynamic camera shots, some of which are deliberately suggestive of the 'helmet-cam' style of *Our War*. Significantly, some episodes were also made available online, with the added attraction of enabling audience interaction: viewers could *choose* which characters to follow, and the plots could deviate from that aired on television. Such an approach might be critiqued as ahistorical. But understood as a televisual memorial, *Our World War* is in essence the same – in point and purpose – to *The Great War*. Whereas the latter enabled viewers to remember in a manner conducive to the moment (e.g. through the use of image and testimony), *Our World War* responds to the contemporary interest in speed, sound, pace, and interactivity, all communicative qualities and dynamics similarly being explored at present by many museum curators (see Chapter 2).

Between these two poles – *37 Days* as the past replayed, and *Our World War* as the past remade – stands one other BBC drama, aired across five days in the week immediately preceding Remembrance Day 2014, and specifically targeted at a young adult audience: *The Passing Bells* (BBC 2014). The story centres around two key characters – one British, one German – whose lives connect and interact in various ways, but who do not actually meet face-to-face until the final scenes of the final episode, when they engage in mortal combat in no-man's land, just minutes before the Armistice is due to come into force. They die, each other's assailant, locked in an embrace in which the audience is encouraged to see their commonality; their essential *sameness*. This is affirmed in the final scene, which clearly owes its inspiration to Gance's *J'Accuse* (1919): the dead – British and German – rise from the grave and, arm in arm, walk into the sunlight. Much like the closing credits of *Blackadder Goes Forth*, the picture then fades and is replaced by a scene of a military cemetery in France.[44]

Filmed in Poland and involving significant Polish production input, the series is clearly marked by contemporary discussions about immigration (often connected to Poles) as well as the more general debates – now intensified post-Brexit – about Britain's place in Europe. Indeed, so intent are the production team to emphasize the essential similarity of the two leads that historical and cultural distinctions are flattened. Thus, similar to Remarque's *All Quiet on the Western Front* (1931) *all* the characters, regardless of nationality, speak in English (and occasionally regionally reflected English). As a result, we are not fully aware that one of the leads is German until he dons the uniform of the Kaiser's Empire. Some elements of the narrative and screenplay even seem designed to deliberately encourage this apparent sleight of hand: the first episode begins with scenes of the sort of pre-war, rural, Edwardian summer idyll long a common feature of British memory of the war. But, as we later realize, this idyll is actually in *Germany*. In the *Passing Bells*, then, the national memory of the war is complicated by joining the British experience with that of Germany, and commendable though this intervention might be, it does result in a problematic simplifying of the war's causes (there is no attempt to offer anything in the way of a political account of the conflict's *origins*). The memory of the war is thoroughly present-orientated (and, for some critics, 'patronising',[45] even if the drama – like that of *37 Days* – is, in aesthetic terms, historically accurate.)

Reflection and remembrance

The other two-pronged theme apparent from a survey of early twenty-first British television productions connected to the First World War concerns what I term 'reflection' and 'remembrance'. By this, I mean that some television programmes – both documentary and dramatic – have sought to reflect on the traumas and tragedies of the war, while others have offered some thought provoking interventions into the very politics of remembrance.

The attempt at the turn of the twenty-first century to offer sober reflection on the war perhaps begins with Pat Barker's *Regeneration* trilogy, the first part of which was adapted into a TV released film in 1997. Like the book upon which it was based, this film revisits the war through the prism of psychological trauma, and specifically via what psychiatrists after the 1980s were encouraged to define as 'Post-Traumatic Stress Disorder' (called 'Shell Shock' during the First World War).[46] The film tells the story of the meeting between Siegfried Sassoon (James Wilby) and Wilfred Owen (Stuart Bunce) in Craiglockhart military hospital, where the former has been sent by senior officers hopeful that his political protest against the war might be quietly redefined as mental illness. What follows are some difficult discussions between Sassoon and his doctor, William Rivers (Jonathan Pryce), a man caught in his own 'traumatic' catch-22: he listens to his patients recount the horrors of war (becoming disturbed himself) to 'cure' them so that they might be returned to that horror. Similar 1990s interest in the psychological trauma of the war was also apparent in Sebastian Faulks's novel *Birdsong* (1993), which begins with a late-twentieth-century character discovering the relics and letters of a First World War era relative. Faulks's book was also adapted for television by the BBC in 2012, and not unlike Barker's story, *Birdsong* (BBC 2012) is driven by poignant and often powerful explorations of grief, loss, and memory.

If explorations of time and trauma first emerged in the 1990s, several of the television series aired in and around the centennial of the war have developed these themes further. Indeed, if *The Great War* was the first televisual monument to the war; and if the productions of the 1980s were Cold War era 'screen memorials' to the tragedy of 1914–18; then the reflective impulse of the late 1990s – the moment when living connection to the conflict was increasingly severed – has resulted in several recent television productions purposefully examining not just the psychology of memory, but also its *politics*. We are now in an era in which television does not just make and mediate memory, but also interrogates it.

Initiating this trend was Ian Hislop's documentary series, *Not Forgotten* (Channel 4 2005), which explores the impact of the First World War on British society via engaging discussions of some of the memorials the conflict bequeathed. More revealing, however, are those recent *dramas* which have affected to do likewise. Two television series stand out, for each explored similar issues, but in different ways: Julian Fellowes' *Downton Abbey* (ITV 2010–15) and Peter Moffat's *The Village* (BBC 2013–14). In both series, the war loomed large. In the former – which revisits the themes of *Upstairs, Downstairs* (1971–5), exploring the lives and loves of an Edwardian Estate – the war is the culmination of the first series, and the conflict remains 'present' right through to the fifth and final series. In *The Village*, the conflict is similarly the backdrop to the events unfolding in a fictional, rural, northern community, all of which are told in 'flashback' by one of the central characters – Bert Middleton – whose 'route' into the past is frequently the moving image (significantly, in his youthful incarnation, Bert emerges as a keen photographer). But for all their differences of form and focus, one issue stood out in both series: the ways in which Edwardian communities negotiated – and remembered – the war's trauma through planned and purposeful acts of commemoration. Both series devoted significant time and space to recounting post-war efforts to build memorials.

In *Downton*, the story unfolds over several episodes (during Season 5, which aired in 2014), and sees the established authority of the benign and paternal squire (Lord Grantham, played by Hugh Bonneville) pitted against that of his Butler (Mr Carson, played by Jim Carter) the elected head of the memorial committee. The Lord desires that the village's memorial be erected at the community's centre, close to the church. Placed there, he believes, it will serve as a daily reminder and ensure that the dead continue to be a part of the village's life and future. The Butler disagrees. For him, something unique and useful must be set aside, and together with at least one grieving mother he plans to convert the village cricket pitch into a dedicated memorial garden.[47] This engaging take on 1920s era debates between advocates of 'monumental' and 'utilitarian' memorials is won by the Lord, but only following the intervention of a different representative of the contemporary gendered claim on the dead: a bereaved wife insists that her son 'needs' daily access to his fallen father; this can only come with a memorial in the village centre. Before the project is completed, one last problem intervenes: a member of the Lord's household staff (the cook) requests that her nephew – dishonoured by his execution for desertion – be included on the memorial. The young man in question has been excluded from the memorial established in his home community, and so his aunt hopes that familial pride might be restored by the inscription of his name in Downton. While sympathetic, the head of the memorial committee – the Butler – refuses. Honour is only saved, and the excluded remembered, by the actions of Lord Grantham, who commissions, funds, and builds a separate memorial to the nephew shot at dawn, confirming his supreme benevolence. Here is an engaging exploration of the post-war politics of memory; of the debates, discussions, deliberations and disagreements that emerged in the attempt to create the memorial landscape discussed at the start of this chapter.

Even more powerful is the way very similar issues were explored in *The Village*, a contemporary of *Downton Abbey*, but which recounts history not from the perspective of the Lord of the Manor, but from that of a farming family attempting to hack out an existence from the unforgiving moorland of northern England. Where *Downton Abbey* offers glamour and glitz, *The Village* offers hurt, hope and resilience. This is especially the case for the final episode of the first series, which sees the family at the centre of the series dealing with the pain of having lost a son during the war due to his execution for cowardice (that theme again: present in *The Monocled Mutineer* and *Blackadder Goes Forth*, *Our World War*, as well as others such as *Private Peaceful* (2012), and of course *Downton Abbey* itself).[48] Into their world comes more trouble, and more trauma, in the form of the old village school teacher, recently released from prison where he served out the war as a Conscientious Objector. The problems presented by his presence, and by the circumstances of the family's dead son, are then accentuated by on-going plans for the village's war memorial. The 'shirker' is rejected by a community grieving for those he taught, but did not follow into war. The family's executed son – Joe – is ignored, and the manner of his death unspoken. The surviving veterans and grieving wives and mothers dispute the form the memorial should take, its symbolism, symmetry and location.

FIGURE 13.2 *The memorial dedication ceremony,* Downton Abbey *(Season 5, Episode 8, 2014)*

But the real power of the episode lies in the skill with which the writers recover the process through which those 45,000 glazed, granite and marble markers were built in the 1920s. The real power is how, after almost a century, this televisual 'screen memorial' deploys all the potential of the medium to actively engage with the politics and process of memory. Of particular note are the subtle questions the episode asks about who, and what, such memorials are designed to 'remember'. In one scene, the local aristocrat asks her veteran son about the proposed memorial's symbolism: 'what is the meaning of the four helmets placed at the top?' 'Pathos', replies her former infantry subaltern son. Before he goes on to offer bitter and pointed comments about what other 'things' might have been incorporated into the memorial's symbolism: intestines, blue bottle flies, blood. In another scene, the father of Joe pleas for the inclusion of his dishonoured son on the planned memorial, something ultimately agreed to – as in *Downton Abbey* – by the local figures of authority (including, on this occasion, the Lady of the Manor). Then, on dedication day itself, a more subtle question is asked about the form and function of a memorial. In the days and weeks before the ceremony, Spanish flu sweeps through the village, and the three young girls of one mother – who also lost a son in the war – fall ill. The mother nurses them, but only two survive. In the hours before she must bear witness to the dedication of a war memorial inscribing the name of her only son, she quietly picks up her dead young daughter, wraps her in a blanket, and lays her outside in the yard. She returns to nurse the two daughters that remain, and is later seen at the memorial dedication.

Here, the audience is clearly asked to ponder the lot of the early-twentieth-century working class, for whom death was – in a way more

FIGURE 13.3 *The memorial dedication ceremony,* The Village *(Episode 6, BBC 2013)*

profound than the cliché suggests – a part of life. But we are also invited to ponder an important issue connected to the meaning of death. The fallen son gets a memorial in the town centre; the fallen daughter a blanket in the yard. One is to be remembered, as Kipling said, for 'evermore'; the other – a victim of an infection that killed more than war itself – lingers only in the shadows of history. All acts of commemoration simultaneously demand an act of forgetting; we cannot remember and represent *everything*.[49] We make decisions, selections, reductions. The result of the decisions made in the 1920s – a landscape of monumental memory – hides this fact. The stone and granite monuments marking villages and towns throughout the country communicate the concrete. But in skilled hands, our contemporary landscape of memory – which is televisual – allows us to recover the contested politics through which this concrete was made. Television – a communicative form so often criticized for being complicit in the creation of a culture of amnesia – in actual fact reveals itself as perhaps the preeminent media of memory (see also Chapter 3). On screen, the past can certainly invade the present, but the present can also rediscover, reconsider, and reconstruct the past. It was this act of engaged televisual reconstruction that the former Secretary of State for Education found so problematic. Through television, each age can revisit the First World War past, asking new questions, and interrogating old assumptions. Long may it continue.

Notes

1   See M. Gove, 'Why does the Left insist on belittling true British heroes?', *Daily Mail*, 2 January 2014. Also available online: http://www.dailymail. co.uk/news/article-2532923/Michael-Gove-blasts-Blackadder-myths-First-World-War-spread-television-sit-coms-left-wing-academics.html (accessed 30/4/16).

2   Ibid.

3   For the response of Sir Tony Robinson see: http://www.bbc.co.uk/news/ uk-politics-25612369 (accessed 30 April 2016).

4   For Ben Elton's response see: http://www.bbc.co.uk/news/entertainment-arts-29914919 (accessed 30 April 2016)

5   For Jeremy Paxman's criticism of Gove, see http://www.independent.co.uk/ news/people/news/a-charlatan-who-scores-cheap-political-points-jeremy-paxman-reopens-war-of-words-with-michael-gove-9190705.html (accessed 30 April 2016)

6   For David Mitchell's delightful critique, see http://www.theguardian.com/ commentisfree/2014/jan/12/michael-gove-blackadder-first-world-war-david-mitchell (accessed 30 April 2016)

7   Evans was the expert witness for the Professor Deborah Lipstadt defence team during the highly public Libel action brought against her (and Penguin

Books) by Holocaust denier David Irving in 2000. Shortly before this trial, Evans had also published on the professional and public responsibility of the historian. See R. Evans, *In Defence of History* (London: Granta, 1997).

8   For Richard Evans comprehensive and professional take down, see http://www.theguardian.com/books/2014/jan/06/richard-evans-michael-gove-history-education (accessed 30 April 2016).

9   For the origins of the IWM, see G. Kavanagh, 'Museum as Memorial: The Origins of the Imperial War Museum', *Journal of Contemporary History* 23 (1988): 77–97.

10   See R. Brooke, 'The Soldier' (1914)', *1914 and Other Poems* (London: Read Books Ltd, 2015).

11   For details about post-1918 government sponsored memorials, see P. Longworth, *The Unending Vigil: A History of the Commonwealth War Graves Commission, 1916–1967* (London: Constable, 1967); D. Crane, *Empires of the Dead* (London: William Collins, 2014); G. Stamp, *The Memorial to the Missing of the Somme* (London: Profile Books, 2016).

12   See A. King, *Memorials of the Great War in Britain: The Symbolism and Politics of Remembrance* (Oxford: Berg, 1998).

13   For some details of these various commemorative activities, see King, *Memorials of the Great War in Britain*.

14   See N. Hansen, *The Unknown Soldier: The Story of the Missing of the Great War* (London: Corgi, 2007).

15   See W. Owen, 'Dulce et Decorum Est' (1920).

16   See: J. Bartlett and K. M. Ellis, 'Remembering the Dead in Northrop: First World War Memorials in a Welsh Parish', *Journal of Contemporary History* 34 (2) (1999): 231–42; J. Davies, 'Reconstructing Enmities; War and War Memorials, The Boundary Markers of the West', *History of European Ideas* 19 (1–3) (1994): 47–52; K. Inglis, 'The Homecoming: The War Memorial Movement in Cambridge, England', *Journal of Contemporary History* 27 (4) (1992a): 583–606; K. Inglis, 'War Memorials: Ten Questions for Historians', *Guerres Mondiales et Conflits Contemporains* 42 (167) (1992b): 5–21.

17   See B. Bushaway, 'Name upon Name; the Great War and Remembrance', in *Myths of the English*, ed. R. Porter (Cambridge: Polity Press, 1992), 136–67; T. Laqueur, 'Memory and Naming in the Great War', in *Commemorations: The Politics of National Identity*, ed. J. R. Gillis (Princeton: Princeton University Press, 1993), 150–67.

18   P. Fussell, *The Great War and Modern Memory* (Oxford: Oxford University Press, 2000), esp. 231–69.

19   See, for instance, the prose and poetry of Siegfried Sassoon, as well as the work of Edmund Blunden and Edward Thomas.

20   For the 'traditional' qualities of post-1918 commemoration, see J. Winter, *Sites of Memory, Sites of Mourning: The Great War in European Cultural History* (Cambridge: Cambridge University Press, 1995).

21   See Samuel Hynes, *A War Imagined: The First World War and English Culture* (London: Pimlico, 1992).

22   See E. Hanna, *The Great War on the Small Screen: Representing the First World War in Contemporary Britain* (Edinburgh: Edinburgh University Press, 2009), 32–61, esp. 33–47.

23   See A. Clark, *The Donkeys* (London: Hutchinson, 1961). For some details of the controversy, see A. Danchev, '"Bunking" and Debunking: The Controversies of the 1960s', in *The First World War and British Military History*, ed. B. Bond (Oxford: Oxford University Press, 1991), 268.

24   Hanna, *The Great War on the Small Screen*, 33–6. See also M. Connelly, 'The Devil is Coming', *Historical Journal of Film, Television and Radio* 22 (1) (2002): 21–8.

25   B. Liddell-Hart, Letter of Resignation, *The Times*, 19 September 1964.

26   For details about the production and reception of this film, see N. Reeves, 'Official British War Propaganda', in *The First World War and Popular Cinema*, ed. M. Paris (Edinburgh: Edinburgh University Press, 1999), 27–50.

27   For some details about this film, see A. Kelly, *Cinema and the Great War* (London: Routledge, 1997), 101–6.

28   D. Williams, *Media, Memory and the First World War* (Montreal: McGill University Press, 2009), esp. 38–44.

29   Williams, *Media, Memory and the First World War*, 31.

30   For the idea of the 1960s–1970s as a 'transitional' moment in the memory of the First World War see D. Todman, *The Great War, Myth and Memory* (London: Hambledon and Hambledon, 2005), 225.

31   See D. Sandbrook, *Never Had it So Good: A History of Britain from Suez to the Beatles* (London: Abacus, 2010).

32   Fussell, *The Great War and Modern Memory*, 3–7.

33   Ibid., 25–9.

34   A similar, albeit less provocative, interrogation of this idea was also provided by the television animation of Michael Foreman's *War Game* (2001), which sees a team of Suffolk footballers enlist in 1914, witness the Christmas Truce, and then meet their death going over the top.

35   Hanna, *The Great War on the Small Screen*, 116–25.

36   Ibid., 116–17.

37   B. Elton, http://www.bbc.co.uk/news/entertainment-arts-29914919 (accessed 30 April 2016).

38   Although please note this is by no means exhaustive; the sheer quantity of centenary connected programme makes this prohibitive

39   Williams, *Media, Memory and the First World War*, 38–9.

40   Hanna, *The Great War on the Small Screen*, 143–62.

41   Ibid., 145–6.

42   J. Ford, *The Fourth Bear* (London: Hodder, 2007).

43   Hanna, *The Great War on the Small Screen*, 159.

44   Although strangely, the cemetery chosen is American, despite the fact that the dead we see resurrected are obviously British and German.

45   The reviews were mixed, with some critics finding it patronising, and others thinking it 'profound'. See *Independent*, 6 November 2014. Available online: http://www.independent.co.uk/arts-entertainment/tv/reviews/the-passing-bells-bbc1-tv-review-the-first-world-war-drama-for-children-9844991.html (accessed 30 April 2016); *Sunday Express*, 9 November 2014. Available online: http://www.express.co.uk/showbiz/tv-radio/533067/Passing-Bells-Downton-Abbey-All-Star-Choir (accessed 30 April 2016); *Daily Mirror*, 2 February 2014. Available online: http://www.mirror.co.uk/tv/tv-news/passing-bells-portrays-horror-great-4538234 (accessed 30 April 2016).

46   See P. Hagopian, *The Vietnam War in American Memory: Veterans, Memorials and the Politics of Healing* (Amherst, MA: University of Massachusetts Press, 2009).

47   This is a gesture which perhaps owes something to the earlier ITV production, *1914 All Out* (1987) which follows the destruction of a Yorkshire cricket team in the trenches, and which concludes with scenes of a post-war match – absent of the fallen. The picture then shifts to a close-up of the village war memorial, before the camera pans out to reveal an 1980s village scene.

48   Tellingly, a memorial to those Shot at Dawn was dedicated in 2001, while all those executed for 'cowardice' were pardoned by the government in 2006.

49   This is an idea also explored in the film version of Alan Bennett's *The History Boys* (2006), which in one scene sees the young, energetic and provocative history teacher, Tom Irwin (Stephen Campbell Moore) tell his students that war memorials were deliberately built after 1918 in order to 'forget'.

CHAPTER FOURTEEN

Presenting the past: New directions in television history

Nicola Bishop

Television history has long been an important part of the daily programming, and its influence, it appears, is ever increasing. Not only is there an impressive quantity of popular history programming on contemporary television screens, but the authority that televised histories offer exceeds other educational outlets. In *Television Histories*, Gary Edgerton says that his first assumption on the topic is that 'television is the principal means by which most people learn about history today'.[1] Indeed, as Tristram Hunt observed in 2006, public demand for 'living history' has promoted interactive, engaging, and entertaining history programming across the board, filling the schedules with high (and low) quality documentaries, docu-dramas, docu-soaps, and even reality television shows.[2] Despite the preponderance of the format over the last forty years, discussion about the role that television history plays, and particularly its relationship with 'academic' or 'professional' history, continues to dominate critical discussions (see Chapter 2). This chapter will offer an overview of how those arguments have come to capture the potential antagonism between television and history and survey the fundamental question: can 'good' history make 'good' television – and conversely, is 'good television' ever 'good history'? At the same time, it will discuss developments in television history – specifically in the UK – arguing that generic hybridity has created a new informal historicity that reaches a much wider audience than traditional documentary. It is in this new strand of nostalgic heritage programming that the impact of television has become even more prominent.

For as long as television has offered historical discourse, there has been cross-discussion between historians and television producers about the presentation of the past. The main points of argument have remained surprisingly consistent across the last half-century. The landmark documentary *The Great War* (BBC 1964) is a good case study, marking for many a turning point in observational programming (see also Chapter 13). Influenced by the shift in the 1960s towards social history (a move orchestrated from within universities as a response to the expansion of the Higher Education sector), the series foregrounded the 'ordinary Tommy', drawing upon interviews, unedited footage, diaries and other ephemera rather than the accounts of those in charge. Alongside these innovations in source material, the series also pioneered early audio-visual features; a stirring soundtrack, news footage and photographed stills. *The Great War* became an exploration of the televisual medium and how it might success-fully present history to a wider audience.[3] At the same time, the response to this programme demonstrates much of the status of television within the discipline of history. Acknowledged as a ground-breaking moment in television, it was also criticized in a number of ways (as all such documen-taries continue to be).

The first, and most prominent, of the criticisms frequently levelled at television history is the ability of a popular, visual format to offer what is termed 'historical accuracy'. *The Great War* was created with historians on team (although they often did not agree on pivotal events), in conjunction with the Imperial War Museum, and making use of archival material. In those terms, *The Great War* was 'good history', although many series are interrogated by professional historians for errors in fact and represen-tation. The BBC's *A History of Syria with Dan Snow* (2013), as a more recent example, was criticized for being 'biased' and 'inaccurate' while a BBC Trust complaint about inaccuracy was upheld.[4] In contemporary documentary, where increasingly a well-known historian or media person-ality is used as a figurehead, the reliability of information is passed from the programme producers/creators (or even the channel) to the presenter; thus, in order to uphold ideas of historical legitimacy, the presenter is held accountable. *Absolute Power* (BBC 2003), a British comedy series created by Mark Tavener and adapted for both radio and television, has an episode called 'History Man' – first aired in 2003 on BBC4 – which parodies this relationship between documentary, presenter, and 'truth'.

In the episode, Nigel Harting, an Oxbridge scholar, records a programme promising 'the most astonishing revelation to hit documentary television'; a revelation that is, in fact, based on forged letters. To overshadow potential scandal, PR company Prentiss-McCabe fake an affair involving Harting and a minor celebrity and sell the story to the tabloids: Stephen Fry's character, Charles Prentiss, says, 'as a media commodity, Nigel goes nuclear'.[5] This parody of the historical documentary pokes fun both at the relationship between documentary and 'truth' but also at the cult of celebrity that increasingly sees television historians turned into a 'brand'. N. C. Fleming talks about Niall Ferguson's *Empire: How Britain Made the Modern World* (Channel 4: also, note, aired early in 2003) and the way in which Ferguson was used as a 'vehicle for selling his series' due to his 'relative youth and notoriety'.[6] His series, too, was confrontational, with Linda

Colley arguing that Ferguson 'stack[ed] the deck' against the 'dark sides of his subject'; in effect, offering a revision of Empire as an 'essential engine of modernity'.[7] Assessed for accuracy, integrity, and evidence, as well as likeability, charisma and personality, television historians must tread a fine line between, as Bell and Gray argue, 'act[ing] as a conduit for historical truth', while also maintaining a popularity (or at least prominence) within modern media.[8]

Just as television history is examined for its 'factual accuracy', it is also assessed on the ability of a visual narrative to offer depth. By this, scholars expect a television series to offer multiple readings, interpretations and arguments, rather than giving a static narrative that informs the audience of the 'truth'. In part, this is to counter the impression of television as a 'passive illustrative' medium, but it also about encouraging what Bell and Gray refer to as 'mindful' television (rather than 'mindless' viewing).[9] In this sense, a series focusing on a topic such as the British Empire has to contrive to cover as much nuance and detail as a monograph; a feat that is made more difficult by the fact that scholarly, academic writing mostly feeds a specialized reading into a complex web of other articulated ideas and evidence. A television series, by nature of its having a generalist audience (who may have read extensively on the subject, visited museums and heritage sites, watched other documentaries on the subject, studied for A-levels, at degree level, or even postgraduate level, or who may know *nothing* about the topic), has to attempt to communicate coherently a meticulous argument while contextualizing debates surrounding the topic. While producers, directors, and presenter-historians often take the blame

FIGURE 14.1 *Historian Nigel Harting (Stephen Boxer) examines the sources.* Absolute Power, *'The History Man' (BBC 2003)*

for a series that offers a 'linear' representation of information rather than a multi-dimensional one, it is in the audience that the limitation rests, rather than the medium. Historians, on the other hand, offer their interpretations not just *to* a reader, but *in dialogue with* a network of specialist researchers.

The non-specialization of the audience also restricts the tone of television history. In order to engage an audience across a lengthy series, they must 'capture [their] imagination'.[10] What this has resulted in is an emotional tone that academic history would strive to avoid. As Chapter 13 also noted, the intention of the producer, Tony Essex, to depict the war as an 'epic tragedy' ultimately 'overpowered' the 'rigorously revisionist script'.[11] In this sense, just as *The Great War* succeeded in reaching the depth that professional history demands in terms of engaging with the historiography and offering a counter-narrative, this was lost because of the requirement of 'good television' that equally required a personal engagement with the audience which was most easily formulated (particularly given the subject matter) through emotion.

The Great War (or Ferguson's *Empire*) is also emblematic of the type of history most often presented through television. As television producer, Steve Humphries puts it: '[t]elevision history is at its best when telling epic stories'.[12] It is for this reason, as Hunt suggests, that 'military conflict hold[s] centre stage', alongside subjects such as Empire, royal dynasties, and other particularly 'impactful' narratives within British history.[13] These histories are easily chronicled, turned into 'smaller, accessible story-lines' that can be formed in episodic length, offering digestible nuggets of chronology, context, and themes.[14] Jeremy Paxman's *Empire* (BBC 2012), for example, was criticized for attempting to move away from a straightforwardly sequential discussion and towards a thematic discourse. This left the viewer disorientated, argued Michael White, with the fast pace of the travel ('India to Egypt to Palestine in an hour') confusing the account.[15]

In his review, White raises several key issues about the programme that are worth reiterating here: that television personalities do not necessarily know enough about historical topics to 'do the biz'; that formal documentaries should challenge their audience and offer more than a lukewarm and two-dimensional account; and that, offering multiple voices and revisions would create a historiographical debate.[16] In a similar vein, Hunt has drawn attention to the social histories of the *'long duree'* – the counter-discourses of those often ignored (children, society, the working classes) – that are rare in television history because they fail to placate the 'furious demands of narrative' that are so essential to the format.[17] Audiences require the 'twin dictates of narrative and biography' that provide the chronological framework and the personal connection recognizable from the history taught in school.[18] Recent programmes such as the celebrity-focused ancestry format, *Who Do You Think You Are?* (BBC 2004–) or the docu-drama and TV movie *Churchill's Secret* (2016), that tells the story of Churchill's concealed stroke of 1953, provide this sense of lineage and personal drama.

The necessity for 'a well-constructed plot' also begins to impact upon the way in which history is represented.[19] A good example is Dan Snow's *The Vikings Uncovered* (BBC 2016): along with a 'space archaeologist', Snow attempts to prove that the Vikings had settled in North America. The crux of the programme centres on awaiting the results of carbon dating of the (potentially) most 'westerly Viking settlement ever discovered'.[20] Fulfilling a well-known narrative, the first two tests prove inconclusive, but the final and third test shows the presence, not of the smithing slag that was expected, but of bog iron ore that has been 'processed for something'.[21] What is most interesting about this example, however, is the consequent 'summing up' – the grand point of narrative: the conclusion. The tests find traces of bog iron ore, but Snow's ending summary offers the following: 'This fragment of bog ore is the proof we've been waiting for. Hundreds of years before Columbus, Viking pioneers like Leif Erikson came to Point Rosee. They smelted metal to mend their ships in workshops just like those we've seen on our journey across the Atlantic'.[22] This demonstrates the typical narrative function of the 'happy ending' – the claims that Snow makes move much further than the evidence found can take him, but it is a critical part of the televisual format, just as the tension created while the test results are awaited replicates the gameshow. While offering an easy criticism of television, the latent narrative arc apparent in this example can also be used to understand the stance of traditional historiography.

While history 'in text' and 'on screen' are often set against one another, it would be counter-intuitive to see academic history as a form that ignores this central 'humanizing' or 'fictionalizing' premise. Scholarly, written history must similarly construct a narrative that mirrors its fictional counterpart (see also Chapter 2). Without getting too drawn into the centuries-long debate about the relationship between literature and history, the devices that enable the construction of an engaging and meaningful argument (or plot) are equally applicable. The construction of a thesis statement, or line of intent, serves the same function as the opening line of a television show, just as the introduction for both must (either visually or through prose) set the scene, offer an argument or revision, and set out the parameters and players of the content. Where historians often criticize television history for offering too firm a vision (see, for example, the response to *The World at War* that 'the commentary left us in no doubt as to what we should think'),[23] the conclusion to formal academic writing gives an equally mediated overview. As Hayden White argues, in his influential 1988 essay, 'Historiography and Historiophoty', both types of history – in scholarly writing and in visual or filmic discourse – can offer only a relative 'truth' when compared to 'reality' itself (see also Chapter 1).[24] Ultimately, as Gary Edgerton puts it, both history and its televisual counterpart are, 'more about telling stories inspired by contemporary perspectives than recapturing and conveying any kind of objective truth about the past'.[25] The discussions that surround integrity, accuracy, and 'factual' basis within television history, only serve to illuminate the fragility of the narrative that formal history can offer.

Finally, *The Great War* is a pertinent case study because, as Chapter 13 explained, it was a commemorative memorial of the fiftieth anniversary of the First World War. *The Great War* thus presents an artefact that is complicated at its inception because it also relies on memory – both individual and collective – and that, in and of itself, carries a complex historical meaning. If history can only offer storytelling rather than 'objective truth', then memory further muddies the metaphorical waters. Even first-hand oral accounts and interviews, as professional historians are well aware, are in danger of self-narration – from the way in which, for example, we construct our own personal history or memory to fulfil the expectations of storyline, even before issues of time lapse, forgetfulness, and the distortion of collective impressions are taken into consideration (see Chapter 3). The response to series such as these (that focus on memorable history), is grounded in individual expectation, derived from personal and collective memory. As a result, criticisms from viewers mostly focus on the omission of events that were prominent in their own view, but which were considered minor in the grand scheme of the events.[26]

More broadly, Hunt has talked about recent trends in popular history that derive from the 'millennial spirit of introspective self-doubt over questions of national identity' (see also Chapters 4 and 12);[27] our secular dissection of the past looks to redraw the lines of connection with a stable sense of historical self. In this sense, we turn to the past, and a particular representation of our collective identity (think, particularly, of concepts such as the 'blitz spirit'), to provide a stronger sense of the contemporary self. In the same way, popular history, as Jerome de Groot explores, is a method which allows an individual and intimate connection with understanding the past, and a collective and societal endeavour that allows us as a community to fill in the gaps of known experience. The 'commodification' of history (as seen in the burgeoning television market but also in live 'heritage' – museums, stately homes, online genealogy websites and so on), then becomes an act of collective interpretation, in which the national identity is redefined and reinterpreted, as well as an individualist impulse to understand 'our' past.[28]

It is, perhaps, this freedom to revise and reinterpret the past that precipitates the antagonism between television (or popular) history and the academic discipline. Much of professional history's issue with popular forms rests on the nineteenth-century creation of the discipline as an empirical subject and a subsequent defensiveness against the loss of authority. The legitimacy of the historian, as de Groot argues, is being 'eroded due to shifts in technology, theory, and access', and the discipline's response to the democratization of the subject shows resistance to claims of inferiority.[29] The popularization of historical knowledge, and the ability for audiences to engage first-hand in 'discovering' the past, reduces the divide between knowledge and expertise. Television history, and its relationship with popular or public history, has become emblematic of this technologically driven dissemination of information, intensifying the disapproval of traditional historians who argue that television can only offer an 'impoverished "information load"' that struggles to present the 'complex, qualified, and critical dimensions of historical thinking about events'.[30] At the same time, television argues that it can offer something more tangible than written history, by turning to sources that animate our understanding of events in a new way. Indeed, several history programmes demonstrate the pioneering nature of popular history: as James Chapman argues, television was an advocate of oral history 'long before it became fashionable among historians'.[31] The most frequently cited example of this is the landmark 1970s documentary, *The World at War* (BBC 1973–4) (see also Chapter 11). Ultimately, the debate becomes about more than who is recording the 'best' history: it is about ownership of the relationship that individuals can have with the past. However, as Keith Jenkins asks: 'Why is the professional historian ... seemingly alone in being able to determine the proper answer to the question "what is history?"'[32]

New directions in television history

Developments within television history have reasserted this democratization of the past. If the 'commodification' of history is seen as a negative and commercialized move, it is also, more positively, symptomatic of a deeper interest in understanding, preserving and protecting our heritage. To coincide with the general boom in interest in history more generally, television has diversified, offering the sort of bite-size 'docu-lite' history segments within magazine format programmes that appeal to an interested but non-specializing audience. Simultaneously, the documentary form itself has evolved, influenced by the traits and characteristics of other sub-genres such as the docu-drama, docu-soap, and reality television. This cross-fertilization of ideas and visual aesthetics, combined with a postmodern playfulness, has made television history much more self-aware. While some critics have viewed this as a retrograde step (see, for instance, 'Perspective A' in Dafydd Sills-Jones's TV producer account of changes in history documentaries),[33] it also marks the method by which television history, in its various guises, has continued to find relevance for audiences, despite the many changes to television itself. Current 'factual' history programming can now be understood as fitting into three broad categories: traditional history documentary, the docu-lite, and reality history.[34]

The first, and most conventional, type of history documentary continues to strive after the heady heights of academic recognition. BBC 4 has become the hub of the formal history documentary, presented ostensibly by esteemed scholars who offer carefully researched arguments. This format has been influenced to some extent, as has all of television, by genre hybridization, as well as other media conventions such as the cult of celebrity. The status of the scholar-presenter has evolved to include not only practicing academics (professorial figures who are specialists in their field), but also media figures who have become synonymous with the scholar-presenter style. Dan Snow (whose Twitter username is @thehistoryguy), for example, finished his formal education after obtaining a first-class undergraduate honours degree in History from Oxford, but his established reputation as a history television presenter sees him frequently labelled as a historian. In this sense, history television has simply conformed to the cult of the presenter typical of non-fictional television: from Kirstie and Phil (house buying), Kevin McCloud (house building), and Dominic Littlewood (bad building).[35]

A BBC 4 history documentary will increasingly rely on the new foci derived from more popular entertainment formats, but the presenter (while fulfilling certain aspects of entertainer) also offers an academic argument grounded in conventional, and often empirical, research and with a strong thesis. In BBC 4's *Empire of the Tsars: Romanov Russia with Lucy Worsley* (BBC 2016), for instance, Lucy Worsley dresses up, circles monuments and sites under discussion and engages in 'informal' conversations with relevant talking heads. Her narrative is immersed in the landscape of the subject – in this case, the palaces of the Russian aristocracy – featuring outdoor shots of monuments and architecture as well as close-ups of minutia and artefacts. There is even a scene filmed in an archive (a key setting in nearly all contemporary history programmes) where Worsley whispers as she touches documents about the Tsars' pasts. This is an active history (or 'living history' as Aaltonen and Kortti term it);[36] as we learn about locations, the historian must be in them, must move about them, and engage with their features. At the same time, the focus often remains on the presenter over the landscape; Worsley dresses the part (in this instance in brown furs and with striking red lipstick), and the camera consequently zooms in on this aesthetic, leaving the location as a blurry background. Indeed, Bell and Gray argue that this is a particularly gendered trait; where male presenters are authoritative and paternalist, female historians are 'marketed in terms of youth, glamour, travel and tourism'.[37]

It is of note, also, that Worsley's name is becoming a more recurrent feature in the titles of her programmes; this marks both the presenter's individual style (acting as a recommendation to potential audiences) and serves as a reminder of 'brand identity' (see, for instance, *Lucy Worsley's Reins of Power* [BBC 2015] and *When Lucy Met Roy* [BBC 2015]). The informality of the titles reflects the diverse domestic and social history which she more usually engages with (see *Cake Bakers and Trouble Makers, Lucy Worsley's 100 Years of the WI* [BBC 2015], *A Very British Romance* [BBC 2015], *Dancing Cheek to Cheek: An Intimate History of Dance*

[BBC 2014]). Compared to, for example, other historians' programme titles (Simon Schama's *A History of Britain* [BBC 2000–2] and David Starkey's *Magna Carta* [BBC 2015]), which, as de Groot suggests both signal ownership as well as marking the historian as a 'cultural gatekeeper', the perceived familiarity of Worsley's titles suggest a less instructive tone.[38] Likewise, Russian historians are interviewed to add weight in the *Empire of the Tsars* but in a new style; rather than the formal 'talking head', a casual, conversational 'encounter' is re-enacted in a corridor.

The second category of television as history can be termed the 'docu-lite'; a magazine-style blend of a variety of interconnected and complementary subthemes such as heritage, nostalgia, geography, ecology, biography and anthropology, in a light-entertainment format. These programmes have eschewed the formality of television history, but do still attempt to offer a specialist (if employed in a generalist way) strand of knowledge. They are often supported by leading academics who give 'gobbets' of information, and they are overwhelming structured, not by chronology, but by an interdisciplinary topography. The docu-lite is, perhaps, the most important development in television history in recent years; following the format of general geographical interest programmes such as *Coast* (BBC 2005–) and *Countryfile* (BBC 1988–), they are an example of the type of programmes that, as Helen Wheatley points out, have very quickly come to fill television schedules in the High Definition age.[39] More importantly, they are not network or channel-centric; in the UK, Channel 4 seems to have taken the lead in producing many types of docu-lite but the way was marked by the BBC (who still produce a lot of their own magazine-format shows), and ITV and Channel 5 are increasingly exploring this style. Indeed, the creation of Freeview channel Yesterday serves as an outlet for many of these docu-lite programmes, charting the rise of the format from the early noughties to the present day. It regularly shows, for example, Michael Portillo's long-running *Great British Railway Journeys* (BBC 2010–), a very typical docu-lite that follows an 1863 Bradford railway guide, stopping at points of interest and historical importance along the line.

The docu-lite is more likely to use an informed but non-specialist narrator; Michael Portillo is a good example, Tony Robinson is another. Robinson's role as presenter on *Time Team* (Channel 4 1994–2014) gave him gravitas in the type of 'active' history that the archaeology programme necessitated (and means that he now has a host of honorary academic awards). This emphasis on the active presenter is fundamental to the docu-lite as a reminder of the format's development from the natural sciences and geography. Programmes such as Tony Robinson's *Walking Through History* (Channel 4 2013–) and *Britain's Lost Routes with Griff Rhys Jones's* (BBC 2012) are centred around the active narrator; the structure of the episodes rests on their journey and the points of interest encountered along the way. This way, an episode based in, say, the Lake District, can cover literary history (William Wordsworth, Wainwright's guides), architectural history, regional history (of, say, the Mountain Rescue or Kendal Mint cake), and various local traditions and festivities. Others, such as *B-Road Britain* with Robbie Coltrane (ITV 2007), Clare Balding's *Britain by Bike* (BBC 2010), and Richard Wilson's *Britain's Best Drives* (BBC 2009) are formed along the same lines. The personality-presenter (in most of these cases, an actor), follows a familiar narrative in these instances; each is following a nostalgic route into a 'lost' Britishness – indeed, Balding and Wilson, like Portillo, both make use of 1940s/1950s guide books to structure their series. In all of these cases, History has become 'Heritage' or 'Nostalgia'; reigniting a particular sense of a glorified national past. In 2006, Hunt called a typical by-line for these programmes: 'a journey back in time to discover what it was really like' – similar indeed to Robbie Coltrane's: 'I will be travelling … off the beaten track. The way that we would have done fifty years ago. And I'll be trying to find the real heart and soul along the way.'[40]

While at times, it appears that the 'hard grind of archival research [has been exchanged] for the stock recycling of easy images, lazy ideas, and familiar talking-heads', there is also a dynamism in these new popular histories.[41] While Hunt criticized the focus on event history, the new docu-lites do offer a bottom-up story, drawing heavily on the story-telling style of oral and early forms of history. Due to the geographical organizing principle, the programmes also give a more localized or regional analysis, and, as a result, interviews are usually conducted with local historians, community figures or interested individuals. *Penelope Keith's Hidden Villages* (Channel 4 2014), while offering both an overview of changes to Britain's villages in terms of architecture, size, community, and customs, and a nostalgic 'trip

FIGURE 14.2 *Tony Robinson admires the view,* Walking Through History *(Channel 4 2013)*

down memory lane', presents a type of history that formal documentary would eschew. Many of these programmes also contribute to the sense of collective history that is often intrinsically connected to nostalgia. *Great Canal Journeys* (Channel 4 2014–), for example, while self-aware in many respects about the function of memory (chronicling, as it does, Prunella Scales' dementia), exists both as a nostalgic exercise for the presenters, and a 'golden age' history of the various canal routes – and associated stopping points – along which they pass. Stills of a young Timothy West, Prunella, and their family on canal boat holidays subtly analyse the passing of time, the relativity of history, and the collective emotionality of honeyed personal memories.

'Docu-lite' has little by way of argument or thesis, offering instead more general (if local) knowledge and information. In the amalgamation of topics covered by the magazine style, the programmes can speak to many multiple demographics without focusing too closely on any one. The short attention spans of twenty-first-century audiences further the suggestion that the docu-lite format is the history documentary of the future. Indeed, when considering that *The Great War* unfolded over twenty-six episodes, it is difficult to image a contemporary television history engaging an audience for such a prolonged period (Simon Schama's *A History of Britain* [BBC 2000–2] is perhaps an exception. But even here the production's fifteen episodes were split across three series). Instead, history documentary even in its more formal incarnation has altered to meet the needs of its audience, moving rapidly through landscapes, periods, movements, and presenters, in order to keep pace with contemporary attention spans.

The third strand of television history, which looked set to diversify and proliferate following the beginnings of reality television (particularly *1900s House* [Channel 4, 1999]), is what Aaltonen and Kortti have called the 'reality-experiential history documentaries', in which participants become immersed in a 're-enactment' of history.[42] Part social experiment, but with an underlying intention also to experience history 'as it was lived', the format is designed to pique audience interest in ordinary people who can relate to the families involved. As Annette Hill suggests, the programmes are also intended as a historical contextualization, allowing 'audiences to criti-cally reflect on "the way things have changed" in society'.[43] Programmes such as Channel 4's *Back in Time for Dinner* (2015) which looks at the more recent past (from the 1940s onwards), is deeply rooted, like the docu-lite, in nostalgia, but it also encourages this 'reflection' on progress. The family sample domestic life (leisure, household appliances and food fashions) from each decade of the second half of the twentieth century. Once more, this type of social and domestic history marks a change of direction – indeed, reality-experiential history works best when it engages with the 'ordinary'. Even where forays have been made into war history, the emphasis has stayed with the experience of the ground troops (see *The Trench* [BBC 2002] and *Lads Army* [BBC 2002]).

The success of these ventures appears to rest on the subject matter. As Hanna discusses, *The Trench* was incredibly controversial, 'provok[ing] a heated debate among academics, broadcasters and journalists', and 'beset by negative publicity' (see also Chapter 13).[44] The BBC's *The Slum* (announced in January 2016), seems set to offer historical 'poverty porn', 'chart[ing] the story of what life was really like for poor Victorians [through] immersive experience', and it looks set to court similar controversy.[45] Indeed, it looks possible that BBC2 are not averse to tackling notions of polemic: the abstract draws parallels with contemporary notions of poverty, inviting the audience to 'raise provocative questions about what kind of safety net the poorest should have'.[46] *Back in Time for Dinner*, on the other hand, given its less divisive subject matter (it is, after all a 'time-travelling culinary show')[47] has still mustered up an audience three million strong because it is nostalgic-infotainment (again, offering a reality spin on the docu-lite format).

Contemporary history on television is driven by the pragmatism of the presenter, the movement around historical sites and the reliance on props (or relevant objects, settings and even costume) to offer a narrative or storytelling format. It is also driven by interest in a burgeoning popular heritage and nostalgia market that promotes personal engagement and interest in social and cultural histories of the 'everyday'. Combined, the new television histories are dependent on a scholar-driven, but media-led process, in which the television historian (increasingly defined as a 'media' historian) is both crucial to the success of the format, while fundamentally being defined by the expectations of the media and its audience. Figures such as David Starkey and Simon Schama are criticized by Fleming as becoming part of the new celebrity culture, but they are also, if not participating in a 'revival of the public intellectual', acting as a mediator between academia and popular or public history.[48] Television history has been criticized for struggling to add depth, or trivialized because historians court the publicity of the media, but the importance of strong history television in acting as a 'populariser of academic ideas' should encourage further cooperation.[49] Now that academic worth is judged through the measurable public 'impact' of research, it is clear that television history has quantifiable strength in this area – having the ability to reach wide audiences and disseminate information. In doing so, television fulfils the remit that academic history claims it also prioritizes: being a conduit for education.

How, then, are we to dissect and deconstruct contemporary history on television? Edgerton suggests that rather than simply criticizing television history, the responsibility lies with professional historians to reinforce the groundworks of interpretation, analysis and accuracy in supporting new, creative methods of representing the past. Ultimately, as Edgerton argues:

"Television as historian" should never be feared as the "last word" on any given subject, but viewed as a means by which unprecedentedly large audiences can become increasingly aware of and captivated by the stories and figures of the past.[50]

Ensuring the popularity of history as a discipline may seem beneath the attention of professional scholars, but it is also fundamentally self-serving: if television offers 'bad history', then 'good history' must help to shape a more nuanced and appropriate form, learning to embrace the methods and technologies of the digital age in order to create a well-informed general audience. As scholars of history, we must continue to deconstruct television history, just as we would any other visual or textual 'source', but we must also engage in a constructive discourse that continues to reshape and innovate the practice of presenting the past.

Notes

1   G. R. Edgerton, 'Introduction: Television as Historian: A Different Kind of History Altogether', in *Television Histories: Shaping Collective Memory in the Media Age,* ed. Gary R. Edgerton and Peter C. Rollins (Lexington: University Press of Kentucky, 2001), 1.

2   T. Hunt, 'Reality, Identity and Empathy: The Changing Face of Social History Television', *Journal of Social History* 39 (3) (Spring 2006): 843.

3   Although James Chapman's article on the production and reception does demonstrate the narrative of success is more nuanced than it might appear. Chapman, 'Television and History: *The World at War*', *Historical Journal of Film, Radio and Television* 31 (2) (June 2011): 247–75.

4   'BBC Documentary, A History of Syria with Dan Snow was "biased and inaccurate" say critics', 17 March 2013. Available online: http://www.huffingtonpost.co.uk/2013/03/17/bbc-documentary-history-snow_n_2896575.html (accessed 28 April 2016); 'BBC Rapped Over Dan Snow Documentary', 7 November 2013. Available online: http://www.bbc.co.uk/news/entertainment-arts-24849738 (accessed 28 April 2016).

5   'History Man', *Absolute Power,* dir. John Morton (BBC 2003).

6   N. C. Fleming, 'Echoes of Britannia: Television History, Empire and the Critical Public Sphere', *Contemporary British History* 24 (1) (March 2010): 1–22.

7   L. Colley, 'Into the Belly of the Beast', *Guardian,* 18 January 2003. Available online: http://www.theguardian.com/books/2003/jan/18/featuresreviews.guardianreview5 (accessed 28 April 2016).

8   E. Bell and A. Gray, 'History on Television: Charisma, Narrative and Knowledge', in *Re-viewing Television History,* ed. H. Wheatley (London; I.B. Tauris, 2007), 149.

9   Bell and Gray, 'History on Television', 153.

10 E. Hanna, *The Great War on the Small Screen: Representing the First World*

War in Contemporary Britain (Edinburgh: Edinburgh University Press, 2009), 37.

11   Hanna, *The Great War on the Small Screen*, 33–5.

12   Hunt, 'Reality, Identity and Empathy', 847.

13   Ibid.

14   T. Downing, 'History on Television: The Making of 'Cold War', 1998', *Historical Journal of Film, Radio and Television* 18 (3) (1998): 326.

15   M. White, 'Jeremy Paxman's Empire: A Wasted Chance We Need to Take', *Guardian,* 28 February 2012. Available online: http://www.theguardian.com/tv-and-radio/tvandradioblog/2012/feb/28/jeremey-paxman-empire-wasted-chance (accessed 28 April 2016).

16   White, 'Jeremy Paxman's Empire'.

17   Hunt, 'Reality, Identity and Empathy', 849.

18   Edgerton, 'Introduction', 2.

19   Ibid.

20   'The Vikings Uncovered', http://www.bbc.co.uk/programmes/b076r0sr (accessed 28 April 2016).

21   *The Vikings Uncovered*, dir. Harvey Lilley (BBC 2016).

22   Ibid.

23   Chapman, 'Television and History', 256.

24   Hayden White, 'Historiography and Historiophoty', *The American Historical Review* 93 (5) (December 1988): 1193–9.

25   Edgerton, 'Introduction', 3.

26   See, for example, Chapman's discussion of viewer responses to *The World at War*.

27   Hunt, 'Reality, Identity and Empathy', 844.

28   Jerome de Groot, *Consuming History: Historians and Heritage in Contemporary Popular Culture* (New York: Routledge, 2009), 2.

29   De Groot, *Consuming History*, 2.

30   White, 'Historiography and Historiophoty', 1195, 1193.

31   Chapman, 'Television and History', 254.

32   K. Jenkins, *Re-thinking History* (London: Routledge, 2003), 38.

33   Perspective A includes comments such as: 'a lessoning of the intellectual content, a move towards celebrity narrative history [...] transatlantic funding infantilized the content of history documentary, less time and money spent on research'. Dafydd Sills-Jones, 'Before the History Boom: Revisiting UK Television History Documentary Production', *Critical Studies in Television* 1 (1) (2016): 91.

34   There are clearly further categorisations within drama that focus on historical narratives – these would also include the staged re-enactments of programmes like *The Great Fire* (directed by Jon Jones ITV 2014).

35   Kirstie Allsopp and Phil Spencer co-host *Location, Location, Location*

(Channel 4 2000–) and *Relocation, Relocation* (Channel 4 2003–), Kevin McCloud fronts *Grand Designs* (Channel 4 1999–) and Dominic Littlewood hosts *Cowboy Builders* (Channel 5 2009–).

36   J. Aaltonen and J. Kortti, 'From Evidence to Re-enactment: History, Television and Documentary Film', *Journal of Media Practice* 16 (2) (2015): 120.

37   Bell and Gray, 'History on Television', 150.

38   De Groot, *Consuming History*, 18.

39   H. Wheatley, 'Beautiful Images in Spectacular Clarity: Spectacular Television, Landscape Programming and the Question of (Tele)visual Pleasure', *Screen* 52 (2) (Summer 2011): 233–48.

40   'Episode 1', *Robbie Coltrane's B-Road Britain*, dir. Konrad Begg (ITV 2007).

41   Hunt, 'Reality, Identity and Empathy', 846.

42   Aaltonen and Kortti, 'From Evidence to Re-enactment', 120–2.

43   A. Hill, *Reality TV: Audiences and Popular Factual Television* (London: Routledge, 2005), 102.

44   E. Hanna, 'Reality-Experiential History Documentaries: *The Trench* (BBC 2002) and Britain's Modern Memory of the First World War', *Historical Journal of Film, Radio and Television* 27 (4) (2007): 532.

45   'BBC Two announces ambitious new living history series – *The Slum*' (22 January 2016). Available online: http://www.bbc.co.uk/mediacentre/latestnews/2016/bbc-two-the-slum (accessed 29 April 2016).

46   Ibid.

47   T. Conlan, 'Back in Time for Dinner may get sequel'. *Guardian* (19 April 2015). Available online: http://www.theguardian.com/tv-and-radio/2015/apr/19/back-time-dinner-sequel-giles-coren-robshaw (accessed 29 April 2016).

48   Fleming, 'Echoes of Britannia', 2.

49   G. R. Edgerton, 'Mediating Thomas Jefferson: Ken Burns as Popular Historian', in *Television Histories: Shaping Collective Memory in the Media Age*, ed. G. R. Edgerton and P. C. Rollins (Lexington: University Press of Kentucky, 2001), 173.

50   Edgerton, 'Introduction', 9.

FILMOGRAPHY

10 Days to D-Day (2004), [TV programme] Channel 4.

12 Years a Slave (2013), [Film] Dir. Steve McQueen, USA: Regency Enterprises, River Road Entertainment, Plan B Entertainment, New Regency Pictures in association with Film4.

37 Days (2014), [TV programme] BBC.

1492: Conquest of Paradise (1992), [Film] Dir. Ridley Scott, France and Spain: Gaumont, Légende Entreprises, France 3 Cinéma, Due West and Cyrkfilms.

1612 (2007), [Film] Dir. Vladimir Khotinenko, Russia: Central Partnership, Golden Eagle, Renova-Media and Three T Productions.

1900s House (1999), [TV programme] Channel 4.

1914 All Out (1987), [TV programme] ITV.

A Canterbury Tale (1944), [Film] Dir. Michael Powell and Emeric Pressburger, UK: The Archers.

A History of Britain (2000–2), [TV programme] BBC.

A History of Syria with Dan Snow (2013), [TV programme] BBC.

A Taste of Honey (1962), [Film] Dir. Tony Richardson, UK: Woodfall Film Production.

A Very British Romance (2015), [TV programme] BBC.

Absolute Power (2003), [TV programme] BBC.

Adventures of Superman (1952–8), [TV programme] ABC.

Alexander Nevsky (1938), [Film] Dir. Sergei Eisenstein and Dmitri Vasilyev, Soviet Union: Mosfilm.

All Quiet on the Western Front (1930), [Film] Dir. Lewis Milestone, USA: Universal Pictures.

Amadeus (1984), [Film] Dir. Milos Forman, USA: The Saul Zaentz Company in association with AMLF.

Amistad (1997), [Film] Dir. Steven Spielberg, USA: DreamWorks SKG in association with Home Box Office.

Apocalypse Now (1979), [Film] Dir. Francis Ford Coppola, USA: Zoetrope Studios.

Aristocrats (1999), [TV programme] BBC, Irish Screen and PBS.

Avengers Assemble (2012), [Film] Dir. Joss Whedon, USA: Marvel Studios in association with Paramount Pictures.

Back in Time for Dinner (2015), [TV programme] Channel 4.

Band of Angels (1957), [Film] Dir. Raoul Walsh, USA: Warner Bros.

Band of Brothers (2001), [TV programme] HBO.

Batman (1943), [Film] Dir. Lambert Hillyer, USA: Columbia Pictures Corporation.

Batman (1966), [Film] Dir. Leslie H. Martinson, USA: Twentieth Century Fox Film Corporation, William Dozier Productions and Greenlawn Productions.

Batman (1966–8), [TV programme] ABC.

Batman (1989), [Film] Dir. Tim Burton, USA: Warner Bros and The Guber-Peters Company in association with PolyGram Filmed Entertainment.

Battleship Potemkin (1925), [Film] Dir. Sergei M. Eisenstein, Soviet Union: Mosfilm.

Beloved (1998), [Film] Dir. Jonathan Demme, USA: Harpo Films, Clinica Estetico and Touchstone Pictures.

Bend It Like Beckham (2002), [Film] Dir. Gurinder Chadha, UK: Kintop Films.

Bhaji on the Beach (1993), [Film] Dir. Gurinder Chadha, UK: Film4.

Billy Elliot (2000), [Film] Dir. Stephen Baldry, UK: StudioCanal, Working Title Films, BBC Films and Tiger Aspect Productions in association with Arts Council of England and WT2 Productions.

Billy Liar (1963), [Film] Dir. John Schlesinger, UK: Vic Films Productions in association with Waterfall Productions.

Birdsong (2012), [TV programme] BBC.

Black Hawk Down (2001), [Film] Dir. Ridley Scott, USA: Revolution Studios and Jerry Bruckheimer Films in association with Scott Free Productions.

Blackadder Goes Forth (1989), [TV programme] BBC2.

Blackadder II (1985), [TV programme] BBC2.

Blackadder III (1987), [TV programme] BBC2.

Blade (1998), [Film] Dir. Stephen Norrington, USA: Amen Ra Films, Imaginary Forces, Marvel Enterprises and New Line Cinema.

Brassed Off (1996), [Film] Dir. Mark Herman, UK: Channel Four Films, Miramax and Prominent Features.

Braveheart (1995), [Film] Dir. Mel Gibson, USA: Icon Entertainment International, The Ladd Company and B.H. Finance C.V.

Brief Encounter (1945), [Film] Dir. David Lean, UK: Cineguild.

Britain by Bike (2010), [TV programme] BBC.

Britain's Best Drives (2009), [TV programme] BBC.

Britain's Lost Routes with Griff Rhys Jones's (2012), [TV programme] BBC.

B-Road Britain (2007), [TV programme] ITV.

Brothers in Trouble (1995), [Film] Dir. Udayan Prasad, UK: Renegade Films.

Burma's Ascot (1924), [Newsreel] British Pathé.

Cake Bakers and Trouble Makers, Lucy Worsley's 100 Years of the WI (2015), [TV programme] BBC.

Captain America (1944), [Film] Dir. Elmer Clifton and John English USA: Republic Pictures.

Caravaggio (1986), [Film] Dir. Derek Jarman, UK: British Film Institute (BFI) in association with Channel Four Television.

Churchill's Secret (2016), [Film], Dir. Charles Sturridge, UK: Daybreak Pictures and Masterpiece.

Coast (2005–), [TV programme] BBC.

Cottage to Let (1941), [Film] Dir. Anthony Asquith, UK: Gainborough Pictures.

Countryfile (1988–), [TV programme] BBC.

Cowboy Builders (2009–), [TV programme] Channel 5.

Cruel Intentions (1999), [Film] Dir. Roger Kumble, USA: Columbia Pictures Corporation, Cruel Productions LLC, Newmarket Capital Group and Original Film.

Crusade in Europe (1949), [TV programme] ABC.

Cyrano de Bergerac (1990), [Film] Dir. Jean-Paul Rappeneau, France: Caméra One, Centre National de la Cinématographie (CNC), DD Productions, Films A2, Hachette Première, Investors Club, Sofinergie 1 and Union Générale Cinématographique (UGC).

Dad's Army (1968–77), [TV programme] BBC.

Dancing Cheek to Cheek: An Intimate History of Dance (2014), [TV programme] BBC.

Dangerous Liaisons (1988), [Film] Dir. Stephen Frears, USA: Lorimar Film Entertainment, NFH Productions and Warner Bros.

Danton (1983) Andrzej Wajda, France: Gaumont, TF1 Films Production, S.F.P.C., T.M. and Les Films du Losange in association with Zespól Filmowy "X".

D-Day, the Sixth of June (1956), [Film] Dir. Henry Koster, USA: Twentieth Century–Fox.

D-Day Plus 20 Years: Eisenhower Returns to Normandy (1964), [TV programme] CBS.

D-Day: The Normandy Invasion (1944), [Film] Dir. Frank Capra, USA: US Coast Guard.

'D-Day' Victory at Sea (1953), [TV programme] National Broadcasting Company, 15 February.

'D-Day' You Are There (1955), [TV programme] CBS, 6 March.

Deadwood (2006), [TV programme] HBO.

Desert Victory (1943), [Film] Dir. Roy Boulting and David MacDonald, UK: Royal Air Force Film Production Unit and The Army Film & Photographic Unit.

Django Unchained (2012), [Film] Dir. Quentin Tarantino, USA: The Weinstein Company and Columbia Pictures.

Dockers (1999) [Film] Dir. Bill Anderson, UK: Channel Four Films.

Downton Abbey (2010–15), [TV programme] ITV.

Dr Strangelove or: How I Learned to Stop Worrying and Love the Bomb (1964), [Film] Dir. Stanley Kubrick, USA: Columbia Pictures Corporation and Hawk Films.

East is East (1999), [Film] Dir. Damien O'Donnell, UK: Film4.

Edge of Tomorrow (2014), [Film] Dir. Doug Liman, USA: Warner Bros.

Elizabeth I (2005), [TV programme] HBO and Channel 4.

Elizabeth R (1971), [TV programme] BBC.

Empire (2012), [TV programme] BBC.

Empire of the Tsars: Romanov Russia with Lucy Worsley (2016), [TV programme] BBC.

Empire: How Britain Made the Modern World (2003), [TV programme] Channel 4.

Fawlty Towers (1975–9), [TV programme] BBC.

Fire Over England (1937), [Film] Dir. William K. Howard, UK: London Film Productions.

Fires were Started (1943), [Film] Dir. Humphrey Jennings, UK: Crown Film Unit.

Football Factory (2004), [Film] Dir. Nick Love, UK: Vertigo Films and Rockstar Games.

For Massa's Sake (1911), [Film] Dir. Joseph A. Golden, USA: Pathé Frères

Four Weddings and a Funeral (1994), [Film] Dir. Mike Newell, UK: PolyGram Filmed Entertainment, Channel Four Films and Working Title Films.

Fury (2014), [Film] Dir. David Ayer, USA: Columbia Pictures, Le Grisbi Productions, Crave Films, Huayi Brothers Media in association with QED International and LStar Capital.

Glory (1989), [Film] Dir. Edward Zwick, USA: TriStar Pictures and Freddie Fields Productions.

Gone with the Wind (1939), [Film] Dir. Victor Fleming, George Cukor and Sam Wood, USA: Selznick International Pictures in association with Metro-Goldwyn-Mayer (MGM).

Grand Designs (1999–), [TV programme] Channel 4.

Great British Railway Journeys (2010–), [TV programme] BBC.

Great Canal Journeys (2014–), [TV programme] Channel 4.

Green Street (2005), [Film] Dir. by Lexi Alexander, USA: Oddlot Entertainment.

Guess Who's Coming to Dinner (1967), [Film] Dir. Stanley Kramer, USA: Columbia Pictures Corporation.

Handsworth Songs (1986), [Film] Dir. John Akomfrah, UK: Black Audio Film Collective.

Hello India (1933), [Newsreel] British Pathé.

Henri 4 (2010), [Film] Dir. Jo Baier, Germany: Ziegler Film & Company, GéTéVé, Institut del Cinema Català (ICC), Wega Film, Westdeutscher Rundfunk (WDR), Bayerischer Rundfunk (BR), Südwestrundfunk (SWR), Mitteldeutscher Rundfunk (MDR), Norddeutscher Rundfunk (NDR), Österreichischer Rundfunk (ORF), Degeto Film, France 2 (FR2), B.A. Produktion, MMC Independent, in association with ARTE.

His Trust Fulfilled: The Faithful Devotion and Self-Sacrifice of an Old Negro Servant (1911), [Film] Dir. D.W. Griffith, USA: Biograph.

History of Britain, (2000–2), [TV programme] BBC.

Human Traffic (1999), [Film] Dir. Justin Kerrigan, UK: Irish Screen and Fruit Salad Films.

Ike: Countdown to D-Day (2004), [Film] Dir. Robert Harmon, USA: A&E Television Networks.

In Slavery Days (1913), [Film] Dir. Otis Turner, USA: Rex Motion Picture Company.

In Which We Serve (1942), [Film] Dir. Noel Coward and David Lean, UK: Two Cities Films.

India Today – The Empire's Greatest Problem (1929), [Newsreel] British Pathé.

Indian Town Studies (1937), [Newsreel] British Pathé.

Isabel (2012–14), [TV programme] TVE.

Ivan the Terrible (1944), [Film] Dir. Sergei M. Eisenstein, Soviet Union: Mosfilm and TsOKS.

J'Accuse (1919), [Film] Dir. Abel Gance, France: Pathé Frères.

Jefferson in Paris (1995), [Film] Dir. James Ivory, USA: Touchstone Pictures and Merchant Ivory Productions.

Jezebel (1938), [Film] Dir. William Wyler, USA: Warner Bros.

JFK (1991), [Film] Dir. Oliver Stone, USA: Warner Bros, Ixtlan and Camelot in association with Canal+, Regency Enterprises and Alcor Films.

John Adams (2008), [TV programme] HBO.

Kanal (1957), [Film] Dir. Andrzej Wajda, Poland: Zespól Filmowy "Kadr"

Kes (1969), [Film] Dir. Kenneth Loach, UK: Kestrel Films and Woodfall Film Productions.

Kingdom of Heaven (2005), [Film] Dir. Ridley Scott, USA: Twentieth Century Fox Film Corporation, Scott Free Productions, BK, KOH, Reino del Cielo, Studio Babelsberg, Calle Cruzada, Dune Films and Kanzaman in association with Inside Track 3.

Kitchener's Great Army in the Battle of the Somme (1916), [Film] Dir. Geoffrey Malins, UK: British Topical Committee for War Films.

La Reine Margot (1994), [Film] Dir. Patrice Chéreau, France: Renn Productions, France 2 Cinéma, D.A. Films, N.E.F. Filmproduktion und Vertriebs (I), Degeto Film, Arbeitsgemeinschaft der öffentlich-rechtlichen Rundfunkanstalten der Bundesrepublik Deutschland (ARD), WMG Film, RCS Films & TV, Centre National de la Cinématographie (CNC), Canal+ and Miramax.

Lads Army (2002), [TV programme] BBC.

Let George Do It (1940), [Film] Dir. Marcel Varnel, UK: Associated Talking Pictures (ATP), Ealing Studios.

Letter to Brezhnev (1985), [Film] Dir. Chris Bernard, UK: Channel Four Films, Palace Pictures and Yeardream.

Life in Rangoon (undated), [Newsreel] British Pathé.

Lincoln (2013), [Film] Dir. Steven Spielberg, USA: DreamWorks SKG, Twentieth Century Fox Film Corporation, Reliance Entertainment, Amblin Entertainment, The Kennedy/Marshall Company and Walt Disney Studios Motion Pictures, in association with Participant Media and Dune Entertainment.

Location, Location, Location (2000–), [TV programme] Channel 4.

Love on the Dole (1941), [Film] Dir. John Baxter, UK: British National Films.

Love Story (1944), [Film] Dir. Leslie Arliss, UK: Gainsborough Pictures.

Lucy Worsley's Reins of Power (2015), [TV programme] BBC.

Made in Britain (1983), [Film] Dir. Alan Clarke, UK: Central Independent Television.

Madonna of the Seven Moons (1945), [Film] Dir. Arthur Crabtree, UK: Gainsborough Pictures.

Magna Carta (2015), [TV programme] BBC.

Magnificent Century ('Muhtesem Yüzyi') (2011–14), [TV programme] Kanal D.

Mandingo (1975), [Film] Dir. Richard Fleischer, USA: Dino De Laurentiis Company and Paramount Pictures.

Marie-Antoinette (2006), [Film] Dir. Sofia Coppola, USA: Columbia Pictures Corporation and American Zoetrope in association with Pricel and Tohokushinsha Film Corporation (TFC).

Mary, Queen of Scots (1971), [Film] Dir. Charles Jarrott, UK: Universal Pictures.

Mary of Scotland (1936), [Film] Dir. John Ford, Leslie Goodwins, USA: RKO Radio Pictures.

Meet Me in St. Louis (1944), [Film] Dir. Vincente Minnelli, USA: Metro-Goldwyn-Mayer.

Millions Like Us (1943), [Film] Dir. Sidney Gilliat and Frank Launder, UK: Gainsborough Pictures.

My Beautiful Laundrette (1985), [Film] Dir. Stephen Frears, UK: Working Title Films, SAF Productions and Channel Four Films.

My Son the Fanatic (1997), [Film] Dir. Udayan Prasad, UK: Arts Council of England, BBC Films, British Broadcasting Corporation, Canal+, Image International, UGC DA International and Zephyr Films.

News of the Day, Invasion Extra! (1944), [Newsreel] Metro-Goldwyn-Mayer.

Nightjohn (1996), [Film] Dir. Charles Burnett, USA: Hallmark Entertainment, Sarabande Productions and Signboard Films Production Inc.

Not Forgotten (2005), [TV programme] Channel 4.

Oh! What a Lovely War (1969), [Film] Dir. Richard Attenborough, UK: Accord Productions

Old Bill and Son (1941), [Film] Dir. Ian Dalrymple, UK: Legeran.

Orlando (1992), [Film] Dir. Sally Potter, USA: Adventure Pictures, Lenfilm Studio, Mikado Film, Rio and Sigma Film Productions.

Our War (2011), [TV programme] BBC.

Our World War (2014), [TV programme] BBC.

Passport to Pimlico (1949), [Film] Dir. Henry Cornelius, UK: J. Arthur Rank Organisation and Ealing Studios.

Paths of Glory (1957), [Film] Dir. Stanley Kubrick, UK: Bryna Productions.

Patton (1970), [Film] Dir. Franklin J. Schaffner, USA: Twentieth Century Fox Film Corporation.

Pearl Harbor (2001), [Film] Dir. Michael Bay, USA: Touchstone Pictures and Jerry Bruckheimer Films.

Penelope Keith's Hidden Villages (2014), [TV programme] Channel 4.

Peter Moffat's The Village (2013–14), [TV programme] BBC.

Power of Art (2006), [TV programme] BBC.

Private Peaceful (2012), [Film] Dir. Pat O'Connor, UK: Fluidity Films.

Regeneration/ Behind the Lines (1997), [Film] Dir. Gillies MacKinnon, UK: BBC.

Relocation, Relocation (2003–), [TV programme] Channel 4.

Ridicule (1996), [Film] Dir. Patrice Leconte, France: Epithète Films, Cinéa, France 3 Cinéma and Cineplex Odeon Films.

Rita, Sue and Bob Too (1986), [Film] Dir. Alan Clarke, UK: British Screen Productions, Channel Four Films and Umbrella Films.

Room at the Top (1959), [Film] Dir. Jack Clayton, UK: Romulus Films and Remus.

Roots (1977), [TV programme] ABC.

Rough Crossings: Britain, the Slaves and the American Revolution (2005), [TV programme] BBC.

Sally Hemings: An American Love Story (2000), [Film] Dir. Charles C. Haid, USA: Inspired Studio.

Sankofa (1993), [Film] Dir. Haile Gerima, USA: Channel Four Films, Diproci, Ghana National Commission on Culture, Mypheduh Films, Negod-Gwad Productions, Norddeutscher Rundfunk (NDR) and Westdeutscher Rundfunk (WDR).

Saturday Night and Sunday Morning (1960), [Film] Dir. Karel Reisz, UK: Woodfall Film Productions.

Saving Private Ryan (1998), [Film] Dir. Steven Spielberg, USA: DreamWorks Pictures and Paramount Pictures.

Schindler's List (1993), [Film] Dir. Steven Spielberg, USA: Universal Pictures and Amblin Entertainment.

Secrets of India (1934), [Newsreel] British Pathé.

Shaft (1971), [Film] Dir. Gordon Parks, USA: Metro-Goldwyn-Mayer (MGM) and Shaft Productions Ltd.

Ships with Wings (1941), [Film] Dir. Sergei Nolandov, UK: Ealing Studios.

Singin' in the Rain (1951), [Film] Dir. Gene Kelly and Stanley Donan, USA: Metro-Goldwyn-Mayer.

Slave Ship (1937), [Film] Dir. Tay Garnett, USA: Twentieth Century Fox Film Corporation.

So Red the Rose (1935), [Film] Dir. King Vidor, USA: Paramount Pictures.

Solomon Northup's Odyssey (1984), [TV programme] PBS.

Song of the South (1946), [Film] Dir. Wilfred Jackson and Harve Foster, USA: Walt Disney Productions.

Souls and Sea (1937), [Film] Dir. Henry Hathaway, USA: Paramount Pictures.

Spider-Man (2002), [Film] Dir. Sam Raimi, USA: Columbia Pictures, Marvel Enterprises and Laura Ziskin Productions.

Spider-Man 2 (2004), [Film] Dir. Sam Raimi, USA: Columbia Pictures, Marvel Enterprises and Laura Ziskin Productions.

Spider-Man 3 (2007), [Film] Dir. Sam Raimi, USA: Columbia Pictures, Marvel Enterprises and Laura Ziskin Productions.

'Steven Spielberg', *Inside the Actors Studio* (1999), [TV programme] Bravo Channel.

Superman (1941–3), [Film] Dir. Max and Dave Fleischer, USA: Fleischer Studios.

Superman (1978), [Film] Dir. Richard Donner, USA: Dovemead Films, Film Export A.G. and International Film Production.

The Age of Regency (2011), [TV programme] BBC.

The Americanization of Emily (1964), [Film] Dir. Arthur Hiller, USA: Metro-Goldwyn-Mayer.

The Bells Go Down (1943), [Film] Dir. Basil Dearden, UK: Ealing Studios.

The Big Red One (1980), [Film] Dir. Samuel Fuller, USA: United Artists.

The Birth of a Nation (1915), [Film] Dir. D. W. Griffith, USA: David W. Griffith Corp. and Epoch Producing Corporation.

The Borgias (2011–13), [TV programme] Showtime.

The Civil War (1990), [TV programme] PBS.

The Colditz Story (1954), [Film] Dir. Guy Hamilton, UK: Ivan Foxwell Productions.

The Cruel Sea (1953), [Film] Dir. Charles Frend, UK: J. Arthur Rank Organisation and Ealing Studios.

The Dam Busters (1955), [Film] Dir. Michael Anderson, UK: Associated British Picture Corporation (ABPC).

The Deer Hunter (1978), [Film] Dir. Michael Cimino, USA: EMI Films and Universal Pictures.

The Devils (1971), [Film] Dir. Ken Russell, USA: Russo Productions.

The Evil Dead (1981), [Film] Dir. Sam Raimi, USA: Renaissance Pictures.

The Evil Dead 2 (1987), [Film] Dir. Sam Raimi, USA: Renaissance Pictures and De Laurentiis Entertainment Group (DEG).

The Firm (1989), [Film] Dir. Alan Clarke, UK: BBC.

The First of the Few (1942), [Film] Dir. Leslie Howard, UK: British Aviation Pictures.

The Foreman went to France (1942), [Film] Dir. Charles Frend, UK: Ealing Studios

The Full Monty (1997), [Film] Dir. Peter Cattaneo, UK: Redwave Films, Channel Four Films and Twentieth Century Fox Film Corporation.

The Gathering Storm (2002), [TV programme] BBC and HBO.

The Gentle Sex (1943), [Film] Dir. Leslie Howard and Maurice Elvey (uncredited), UK: Two Cities Films, Concanen Productions, Derrick De Marney Productions.

The Great Fire (2014), [TV programme] ITV.

The Great War (1964), [TV programme] BBC.

The History Boys (2006), [Film] Dir. Nicholas Hyter, UK: Fox Searchlight Pictures, DNA Films, BBC Two Films and National Theatre in association with UK Film Council.

The Iron Lady (2012), [Film] Dir. Phyllida Lloyd, UK: Pathé, Film4, UK Film Council, The Weinstein Company, Yuk Films and DJ Films in association with Goldcrest Pictures.

The King and I (1956), [Film] Dir. Walter Lang, USA: Twentieth Century Fox.

The Ladykillers (1955), [Film] Dir. Alexander Mackendrick, UK: The Rank Organisation and Ealing Studios.

The Lamp Still Burns (1943), [Film] Dir. Maurice Elvey, UK: Two Cities Films.

The Last Kingdom (2015), [TV programme] BBC.

The Legend of Nigger Charley (1972), [Film] Dir. Martin Goldman, USA: Paramount Pictures.

The Lion has Wings (1939), [Film] Dir. Adrian Brunel, Brian Desmond Hurst, Michael Powell and Alexander Korda, UK: London Film Productions.

The Longest Day (1962), [Film] Dir. Ken Annakin, Andrew Marton, Bernhard Wicki, and Darryl F. Zanuck, USA: Darryl F. Zanuck Productions and Twentieth Century Fox Film Corporation.

The Madness of King George (1994), [Film] Dir. Nicholas Hytner, UK: The Samuel Goldwyn Company, Channel Four Films and Close Call Films.

The Man in the Iron Mask (1998), [Film] Dir. Randall Wallace, USA: United Artists Corporation.

The Mission (1986), [Film] Dir. Roland Joffe, USA: Warner Bros., Goldcrest Films International, Kingsmere Productions Ltd., Enigma Productions and AMLF.

The Monocled Mutineer (1986), [TV programme] BBC.

The New World (2005), [Film] Dir. Terrence Malick, USA: New Line Cinema, Sunflower Productions, Sarah Green Film, First Foot Films and The Virginia Company LLC.

The Passing Bells (2014), [TV programme] BBC.

The Patriot (2000), [Film] Dir. Roland Emmerich, USA: Columbia Pictures Corporation, Centropolis Entertainment, Mutual Film Company and Global Entertainment Productions GmbH & Company Medien KG.

The Private Lives of Elizabeth and Essex (1939), [Film] Dir. Michael Curtiz, USA: Warner Bros.

The Return of Martin Guerre (*Le Retour de Martin Guerre*) (1982), [Film] Dir. Daniel Vigne, France: Dussault, France 3 (FR 3) and Société Française de Production (SFP).

The Slum (2016), [TV programme] BBC.

The Sound of Music (1965), [Film] Dir. Robert Wise, USA: Twentieth Century Fox.

The Summer Stock (1950), [Film] Dir. Charles Walters, USA: Metro-Goldwyn-Mayer.

The Taking of Power by Louis XIV (*Le Prise de Pouvoir de Louis XIV*) (1966), [Film] Dir. Roberto Rossellini, France: Office de Radiodiffusion Télévision Française (ORTF).

The Terminal (2004), [Film] Dir. Steven Spielberg, USA: DreamWorks SKG, Amblin Entertainment and Parkes+MacDonald Image Nation.

The Titfield Thunderbolt (1953), [Film] Dir. Charles Crichton, UK: J. Arthur Rank Organisation, Ealing Studios and Michael Balcon Productions.

The Trench (2002), [TV programme] BBC.

The True Glory (1945), [Film] Dir. Garson Kanin, UK and USA: Ministry of Information (UK) and US Office of War Information.

The Tudors (2007–10), [TV programme] Showtime.

The Vikings Uncovered (2016), [TV programme] BBC.

The Vikings (2014), [TV programme] HBO.

The War Game (1965), [TV programme] BBC.

The Way to the Stars (1945), [Film] Dir. Anthony Asquith, UK: Two Cities Films

The White Queen (2013), [TV programme] BBC.

The Wizard of Oz (1939), [Film] Dir. Victor Fleming, USA: Metro-Goldwyn-Mayer.

The World at War (1973–4), [TV programme] Thames Television and the Imperial War Museum.

The World at War (1973–4), [TV programme] BBC.

This Happy Breed (1944), [Film] Dir. David Lean, UK: Noel Coward-Cineguild (in association with) Two Cities Films (as a Prestige Production).

This Sporting Life (1963), [Film] Dir. Lindsay Anderson, UK: Independent Artists and Julian Wintle/Leslie Parkyn Productions.

Through India and Burma with H.R.H. The Prince of Wales (1922), [Newsreel] British Pathé.

Time Team (1994–2014), [TV programme] Channel 4.

Tony Robinson's Walking Through History (2013–), [TV programme] Channel 4.

Tora, Tora, Tora (1970), [Film] Dir. Richard Fleischer, Kinji Fukasaku and Toshio Masuda, USA: Twentieth Century Fox Film Corporation, Elmo Williams-Richard Fleischer Production and Toei Company.

Trainspotting (1995), Danny Boyle, [Film] Dir. UK: Channel Four Films, Figment Films and The Noel Gay Motion Picture Company.

Uncle Tom's Cabin (1914), [Film] Dir. William Robert Daly, USA: World Film.

Uncle Tom's Cabin (1927), [Film] Dir. Harry A. Pollard, USA: Universal Pictures.

Uncle Tom's Cabin (1987), [TV programme] Showtime.

Uncle Tom's Cabin: Slavery Days (1903), [Film] Dir. Edwin S. Porter, USA: Edison Manufacturing Company.

United 93 (2006), [Film] Dir. Paul Greengrass, USA: Universal Pictures, StudioCanal, Sidney Kimmel Entertainment and Working Title Films.

Upstairs, Downstairs (1971–5), [TV programme] BBC.

Valmont (1989), [Film] Dir. Milos Forman, USA: Renn Productions and Timothy Burrill Productions.

Vatel (2000), [Film] Dir. Roland Joffe, France: Légende Entreprises, Gaumont, Canal+, Nomad Films, TF1 Films Production and Timothy Burrill Productions.

Victory at Sea (1953), [TV programme] National Broadcasting Company.

Wake Island (1942), [Film] Dir. John Farrow, USA: Paramount Pictures.

War Game (2001), [Film] Dir. Dave Unwin, UK: Illuminated Film Company and Scala Productions in association with Film Council, Channel 4 Television Corporation and Infiniss.

Waterloo Road (1945), [Film] Dir. Sidney Gilliat, UK: Gainsborough Pictures.

We Dive at Dawn (1943), [Film] Dir. Anthony Asquith, UK: Gainsborough Pictures, Gaumont British Picture Corporation.

Went the Day Well (1942), [Film] Dir. Alberto Cavalcanti, UK: Ealing Studios.

When Lucy Met Roy (2015), [TV programme] BBC.

Who Do You Think You Are? (2004–), [TV programme] BBC.

With our King and Queen through India (1912), [Newsreel] British Pathé.

Wolf Hall (2015), [TV programme] BBC.

Wonder Woman (1975–9), [TV programme] ABC.

World Trade Center (2006), [Film] Dir. Oliver Stone, USA: Paramount Pictures, Double Feature Films Intermedia Films, Ixtlan, Kernos Filmproduktionsgesellschaft & Company and Saturn Films.

World Troubles 1914–1934 (1934), [Newsreel] British Pathé.

X-Men (1999), [Film] Dir. Bryan Singer, USA: Twentieth Century Fox Film Corporation, Marvel Enterprises, Donners' Company, Bad Hat Harry Productions, Springwood Productions and Genetics Productions.

BIBLIOGRAPHY

Books and journals

'12 Years a Slave: An ALH Forum'. *American Literary History* 26 (2) (2014): 317–84.

Aaltonen, J. and J. Kortti. 'From Evidence to Re-enactment: History, Television and Documentary Film'. *Journal of Media Practice* 16 (2) (2015): 108–25.

Aldgate A. and J. Richards. *Britain Can Take It: The British Cinema in the Second World War*. Edinburgh: Edinburgh University Press, 1994.

Allen, R. C. *Channels of Discourse: Television and Contemporary Criticism*. Chapel Hill, NC: University of North Carolina Press, 1987a.

Allen, R. C. 'Introduction: Talking about Television'. In *Channels of Discourse: Television and Contemporary Criticism*, ed. R. C. Allen, 1–16. Chapel Hill, NC: The University of North Carolina Press, 1987.

Allen, R. C. "Reader-Oriented Criticism". In *Channels of Discourse: Television and Contemporary Criticism*, ed. R. C. Allen, 74–112. Chapel Hill, NC: University of North Carolina Press, 1987.

Althaus, S. L. 'The Forgotten Role of the Global Newsreel Industry in the Long Transition from Text to Television'. *The International Journal of Press/Politics* 15 (2) (2010): 193–218.

Altman, C. F. 'Towards a Historiography of American Film'. *Cinema Journal* 16 (Spring 1977): 1–25.

Altman, R. *The American Film Musical*. Bloomington: Indiana University Press, 1987.

Ambrose, S. *D-Day, June 6, 1944: The Climactic Battle of World War II*. New York: Simon & Schuster, 1994.

Ambrose, S. '*The Longest Day* (US, 1962): "Blockbuster" History'. In *World War II, Film, and History*, ed. J. Whiteclay Chambers II and D. Culbert, 97–106. New York: Oxford University Press, 1996.

Anderegg, M., ed. *Inventing Vietnam: The War in Film and Television*. Philadelphia: Temple University Press, 1991.

Anderson, B. *Imagined Communities: Reflections on the Origin and Spread of Nationalism*. London: Verso, 2003.

Anderson, L. 'The Porous Boundaries of Newsreel Memory Research'. In *Cathedrals of the Movies: A History of British Cinemas and Their Audiences*, ed. D. Atwell, 71–86. London: Architectural Press, 1980.

Anderson, S. 'History TV and Popular Memory'. In *Television Histories: Shaping Collective Memory in the Media Age,* ed. G. R. Edgerton and R. C. Rollins, 19–36. Lexington: University of Kentucky Press, 2001.

Anglo Saxon Chronicle: Peterborough Manuscript, AD 793.

Anglo Saxon Chronicle: Peterborough Manuscript, AD 872.

Ashcroft, B., G. Griffiths and H. Tiffin. *Key Concepts in Post-Colonial Studies.* London: Routledge, 1998.

Aspinall, S. 'Women, Realism and Reality in British Films, 1943–53'. In *British Cinema History*, ed. J. Curran and V. Porter, 272–93. London: Weidenfeld and Nicolson, 1983.

Bale, J. and M. Cronin. 'Introduction: Sport and Postcolonialism'. In *Sport and Postcolonialism*, ed. J. Bale and M. Cronin, 1–14. Oxford: Berg, 2003.

Ball, J. C. *Satire and the Postcolonial Novel: V. S. Naipaul, Chinua Achebe, Salman Rushdie.* London: Routledge, 2003.

Barber, S. 'The Formation of Cultural Attitudes: The Example of the Three Kingdoms in the 1650s'. In *The Stuart Kingdoms in the Seventeenth Century: Awkward Neighbours*, ed. A. I. Macinnes and J. Ohlmeyer, 169–85. Dublin: Four Courts Press, 2002.

Barber S. and C. M. Peniston-Bird (eds), *History Beyond the Text: A Student's Guide to Approaching Alternative Sources.* London: Routledge, 2009.

Barrett, J. *Shooting the Civil War: Cinema, History and American National Identity National Television and Civil War.* New York: I.B. Tauris, 2009.

Barry, P. *Beginning Theory: An Introduction to Literary and Cultural Theory*, 3rd edn. Manchester: Manchester University Press, 2009.

Barthes, R. *Mythologies.* London: Grant and Cutler, 1994.

Bartlett, J. and K.M. Ellis. 'Remembering the Dead in Northrop: First World War Memorials in a Welsh Parish'. *Journal of Contemporary History* 34 (2) (1999): 231–42.

Basinger, J. *The World War II Combat Film: Anatomy of a Genre, Updated Filmography by J. Arnold.* New York: Columbia University Press, 1986; Middletown: Wesleyan University Press, 2003.

Batuman, E. 'Ottomania: A Hit TV Show Reimagines Turkey's imperial Past'. *New Yorker*, 17 February 2014.

Beaumont, R. A. 'Images of War: Films as Documentary History'. *Military Affairs* 35 (1971): 5–7.

Beik, W. 'The Absolutism of Louis XIV as Social Collaboration'. *Past and Present* 188 (2005): 195–224.

Bell, E. and A. Gray. 'History on Television: Charisma, Narrative and Knowledge'. In *Re-viewing Television History*, ed. H. Wheatley, 142–55. London: I.B. Tauris, 2007.

Benjamin, J. R. *A Student's Guide to History*, 10th edn. New York: Bedford/St. Martin's, 2007.

Benson, J. *The Working Class in Britain 1850–1939.* London: I.B. Tauris, 2003.

Berlin, I. 'Glory Be'. *Radical History Review* 53 (1992): 141–8.

Bernstein, M. 'Nostalgia, Ambivalence, Irony: Song of the South and Race Relations in 1946 Atlanta'. *Film History* 8 (1996): 219–36.

Best, B. *Reporting the Second World War.* Barnsley: Pen & Sword, 2015.

Bhabha, H. K. *Nation and Narration.* London: Routledge, 1990.

Bhattacharya, S. *Propaganda and Information in Eastern India, 1939–45: A Necessary Weapon of War.* London: Routledge, 2001.

Bibler, M. 'Always the Tragic Jezebel: New Orleans, Katrina, and the Layered Discourse of a Doomed Southern City'. *Southern Cultures* 14 (2) (2008): 6–27.

Blackburn, S. *Truth: A Guide for the Perplexed*. London: Penguin Books, 2006.

Bodnar, J. '*Saving Private Ryan* and Postwar Memory in America'. *American Historical Review* 106 (3) (2001): 805–17

Bogle, D. *Toms, Coons, Mulattoes, Mammies, & Bucks: An Interpretive History of Blacks in American Films*. New York: Continuum, 2003.

Bottomore, S. "An Amazing Quarter Mile of Moving Gold, Gems and Genealogy': Filming India's 1902/03 Delhi Durbar'. *Historical Journal of Film, Radio and Television* 15 (4) (1995): 495–515.

Bottomore, S. 'News before the Newsreels: The British Pioneers'. In '*The Story of the Century*': *An International Newsfilm Conference*, 14–16. London: BUFVC, 1996.

Bottomore, S. "Have You Seen the Gaekwar, Bob?': Filming the 1911 Delhi Durbar'. *Historical Journal of Film, Radio and Television* 17 (3) (1997): 309–45.

Boulton, J. T. and T. O. McLoughlin, eds. *News from Abroad: Letters Written by British Travellers on the Grand Tour, 1728–1771*. Eighteenth Century Worlds, no. 3; Liverpool: Liverpool University Press, 2012. Available online: universitypublishingonline.org (accessed 26 August 2015).

Braudy, L. *The World in a Frame: What We See In Films*. Chicago: University of Chicago Press, 2002.

Braudy, L. *Film Theory and Criticism: Introductory Readings*, 6th edn. New York: Oxford University Press, 2004.

Brinkley, D. *The Boys of Pointe du Hoc: Ronald Reagan, D-Day, and the U.S. Army 2nd Rangers Battalion*. New York: HarperPerennial, 2005.

Brooke, R. *1914 and Other Poems*. London: Read Books Ltd, 2015.

Burgoyne, R. *The Hollywood Historical Film*. Malden, MA: Blackwell, 2008.

Burks, R. E. '*Gone with the Wind*: Black and White in Technicolor'. *Quarterly Review of Film Video* 21 (1) (2004): 53–73.

Burns, J. *Cinema and Society in the British Empire, 1895–1940*. New York: Palgrave Macmillan, 2013.

Bushaway, B. 'Name upon Name; the Great War and Remembrance'. In *Myths of the English*, ed. R. Porter, 136–67. Cambridge: Polity Press, 1992.

Butler, J. *Precarious Life: The Power of Mourning and Violence*. London: Verso, 2006.

Cacqueray, E. de. 'New Slants on Gender and Power Relations in British Second World War Films'. *Miranda* 2 (2010): 2–14.

Calder, A. *The Myth of the Blitz*. London: Pimlico, 1992.

Campan, J. L. H. *The Private Life of Marie Antoinette. A Confidante's Account*. Warwick, NY: 1500 Books, 2006.

Cannadine, D. *Class in Britain*. London: Penguin, 2000.

Castonguay, J. 'Conglomeration, New Media and the Cultural Production of the "War on Terror"'. *Cinema Journal* 43 (4) (2004): 102–8.

Cavell, S. *The World Viewed: Reflections on the Ontology of Film*. Cambridge: Harvard University Press, 1979.

CCRT (Community Cohesion Review Team). 'Community Cohesion: A Report of the Independent Review Team, chaired by Ted Cantle' (2001). Available online: http://resources.cohesioninstitute.org.uk/Publications/Documents/Document/DownloadDocumentsFile.aspx?recordId=96%26file=PDFversion (accessed 16 December 2014).

Certeau, M. de. *The Possession at Loudun*, trans. M. B. Smith. Chicago: University of Chicago Press, 2000.

Chandler, D. *Semiotics: The Basics*, 2nd edn. New York: Routledge, 2007.

Chapman, J. *The British Can Take it: Cinema, State and Propaganda*. London: I.B. Tauris, 2000a.

Chapman, J. *The British at War: Cinema, State and Propaganda, 1939–1945*. London: I.B. Taurus, 2000b.

Chapman, J. *Film and History*. London: Routledge, 2007.

Chapman, J. 'Television and History: The World at War'. *Historical Journal of Film, Radio and Television* 31 (2) (2011): 247–75.

Chapman, J. M. Glancy and S. Harper (eds). *The New Film History: Sources, Methods, Approaches*. New York: Palgrave Macmillan, 2007.

Childers, T. *Soldier from the War Returning: The Greatest Generation's Troubled Homecoming from World War II*. Boston: Houghton Mifflin Harcourt, 2009.

Chopra-Gant, M. *Cinema and History: The Telling of Stories*. London: Wallflower Press, 2008.

Clark, A. *The Donkeys*. London: Hutchinson, 1961.

Classen, C. and W. Kansteiner. 'Truth and Authenticity in Contemporary Historical Culture: An Introduction to Historical Representation and Historical Truth'. *History and Theory* 47 (2) (2009): 1–4.

Cohn, L. 'Long Roundabout to "Big Red", Fuller's First Major Pic in 16 Yrs'. *Variety*, 8 July 1980.

Colley, L. *Britons: Forging the Nation 1707–1837*. London: Vintage, 1996.

Colls, R. *Identity of England*. Oxford: Oxford University Press, 2002.

Confino, A. 'Collective Memory and Cultural History: Problems of Method'. *American Historical Review* 102 (5) (1997): 1386–403.

Conlan, T. 'Back in Time for Dinner may get sequel'. *Guardian*, 19 April 2015. Available online: http://www.theguardian.com/tv-and-radio/2015/apr/19/back-time-dinner-sequel-giles-coren-robshaw (accessed 29 April 2016).

Connelly, M. 'The Devil is Coming'. *Historical Journal of Film, Television and Radio* 22 (1) (2002): 21–8.

Connelly, M. *We Can Take It!: Britain and the Memory of the Second World War*. London: Routledge, 2004.

Considine, S. *Mad as Hell: The Life and Work of Paddy Chayefsky*. New York: Random House, 1994.

Cooper, F. and A. L. Stoler. *Tensions of Empire: Colonial Cultures in a Bourgeois World*. Berkeley: University of California Press, 1997.

Coronation Durbar, Delhi 1911. Official Directory with Maps. Calcutta: Government Printing, 1911.

Coras, J. de. *Arrest Memorable, du Parlement de Tolose, Contenant une histoireprodigieuse, de nostre temps, avee cent belles, & doctes Annotations, de monsieur maistre Jean de Coras, Conseiller en ladite Cour, & rapporteur du proces. Prononce es Arrestz Generaulx le xii Septembre*. Lyon: Antoine Vincent, 1561. [Published as 'Arrest Memorable du Parlement de Toulouse' in 1561.]

Crane, D. *Empires of the Dead*. London: William Collins, 2014.

Crary, J. 'Spectacle, Attention, Counter-Memory'. *October* 50 (1989): 96–107.

Crawford, K. 'Love, Sodomy and Scandal: Controlling the Sexual Reputation of Henri III'. *Journal of the History of Sexuality* 12 (X) (2003): 513–42.

Cripps, T. 'The Unformed Image: The Negro in the Movies before Birth of a Nation'. *Maryland Historian* 2 (1) (1971): 13–26.

Cripps, T. *Making Movies Black: The Hollywood Message Movie from World War II to the Civil Rights Era*. New York: Oxford University Press, 1993a.

Cripps, T. *Slow Fade to Black: The Negro in American Film, 1900–1942*. New York: Oxford University Press, 1993b.

Crofts, S. 'Not a Window on the Past: How Films and Television Construct History'. *Film and History: An Interdisciplinary Journal of Film and Television* 17 (4) (1987): 90–5.

Culler, J. *Literary Theory: A Very Short Introduction*, 2nd edn. New York: Oxford University Press, 2011.

Cummings, B. *War and Television*. New York: Verso: 1992.

D'Este, C. *Decision in Normandy*. Old Saybrook, CT: Konecky and Konecky, 1983.

Danchev, A. '"Bunking" and Debunking: The Controversies of the 1960s'. In *The First World War and British Military History*, ed. B. Bond, 263–88. Oxford: Oxford University Press, 1991.

Davies, J. 'Reconstructing Enmities; War and War Memorials, The Boundary Markers of the West'. *History of European Ideas* 19 (1–3) (1994): 47–52.

Davis, J. J. *Defining Culinary Authority: The Transformation of Cooking in France, 1650–1830*. Baton Rouge: Louisiana State University Press, 2013.

Dawson, A. *Historical Insights: Focus on History: Hollywood For Historians*. Coventry: History at the Higher Education Academy, 2009.

Dengel-Janic, E. and L. Eckstein. 'Bridehood Revisited: Disarming Concepts of Gender and Culture in Recent Asian British Film'. In *Multi-ethnic Britain 2000+: New Perspectives in Literature, Film and the Arts*, ed. L. Eckstein, 45–64. Amsterdam: Rodopi, 2008.

Department for Culture, Media and Sport. 'Cultural Test for British Films; Final Framework' (2015 [2005]). Available online: http://old.culture. gov.uk/images/publications/CulturalTestFilm.pdf (accessed 22 November 2015).

Deprez, C. 'India'. In *The Concise Routledge Encyclopedia of the Documentary Film*, ed. I. Aitken, 400–6. London: Routledge, 2013.

DeVos, A. '"Expect the Truth': Exploiting History with Mandingo'. *American Studies* 52 (2) (2013): 127–33.

Di Maggio, P. 'Culture and Cognition'. *Annual Review of Sociology* 23 (1997): 263–87.

Diefendorf, B. B. *The St. Bartholomew's Day Massacre: A Brief History with Documents*. Boston and New York: Bedford/St. Martin's, 2008.

Dittmer, J. *Captain America and the Nationalist Superhero: Metaphors, Narratives, and Geopolitics*. Philadelphia: Temple University Press, 2013.

Doane, M. A. 'Information, Crisis, Catastrophe', in *Logics of Television*, ed. P. Mellencamp, 226–7. Bloomington: Indiana University Press, 1990.

Doane, M. A. 'Information, Crisis, Catastrophe'. In *The Historical Film: History and Memory in Media*, ed. M. Landy, 269–85. New Brunswick, NJ: Rutgers University Press, 2001.

Dobson, M. and N. J. Watson. *England's Elizabeth: An Afterlife in Fame and Fantasy*. Oxford: Oxford University Press, 2002.

Doherty, T. *Projections of War: Hollywood, American Culture, and World War II*, rev. edn. New York: Columbia University Press, 1999.

Doherty, T. 'The New War Movies as Moral Rearmament: Black Hawk Down and We Were Soldiers'. In *The War Film*, ed. R. Eberwein, 214–22. New Brunswick, NJ: Rutgers University Press, 2005.

Dolski M. R. "Portal of Liberation' D-Day Myth as American Self-Affirmation'. In *D-Day in History and Memory: The Normandy Landings in International Remembrance and Commemoration*, ed. M. R. Dolski, S. Edwards, and J. Buckley, 43–84. Denton: University of North Texas Press, 2014.

Dolski, M. R. '"To Set Free a Suffering Humanity": D-Day in American Remembrance'. Ph.D. diss., Temple University, Philadelphia, 2012.

Dolski, M. R. *D-Day Remembered: The Normandy Landings in American Collective Memory*. Knoxville: University of Tennessee Press, 2016.

Dolski, M., S. Edwards and J. Buckley. *D-Day in History and Memory: The Normandy Landings in International Remembrance and Commemoration*. Denton: University of North Texas Press, 2014.

Dombrowski, L. *The Films of Samuel Fuller: If You Die, I'll Kill You!* Middletown, CT: Wesleyan University Press, 2008.

Doran, S. *Monarchy and Matrimony: The Courtships of Elizabeth I*. London: Routledge, 1995.

Doran, S. and T. Freeman. *The Myth of Elizabeth*. Basingstoke: Palgrave Macmillan, 2003.

Doran, S. and T. S. Freeman. *Tudors and Stuarts on Film: Historical Perspectives*. Basingstoke: Palgrave Macmillan, 2009.

Downing, T. 'History on Television: The Making of "Cold War", 1998'. *Historical Journal of Film, Radio and Television* 18 (3) (1998): 325–32.

Downing, T. 'History on Television: The Making of Cold War, 1998'. In *The Historical Film: History and Memory in Media*, ed. M. Landy, 294–6. New Brunswick, NJ: Rutgers University Press, 2001.

Downing, T. 'Bringing in the Past to the Small Screen'. In *History and the Media*, ed. D. Cannadine, 7–19. New York: Palgrave MacMillian, 2004.

Doyle, W. *Aristocracy and Its Enemies in the Age of Revolution*. Oxford: Oxford University Press, 2009.

Du Bois, W. E. B. *The Souls of Black Folk*. Chicago: A. C. McClurg & Co., 1903. Available online: http://docsouth.unc.edu/church/duboissouls/dubois.html (accessed 28 June 2015).

Durkheim, E. *The Elementary Forms of the Religious Life*. Oxford: Oxford University Press, 2001 [1912].

Dyer, R. *Only Entertainment*. London: Routledge, 1992.

Dyer, R. *In the Space of a Song: The Uses of Song In Film*. London: Routledge, 2012.

Eckstein, L. 'The Pitfalls of Picturing Atlantic Slavery: Steven Spielberg's Amistad vs Guy Deslaurier's The Middle Passage'. *Cultural Studies Review* 14 (1) (2008): 72–84.

Edgerton, G. R. 'Introduction: Television as Historian: A Different Kind of History Altogether'. In *Television Histories: Shaping Collective Memory in the Media Age*. ed. G. R. Edgerton and P. C. Rollins, 1–18. Lexington: University Press of Kentucky, 2001.

Edgerton, G. R. 'Mediating Thomas Jefferson: Ken Burns as Popular Historian'. In *Television Histories: Shaping Collective Memory in the Media Age*, ed. G. R. Edgerton and P. C. Rollins, 169–92. Lexington: University Press of Kentucky, 2001.

Edgerton, G. R. and P. C. Rollins. *Television Histories: Shaping Collective Memory in the Media Age*. Lexington: University of Kentucky, 2003.

Edison, T. A. 'Uncle Tom's Cabin Film Catalogue'. New York: Edison

Manufacturing Co., 1903. Available online: http://utc.iath.virginia.edu/onstage/films/ficattaeat.html (accessed 28 June 2015).

Egerton, D. R. 'Jefferson in Paris'. *American Historical Review* 100 (4) (1995): 1202–3.

Ehrenhaus, P. 'Why We Fought: Holocaust Memory in Spielberg's Saving Private Ryan'. *Critical Studies in Media Communication* 18 (2001): 321–37.

Eisenhower, D. D. 'Order of the Day'. 6 June 1944.

Eisenhower, D. D. *Crusade in Europe.* New York: Doubleday, 1997 [1948].

Eley, G. 'Finding the People's War: Film, British Collective Memory, and World War II'. *American Historical Review* 106 (3) (2001): 818–38.

Elliot, P. 'The Weak and the Wicked: Non-conscripted Masculinities in 1940s British Cinema'. In *The Home Front in Britain: Images Myths and Forgotten Experiences since 1914,* ed. M. E Andrews and J. Lomas, 170–84. Basingstoke: Palgrave Macmillan, 2014.

Emad, C. M. 'Reading Wonder Woman's Body: Mythologies of Gender and Nation', *The Journal of Popular Culture* 39 (6) (2006): 954–84.

Evans, R. *In Defence of History.* London: Granta, 1997.

Falkowska, J. and A. Wajda. *History, Politics and Nostalgia in Polish Cinema.* Oxford and New York: Berghahn, 2008.

Farmer, S. *Martyred Village: Commemorating the 1944 Massacre at Oradour-sur-Glane.* London: University of California Press, 1999.

Ferro, M. 'The Fiction Film and Historical Analysis'. In *The Historian and Film,* ed. P. Smith, 80–94. Cambridge: Cambridge University Press, 1976.

Ferro, M. 'Does a Filmic Writing of History Exist?'. *Film and History: An Interdisciplinary Journal of Film and Television* 17 (4) (1987): 81–9.

Ferro, M. *Cinema and History,* trans. N. Greene. Detroit: Wayne State University Press, 1988.

Feuer, J. 'Genre Study and Television'. In *Channels of Discourse: Television and Contemporary Criticism,* ed. R. C. Allen, 113–33. Chapel Hill, NC: University of North Carolina Press, 1987.

Feuer, J. 'The Self-Reflexive Musical and the Myth of Entertainment.' In *The Film Genre Reader II,* ed. B. K. Grant, 441–55. Austin: University of Texas Press, 1995.

Finkel, D. *Thank You for Your Service.* New York: Farrar, Straus and Giroux, 2013.

Finkelman, P. 'Glory'. *Journal of American History* 77 (3) (1990): 1108.

Finlay, R. 'The Refashioning of Martin Guerre'. *The American Historical Review* 93 (3) (1988): 553–71.

Fishbein, L. 'Roots: Docudrama and the Interpretation of History'. In *Why Docudrama? Fact-Fiction on Film and TV,* ed. R. A. Rosenthal, 271–95. Carbondale, IL: Southern Illinois University Press, 1999.

Flanzbaum, H. *The Americanization of the Holocaust.* Baltimore: Johns Hopkins University Press, 1999.

Fleming, N. C. 'Echoes of Britannia: Television History, Empire and the Critical Public Sphere'. *Contemporary British History* 24 (1) (March 2010): 1–22.

Flinn, C. *The Sound of Music.* London: Palgrave Macmillan, 2015.

Ford, E. H. and D. C. Mitchell. *Royal Portraits in Hollywood: Filming the Lives of Queens.* Lexington: University Press of Kentucky, 2009.

Ford, J. *The Fourth Bear.* London: Hodder, 2007.

Fortier, A. *Multicultural Horizons: Diversity and the Limits of the Civil Nation*. London: Routledge. 2008.

Francis, M. *The Flyer: British Culture and the Royal Air Force 1939–1945*. Oxford and New York: Oxford University Press, 2008.

Fraser, A. *Marie Antoinette: The Journey*. London, Weidenfeld & Nicolson, 2001.

Frick, J. W. *Uncle Tom's Cabin on the American Stage and Screen*. Basingstoke: Palgrave MacMillan, 2012.

Froula, A. and S. Takacs. *American Militarism on the Small Screen*. London: Routledge, 2016.

Frykenberg, R. E. 'The Coronation Durbar of 1911: Some Implications'. In *Delhi through the Ages: Selected Essays in Urban History, Culture and Society*, ed. R. E. Frykenberg, 369–90. Delhi: Oxford University Press, 1993.

Fuller, S., C. Lang Fuller and J. H. Rudes. *A Third Face: My Tale of Writing, Fighting, and Filmmaking*. New York: Knopf, 2002.

Fussell, P. *The Great War and Modern Memory*. Oxford: Oxford University Press, 2000.

Garrity, H. A. 'The French Revolution and the Seventh Art'. *The French Review* 62 (6) (May 1989): 1041–51.

Gates, H. L. 'An Unfathomable Place: A Conversation with Quentin Tarantino about Django Unchained (2012)'. *Transition* 112 (2013): 54.

Gedi, N. and Y. Elam. 'Collective Memory – What is it?'. *History and Memory* 8 (1) (1996): 30–50.

Geraghty, C. 'Masculinity'. In *National Fictions: World War Two in British Films and Television*, ed. G. Hurd, 63–7. London: British Film Institute, 1984.

Gerima, H. and P. Woolford. 'Filming Slavery'. *Transition* 64 (1994): 101.

Ghuman, N. *Resonances of the Raj. India and the English Musical Imagination, 1897–1947*. Oxford: Oxford University Press, 2014.

Gillett, P. *The British Working Class in Postwar Film*. Manchester: Manchester University Press, 2003.

Glancy, M. *When Hollywood Loved Britain: The Hollywood 'British' Film, 1939–45*. Manchester: Manchester University Press, 2013.

Gledhill, C. and G. Swanson. 'Gender and Sexuality in Second World War Films – A Feminist Approach'. In *National Fictions: World War Two in British Films and Television*, ed. G. Hurd, 56–62. London: BFI, 1984.

Gledhill, C. *Home Is Where the Heart Is: Essays on Melodrama and the Woman's Film*. London: British Film Institute, 1987.

Gledhill, C. and G. Swanson. *Nationalising Femininity: Culture, Sexuality, and British Cinema in the Second World War*. Manchester: Manchester University Press, 1996.

Glendinning, S. *Derrida: A Very Short Introduction*. New York: Oxford University Press, 2011.

Goodrum, M. *Superheroes and American Self Image: From War to Watergate*. London: Routledge, 2016.

Gordon-Reed, A. *Thomas Jefferson and Sally Hemings: An American Controversy*. Charlottesville: University of Virginia Press, 1997.

Gordon-Reed, A. 'Did Sally Hemings and Thomas Jefferson Love Each Other?'. *American Heritage* 58 (5) (2008a). Available online: http://www.americanheritage.com/content/didsallyhemingsandthomasjeffersonlove eachother? (accessed 18 June 2015).

Gordon-Reed, A. *The Hemingses of Monticello*. New York: W. W. Norton, 2008b.

Graburn, N. 'A Quest for Identity'. *Museum International* 50 (3) (1998): 13–18

Gray, A. and E. Bell. *History on Television*. London: Routledge, 2013.

Groot, J. de *Consuming History: Historians and Heritage in Contemporary Popular Culture*. New York: Routledge, 2009.

Guerrero, E. *Framing Blackness: The African American Image in Film*. Philadelphia: Temple University Press, 1993.

Hadden, S. 'How Accurate is the Film?'. *The History Teacher* 31 (3) (1998): 374–79.

Hagen, W. '*Apocalypse Now* (1979): Joseph Conrad and the Television War'. In *Hollywood as Historian: American Film in a Cultural Context*, ed. P. C. Rollins, 230–45. Lexington: University Press of Kentucky, 1983.

Hagopian, P. *The Vietnam War in American Memory: Veterans, Memorials and the Politics of Healing*. Amherst, MA: University of Massachusetts Press, 2009.

Halbwachs, M. *On Collective Memory*. London: University of Chicago Press, 1992.

Hall, C. *Cultures of Empire. A Reader*. Manchester: Manchester University Press, 2000.

Hallam, J. 'Film, Class and National Identity: Re-imagining Communities in the Age of Devolution'. In *Past and Present*, ed. J. Ashby and A. Higson, 261–73. London: Routledge, 2000.

Hammerton, J. 'The Spice of the Perfect Programme. The Weekly Magazine Film during the Silent Era'. In *Young and Innocent? The Cinema in Britain, 1896–1930*. ed. A. Higson, 162–82. Exeter: Exeter University Press, 2002.

Hanley, T. *Wonder Woman Unbound: The Curious History of the World's Most Famous Heroine*. Chicago: Chicago Review Press, 2014.

Hanna, E. 'Reality-Experiential History Documentaries: *The Trench* (BBC 2002) and Britain's Modern Memory of the First World War'. *Historical Journal of Film, Radio and Television* 27 (4) (2007): 531–47.

Hanna, E. *The Great War on the Small Screen: Representing the First World War in Contemporary Britain*. Edinburgh: Edinburgh University Press, 2009.

Hansen, N. *The Unknown Soldier: The Story of the Missing of the Great War*. London: Corgi, 2007.

Harmetz, A. *The Making of the Wizard of Oz*. Chicago: Chicago Review Press, 2013.

Harper, S. *Women in British Cinema, Mad, Bad and Dangerous to Know*. London and New York: Continuum, 2000.

Harris, M. *Five Came Back: A Story of Hollywood and the Second World War*. London: Canongate, 2015.

Harrison, G. A. *Cross-Channel Attack, U.S. Army in World War II: European Theater of Operations*. 1951; repr., New York: BDD, 1993. Available online: http://history.army.mil/html/books/007/7-4-1/index.html (accessed 21 March 2016).

Harrisson, T. 'Films and the Home Front. The Evaluation of their Effectiveness by Mass-observation'. In *Propaganda, Politics and Film, 1918–1945*, ed. N. Pronay and D. W. Spring, 234–45. London: Macmillan, 1982.

Henshall, N. 'The Myth of Absolutism'. *History Today* 42 (6) (June 1992): 40–7.

Higashi, S. 'Melodrama, Realism, and Race: WW2 Newsreels and Propaganda Films'. *Cinema Journal* 37 (3) (1998): 38–61.

Higonnet, M. R. and P. Higonnet. 'The Double Helix'. In *Behind the Lines, Gender and the Two World Wars,* ed. M. R. Higonnet, J. Jenson, S. Michel and M. Collins Weitz, 31–47. Yale: Yale University Press, 1988.

Higson, A. *Waving the Flag: Constructing a National Cinema in Britain.* Oxford: Clarendon Press, 1995.

Hiley, N. 'Audiences in the Newsreel Period'. In *'The Story of the Century': An International Newsfilm Conference,* 59–62. London: BUFVC, 1996.

Hill, A. *Reality TV: Audiences and Popular Factual Television.* London: Routledge, 2005.

Hill, J. *Sex, Class and Realism: British Cinema 1956–1963.* London: BFI, 1986.

His Royal Highness The Duke of Connaught in India 1921. Being a Collection of the Speeches Delivered by His Royal Highness. Calcutta: Superintendent Government Printing, 1921.

Hitchcock, W. I. *The Bitter Road to Freedom: A New History of the Liberation of Europe.* New York: Free Press, 2008.

Hobbes, T. *Of Man, Being the First Part of Leviathan.* Vol. XXXIV, Part 5. The Harvard Classics; New York: P. F. Collier & Son, 1909–14. Available online: http://www.bartleby.com/34/5/13.html (accessed 25 August 2015).

Hobsbawm, E. and T. Ranger (eds). *The Invention of Tradition.* Cambridge: Cambridge University Press, 1983.

Holdsworth, A. '"Television Resurrections": Television and Memory'. *Cinema Journal* 47 (3) (2008): 137–44.

Holloway, D. *9/11 and the War on Terror.* Edinburgh: Edinburgh University Press, 2008.

Holtorf, C. *Archaeology is a Brand! The Meaning of Archaeology in Contemporary Popular Culture.* Oxford: Archaeopress, 2006.

Horne, G. 'Glory'. *American Historical Review* 95 (4) (1990): 1141–3.

Hoskins, A. 'New Memory: Mediating History', *Historical Journal of Film, Radio and Television* 21 (4) (2001): 333–46.

Howarth, D. *Dawn of D-Day: These Men Were There, 6 June 1944.* 1959; repr., Mechanicsburg, PA: Stackpole Books, 2001.

Howell, C. '"Tricky" Connotations: Wonder Woman as DC's Brand Disruptor'. *Cinema Journal* 55 (1) (2015): 141–9.

Howells, R. and R. Matson. *Using Visual Evidence.* Berkshire: Open University Press, 2009.

Howlett, P. and Great Britain Central Statistical Office. *Fighting with Figures.* London: H.M.S.O., 1995.

Hughes, W. 'The Evaluation of Film as Evidence'. In *The Historian and Film,* ed. P. Smith, 65–74. Cambridge: Cambridge University Press, 1976.

Hughes-Warrington, M. *History Goes to the Movies: Studying History on Film.* London: Routledge, 2006.

Hunt, T. 'How does Television Enhance History?'. In *History and the Media,* ed. D. Cannadine, 88–102. New York: Palgrave MacMillian, 2004.

Hunt, T. 'Reality, Identity and Empathy: The Changing Face of Social History Television', *Journal of Social History* 39 (3) (Spring 2006): 843–58.

Hutton, P., 'Sigmund Freud and Maurice Halbwachs: The Problem of Method in Historical Psychology'. *The History Teacher* 27 (2) (1994): 145–58.

Huyssen, A. *Twilight Memories: Marking Time in a Culture of Amnesia.* London: Routledge, 1995.

Huyssen, A. *Present Pasts: Urban Palimpsests and the Politics of Memory*. Stanford, CA: Stanford University Press, 2003.

Hynes, S. *A War Imagined: The First World War and English Culture*. London: Pimlico, 1992.

Ilott, S. *New Postcolonial British Genres: Shifting the Boundaries*. London: Palgrave Macmillan, 2015.

Inge, M. T. 'Walt Disney's *Song of the South* and the Politics of Animation'. *Journal of American Culture* 35 (3) (2012): 219–30.

Inglis, K. 'The Homecoming: The War Memorial Movement in Cambridge, England'. *Journal of Contemporary History* 27 (4) (1992a): 583–606.

Inglis, K. 'War Memorials: Ten Questions for Historians'. *Guerres Mondiales et Conflits Contemporains* 42 (167) (1992b): 5–21.

Irwin-Zarecka, I. *Frames of Remembrance: The Dynamics of Collective Memory*. New Brunswick: Transaction Publishers, 1994.

Isaacs, J. 'Television History'. *History Today* 58 (9) (2008): 17.

Jackson, A. *The Colonial Film Archive and the British Empire at War, 1939–1945*. London: King's College, 2010. Available online: https://britishempireatwardotorg.files.wordpress.com/2012/09/the-empire-at-war-on-film1.pdf (accessed 4 May 2016).

Jackson, R. 'The Celluloid War before The Birth: Race and History in Early American Film'. In *American Cinema and the Southern Imaginary*, ed. D. E. Barker and K. McKee, 27–51. Athens, GA: University of Georgia Press, 2011.

James, R. 'Popular Film-going in Britain in the Early 1930s'. *Journal of Contemporary History* 46 (2) (2011): 271–87.

Jarvie, I. 'The Burma Campaign on Film'. *British Journal of Film, Radio and Television* 8 (2) (1988): 55–73.

Jeffrey, J. R. '*Amistad* (1997): Steven Spielberg's "True Story"'. *Historical Journal of Film, Radio and Television* 21 (1) (2001): 77–96.

Jenkins, K. *Re-thinking History*. London: Routledge, 2003.

Johnson, C. *Blowback: The Costs and Consequences of American Empire*. New York: Holt Paperbacks, 2001.

Johnson, H. *Sleepwalking Through History: America in the Reagan Years*. New York: Anchor Books, 1992.

Jones, S. G. *The British Labour Movement and Film, 1918–1939*. London: Routledge & Kegan Paul, 1987.

Jordanova, L. *History in Practice*. London: Bloomsbury Academic, 2010.

Jouanna, A. *The Saint Bartholomew's Day Massacre: The Mysteries of a Crime of State*, trans. J. Bergin. Manchester: Manchester University Press, 2013.

Kansteiner, W. 'Finding Meaning in Memory: A Methodological Critique of Collective Memory Studies'. *History and Theory* 4 (2) (2002): 179–97.

Kaplan, R L. 'Spider-Man in Love: A Psychoanalytic Interpretation'. *The Journal of Popular Culture* 44 (2) (2011): 291–313.

Kaufman, G. *Meet Me in St. Louis*. London: BFI, 1994.

Kaufman, G. 'Royal Flush'. *New Statesman* 11 (524) (2 October 1998): 36–7.

Kaul, C. *Reporting the Raj: The British Press and India, c. 1888–1922*. Manchester: Manchester University Press, 2003.

Kaul, C. *Media and the British Empire*. London: Palgrave Macmillan, 2006.

Kaul, C. *Communications, Media and the Imperial Experience. Britain and India in the Twentieth Century*. London: Palgrave Macmillan, 2014.

Kavanagh, G. 'Museum as Memorial: The Origins of the Imperial War Museum'. *Journal of Contemporary History* 23 (1988): 77–97.

Kellner, D. 'The Horrors of Slavery and Modes of Representation in *Amistad* and *12 Years a Slave*', *Jump Cut: A Review of Contemporary Media* 56 (2014). Available online: http://ejumpcut.org/currentissue/Kellner12YearsSlave/text.html (accessed 10 June 2015).

Kelly, A. *Cinema and the Great War*. London: Routledge, 1997.

Kershaw, A. *The Bedford Boys: One American Town's Ultimate D-Day Sacrifice*. Cambridge, MA: Da Capo Press, 2003.

Keser, R. 'The Greatest Film About Race Ever Filmed in Hollywood: Richard Fleischer's Mandingo'. *Bright Lights Film Journal*, 30 July 2014. Available online: http://brightlightsfilm.com/greatestfilmraceeverfilmedhollywoodrichard fleischersmandingo (accessed 28 June 2015).

King, A. *Memorials of the Great War in Britain: The Symbolism and Politics of Remembrance*. Oxford: Berg, 1998.

Knapp, R. *The American Musical and the Formation of American Identity*. Princeton: Princeton University Press, 2006.

Koppes, C. R. *Hollywood Goes to War: How Politics, Profits and Propaganda Shaped World War II Movies*. London: I.B. Tauris, 1988.

Korte, B. and C. Sternberg. *Bidding for the Mainstream: Black and Asian British Film since the 1990s*. Amsterdam: Rodopi, 2004.

Kozloff, S. R. 'Narrative Theory and Television'. In *Channels of Discourse: Television and Contemporary Criticism*, ed. R. C. Allen, 42–73. Chapel Hill, NC: University of North Carolina Press, 1987.

Kramer, L. *Musical Meaning: Towards A Critical History*. Berkeley: University of California Press, 2002.

Kuhn, A. *An Everyday Magic, Cinema and Cultural Memory*. London and New York: I.B. Tauris, 2002.

Kuhn, A. *'Living within the Frame'*. An Inaugural Lecture delivered at the University of Lancaster. Lancaster: University of Lancaster Pamphlet, 2003.

Laclos, P. C. de. *Les Liaison dangereuses* (1782), trans. H. Constantine. London: Penguin Classics, 2007.

Lant, A. *Blackout: Reinventing Women for Wartime British Cinema*. Princeton: Princeton University Press, 1991.

Lant, A. 'Britain and the End of Empire'. In *The Oxford History of World Cinema*, ed. G. Nowell-Smith, 361–74. Oxford: Oxford University Press, 1996.

Laqueur, T. 'Memory and Naming in the Great War', in *Commemorations: The Politics of National Identity*, ed. J. R. Gillis, 150–67. Princeton: Princeton University Press, 1993.

Latham, B. *Elizabeth I in Film and Television. A Study of Major Portrayals*. Jefferson: McFarland, 2011.

Lee, S. and S. Ditko et al. *Amazing Fantasy* #15. Marvel Comics: New York, 1962.

Leff, L. J. 'A Test of American Film Censorship: Who's Afraid of Virginia Woolf? (1966)'. In *Hollywood as Historian: American Film in a Cultural Context*, ed. P. C. Rollins, 211–29. Lexington: University Press of Kentucky, 1983.

Leff, L. J. '*Gone with the Wind* and Hollywood's Racial Politics'. *Atlantic Monthly* 284 (6) (1999): 109.

Lemay, K. C. 'Gratitude, Trauma, and Repression: D-Day in French Memory'.

In *D-Day in History and Memory: The Normandy Landings in International Remembrance and Commemoration,* ed. M. R. Dolski, S. Edwards and J. Buckley, 159–88. Denton: University of North Texas Press, 2014.

Leonard, M. 'Britain™: Renewing our identity'. *Demos,* 1 May 1997. Available online: http://www.demos.co.uk/files/britaintm.pdf (accessed 29 April 2015).

Lepore, J. *The Secret History of Wonder Woman.* London: Scribe Publications, 2015.

Lewis, A. *Omaha Beach: A Flawed Victory.* Chapel Hill, NC: University of North Carolina Press, 2001.

Loe, L., A. Boyle, H. Webb, and D. Score. *'Given to the Ground': A Viking Massive Grave on Ridgeway Hill, Weymouth.* Dorset: Dorset National History and Archaeology Society, 2014.

Longino Farrell, M. 'Writing Letters, Telling Tales, Making History: Vatel's Death Told and Retold'. *The French Review* 66 (2) (1992): 229–42.

Longworth, P. *The Unending Vigil: A History of the Commonwealth War Graves Commission, 1916–1967.* London: Constable, 1967.

Loomis, S. *Paris in the Terror.* Philadelphia, Lippincott, 1964.

Low, R. *History of British Film,* vols 4–6. London: Routledge, 1971–1985.

Lowenthal, D. *The Heritage Crusade and the Spoils of History.* Cambridge: Cambridge University Press, 1989.

MacKenzie, J. *Propaganda and Empire. The Manipulation of British Public Opinion, 1880–1960.* Manchester: Manchester University Press, 1984.

Majumdar, N. 'Film Fragments, Documentary History, and Colonial Indian Cinema'. *Canadian Journal of Film Studies* 16 (1) (2007): 63–79.

Manvell, R. *Films and the Second World War.* London: Dent, 1974.

Mapp, E. *Blacks in American Films: Today and Yesterday.* Metuchen, NJ: Scarecrow Press, 1972.

Marcus, L. S., J. Mueller and M. B. Rose, eds. *Elizabeth I. Collected Works.* Chicago: University of Chicago Press, 2000.

Maroto, M. C. *Film, Memory and the Legacy of the Spanish Civil War.* London: Palgrave Macmillan, 2011.

Marwick, A. *Class: Image and Reality,* 2nd edn. Basingstoke: Macmillan, 1990.

Mason, B. J. 'The New Films: Culture or Con Game? Rash of 'Black' Movies Draws both Condemnation and Praise'. *Ebony,* December 1972, 60–6.

Mason, L. and T. Rizzo. *The French Revolution: A Document Collection.* Boston: Houghton-Mifflin, 1999.

May, G. *Bending Toward Justice: The Voting Rights Act and the Transformation of American Democracy.* New York: Basic Books, 2013.

May, L. *The Big Tomorrow: Hollywood and the Politics of the American Way.* Chicago: University of Chicago Press, 2002.

McClelland, J. L. 'Connectionist Models of Memory'. In *The Oxford Handbook of Memory,* ed. E. Tulving and F. I. M. Craik, 583–96. New York: Oxford University Press, 2000.

McKeachie, W. J. *McKeachie's Teaching Tips: Strategies, Research, and Theory for College and University Teachers,* 11th edn. New York: Houghton Mifflin Company, 2002.

McKernan, L. 'Newsreels in the Silent Era'. In *'The Story of the Century': An International Newsfilm Conference,* 17–22. London: BUFVC, 1996.

McKernan, L. 'Putting the World before You: The Charles Urban Story". In

Young and Innocent? The Cinema in Britain, 1896–1930, ed. A. Higson, 65–76. Exeter University Press, 2002a.

McKernan, L. *Yesterday's News: British Cinema Newsreel Reader.* London: BUFVC, 2002b.

McKernan, L. "The Modern Elixir of Life': Kinemacolor, Royalty and the Delhi Durbar'. *Film History: An International Journal* 21 (2) (2009): 122–36.

McKernan, L. *Charles Urban. Pioneering the Non-fiction Film in Britain and America, 1897–1925.* Exeter: University Press, 2014.

McLoone, M. 'Internal Decolonisation? British Cinema in the Celtic Fringe'. In *The British Cinema Book*, 2nd edn, ed. R. Murphy, 184–90. London: British Film Institute, 2001.

McManus, J. C. *The Dead, or The Americans at D-Day: The American Experience at the Normandy Invasion.* New York: Forge, 2004.

McManus, J. C. *The Dead and Those About to Die: D-Day; The Big Red One at Omaha Beach.* New York: New American Library, 2014.

McNeil, W. H. 'Mythistory, or Truth, Myth and History and Historians'. *American Historical Review* 91 (1) (1986): 1–10.

Mears, N. 'Love-making and Diplomacy: Elizabeth I and the Anjou Marriage Negotiations, c. 1578–1582'. *History* 86 (284) (2001): 442–66.

Meroney, J. and S. Coons. 'The Man Who Brought War to Hollywood'. theAtlantic.com, 27 August 2010. Available online: http://www.theatlantic.com/culture/archive/2010/08/the-man-who-brought-war-to-hollywood/62070/1/# (accessed 18 January 2011).

Miller, R. *Nothing Less Than Victory: The Oral History of D-Day.* New York: William Morrow, 1993.

Milne, E. *Letters, Postcards, Email. Technologies of Presence.* London: Routledge, 2010.

Mitford, N. *The Sun King.* London: Vintage Classics, 2011 [1966].

Monaco, J. *How to Read a Film. The Art, Technology, Language, History and Theory of Film and Media.* New York'. Oxford: Oxford University Press, 2009 [1981].

Monaghan, D. 'Margaret Thatcher, Alan Bleasdale, and the Struggle for Working-Class Identity'. *Journal of Popular Film and Television* 29 (1) (2001): 1–11.

Monson, I. 'Doubleness and Jazz Improvisation: Irony, Parody and Ethnomusicology'. *Critical Inquiry* 20 (2) (1994): 283–313.

Monteith, S. 'Sally Hemings in Visual Culture: A Radical Act of the Imagination?'. *Slavery & Abolition* 29 (2) (2008): 233–46.

Morris, W. 'At Henry Parkes Motel'. *Cultural Studies* 2 (1998): 1–47.

Murphy, R. *Realism and Tinsel: Cinema and Society in Britain, 1939–48.* London and New York: Routledge, 1989.

Naremore, J. *The Films of Vincente Minnelli.* Cambridge: Cambridge University Press, 1993.

Navickas, K. 'What Happened to Class? New Histories of Labour and Collective Action in Britain'. *Social History* 36 (2011): 192–204.

Neisser, U. 'Snapshots or Benchmarks'. In *Memory Observed: Remembering in Natural Contexts*, ed. U. Neisser, 43–9. San Francisco: W. H. Freeman and Co., 1982.

Neisser, U. and L. K. Libby. 'Remembering Life Experiences', in *The Oxford*

Handbook of Memory, ed. E. Tulving, 315–32. Oxford: Oxford University Press, 2000.

Nietzsche, F. *The Will to Power*, ed. W. Kaufmann. London: Weidenfeld and Nicolson, 1967.

Nora, P. 'General Introduction: Between Memory and History'. In *Realms of Memory: Rethinking the French Past, Volume I*, ed. P. Nora and L. Krtizman, 1–20. New York: Columbia University Press, New York, 1996.

Northup, S. *Twelve Years a Slave: Narrative of Solomon Northup, a Citizen of New-York, Kidnapped in Washington City in 1841 and Rescued in 1853, from a Cotton Plantation near the Red River in Louisiana.* Auburn, NY: Derby and Miller, 1853. Available online: http://docsouth.unc.edu/fpn/northup/northup. html (accessed 28 June 2015).

Novick, P. *That Noble Dream: The "Objectivity Question" and the American Historical Profession.* New York: Cambridge University Press, 1988.

Novick, P. *The Holocaust in American Life.* New York: Houghton Mifflin, 1999.

Nowell-Smith, G. 'On History and the Cinema'. *Screen* 3 (2) (1990): 160–71.

O'Connor, J. 'Special Report. The Moving-Image Media in the History Classroom'. *Film and History: An Interdisciplinary Journal of Film and Television* 16 (3) (1986): 49–54.

Ohmann, R. *Selling Culture: Magazines, Markets, and Class at the Turn of the Century.* New York: Verso, 1996.

Osterberg, B. *Colonial America on Film and Television.* London: McFarland, 2001.

Owen, A. S. 'Memory, War and American Identity: Saving Private Ryan as Cinematic Jeremiad'. *Critical Studies in Media Communication* 19 (2002): 259–65.

Owen, W. 'Dulce et Decorum Est' (1920)

Paris, M. *From the Wright Brothers to Top Gun.* Manchester: Manchester University Press, 1995.

Paris, M. *The First World War and Popular Cinema.* Edinburgh: Edinburgh University Press, 1999.

Paris, M. 'Reconstructing D-Day: 6 June 1944 and British Documentary Films'. In *The Normandy Campaign 1944: Sixty Years On*, ed. J. Buckley, 207–9. New York: Routledge, 2006.

Paterson, C., A. Parsons, R. Newman, N. Johnson and C. Howard Davis. *Shadows in the Sand: Excavation of a Viking-age cemetery at Cumwhitton, Cumbria.* Lancaster: Oxford Archaeology North, 2014.

Peters, I. 'What's Happening: "Mandingo" ... Sick, Brutal!'. *Baltimore Afro-American*, 31 May 1975.

Plain, G. *John Mills and British Cinema: Masculinity, Identity and Nation.* Edinburgh: Edinburgh University Press, 2006.

Ponting, C. *1940: Myth and Reality.* Chicago: Ivan R. Dee. 1993.

Porter, B. *The Absent-Minded Imperialists. Empire, Society and Culture in Britain.* Oxford: Oxford University Press, 2004.

Porter, L. *Coltrane: His Life and Music.* Ann Arbor: University of Michigan Press, 1998.

Prados, E. F. U.S. Navy Memorial Foundation, eds. *Neptunus Rex: Naval Stories of the Normandy Invasion, June 6, 1944.* Novato, CA: Presidio Press, 1998.

Prince, S. 'A Brief History of Film Violence'. In *Violence in Film and Television*, ed. J. D. Torr, 21–8. San Diego, CA: Greenhaven Press, Inc., 2002.

Pronay, N. 'British Newsreels in the 1930s, pt. 1: Audience and Producers'. *History* 56 (3) (1971): 411–18.

Pronay, N. 'The Newsreels: The Illusion of Actuality'. In *The Historian and Film*, ed. P. Smith, 95–120. Cambridge: Cambridge University Press, 1976.

Pronay, N. 'The Newsmedia at War'. In *Propaganda, Politics and Film, 1918–1945*, ed. N. Pronay and D. W. Spring, 173–208. London: Macmillan, 1982.

Pronay, N. 'The Moving Picture and Historical Research: The State of the Art'. *Journal of Contemporary History* 18 (3) (1983): 365–95.

Railton, S. 'Uncle Tom's Cabin on Film 1: The Silent Era' (2007). Available online: http://utc.iath.virginia.edu/interpret/exhibits/utconfilm/utconfilm.html (28 June 2015)

Reeves, N. 'Official British War Propaganda'. In *The First World War and Popular Cinema*, ed. M. Paris, 27–50. Edinburgh: Edinburgh University Press, 1999.

Rehling, N. '"It's About Belonging": Masculinity, Collectivity, and Community in British Hooligan in Films'. *Journal of Popular Film and Television* 39 (4) (2011): 162–73.

Reid, M. A. 'Haile Gerima: "Sacred Shield of Culture"'. In *Contemporary American Independent Film: From the Margins to the Mainstream*, ed. C. Holmlund and J. Wyatt, 141–54. Athens, GA: University of Georgia Press, 2011.

Renan, E. 'What is a Nation?', 11 March 1882. Available online: http://ucparis.fr/files/9313/6549/9943/What_is_a_Nation.pdf (accessed 30 April 2016).

Richards, J. 'Film and Television, the Moving Image'. In *History Beyond the Text: A Student's Guide to Approaching Alternative Sources*, ed. S. Barber and C. M. Peniston-Bird, 72–88. London: Routledge, 2009.

Richards, J. 'Signposts: History Films', *History Today* 61 (10) (2011)

Richards, J. *Films and British National Identity from Dickens to Dad's Army*. Manchester: Manchester University Press, 1997.

Richards, J. and A. Aldgate. *Best of British: Cinema and Society from 1930 to the Present*. London: I.B. Tauris, 2002.

Richards, J. and D. Hadley. 'Viking Torksey: Inside the Great Army's Winter Camp'. *Current Archaeology* 281 (2013): 12–19.

Richards, J., D. Sheridan and Mass-Observation. *Mass-Observation at the Movies (Cinema and Society)*. London and New York: Routledge & Kegan Paul, 1987.

Richardson, N. 'The Gospel According to Spider-Man'. *The Journal of Popular Culture* 37 (4) (2004): 694–703.

Robb, L. *Men at Work: The Working Man in British Culture, 1939–1945*. London: Palgrave Macmillan, 2015.

Robinson, C. J. 'In the Year 1915: D. W. Griffith and the Whitening of America'. *Social Identities: Journal for the Study of Race, Nation and Culture* 3 (2) (1997): 161–92.

Rocchio, V. *Reel Racism: Confronting Hollywood's Construction of Afro-American Culture*. Boulder, CO: Westview Press, 2000.

Roeder, Jr., G. H. *The Censored War: American Visual Experience During World War Two*. New Haven, CT: Yale University Press, 1993.

Rogin, M. '"The Sword Became a Flashing Vision": D. W. Griffith's The Birth of a Nation'. *Representations* 9 (1985): 150–95.

Rollins, P. C. and J. E. O'Connor. *Why We Fought: America's Wars in Film and History*. Lexington: University Press of Kentucky, 2008.

Roosevelt, F. D. 'D-Day Prayer', 6 June 1944. Available online: http://www. historyplace.com/speeches/fdr-prayer.htm (accessed 19 November, 2009).

Rose, S. O. *Which People's War*. Oxford, Oxford University Press, 2003.

Rose, S. O. 'Temperate Heroes: Concepts of Masculinity in Second World War Britain'. In *Masculinities in Politics and War: Gendering Modern History*, ed. S. Dudink, K. Hagemann and J. Tosh, 177–98. Gender in History; Manchester: Manchester University Press, 2004.

Rosen, G. '"Amistad" and the Abuse of History'. *Commentary* 105 (2) (1998): 46–51.

Rosenberg, E. *A Date Which Will Live: Pearl Harbor in American Memory*. London: Duke University Press, 2003.

Rosenheim, S. 'Interrotroning History: Errol Morris and the Documentary of the Future'. In *The Historical Film: History and Memory in Media*, ed. M. Landy, 316–29. New Brunswick, NJ: Rutgers University Press, 2001.

Rosenstone, R. A 'History in Images/History in Words: Reflections on the Possibility of Really Putting History onto Film'. *The American Historical Review* 93 (1988): 1173–85.

Rosenstone, R. A. *Visions of the Past: The Challenge of Film to Our Idea of History*. Cambridge: Harvard University Press, 1995.

Rosenstone, R. A. 'The Historical Film: Looking at the Past in a Postliterate Age'. In *The Historical Film: History and Memory in Media*, ed. M. Landy, 50–66. New Brunswick, NJ: Rutgers University Press, 2001.

Rosenstone, R. A. *History on Film, Film on History*, 2nd edn. New York: Pearson, 2012.

Rousso, H. *The Vichy Syndrome: History and Memory in France since 1944*, trans. A. Goldhammer. Cambridge: Harvard University Press, 1996.

Rowson, S. 'A Statistical Survey of the Cinema Industry in Great Britain in 1934'. *Journal of the Royal Statistical Society* 99 (2) (1936): 67–129.

Roy, S. 'Moving Pictures: The Post-Colonial State and Visual Representation of India'. *Contributions to Indian Sociology* 36 (1–2) (2002): 233–63.

Rushdie, S. *The Wizard of Oz*. London: Palgrave Macmillan, 2012.

Rushton, R. *The Politics of Hollywood Cinema*. London: Palgrave Macmillan, 2013.

Ryan, C. *The Longest Day*. New York: Simon & Schuster, 1959.

Samuel, R. *Theatres of Memory: Past and Present in Contemporary Culture*. London: Verso, 2012.

Sandbrook, D. *Never Had it So Good: A History of Britain from Suez to the Beatles*. London: Abacus, 2010.

Schedule of Reserved Occupations (Provisional). London: His Majesty's Stationery Office, 1939.

Schickel, R. 'Television: Viewpoint: Middlebrow Mandingo'. *Time*, 24 January 1977.

Schickel, R. 'Belated Victory: The Big Red One'. *Time*, 21 July 1980.

Schütz, A. 'Making Music Together: A Study in Social Relationship'. *Social Research* 18 (1) (1951): 76–97.

Scott, E. C. 'The Horrors of Remembrance: The Altered Visual Aesthetic of Horror in Jonathan Demme's Beloved'. *Genders* 40 (2004). Available online:

http://www.iiav.nl/ezines/web/GendersPresenting/2005/No41/genders/g40_scott.
html (accessed 10 June 2015)

Seiter, E. 'Semiotics and Television'. In *Channels of Discourse: Television and Contemporary Criticism*, ed. R. C. Allen, 17–41. Chapel Hill, NC: University of North Carolina Press, 1987.

Shapiro, S. 'Roland Joffé's Vatel: Refashioning the History of the Ancien Régime'. In *Studies in Early Modern France*, ed. A. L. Birberick and R. Ganim, 77–88, vol. 10. Rockwood Press, Charlottesville, 2005.

Sherman, D. *The Construction of Memory in Interwar France*. London: University of Chicago Press, 1999.

Sills-Jones, D. 'Before the History Boom: Revisiting UK Television History Documentary Production'. *Critical Studies in Television* 1 (1) (2016): 78–95.

Sklar, R. *Movie-Made America: A Cultural History of American Movies, Revised and Updated*. New York: Vintage, 1994.

Slocum, J. D. 'Cinema and the Civilizing Process: Rethinking Violence in the World War II Combat Film'. *Cinema Journal* 44 (Spring 2005): 35–63.

Smith, K. A. 'Espionage in British Popular Culture of the 20th Century: Gender, Moral Ambiguity and the Inextricability of Fact and Fiction'. Ph.D. diss., Lancaster University, Lancaster, 2016.

Smith, M. *Britain and 1940: History, Myth and Popular Memory*. London: Routledge, 2000.

Smith P. *The Historian and Film*. Cambridge: Cambridge University Press, 1976.

Smith, V. 'Black Life in the Balance: *12 Years a Slave*'. *American Literary History* 26 (2) (2014): 362–6.

Snead, J. 'White Screens, Black Images: Hollywood from the Dark Side', ed. C. MacCabe and C. West. New York: Routledge, 1994.

'Sol [Standards of Learning] Education Packet'. National D-Day Memorial Foundation, 2002.

Sorlin, P. *The Film in History: Restaging the Past*. Totowa, NJ: Barnes & Noble Books, 1980.

Sperb, J. 'Reassuring Convergence: Online Fandom, Race, and Disney's Notorious Song of the South'. *Cinema Journal* 49 (4) (2010): 25–45.

Spicer, A. *Typical Men: The Representation of Masculinity in Popular British Cinema*. London and New York: I.B. Tauris, 2003.

Spiller, R. J. 'War in the Dark'. *American Heritage* (February/March 1999). Available online: http://www.americanheritage.com/articles/magazine/ah/1999/1/1999_1_41.shtml (accessed 2 September 2009).

Stam, R. *Film Theory: An Introduction*. Malden, MA: Wiley-Blackwell, 2000.

Stamp, G. *The Memorial to the Missing of the Somme*. London: Profile Books, 2016.

Starkey, D. *Henry: Virtuous Prince*. London: Harper Press, 2008.

Stern, J. 'What's Wrong with HBO's Dramatization of John Adams's Story'. *History News Network*, 27 October 2008. Available online: http://historynewsnetwork.org/article/56155 (accessed 19 April 2016).

Stevens, J. D. 'The Black Reaction to Gone with the Wind'. *Journal of Popular Film* 2 (4) (1973): 366–72.

Stokes, M. D. W. *Griffith's The Birth of a Nation: A History of 'the Most Controversial Motion Picture of all Time'*. New York: Oxford University Press, 2007.

Stokes, M. *American History through Hollywood Film: From the Revolution to the 1960s*. London: Bloomsbury Academic, 2013.

Street, S. *British National Cinema*, 2nd edn. London: Routledge, 2008.

Sturken, M. *Tangled Memories: The Vietnam War, The AIDS Epidemic, and the Politics of Remembering*. London: University of California Press, 1997.

Suid, L. *Guts & Glory: The Making of the American Military Image in Film*, rev. edn. Lexington: University Press of Kentucky, 2002.

Summerfield, P. *Women Workers in the Second World War: Production and Patriarchy in Conflict*. London and New York: Routledge, 1989.

Sutherland, N. M., ed. 'Catherine de Medici: The Legend of the Wicked Italian Queen'. In *Princes, Politics and Religion, 1547–1589*, ed. N. M. Sutherland, 237–50. London: Hambledon, 1984.

Swann, P. *The British Documentary Film Movement*. Cambridge: Cambridge University Press, 1989.

Tancock, L., trans. *Selected Letters*. London: Penguin, 1982.

Taylor, J. *The Generalissimo*. Cambridge, MA: Harvard University Press, 2009.

Taylor, P. 'Introduction' in *Britain and the Cinema in the Second World War*, ed. S. Taylor. Basingstoke: Macmillan, 1988.

Taylor, P. *Britain and the Cinema in the Second World War*. Basingstoke: Macmillan, 1988.

Terkel, S. *'The Good War': An Oral History of World War II*. New York: New Press, 1984.

Thompson, A. *Britain's Experience of Empire in the Twentieth Century*. Oxford: Oxford University Press, 2011.

Thompson, J. 'After the Fall: Class and Political Language in Britain 1780–1900'. *Historical Research* 39 (1996): 785–806.

Tillyard, S. K. *Aristocrats: Caroline, Emily, Louisa and Sarah Lennox, 1740–1832*. London: Chatto & Windus, 1994.

Todman, D. *The Great War, Myth and Memory*. London: Hambledon and Hambledon, 2005.

Tolson, M. '*Gone with the Wind* is More Dangerous than Birth of a Nation'. In *American Movie Critics: An Anthology from the Silents until Now*, ed. P. Lopate 140–2. New York: Library of America, 2008.

Toplin, R. B. 'The Filmmaker as Historian'. *The American Historical Review* 93 (1988): 1210–27.

Toplin, R. B. *Reel History: In Defense of Hollywood*. Lawrence: University Press of Kansas, 2002.

Toplin, R. B. 'Hollywood's D-Day from the Perspective of the 1960s and 1990s: *The Longest Day* and *Saving Private Ryan*'. In *Why We Fought: America's Wars in Film and History*, ed. P. C. Rollins and J. E. O'Connor, 303–13. Lexington: University Press of Kentucky, 2008.

Tosh, J. 'Hegemonic Masculinity and the History of Gender'. In *Masculinities in Politics and War: Gendering Modern History*, ed. S. Dudink, K. Hagemann and J. Tosh, 41–60. Gender and History; Manchester: Manchester University Press, 2004.

Tracy, J. F. 'Revisiting a Polysemic Text: The African American Press's Reception of *Gone with the Wind*'. *Mass Communication Society* 4 (4) (2001): 419–36.

Treacey, M. *Reframing the Past: History, Film and Television*. London: Routledge, 2016.

Trevithick, A. 'Some Structural and Sequential Aspects of the British Imperial Assemblages at Delhi, 1877–1911'. *Modern Asian Studies* (1990): 561–78.

Turner, F. J. 'The Significance of the Frontier in American History'. In *The Frontier of American History*. New York: Henry Holt and Co., 1921.

Tusa, J. 'A Deep and Continuing Use of History'. In *History and the Media*, ed. D. Cannadine, 123–40. New York: Palgrave MacMillian, 2004.

UK Film Council. 'Stories we tell ourselves' (2009). Available online: http://www. bfi.org.uk/sites/bfi.org.uk/files/downloads/bfi-opening-our-eyes-stories-we-tell-ourselves-report-2006.pdf (accessed 30 April 2015).

Urwand, B. *The Collaboration: Hollywood's Pact with Hitler*. London: The Belknap Press of Harvard University Press, 2013.

Vera, H. and A. M. Gordon. *Screen Saviors: Hollywood Fictions of Whiteness*. New York: Roman and Littlefield, 2003.

Vickery, A. 'Golden Age to Separate Spheres? A Review of the Categories and Chronology of English Women's History'. *The Historical Journal* 36 (2) (1993): 383–414.

Ward, P. *Britishness Since 1870*. London: Routledge, 2004.

Wardi, A. J. 'Freak Shows, Spectacles, and Carnivals: Reading Jonathan Demme's Beloved'. *African American* Review 39 (4) (2005): 513–26.

Warren-Findley, J. 'History in New Worlds: Surveys and Results in the United States and Australia'. *American Studies International* XLII (2/3) (2004).

Weber, C. *Queen of Fashion: What Marie-Antoinette Wore to the Revolution*. New York: Henry Holt, 2006.

Weber, S. 'War, Terrorism, and Spectacle, or: On Towers and Caves'. *Grey Room* 7 (2002): 14–23.

Weight, R. *Patriots: National Identity in Britain 1940–2000*. Basingstoke: Macmillan, 2002.

Weinman, J. J. 'Zip-a-dee-doo-don't mention it'. *Maclean's*, 14 May 2007, 63–4.

Weinstein, P. B. 'Movies as the Gateway to History: The History and Film Project'. *The History Teacher* 35 (2001): 27–48.

Welch, D. *Propaganda and the German Cinema, 1933–1945*. London: I.B. Tauris, 2001.

Wheatley, H. 'Beautiful Images in Spectacular Clarity: Spectacular Television, Landscape Programming and the Question of (Tele)visual Pleasure'. *Screen* 52 (2) (Summer 2011): 233–48.

White, H. *Metahistory: The Historical Imagination in Nineteenth Century Europe*. Baltimore: Johns Hopkins University Press, 1975.

White, H. 'Historiography and Historiophoty'. *The American Historical Review* 93 (5) (1988): 1193–9.

White, J. *The Worst Street in North London: Campbell Bank, Islington Between the Wars*. London: Routledge and Kegan Paul, 1986.

Whitlock, F. *The Fighting First: The Untold Story of the Big Red One on D-Day*. Boulder, CO: Westview Press, 2004.

Wieviorka, O. *Normandy: The Landings to the Liberation of Paris*, trans. M. B. DeBevoise. Cambridge: Harvard University Press, 2008.

Williams, D. *Media, Memory and the First World War*. Montreal: McGill University Press, 2009.

Williams, M. 'Brief Encounter'. In *Fifty Key British Films*, ed. S. Barrow and J. White, 50–60. London: Routledge, 2008.

Winter, J. *Sites of Memory, Sites of Mourning: The Great War in European Cultural History*. Cambridge: Cambridge University Press, 1995.

Winter, J. 'Film and the Matrix of Memory'. *The American Historical Review* 106 (2001): 863.

Winter, J. *Remembering War: The Great War between Memory and History in the Twentieth Century*. London: Yale University Press, 2006.

Wollen, P. *Singin' in the Rain*. London: BFI, 1992.

Wood, G. S. *The Purpose of the Past: Reflections on the Uses of History*. New York: Penguin, 2008.

Wood, N. *Vectors of Memory: Legacies of Trauma in Postwar Europe*. Oxford: Berg, 1999.

Woods, P. '"Business as Usual"?: British Newsreel Coverage of Indian Independence and Partition, 1947–1948'. In *Media and the British Empire*, ed. C. Kaul, 145–59. London: Palgrave Macmillan, 2006.

Woods, P. 'Filming the Retreat from Burma, 1942: British Newsreel Coverage'. *Historical Journal of Film, Radio and Television* 35 (3) (2015): 438–53.

Young, J., ed. *The Art of Memory: Holocaust Memorials in History*. New York: Prestel, 1994.

Zemon Davis, N. *The Return of Martin Guerre*. Cambridge: Harvard University Press, 1983.

Zemon Davis, N. 'On the Lame'. *The American Historical Review* 93 (3) (1988a).

Zemon Davis, N. 'Slaves on Screen; "*Amistad*: Controversy about the Film and Its Use"'. *The History Teacher* 31 (3) (1988b): 369–402.

Zemon Davis, N. *Slaves on Screen: Film and Historical Vision*. Cambridge: Harvard University Press, 2000.

Newspaper and magazine articles

'BBC Documentary, A History of Syria with Dan Snow was "biased and inaccurate" say critics'. *Huffington Post*, 17 March 2013. Available online: http://www.huffingtonpost.co.uk/2013/03/17/bbc-documentary-history-snow_n_2896575.html (accessed on 28 April 2016).

'BBC Rapped Over Dan Snow Documentary'. BBC, 7 November 2013. Available online: http://www.bbc.co.uk/news/entertainment-arts-24849738 (accessed on 28 April 2016).

'BBC Two announces ambitious new living history series – The Slum'. BBC, 22 January 2016. Available online: http://www.bbc.co.uk/mediacentre/latestnews/2016/bbc-two-the-slum (accessed on 29 April 2016).

'Blackadder star Sir Tony Robinson in Michael Gove WW1 row'. BBC, 5 January 2014. Available online: http://www.bbc.co.uk/news/uk-politics-25612369 (accessed 30 April 2016).

'Even After *Roots*, Whites Don't See Job Bias Against Blacks Today: Poll'. *Jet*, 19 May 1977, 29.

'New York Beat'. *Jet*, 1 May 1975, 62.

'Operation Overblown'. *Time*, 19 October 1962. Available online: http://www.time.com/time/magazine/article/0,9171,827910,00.html (accessed 28 May 2009).

'Why "Roots" Hit Home'. *Time*, 14 February 1977.

Adams, R., P. Wintour S. and Morris. 'All schools must promote "British values", says Michael Gove'. *Guardian*, 9 June 2014. Available online: http://www.theguardian.com/politics/2014/jun/09/michael-gove-says-all-schools-must-promote-british-values-after-trojan-horse-reports (accessed 16 May 2015).

Ansen, D. 'An Unblinking View of War'. *Newsweek*, 28 July 1980.

Ansen, D. 'Celluloid Soldiers'. *Newsweek*, 13 July 1998. Available online: http://www.newsweek.com/id/93119 (accessed 27 July 2008).

Ascherson, N. 'Why' "Heritage" is Right-Wing'. *Observer*, 8 November 1987.

Batey N. 'The Passing Bells portrays the horror of the Great War through the eyes of young recruits'. *Daily Mirror,* 2 February 2014. Available online: http://www.mirror.co.uk/tv/tv-news/passing-bells-portrays-horror-great-4538234 (accessed 30 April 2016).

Blunkett, D. 'The full text of David Blunkett's speech, made in the West Midlands to highlight the publication of reports into inner-city violence this summer'. *Guardian*, 11 December 2001. Available online: http://www.theguardian.com/politics/2001/dec/11/immigrationpolicy.race (accessed 17 December 2014).

Borsten, J. 'A D-Day Landing by "Big Red One" in Israel'. *LA Times*, 13 August 1978.

Bush, G. W. 'Address to Joint Session of Congress and the Nation'. *Washington Post*, 20 September 2001. Available online: http://www.washingtonpost.com/wp-srv/nation/specials/attacked/transcripts/bushaddress_092001.html (accessed 30 December 2014).

Canby, V. 'Film: "The Big Red One", 5 G.I.s in World War II'. *New York Times*, 18 July 1980.

Colley, L. 'Into the Belly of the Beast'. *Guardian*, 18 January 2003. Available online: http://www.theguardian.com/books/2003/jan/18/featuresreviews.guardianreview5 (accessed 28 April 2016).

Evans, R. J. 'Richard J Evans: Michael Gove shows his ignorance of history – again'. *Guardian,* 6 January 2014. Available online: http://www.theguardian.com/books/2014/jan/06/richard-evans-michael-gove-history-education (accessed 30 April 2016).

Foner, E. 'Hollywood Invades the Classroom'. *New York Times*, 20 December 1997.

Foucault, M. 'Film and Popular Memory'. *Edinburgh Magazine* 2 (1977).

Fussell, P. 'Hell and High Water'. *London Observer*, 2 August, 1998.

Gallagher, P. 'Jeremy Paxman reopens war of words with Michael Gove over the WW1 centenary: "A charlatan" who scores "cheap political points"'. *Independent*, 13 March 2014. Available online: http://www.independent.co.uk/news/people/news/a-charlatan-who-scores-cheap-political-points-jeremy-paxman-reopens-war-of-words-with-michael-gove-9190705.html (accessed 30 April 2016).

Gates, H. L. 'Steve McQueen and Henry Louis Gates Jr. Talk 12 Years a Slave' (Part 1). *The Root*, 24 December 2013. Available online: http://www.theroot.com/articles/culture/2013/12/_12_years_a_slave_henry_louis_gates_jr_interviews_director_steve_mcqueen.1.html (accessed 21 June 2015).

Gates, H. L. 'Steve McQueen and Henry Louis Gates Jr. Talk 12 Years a Slave'

(Part 3). *The Root*, 26 December 2013. Available online: http://www.theroot. com/articles/culture/2013/12/_12_years_a_slave_director_steve_mcqueen_ interviewed_by_henry_louis_gates_1.html (accessed 21 June 2015).

George, N. 'An Essentially American Narrative: A Discussion of Steve McQueen's Film '12 Years a Slave''. *New York Times*, 11 October 2013.

Gove, M. 'Why does the Left insist on belittling true British heroes?'. *Daily Mail*, 2 January 2014. Available online: http://www.dailymail.co.uk/news/ article-2532923/Michael-Gove-blasts-Blackadder-myths-First-World-War- spread-television-sit-coms-left-wing-academics.html (accessed 30/4/16).

Green, T. 'The Black Man as Movie Hero: New films offer a different male image'. *Ebony*, August 1972, 145.

Higgins, B. ''Ryan' Leaves Them Speechless'. *Los Angeles Times*, 23 July 1998.

Infield, T. 'Rating 'Private Ryan'. *Philadelphia Inquirer*, 26 July 1998.

Jones, E. E. 'The Passing Bells, BBC1, TV review: The First World War drama for children'. *Independent*, 6 November 2014. Available online: http://www. independent.co.uk/arts-entertainment/tv/reviews/the-passing-bells-bbc1-tv-review- the-first-world-war-drama-for-children-9844991.html (accessed 30 April 2016).

Kennedy, R. 'The Still-Life Mentor to a Filmmaking Generation'. *New York Times*, 19 October 2006. Available online: http://www.nytimes. com/2006/10/19/arts/design/19lieb.html?_r=0 (accessed 23 December 2014).

Krupa, C. 'Day of Infamy'. *Time*, 12 September 2001. Available online: http:// www.time.com/time/nation/article/0,8599,174502,00.html (accessed 20 January 2016).

Lang, K. 'Ben Elton inspired by Michael Gove Blackadder criticism'. BBC, 5 November 2014. Available online: http://www.bbc.co.uk/news/ entertainment-arts-29914919 (accessed 30 April 2016).

Lee, D. P. 'Where It Hurts: Steve McQueen on Why 12 Years a Slave Isn't Just About Slavery'. *Vulture*, 8 December 2013. Available online: http://www. vulture.com/2013/12/stevemcqueentalks12yearsaslave.html (accessed 21 June 2015).

Lee, J. 'Left Husbands "... and as I was saying to the other lady at No 47 ..."'. *Evening News*, 26 November 1940.

Lee, J. 'Smiling Through / Washing up / "... and soon, after four long years, my darling wife will be in her own dear kitchen again ... I saved you the washing up"'. *Evening News*, 16 October 1944.

Liddell-Hart, B. 'Letter of resignation'. *The Times*, 19 September 1964.

Lippman, J. 'Hollywood's Drill Sergeant to the Stars is a Busy Man'. *Wall Street Journal*, 10 July 1998.

Mathews, J. 'Maneuvering in the Theaters of War: Tales of 2 Battles Pushed Ahead'. *Daily News (New York)*. 8 November 2001.

McCrary, L. 'Watching "Private Ryan", Veterans Relive the Horrors Years from Omaha Beach, Pain Lingers'. *Philadelphia Inquirer*, 6 August 1998.

Morrow, L. 'Cinema: Manhood and The Power of GLORY'. *Time*, 26 February 1990.

Murray, R. 'Writer/Director Sofia Coppola Talks About "Marie Antoinette"'. *About.Entertainment*, 2 January 2016. Available online: http://movies. about.com/od/marieantoinette/a/mariesc101006.htm (accessed 25 August 2015).

Nicholson, G. A. 'What's Happening: A reader's view ... of "Mandingo"'. *Baltimore Afro-American*, 17 June 1975.

Phillips, C. 'Slaves in Spielberg's manacles'. *The Times*, 28 February 1998.

Quinn, B. '*Bend It Like Beckham* to be made into musical'. *Guardian*, 31 October 2014. Available online: http://www.theguardian.com/stage/2014/oct/31/bend-it-like-beckham-musical (accessed 5 January 2015).

Randolph, L. B. 'Oprah and Danny Sizzle in Her First Love Scenes in the Powerful Film "BELOVED"'. *Ebony*, November 1998, 42.

Rich, F. 'Journal; Slavery Is Bad'. *New York Times*, 6 December 1997.

Rickey, C. 'Spielberg's Private Battle In "Saving Private Ryan"'. *Philadelphia Inquirer*, 19 July 1998.

Robinson, T. (2014) 'We're losing all our strong Female characters to Trinity syndrome'. *The Dissolve*, 16 June 2014. Available online: http://thedissolve. com/features/exposition/618-were-losing-all-our-strong-female-characters-to-tr/ (accessed June 2014).

Runcie, C. '*The Last Kingdom*, BBC Two, Review: "The thinking person's Game of Thrones"'. *Daily Telegraph*, 23 October 2015. Available online: http://www.barb.co.uk/whats-new/weekly-top-30? (accessed 15 February 2016).

Scheuer, P. K. '"Gen." Darryl Zanuck Takes Normandy, Reviews Battle'. *L.A. Times*, 1 April 1962.

Smith D. and N. Wade. 'DNA Test Finds Evidence of Jefferson Child by Slave'. *New York Times*, 1 November 1998.

Stephenson, D. 'Passing Bells was "one of the saddest war dramas we've seen"'. *Sunday Express*, 9 November 2014. Available online: http://www.express. co.uk/showbiz/tv-radio/533067/Passing-Bells-Downton-Abbey-All-Star-Choir (accessed 30 April 2016).

Wapshott, N. 'Hollywood Moguls Enlisted to Bolster War Effort'. *The Times*, 10 November 2001.

Weber, C. 'Queen of the Zeitgeist'. *New York Times*, 21 October 2006.

White, A. 'Can't Trust It', *City Arts: New York's Review of Culture*, 16 October 2013. Available online: http://cityarts.info/2013/10/16/canttrustit/ (accessed 21 June 2015).

White, M. 'Jeremy Paxman's Empire: A Wasted Chance We Need to Take'. *Guardian*, 28 February 2012. Available online: http://www.theguardian.com/ tv-and-radio/tvandradioblog/2012/feb/28/jeremey-paxman-empire-wasted-chance (accessed 28 April 2016).

Wiener, R. M. M. 'Ex-soldier Fuller's Dreams Realized in "Big Red One"'. *Boxoffice*, 21 July 1980.

Websites

Box Office Mojo. 'Blade'. Available online: http://www.boxofficemojo.com/ movies/?id=blade.htm (accessed 20 January 2016).

Box Office Mojo. 'Spiderman'. Available online: http://www.boxofficemojo.com/ movies/?id=spiderman.htm (accessed 20 January 2016).

Box Office Mojo. 'X-Men'. Available online: http://www.boxofficemojo.com/ movies/?id=xmen.htm (accessed 20 January 2016).

British Film Institute. 'The Cultural Test for Film'. Available online: http://

www.bfi.org.uk/film-industry/british-certification-tax-relief/cultural-test-film#cultural-test (accessed 22 November 2015).

Exploring Surrey's Past. 'Airfield and Aircraft Production'. Available online: http://www.exploringsurreyspast.org.uk/themes/subjects/military/battle_of_britain/airfield/ (accessed December 2013).

Gallup Poll. 'Presidential Approval Ratings – George W. Bush'. Available online: http://www.gallup.com/poll/116500/presidential-approval-ratings-george-bush.aspx (accessed 31 December 2014).

HBO. 'Behind the Scenes'. Available online: http://www.hbo.com/html/movies/elizabeth/behind-the-scenes/index.html (accessed 25 August 2015).

Internet Movie Database (IMDB). 'Box office/business for Saving Private Ryan (1998)'. Available online: http://www.imdb.com/title/tt0120815/business (accessed 18 March 2007).

National D-Day Memorial. 'D-Day Plaque Project'. Available online: http://www.dday.org/component/content/article/42–the-memorial/programs/75–d-day-programs (accessed 3 October 2014).

Bechdel, A. 'Testy'. Available online: http://dykestowatchoutfor.com/testy (accessed December 2014).

Chadha, G. and S. Freidman (2015), 'Exclusive: A New British Musical About Where We Are Now: Gurinder Chadha and Sonia Friedman on what inspired them to tackle Bend It Like Beckham the musical'. Available online: http://benditlikebeckhamthemusical.co.uk/?gclid=Cj0KEQiAiamlBRCgj8 3PiYm6--gBEiQArnojD8OY81uGgNtQDEKMgO7m0SJ1xzV4U4wR0S-J-Tpx7AYaAqiL8P8HAQ#content (accessed 5 January 2015)

Dalton Hewland, E. (1940–7), [Poster] 'Assembling a Hawker Hurricane'. Available online: http://www.bbc.co.uk/arts/yourpaintings/paintings/assembling-a-hawker-hurricane-205190 (accessed December 2013).

Kealey, E.V. (1915), [Poster] 'Women of Britain say "Go!"'. Available online: http://www.iwm.org.uk/collections/item/object/14592 (accessed 1 March 2016).

Lefebvre, L. 'American D-Day'. Available online: http://www.americandday.org/ (accessed 27 April 2016).

Oliphant, L. (1940–5), [Poster]. 'The Attack Begins in the Factory'/'Back them up!'. Available online: http://www.iwm.org.uk/collections/item/object/20594 (accessed 1 March 2016).

'The National D-Day Memorial'. Available online: https://www.dday.org (accessed 27 April 2016).

'The National WWII Museum'. Available online: http://www.nationalww2museum.org (accessed 27 April 2016).

'Uncle Tom's Cabin in Hollywood: 1929–1959'. Available online: http://utc.iath.virginia.edu/onstage/films/cameos/hollywood.html (accessed 28 June 2015).

Unpublished primary sources

Advanced Fact Sheet on 'The Longest Day', n.d., Folder Ryan, Cornelius Printed Matter The Last Battle #3, Miscellaneous Supplementary Material records, Robert E. and Jean R. Mahn Center for Archives and Special Collections, Ohio University Library, Athens, OH.

Brackett, C. Letter to Robert J. Wright, 6 March 1957. Folder Charles Brackett papers 1.f-[21] D-DAY, THE SIXTH OF JUNE – correspondence, Charles Brackett papers, Special Collections, Margaret Herrick Library, The Academy of Motion Picture Arts and Sciences, Beverly Hills, California. Letter, Cornelius Ryan to Kenneth E. Crouch, 20 August 1963, Folder Ryan, Cornelius, Letters and Correspondence, Zanuck, Darryl F., "The Longest Day" records, Robert E. and Jean R. Mahn Center for Archives and Special Collections, Ohio University Library, Athens, OH.

CBS Productions, Memorandum of Conference with Former President Eisenhower, 27 May 1963, Folder TR Trips – Europe, July 30–August 15, 1963 (1), Principal Files, Dwight D. Eisenhower Presidential Library, Abilene, KS.

Friendly F., Letter to D D. Eisenhower, 26 August 1963. Folder Fr (3), Principal Files, Dwight D. Eisenhower Presidential Library, Abilene, KS.

Memorandum, undated, Folder TR Trips – Europe, July 30–August 15, 1963 (1), Principal Files, Dwight D. Eisenhower Presidential Library, Abilene, KS..

Memorandum, undated, Folder TR Trips – Europe, July 30–August 15, 1963 (3), Principal Files, Dwight D. Eisenhower Presidential Library, Abilene, KS.

Rodat, R. '"Saving Private Ryan" Production Notes & Synopsis', n.d., Folder Saving Private Ryan DreamWorks 1998 (Credits, Synopsis, Productions Notes) (Music Cue Sheet), Core Collections, Margaret Herrick Library, Academy of Motion Picture Arts and Sciences, Beverly Hills, CA.

Ryan, C. Letter to Peter Schwed. 24 February 1959, Folder – The Longest Day Correspondence Release Sheet etc, 'The Longest Day' records, Robert E. and Jean R. Mahn Center for Archives and Special Collections, Ohio University Library, Athens, OH.

'Saving Private Ryan Nomination Sheet for the 1998 Academy Awards'. Core Collections, Margaret Herrick Library, Academy of Motion Picture Arts and Sciences, Beverly Hills, CA.

Shurlock, G. (Production Code Administration) Letter to Frank McCarthy (Twentieth Century Fox), 6 October 1961. Folder – The Longest Day, Film year: 1962 (Twentieth Century Fox, 1962), Production Code Administration records, Special Collections, Margaret Herrick Library, Academy of Motion Picture Arts and Sciences, Beverly Hills, CA.

Shurlock, G. Letter to J. L. Warner, 28 March 1958. Folder – THE BIG RED ONE (Warner Bros., 1958) unproduced, Special Collections, Margaret Herrick Library, Academy of Motion Picture Arts and Sciences, Beverly Hills, CA.

"The Big Red One" Final Production Notes, Lorimar Pictures, undated, Folder – Samuel Fuller's The Big Red One, Lorimar, Core Collections, Margaret Herrick Library, Academy of Motion Picture Arts and Sciences, Beverly Hills, CA

"The Big Red One" Production Notes, Lorimar Pictures, undated, Folder – Samuel Fuller's The Big Red One, Lorimar, Core Collections, Margaret Herrick Library, Academy of Motion Picture Arts and Sciences, Beverly Hills, CA

Transcript of CBS News Special "Some Friends of General Eisenhower," 29 March 1969, Folder – Eisenhower, President, Death of, Robert S. Anderson Papers, Dwight D. Eisenhower Presidential Library, Abilene, KS.

Zanuck, D. F. Letter to Hedda Hopper, 16 January 1961. Folder 62 Zanuck, Darryl F. 1939–1965, Darryl F. Zanuck papers, Special Collections, Margaret Herrick Library, Academy of Motion Picture Arts and Sciences, Beverly Hills, CA.

Zanuck, D. F. Letter to Hedda Hopper, 23 February 1961. Folder 62 Zanuck, Darryl F. 1939–1965, Darryl F. Zanuck papers, Special Collections, Margaret Herrick Library, Academy of Motion Picture Arts and Sciences, Beverly Hills, CA.

INDEX